LET THE RECORD SHOW

LET THE RECORD SHOW
John D. Hansen

Hansen Press
Boise, Idaho USA

Copyright © 2019 Michele Hansen

All rights reserved. This book, or parts thereof, may not be reproduced in any form without permission from the author's agent; exceptions are made for brief excerpts used in published reviews.

Edited by Dorothy Read

Cover and design by Terry Hansen

Hansen Press ▪ Boise Idaho USA

ISBN: 9781798660959

Library of Congress Control Number: 2019914767

Contents

Author's Note xi

Part I: The Early Years

1. It All Started When 1
2. The Airport Farm 3
3. Early Days in the Farmhouse 5
4. Eating on the Farm 9
5. Home Improvements 12
6. The Barnyard 15
7. The Neighbors 17
8. The Only Sibling at Home 19
9. Snow Up to the Telephone Lines 21
10. Working on the Farm 23
11. Mother the Manager 25
12. The Foursome 28
13. Holidays During the Great Depression 30
14. Family Dynamics 32
15. Camping at the Yankee Fork 34
16. Early Trauma 36
17. From the Ashes 38
18. School, at Last 40
19. Country Kid and School Daze 42
20. Nearsightedness and the Joy of Reading 44
21. Parent Days at Eagle Rock School 46

22. Observing the Field Work on the Airport Farm 47
23. The Grain Harvest..50
24. Milk Cows Are Fulltime Work 52
25. The Zenith Brings the News..54
26. The B-17 56
27. Introducing the Osgood Farm and Dad, the Pilot................58
28. Beginning a Year of Transition 61
29. Building the Westside Mutual Canal Company...................63
30. Cleaning the Pipe and Patrolling the Levies 65
31. Farrel Goes to College 68
32. The Unfortunate Tractor Escapade......................................70
33. Holsteins and Guernseys and Bangs Disease 72
34. Help Comes to the Osgood Farm 74
35. Calf Scramble at the War Bonnet Roundup........................77
36. Vacation at Falconberry Ranch 79
37. Farrel, Jr. Joins the Navy 82
38. Supporting the War Effort...84
39. Sixth Grade at Riverside Elementary 88
40. The Potato Harvest..91
41. 1945 Brings Distinction and Tragedy 94
42. Grandma Wahlquist, a.k.a. Aunt Mattis 97
43. The War Ends and Junior High School Begins...................99
44. Advancing from Cub Scout to Boy Scout 103
45. Dad, the Potato Man 106
46. An Eighth Grader's Dream Trip 109
47. At Last, the Dream House 113
48. Swimming and Hunting..116

49. The Stinson	119
50. Hansen-Allen, Inc. Starts Selling Fords	122
51. Ninth Grade at O.E. Bell	125
52. Gus	128
53. Lloyd Beal and I: Future Farmers	130
54. Time Speeds by in High School	135
55. A Sad Ending to a Partnership	137
56. More Time with Dad	139
57. The Infamous Winter of '48	142
58. 1949: Looking to the Future	144
59. Watering Potatoes and Chopping Hay	145
60. Trauma and a Camping Trip	147
61. An Arrival and a Devastating Departure	151
62. Arrangements Must Be Made	155
63. Life Goes on and Mother Manages	158
64. Summer Morphs into Senior Year	160
65. Future Farmers Go AWOL	163
66. The Summer Before College	168

Part II: The College Years

67. College Classes and Sigma Chi	175
68. Home Cooking and Winter Casualties	180
69. The Christmas Special	182
70. Serious Studying and College Dances	184
71. Spring Fever and Sports	186
72. Pranksters	188

73. A Character in the House	190
74. Spring Leads to an Initiation	192
75. More Hijinks	194
76. A Momentous Decision	196
77. Plans Come Together	198
78. First Stop, Washington D.C.	201
79. The Adventure Begins	204
80. Glitches	209
81. Meeting Beirut and AUB	212
82. School Starts	216
83. Dealing with Culture Shock	219
84. Making the Adjustment	221
85. Learning the Arab Perspective on Israel	224
86. Day Trips and Intrigue	227
87. Snapping Shots in Beirut	231
88. Beggars and Bargaining	233
89. Fall Happenings	235
90. Street Demonstrations	237
91. Christmas Vacation in Amman	239
92. A Close Call and a Good Lesson	244
93. The Iranian Connection	246
94. The Egyptian Adventure	249
95. Settling into Second Semester	257
96. Classmates to Remember	259
97. Easter in the Holy Land	262
98. Meeting the Lebstocks	267
99. Travel Complications	269

100. The Kit Kat Club and an Overdue Debt 272
101. Pinned! 274
102. Bearing the Brunt of American Foreign Policy 275
103. The Final Trek Begins 278
104. Touring Istanbul 284
105. To Athens on the SS Adana 286
106. Through Yugoslavia on the Orient Express 288
107. Italy, Switzerland, and Austria 291
108. Germany and an Incredible Coincidence 293
109. The Netherlands 296
110. Through Belgium and Luxembourg and on to Paris 299
111. London, Shannon, and Going Home 303
112. Our Luck Holds 306
113. Everything Changes 310
114. Married! 312
115. Back to School 314
116. Mary Marries George Freund 316
117. Happy Holidays Lead to a Happy Arrival 318
118. An Unexpected Opportunity 321
119. A Family Summer Before Law School 326

Part III: The Law Years

120. First Semester 333
121. An Ambitious Work Schedule 337
122. Summer of 1957 and the Palisades Family Venture 341
123. The Cold War Escalates 345

124. Summer of 1958	348
125. Graduation in Sight; Panic Sets In	352
126. Back Where We Started	356
127. Practicing Law	359
128. Life Before the Bar	363
129. My Turn with Judge Chase Clark	365
130. First Experiences	369
131. Representing Don Antone	374
132. Learning from the Masters	377
133. Introducing Vernon K. Smith	380
134. Decision Time	383
135. First House and a Son	386
136. Practicing Law in Idaho Falls	389
137. Growing the Law Firm of Hansen and Hansen	391
138. Taking on the Corporate World	394
139. Idaho Lawyer Meets the Mob	397
Editor's Note: The Final Chapter	419
More About John	421

AUTHOR'S NOTE

In truth, I know rather little about the lives of my parents and grandparents. Who were these people, really? How did they live; where did they go to school and what did they learn; what did they think and do; what experiences did they have? I assumed that heroic feats, if any, would already be known and would likely have been embellished. I wanted to learn more about the ordinary things, the everyday lives of people when they were children, teenagers, and adults.

My kids deserve to have such information about me and my life, particularly about events that occurred before they were born, when they were young, and after they left home. It is part of their heritage. Occasionally my kids have asked a question or made a comment which revealed a lack of knowledge about me and my early life. I am determined to correct this deficiency.

Two trips helped to spark my interest in recording my personal history: one was a road trip with Farrel and the second, a Memorial Day ride with Mother. Farrel and I drove to Hemet, California a few years ago to attend the funeral of our stepbrother, Riter Taylor. Farrel had left home at age eighteen to begin his pre-med studies at Washington University in St Louis, Missouri. I was nine years old.

After he reached age eighteen, Farrel didn't live at home and only briefly visited. He had limited knowledge of many family events that occurred after he left home. On the other hand, I had limited knowledge of family events which occurred before I was born and while I was young. We talked almost nonstop during the trip, probably more total hours than we had all the previous years put together. We gradually filled in many of the "gaps" in our respective knowledge of family history. It was a fascinating experience and a strong motivation for me to begin this effort.

Farrel has done a remarkable job of preserving family history. He has undertaken thousands of hours of genealogy research, and has hundreds of hours of audio and video interviews of relatives and acquaintances, many of whom are now deceased. Farrel has authored two wonderful books, *A Hansen History* and *A Wahlquist History*. I will not attempt to duplicate his work, as my effort will be to record my own experiences and recollections. I will, however, refer to these books to check certain facts and the chronology in an effort to assure accuracy.

The Memorial Day ride with Mother occurred in the mid-1980s. Together we decorated graves at Fielding Memorial south of Idaho Falls where Dad was buried, and the Shelley Pioneer Cemetery where Grandma and Grandpa Hansen and several of their children were buried. I always enjoyed this annual Memorial Day event, partly because I would often hear details of the lives of those in the graves we decorated.

On this occasion, Mother started talking about her marriage, the move to Firth and her life in those early years. I asked if she would remember the places they had lived, and she thought she would. We drove to Firth and she pointed out the two-room apartment she and Dad had first moved into and the four-room house across the street they next moved into. She was recalling and relating events that I had not heard before.

We then drove to Idaho Falls where she pointed out the house they had moved to on Longfellow Street, now Elva, and to the house the family later lived in, on 12th Street, when I was born. Next, we drove to the site of the house, now torn down, we had lived in on the Airport Farm. Afterwards we returned to her house on the Osgood Farm. During the drive, Mother had uncharacteristically talked almost nonstop about her life during the years when she lived at the various locations we had visited.

When I arrived home I picked up my camera, retraced the route we had taken, and snapped pictures of all the residences and the location of the old farmhouse on the Airport Farm. The next day I went to the Bonneville County Courthouse and made copies of the deeds by which title to the various properties in Bonneville County were acquired and, except the present farm, later sold. I made folders with duplicates of all the photos and documents for Mother and the siblings.

My brother Orval also happens to be writing his life history. I hope that the combined efforts of Farrel, Orval and me, and perhaps of others in the family, will provide a wealth of interesting and valuable information. My endeavor will likely be a work in progress for some time. I will undoubtedly ramble somewhat along the way. The events I relate from my very early years will not always be exactly chronological.

This exercise will undoubtedly help me recall events since forgotten, something I look forward to experiencing. I will try to avoid doing excessive damage to the rules of spelling, punctuation and grammar; however, I make no guarantees. Let me say at the outset, that if any of the facts and events I relate are at variance with those as related by any of my siblings, or other relatives, their recollections must be faulty! Wish me well.

J.D.H.

LET THE RECORD SHOW

Part I:
The Early Years

Chapter 1

It All Started When

I was born March 1, 1933. Herbert Hoover was President of the United States. Franklin D. Roosevelt had been elected by a landslide in early November, 1932; however, at that time the newly-elected President was not inaugurated until March 4 of the following year. America and the entire world were in the midst of the Great Depression which was triggered by the stock market crash in October, 1929, and which continued to deepen thereafter. There was little improvement in the economy until the New Deal programs initiated by President Roosevelt began to kick in, and increased economic activity began due to a world-wide military build-up on the eve of World War II.

I was the sixth child of Farrel and Lily Hansen. Farrel, the oldest, was born November 4, 1924, Orval on August 3, 1926, Norman on December 30, 1927, Reed on October 30, 1929, and Mary on August 26, 1931. Orval was born at home in Firth, Idaho, and all of the others were born at the LDS hospital, since torn down, on Memorial Drive overlooking the Snake River in Idaho Falls, Idaho.

Mother and Dad were married January 9, 1924, at the LDS Temple in Salt Lake City, Utah. At the time of their marriage they both lived in Boise, Idaho, and Dad had been attending the University of Idaho. They moved to Firth in September, 1924, where Dad was employed by the State of Idaho as a potato inspector. After their second son, Orval, was born the family moved to a house on Longfellow Street, now Elva Street, in Idaho Falls. Dad and his brother Heber had jointly purchased a farm near Goshen, east of Shelley, Idaho, on which Heber and his family lived. The two brothers also acquired a small farm along the Snake River west of Firth.

Dad farmed with Heber, and also worked as a potato inspector, trackside buyer, and potato broker in various relationships. Dad later sold his interest in the Goshen farm to his brother Heber, and still later the two of them sold the small farm along the river. In 1936 Dad was hired as general manager of the Idaho Potato Growers Association, a potato marketing cooperative. He continued as general manager of the potato cooperative until he and Mother acquired the Ford Motor Company agency, which he managed until his untimely death at the age of forty-seven, on November 18, 1949.

My very earliest recollection is riding in the car with Mother and Dad one evening when they were going to Goshen to see Uncle Heber and Aunt Myrtle. During the ride, Mother and Dad were talking in quiet, somber tones I had not heard before. I now know that one of them had received a call from Uncle Heber saying Aunt Myrtle was not well. I later learned she had had a miscarriage. Uncle Heber met us at the house. He and Dad hugged, began talking, then both choked up and broke down. Heber's young boys were standing around looking confused, frightened, and anxious. Mother went into the bedroom and spent time with Aunt Myrtle. I just stood around, not knowing what I should do.

Most family members believe that I was too young, at two and a half, to remember the event. I really believe otherwise. I rarely remember my parents showing such emotion, and it had a profound effect on me. The only other time I remember Dad's showing emotion like that was years later, in 1942, when Farrel left home to report for his induction into the US Navy.

Another early recollection was the first and only time I received a spanking from Dad. Both Mary and I were pre-school age. Without asking permission from Mother, we went across the road and played with some of Ed and Alice Petersen's kids. We were not allowed to cross the street, and Mother reported our misbehavior to Dad when he came home from work. He took us outside on the lawn and gave us both a serious spanking. We may well have been too young to cross the road by ourselves, although it had little traffic. I now believe a major factor was that Ed Petersen was an alcoholic who regularly went to town and got drunk. When he came home he would fight with his wife and kids, both physically and verbally. Anyway, Mary and I never repeated our transgression.

About that same time, I had a problem with warts on my hands and nothing we tried seemed to help. One of the neighbors, Art Lundgren, told me that if I rubbed a greasy rag on the warts, and buried the rag without telling anyone, the warts would go away. I found a greasy rag, rubbed as he suggested, and buried the rag near the house. I did tell my sister Mary what I was doing. However, in spite of that, in time the warts disappeared.

Chapter 2

The Airport Farm

Dad and Mother purchased the Airport Farm from Mr. and Mrs. Henry Hurley in 1935 and we lived there until 1942. The south boundary of the farm was a county road which extended from what is now Lindsay Boulevard, west to US Highway 91, now known as the Old Butte Road. The east side of the farm bordered on the Idaho Falls airport, which then consisted of the north-south runway, the log hangar which still exists, and a beautiful log control tower which, sadly, was torn down years ago. Airway Road ran along the south side of the farm.

To have an airport just beyond our east boundary was exciting for the six Hansen kids. We could watch airplanes from the dining room window of our home. One time when Mary and I were quite small, a commercial passenger plane landed and taxied to the south end of the runway. We went over the fence to get a closer look and talked to the airline stewardess. I believe she asked if we would like a ride on the airplane, although we may have asked her, I am not sure. Anyway, the stewardess said we were welcome to ride in the plane to Salt Lake City. She suggested that we pack a suitcase and hurry back to board the plane. We ran home and started to pack some of our things. Mother asked us what we were doing and we told her. She said we could not go. She may have also said that the lady was simply teasing us. Mary and I were sure the offer was real and very disappointed that Mother refused to let us go. About this time the plane took off.

Mother always planted a garden in an area close to the fence along our common boundary with the airport. Watching the airplanes land and take off just beyond the fence was a major distraction when we kids were supposed to be weeding the garden. We would often sneak over to the log hanger to inspect the planes, talk to the airport employees, and daydream about flying. For us, every day was an air show that included the arrival and departure of commercial flights from Salt Lake City.

One day we kids were watching a plane flying over the runway in an erratic pattern. We continued to watch, and suddenly the plane crashed near the fence, a considerable distance north of our house. We ran as hard as we could to the area where the crash occurred, and we noticed someone running from the log hangar to the crash site. When we arrived, we discovered it was only a large model airplane, with a wing span of three to four feet.

Occasionally there was a special air show. During the first air show I can remember, Mary and I were given a plane ride by someone who, for a small fee, was giving rides to the public. The pilot might have been Dad's friend Rudolph Nelson, who was a pioneer aviator in the area. I remember my excitement at the prospect of finally taking a real plane ride, after all of my fantasy flights.

Shortly after the flight started I became airsick and vomited on the floor of the back seat. It was a hot day and I was really embarrassed. As we were leaving the plane, I remember the reaction of the persons who were next in line to take a ride. I also remember the reaction of the pilot! Although I was notorious for experiencing motion sickness when I was small, I finally overcame the problem of air sickness when I started taking flight lessons in high school. During flight lessons, I didn't have time to think about getting sick.

The Airport Farm was acquired by the City of Idaho Falls for airport expansion in a condemnation proceeding a few years later. The expansion included a new SE-NW runway and a new passenger terminal, and the county road called Airway Road, was closed. The only portion of the road that remains today is International Way, which extends from Skyline Drive west to AeroMark, the present fixed-base facility owned and operated by Bob Hoff, brother of my brother Reed's wife, Marilyn.

Chapter 3

Early Days in the Farmhouse

We lived in a two-story frame house which had three large bedrooms upstairs, with a small room Mary and I occupied early on, accessible only through Mother and Dad's bedroom above the living room. Later I was moved to the room occupied by the older brothers, in the northeast corner of the second floor.

The kitchen stove was a magnificent piece. It was large, and had a large water jacket on the back, which provided hot water for washing and bathing. Mother was generally the first one downstairs in the mornings and she would start a fire in the stove. The kitchen was the warmest and friendliest place in the house, particularly during the cold months. Often there would be one or two baby pigs in a cardboard box near the stove, with rags or straw in the bottom of the box. When our sows had litters often one of the baby pigs, called a runt, was smaller than the rest. These smaller pigs had difficulty competing with the rest of the litter for space to nurse. The so-called runts were often brought in to stay near the stove to stay warm and be fed from a small bottle equipped with a nipple. Many of the runts, though not all, were saved.

We bathed, generally, on Saturday night, in a folding rubber tub. The tub was set up in the kitchen and filled with water from the stove water jacket, or reservoir, or from pots heated on the top of the stove. When we were small, Reed and I often bathed in the same water, he always first and me second. I remember quite vividly one time when Reed was drying off after his bath. He bent over and accidentally backed into the small door of the very hot fire box of the Majestic stove. He was "branded" on his rump with a beautifully scrolled M. I thought it was hilarious. However, this was not a feeling Reed shared.

There was also a bedroom in the northwest corner occupied at various times by Mother's brothers Glen, Brent and Grant, my older brothers, and one winter by Oscar "Bob" Anderson who was truly a character out of the old west. I believe he was a friend of the Lundgrens; he had lost everything in a fire and needed a place to stay.

Oscar, who was quite old at the time, had spent most of his life as a cowboy. He wore a leather vest and leather sleeve protectors on his lower arms. He chewed Copenhagen tobacco, which we called snoose. He was a pretty good spitter, although like most "chewers" he had tobacco stains in his otherwise white beard and mustache. During the fall, winter, and spring months he wore long underwear all the time and resisted Mother's attempts to include his underwear in the weekly wash. He was an avid pinochle player. I first learned the card game from Oscar Bob. My older brothers maintained that Oscar Bob had once made an escape from a second story building by leaping onto the back of a horse, and as a consequence had only one testicle. I don't know if the story was true, however I assumed that my brothers were setting me up, hoping I would ask him. I wanted to know the truth, but I never did ask.

Three of my Mother's brothers, Glen, Brent and Grant, stayed with us and helped on the farm for several seasons. They needed the money and we needed the help. Of the three, Uncle Glen spent the most time with us. He was like a member of the family, an older brother rather than an uncle. Mother was close to all of her brothers, and they truly enjoyed each other's company. Glen had a great sense of humor and an infectious laugh. I very much enjoyed being around them and watching the interaction, including the famous food fights at the dining room table. Well, this is a slight exaggeration. Sometimes when Mother asked to have the bread or a roll passed to her at the end of the table, Glen would toss it rather than pass the plate or bowl. Mother would look for an opportunity to toss something back and so on. Both of them laughed like small children. At the same time the "real" kids would watch in fascination, and occasionally follow suit.

All of us kids called Uncle Glen "Uncle Whalebones." I have no idea where the nickname originally came from, but it stuck. He was a tall, lanky, handsome young Swede, who was rather large-boned. He worked very hard, and after lunch he would often try to catch a short nap on the living room floor before going back outside to work. The kids, particularly the younger ones, would sneak up and pester him, and inevitably he would start wrestling with us. He seemed to enjoy these encounters as much as we did. I suspect he often pretended to be asleep and was just waiting for us to pounce on him.

To complete the description of the farmhouse: the main floor consisted of a back porch facing Airway Road. This opened into the living room, and extended along the east side into the dining room. On the west side was the kitchen, which opened into a back porch off of the northwest corner. On the porch was a hand operated cream separator and behind the porch, a supply of coal and wood. When I was too small to split kindling, I was assigned the chore of making sure Mother had an adequate supply of kindling and coal next to the Majestic stove. After the cows were milked, the whole milk was brought to the porch and poured into and run through the cream separator. The cream was saved in small milk cans for delivery and sale to the creamery in town, and the skim milk was fed to our pigs. For years, we drank raw whole milk that was not pasteurized.

The house was poorly insulated and had no basement when we first moved there. It was heated by the Majestic, when in use, and a small heater in the center of the living room which burned fuel oil. There were ceiling vents which allowed some of the warmth generated to move to the upstairs bedrooms, although never enough in winter. Many layers of blankets and much cuddling were essential. The contents of the potty kept in our bedroom closet were often frozen in the morning.

When we first moved into this house, we had no running water or plumbing. Water for washing was ditch water run into a concrete cistern with a dirt floor, just outside the back porch. Drinking water was hauled in from off the farm. We had an outdoor privy at the end of a short path behind the back of the house. The privy was a long way from the upstairs bedrooms, especially in the winter! Mother and Uncle Glen used to tell of being in the dining room, just below the boys' bedroom and catching some of my older brothers peeing out the bedroom window. I have no recollection of being a participant in the activity. One time I did have to confess to Farrel that I was the one who peed in his shoe sometime the night before.

The outhouse was a "two-holer" which faced north, away from the house. It contained reading material, which usually included an old Sears or J.C. Penny catalogue. With the door open, one could watch airplanes landing and taking off. Mary relates that one time she ran to the outhouse, opened the door, pulled down her pants, jumped backwards onto the seat, and sat on Grandpa Hansen's lap. She was really embarrassed; I am sure Grandpa was simply amused.

Another outhouse story has to be told, although Mary would kill me if she knew that I was including it in this narrative. The pit under the outhouse began to fill up, and another pit was dug a short distance farther down the path. The outhouse was moved in position over the new pit, and fresh dirt was thrown in the old pit to bring it level with the adjacent ground. One Sunday only Mary and Norman were home; I believe the rest of the family had gone to town, perhaps to church. Mary hurried down the path to the outhouse, stepped on the fresh dirt, and slid into the old pit.

Mary screamed and Norman came running and pulled her out of the pit. He led her back to the side of the house, turned on the garden hose and washed her off, and then filled the rubber tub with warm water so she could take a bath. Mary was mortified. Even today she has trouble talking about the incident. All six of us kids had a sense of humor and liked to tease one another about a variety of growing-up incidents, but we knew that this particular outhouse incident was off limits, and we respected that. Even today I may have to rethink whether to include this incident in my narrative.

Chapter 4

Eating on the Farm

Mother spent a great deal of time in the kitchen over the Majestic stove. There were always a lot of mouths to feed. This included our family of eight, and whoever else was living with us or helping on the farm. Cooking on the stove was truly a work of art, which Mother had mastered. All of the cooking was done on the Majestic, which was fueled with coal and wood poked into the fire box. The large cast iron top accommodated a variety of pots and pans that were always being shifted to various locations on the stove top, depending on the various heat requirements of whatever was cooking, as some parts of the surface would be hotter than others.

Mother seemed to know instinctively which pot or pan needed to be on a particular part of the stove top to ensure that it would heat properly but not burn. At the same time, Mother was usually baking something in the large oven just beneath the stove top. That something was often a large pan with twelve loaves of bread, or several pies, or a couple dozen rolls. The fire in the firebox had to be maintained to bring the oven to the desired temperature and keep it there. All of this complicated cooking produced wonderful aromas in the kitchen and throughout the house. It also produced a lot of heat which was most welcome in the colder months, however not as welcome during the warm summer months.

In those early years, our food was plentiful and nutritious, although not particularly fancy. Dad had worked in a meat market the one year that he attended the University of Idaho, and had learned to butcher animals and cut and package the meat. Slaughtering a fat steer and a hog was almost an annual ritual when we lived on the farm. When I was pre-school age, I could not watch the killing of the animal, but was fascinated with the rest of the process. With our own beef and pork, chickens and milk, butter from the creamery where we sold our separated cream, and all that was grown and harvested from the garden, we really had about all we needed to survive.

Information about vitamins was just becoming available when Mother began raising a family, and she made a point of learning all she could about good nutrition, and she put her knowledge into practice. We kids were the beneficiaries, even though that meant lining up in the morning for our daily dose of cod liver oil, which we all did for many years.

Breakfast usually consisted of a large pot of cooked oatmeal, milk, and toasted homemade bread with butter and jam. We ate homemade whole wheat or white bread with almost every meal, and often had bread, broken into pieces, in a bowl of milk for supper, which was one of my Dad's favorite meals.

For Sunday breakfast, we often had pancakes, and we kids would engage in a contest to see who could eat the most. Records were set and broken; however, I don't recall the overall winner. And we always had ample amounts of home-grown fruits and vegetables from the garden along with meat, poultry and fresh eggs produced on the farm. We really did not need to buy very much in the way of food.

Mother often told us that she did not know how to cook when she married Dad. She said Dad's mother, Anna Hansen, was a great help in Mother's early efforts to learn to cook. Mother said it also helped that Dad was very patient and never complained. She did say that one time when she had a cooking failure Dad simply suggested that she might want to ask her mother-in-law for advice on that particular recipe, and she did. We considered Mother to be an excellent cook. We always had plenty to eat and we always ate what we were served. I cannot remember anyone in our family being a "picky eater," and to this day I have little or no patience with anyone who is a picky eater.

With our generation, and perhaps there has been some variation for every generation, we kids were told to eat everything on our plate, because "the Chinese are starving." We joked with Mother about this, and questioned how cleaning up our plate would in any way help the situation in China. We never did receive a clear, satisfactory answer.

Let me digress for the moment. In the year 2000, Michele and I had the opportunity to travel to China. During the visit, we had extensive conversations with an older Chinese woman who told us that large numbers of the Chinese people had, in fact, starved to death during the Great Depression and during World War II. As a child, she remembered being told that American children were made to eat extra amounts of food because the Chinese were starving. She said the Chinese people believed that the Americans ate extra food to keep it from being sent to alleviate their suffering. As a result, the Chinese felt humiliated and believed that Americans were cruel. I was astounded and a bit ashamed to learn that something we joked about had in fact been offensive to people who had been suffering such a terrible calamity.

Chapter 5

Home Improvements

Early on, although I don't know the exact year, a well was drilled and a pump installed in the bottom of the cistern which became the pump house. Later the water was piped into the house, and still later a bathroom installed between the kitchen and back porch. The pump was driven by a motor connected by a V belt. Occasionally the water pressure would drop, which was an indication that the belt had been thrown off the pulley. I remember one day when all the other kids were at school and Dad was at his office at the Idaho Potato Growers, Mother climbed down the ladder into the cistern to put the belt back on, and did so without turning the power off. She caught her right index finger in the spinning pulley and it split her nail. She climbed out, wrapped a towel around her bleeding finger, and called Dad. He came home to put the belt back on and to comfort Mother. I don't remember if she went to the doctor, but I do know that her nail was thereafter disfigured by a horizontal split.

The addition of a bathroom required a cesspool which was dug, by hand, by Uncle Glen and others, and when finished was at least twelve feet deep. I carefully watched the progress as the hole became deeper and deeper. Glen later told me that while he and others were digging the cesspool, I asked what they were doing. He told me they were digging a hole to China. He said I replied in a slow drawl, "Well, I think you are just wasting your time." Uncle Glen always laughed his infectious laugh when he retold the story.

The carpenter who put the bathroom into the farmhouse was Charlie Sleppy. I remember watching him and using his saw and some scraps of lumber to make my famous "little man" doll. I still have it, only because Mother saved it and gave it to me years later. You can tell which parts I cut and which parts Mr. Sleppy helped me with. I cut out the head and legs, but when I tried to cut out the arms they broke off. Mr. Sleppy kindly reattached and reinforced the arms for me. This homemade wooden toy became a big part of my life when I was small. His clothes were first colored on with crayons, and later Mother sewed cloth clothes for him. I dressed him and carried him everywhere. I even took him to bed with me, for more years than I like to admit. I don't do that very much anymore!

At some point in time the older boys, with help from an uncle or two, built a tree house in a large tree that was close to the southwest corner of the house, just off the front porch. The tree house seemed elaborate to me. It had a floor of sorts, sides that were two to three feet high, a canvas top, and a ladder that could be pulled up to prevent entry by any one not specifically invited. The boys even put in an electric light and a radio, made possible by an extension cord connected to an outlet in Mary's second floor bedroom. On one occasion Mary and I were given permission to sleep in the tree house. I remember that I became frightened during the night and ended up back in the house. I don't think I ever spent an entire night in the tree house. Reed and I, together with a neighbor boy, built another tree house in a large Cottonwood tree along Airway Road. This tree house was simply a small platform with a wooden box that contained comic books and a few trinkets. It was not grand, but it was our secret place.

The next major home improvement was to excavate under the house for a basement. I remember Uncle Glen and others hauling dirt out from under the farmhouse with a slip scraper that was maneuvered by hand. The scraper had a long cable attached to horses, and the dirt was dumped north of the house. When the basement was finished, a furnace and heating ducts were installed, a major improvement over the oil stove in the living room. The basement also was a great new place to play and to hide.

I was fascinated watching the home improvements, and later the construction of a new barn and corrals, and I enjoyed interacting with the workmen. At about this time I decided I wanted to be a carpenter, and I asked for tools for birthdays and at Christmas time. I really hoped for tools that were more my size, but I always received a full sized hammer, handsaw, or heavy metal square which were, of course, "mine" but always ended up in the farm shop.

As some of you might know, the house I am describing was the same house in the picture painted by Fred Ochi, a well-known local artist. After I finished law school and returned to Idaho Falls, I learned that Fred Ochi had painted it sometime in the 1950's before the old farmhouse was torn down. I was told that the picture had been hanging in the Bonneville Hotel, but when I checked, it was not there. I really wanted to locate and purchase the painting. I was afraid someone outside of our family would buy it first. I talked with Fred

Ochi and he said he would locate the painting. Fred Ochi had paintings hanging in a variety of places, and sometimes he forgot where his paintings were located.

He located the painting and quoted me a price, around two hundred fifty to two hundred seventy-five dollars, which I thought was very high. Fred sensed my surprise at the price, and told me that he had entered the painting in a Western States Art Show and it had received the Best of Show Award. He said he had not planned to sell it, but he would let it go to someone in the Hansen family. He said I could pay him by the month. I agreed to buy it and, in fact, paid a fairly small amount, like ten dollars each month until the full price had been paid. I knew that if I passed up the chance to buy the painting and someone outside the family did, I would regret the decision for the rest of my life.

The price seemed high at the time. I had three small kids, was just beginning to practice law, and had no savings. When I picked up the painting, Donna and I drove to Mother's house and gave it to her. The look on her face was worth the price of the picture. For years, it hung over her couch in the "Round House." Later it followed her to The Good Samaritan and hung in her room until her death. As was her often-expressed wish, on her death the picture became mine and it now hangs over the piano in our present home. I had the painting photographed and I gave framed copies to each of my siblings and to my children. I count locating and buying that painting as one of the best things I have ever done.

Chapter 6

The Barnyard

The Airport Farm consisted of 120 acres on which potatoes, hay and grain were raised and some pasture was maintained. When we first moved to the farm, the outbuildings included an old barn and a collection of pens, corrals, loafing shed, and chicken coop, most of which were later destroyed in a fire. We always had milk cows, pigs, chickens, draft horses, and a pony, and occasionally we raised rabbits. One pony I remember was a buckskin named Buck. We also had a variety of barn cats and a dog. Mother took responsibility for the chickens with help from the younger kids.

We gathered, candled, and sold eggs to neighbors, friends, and a grocery store in town. One of my early chores was helping to gather and "candle" the eggs. Candling required that each egg be placed in front of a bright light bulb that allowed you to see inside the egg. Candling was done to eliminate eggs that contained a blood spot or other evidence of a developing embryo. The candled eggs were put in a large egg crate in multiple layers. One time I was fooling around with a large bearing, about one inch in diameter that I had been using as a "steelie" in marble games. I accidentally dropped the bearing into a nearly full crate of candled eggs. I helped Mother unload the crate, remove the broken eggs, wipe clean those unbroken, and refill the crate. Mother knew it was an accident and said nothing.

We exhibited some of our livestock at the Eastern Idaho State Fair in Blackfoot. One year Orval was involved in caring for and exhibiting our animals at the fair and he also took our pony, Buck. Orval entered the amateur horse race which was held annually on the large oval race track in front of the main grandstand. One night when Orval returned from the fair, he announced that he and Buck received third place in the race. We were very proud of his red ribbon. Later we learned that there were only three horses entered.

At some point, Buck was either sold or given away, I am not sure which. One winter night Mary and I were home alone and a severe blizzard was in progress. We looked out the kitchen window and believed we saw Buck in the yard, covered with snow, and shivering. We grabbed sheets and towels and ran outside to brush him off, and tried without success to move him to the barn. We were bawling because the pony was cold, wet and exposed to the storm.

I believe Mary even called Veva Jackson for advice, but I don't remember if she reached her or what Mrs. Jackson might have suggested. After a while we gave up and went to bed. When the rest of the family arrived home, we told them what had happened but by then the animal was nowhere in sight. The next morning we found a dead horse in the barrow pit a short distance down the road. On closer examination, we discovered that the dead horse was not Buck. Our hearts were in the right place anyway.

Reed and I were in charge of cleaning the chicken coop, a regular Saturday chore. I also helped some with weeding the garden along the west boundary of the airport; however, the distraction of airplanes and the similarity of emerging plants and weeds were always serious problems for me. Often I was excused from hoeing and sent to fetch a cool drink for those who were better at chopping weeds.

Chapter 7

The Neighbors

We had wonderful neighbors when we lived on the Airport Farm. Arthur and Nellie Lundgren and their family lived on a farm across the road, a short distance to the west. Further west of the Lundgren farm lived Ernest and Veva Jackson. The Jacksons had five children: Catherine, Oma Jean, Ernest Jr. (Bud), George and Vonda, all roughly the same ages as the six Hansen children, so we had a number of kids to play with. In good weather we were out of doors almost every evening, playing "Kick the Can" or "No Bears Out Tonight" or "Red Rover, Red Rover" or marbles, or baseball. There was always something. Inside the house, we played board games, Pinochle, Canasta, Chinese Checkers, and Chess. After dinner there was always something going on, and we had a lot of fun. We had little need or time to spend money. Our playtime was limited, however, as there was a lot of work to do on the farm; field work in the summer and fall, and the care of livestock, pigs, and chickens the year around.

Our family was particularly close to the Lundgrens and the Jacksons. As a small child, I was allowed to visit Nellie Lundgren who lived a short distance west on Airway Road. I am sure that on each such occasion Mother called Mrs. Lundgren to alert her I was coming and then watched me carefully during the walk. I liked to visit Mrs. Lundgren. She would always find time to visit with me, and she almost always gave me a cookie or something else good to eat. She seemed very old to me, and probably was, but we were good friends and had long chats. We shared the same birthday, March 1, and I regularly visited her to share a birthday treat and exchange gifts.

Mrs. Lundgren kept a small monkey in a cage, which was fun to watch, but the monkey was quite ill-tempered, as I remember. I believe the monkey belonged to her daughter, Betty. That monkey inspired me to try, repeatedly and unsuccessfully, to persuade Mother and Dad that I should have a pet monkey, too. As a consolation prize, perhaps, or to get me to stop asking, I did receive a toy monkey, which, when a string was pulled, ran up and down a stick.

The John Newmans lived to the east, the Peterson family directly across the street, and just west of them was Jusamite Farms, a Guernsey Dairy owned and operated by Sim Tullet and his family. The Lundgren farm was later purchased by Charles and Helen Reed who had five children: Barbara Jean, Leroy, David, Larry and Shirley. Leroy was a year older, and David, was my age. Leroy stayed out of school one year when he was in elementary school, due to illness. Leroy, David, and I, as well as Vonda Jackson, attended the same schools and we all graduated from Idaho Falls High School in the class of 1951.

Arthur and Nellie Lundgren had four children: Betty, Bruce, Marjorie, and John. When we first became neighbors their youngest son, John Lundgren, was the only one of the children who lived at home, at least most of the time. John was about the same age as my Uncle Glen, and the two of them spent a lot of time together, at work and after work. One night Uncle Glen and John went into Idaho Falls to see a movie at the Paramount Theater. During the movie John Lundgren suffered a heart attack and died instantly. The sudden death of John Lundgren was a devastating blow to Uncle Glen and our entire family; and, of course, to our good friends Nellie and Arthur Lundgren.

Not all of our neighbors had houses to live in. There was what we called a "hobo jungle" or camp, on the bank of the Snake River about a half-mile east of our house. This was not far from where the trains crossed the bridge over the river, and it was a convenient place for those "riding the rails" to hop on and off the trains. Occasionally, one or two of the men would come to the door asking for food in return for work. Mother never turned anyone down. We had a wood pile near the house and we always had a good supply of split wood. Mother and I were often home alone. She would not invite the person or persons into the house, but she would prepare a lunch and put it on the front porch to be eaten. Often I would hang around while they were eating and engage in small talk. The people who came from down by the river were friendly and did not seem out of the ordinary. I don't remember ever being frightened or uneasy around them. Many were well-educated. They were simply out of work. It was hard times.

Chapter 8

The Only Sibling at Home

I have many fond memories of my pre-school years. I believe I was a rather shy, somewhat bashful little boy. Since I spent a lot of time with older brothers and with adults, I was comfortable being around and conversing with older people. I enjoyed playing with my older brothers, mostly Reed, and with Mary, as well as the neighbor kids who were close to my age. At the same time I enjoyed playing or doing things by myself. I believe I was somewhat of a daydreamer.

    I remember lying on my back and watching the clouds pass overhead for long periods of time. I would try to find clouds that were shaped like people or animals. Often I would imagine I was riding on a cloud and traveling around the world, something no doubt triggered by reading the National Geographic magazines we regularly received and saved. I remember spending several hours in a tree near the house trying to nab a curious magpie. Once someone told me that a magpie, if captured, could be tamed and taught to talk, and I thought that would be a great thing to do. The magpie would come close, but never close enough for me to catch him. I do not remember ever being bored when I was a young child.

    Mary started school in 1937, when I was four years old. For the next two years the pattern was much the same. School mornings were frantic and noisy, with five older siblings scrambling to get dressed, do a variety of chores, eat breakfast, gather up schoolbooks and sack lunches, and make a dash for the school bus, which stopped directly in front of the house.

    As soon as the bus left, the house was strangely quiet. Sometime in the confusion Dad would have shaved, dressed and left for his office. Mother later said that when the school bus pulled away and calm was restored, I would often turn to her and say, "Well, we did it again." For the rest of the day I would have Mother to myself. She read to me, taught me some of the fundamentals of cooking and showed me how to stitch patterns onto dish towels, which I often stitched to the arm of the overstuffed chair in which I was sitting.

An interesting aside relates to this overstuffed chair. In later years Mother told me that when she and Dad were first married and moved to a rental apartment in Firth, they had very little furniture. They decided to buy each other a chair. Mother received a rocking chair with wooden arms. We had the chair for many years, although I do not know what finally happened to it. Dad received a large overstuffed chair. Sometime in the mid 1980s Mother told me the story of the chairs and showed me Dad's, which had been upholstered more than once since its purchase. She confirmed that this was the same chair that I had sewn the dish towels to when I was learning to do stitch work. The chair is now located in front of the fireplace in the basement of our present home. It is upholstered in a yellow fabric and in excellent condition. It is hard to believe the chair is over eighty years old!

When I was the only child at home during the day, Mother allowed me to help in the kitchen. Eggnog was a favorite drink. I would crack the eggs, add milk and nutmeg and mix with the egg beater. I often made our lunch, which usually consisted of grilled cheese sandwiches and a bowl of tomato soup. I would pour a can of Campbell's tomato soup into a sauce pan, add milk, and stir while it was heating on the stove. The soup was sometimes scorched. Making lunch seemed kind of complicated then, and I was proud of my contribution. Mother and I ate together and listened to the noontime radio programs, which included the news, a cooking show that provided daily recipes, and an on-going serial, "My Gal Sunday."

If I was outside I would listen for the steam whistle that the folks at the White Star Laundry in Idaho Falls would regularly blow at noon and also at six o'clock, but never on Sundays. If I was inside the house, I would closely watch the clock. I wanted to make sure we didn't miss the programs we regularly listened to: Tom Mix, Jack Armstrong, and the Lone Ranger, among others. The older kids came home from school about the time the afternoon programs were on, and then our activities would take a different direction.

Chapter 9

Snow Up to the Telephone Lines

Winters were severe. We joke about the snow being deeper, the hills steeper, etc., in the "old days." However, we did have very severe winters when we lived on the Airport Farm. Even though we were not far from the city, we were often snowed in for days at a time during the winter months. Roads were narrower than modern roads, and the plows were road graders, which simply pushed the snow into higher and higher banks along the sides of the road. Winds would cause the snow to drift in and make the roads impassable. This again required more plowing, making the banks even higher and easier for the drifting snow to plug up again, and so on. Even main roads such as West Broadway, running west, would often look like topless tunnels in the middle of winter.

Today the wider roads, the use of snow fences and of rotary snow plows, which throw the snow a considerable distance, have changed the landscape in winter. We also often joke about the snow being almost up to the telephone wires. This was true. I remember walking from the house in the direction of what is now Lindsay Boulevard and being able to reach the telephone wires. Of course the poles and wires were not as high as they are today, and the snow banks resulting from the frequent plowing were much higher.

One late afternoon, when I was very young, we had been snowed in quite a while, and I am sure the family was getting "cabin fever." Dad hitched two of our workhorses to the bobsled, and all of the family bundled up in warm clothes and blankets and rode to town. The horses were tied up in an empty lot, and we went to a movie at the Paramount Theater. That was a real treat. After the movie, we climbed in the bobsled and returned home. A few days ago, I was talking with Farrel and mentioned my recollection of the bobsled ride. He remembered the same ride. He said we had been snowed in for over a week, and that the movie we saw was Robin Hood starring Errol Flynn. He has an amazing memory.

On another winter day when the roads were impassable, Dad hitched the horses to the bobsled and we rode to the Coltman area northeast of Idaho Falls to attend the wedding reception for Uncle Brent Wahlquist and his new bride, Irene. I don't remember much about the event except that the bobsled ride seemed to take forever and I had difficulty staying warm.

Chapter 10

Working the Farm

I was impressed that my Dad knew how to harness, hitch up and handle our workhorses. He worked in an office in town, and I don't have any recollection of Dad doing actual farm work, although he often worked with the livestock on his days off. In fact, he did operate the farm the first year we moved from town, and I later learned that in his youth he had had considerable farm work experience. The workhorses seemed huge (and they were huge) and as a small boy I was rather frightened of them. Fortunately, when I was old enough to help in the fields we had made the transition to tractors. My only experience with horses was riding the derrick horse and occasionally the dump rake to put hay windrows into piles, but this was several years later.

I remember when Dad bought what I am quite sure was our first truck, a used Ford. I went with him to the Ford dealership, Bonneville Auto, when he picked up the truck. The truck had been repainted with a fresh coat of black paint and it did not have a truck bed, just the chassis. Dad asked me if I wanted to sit on the chassis and take a ride. I sat between the cab and the rear duals on the driver's side, got black paint on my clothes and was more than a little scared. The ride was short, probably only a few feet, and I then rode in the cab on the drive home. A truck bed, which was a hayrack removed from a horse-drawn wagon, was installed when we were back at the farm.

At harvest time the potatoes were dug with a horse-drawn digger, picked by hand and put into wire baskets and then dumped into burlap sacks. Two baskets of potatoes would generally fill the sack. The sacks would be stood up in two rows far enough apart to allow the truck to drive between the rows. As the truck moved slowly between the two rows, a person on each side, called a "spud bucker," then lifted the sacks onto the truck bed. Another person on the back of the truck would take the sacks, lay each sack on its side, and gradually fill rows of sacks, front to back, until the truck was fully loaded. Then the loaded truck was driven to the potato cellar. At the cellar, men carried the sacks by hand from the truck, walked on planks up to the pile of potatoes and emptied the sacks onto the pile. This was before we had potato conveyers in the cellar.

I was too young to do any farm work when we lived on the Airport Farm. When I was very small, my feet did not reach the brake and clutch pedals. However, I did steer the truck in the field during potato harvest. Since I could not reach the pedals, I would kneel on the seat and grab the steering wheel. The person who was bucking the sacks on the driver's side of the truck would put the truck into its lowest gear, compound, adjust the hand throttle to the right speed, and start the truck in a straight position to go between the two rows of standing sacks. He would then dash back to lift his row of sacks onto the bed of the moving truck. My job was simply to keep the moving truck between the rows of sacks. It does sound easy, doesn't it? In fact, the truck was difficult for me to steer. The deep soft soil often had deep ruts from other machinery and previous trips by the truck.

The truck would often begin to slowly veer toward a row of sacks, most often the row nearest me, which I watched more closely and often crowded. It was very difficult for me to change direction once the truck started moving toward the row of sacks, and I occasionally ran over a sack. When this happened, the bucker on my side would reach in the truck window, grab the steering wheel and steer the truck back onto the right path. Then once again he would dash back to continue lifting his row of sacks onto the truck bed while the truck was still moving. I remember Uncle Glen being the person who was there at times when I was steering, and I am sure there were others. I was never scolded for running over a sack of potatoes. Though chagrined when I did run over a sack, I was very proud to be a working member of the harvest crew. Uncle Glen always told me I was doing a good job.

Chapter 11

Mother, the Manager

I had no appreciation of the fact that times were difficult during those early years, but they really were. Mother and Dad bought the farm and moved from a comfortable home in town to the harsh realities of life on a farm and living in a farmhouse without central heating or inside plumbing. They were both willing to work hard, and with livestock and crop income to supplement Dad's work in town, they believed they would be better able to feed, clothe and educate their six young children, ages two to eleven. Dad operated the farm the first year after its purchase, but he was not really meant to be a farmer. Mother said he was restless when farming, and when offered the position of General Manager of the Idaho Potato Growers, he accepted the job. I am sure the added income was a factor. From then on Mother was the day-to-day farm manager, along with everything else she had to do.

Mother didn't learn to drive a vehicle until after Dad died. When she needed to go into town and Dad was at work or traveling, someone would drive her, usually Uncle Glen, a hired man or a neighbor. Before I attended school, I always went with her. She shopped for groceries at Broulim's Market on Broadway, just west of the present Farrell's men's store, or at the P and H Market on the west side of the Snake River, where Quiznos is now located.

One time I was following her around Broulim's Market while she shopped, and as we were leaving with the groceries, she noticed I had a Guesswhat in my hand. A Guesswhat consisted of two candy kisses and a tiny toy wrapped in paper. It cost either one or two pennies and was a favorite of mine, mainly because of the toy inside. She made me go back into the store and return the treat and apologize to Mr. Broulim, a very tall man, whom I never saw smile. I started bawling before I reentered the store, and didn't stop until long after I had returned to the car. It was a very traumatic experience and a lesson I still remember.

I recall another time a hired man drove Mother and me to town. She needed to hire extra harvest help. The Depression continued, and many able-bodied men, and some not so able bodied, were always looking for work. Many of the job seekers gathered in and around the Lobby Bar, a rather seedy place located on Broadway west of Broulim's Market. Mother, who was young and quite attractive, would take me by the hand and enter the bar, to meet and negotiate with the prospects. I know she was nervous because she squeezed my hand so hard that it hurt. I guess I was her protector; that is, she probably believed that no one would bother her if she was accompanied by a small boy.

The new hired help would follow us out or be picked up at an agreed-upon time to be taken to the farm. They were taken back to town each night and picked up again the next morning. The hired help was paid at the end of each day. Most returned for work the next day; however, there were always a few who would drink up their wages and not show up the next morning. Those who did not show up were readily replaced. The Depression was still a reality, and there were always a lot of able-bodied men looking for any kind of work.

In addition to taking major responsibility for the six children, Mother did most of the hiring and firing and all of the cooking for the help. She also did the banking and paid the bills and raised a large garden and a flock of chickens. I have a vivid recollection of us kids catching live chickens for Mother. She would lay their necks across a chopping block, usually a large tree stump, and chop off their heads with a hatchet or short-handled axe. Occasionally Reed or Norman would offer to help her with this chore. However, as I remember their efforts, though done with enthusiasm, were not always "precise" and Mother often ended up finishing the task.

She would then remove the entrails of the chickens, something the older boys helped with. The chickens were then dunked into a large pot of extremely hot water and the feathers were "plucked" or pulled off the carcass. We all helped with the plucking. Mother would then burn off the small feathers and fuzz that remained, by rolling up a part of an old newspaper, and lighting the paper on fire. She held the rolled-up paper in one hand and the chicken carcass by its legs in the other hand, and singed the carcass. When the paper had burned down to near her hand, she would drop it and stomp the fire out with her shoe. Then she would roll and light another newspaper and continue until all the chickens had been properly singed. Mother would then cut the chickens up into pieces suitable for frying. She often canned meat, but I cannot remember if she ever canned chickens. This was all before the process for freezing vegetables and meats had been perfected. Each year Mother canned a large quantity of fruits and vegetables and jars of meat, for consumption over the winter months.

Chapter 11: Mother, the Manager | 27

Mother made a lot of our clothes. In the evenings, she spread cloth on the table or on the floor, pinned paper patterns to the cloth, cut and sewed and came up with remarkable articles of clothing. She used an old model Singer sewing machine. I was always excited when she would make us new flannel pajamas for winter. Clothes were handed down. With five growing boys close in age, hand-me-down clothing was inevitable. Shoes and overalls, which we all wore when we were young, and a few other things, were purchased at J.C. Penney, Sears & Roebuck or Montgomery Ward stores in town, or ordered through their catalogues. For some reason we used to refer to Montgomery Wards as "Monkey Wards." When the new catalogues came out the old ones often ended up in the outhouse, but only for reading. We always called these catalogues our "wish books."

All farm women worked hard in those days; however, most had husbands working full time on the farm. No one worked harder than Mother, who did her normal chores and also filled the role of a man in the customary farm management responsibilities. Dad worked very hard as well. He went to his office early each morning and stayed all day. He also worked at the office most of the day on Saturday, and occasionally spent part of Sunday there as well. His work required that he travel a fair amount. The Idaho Potato Growers expanded greatly in those years, and branch warehouses were established in several locations in Eastern and Southern Idaho. The successes Mother and Dad achieved during their marriage truly reflected their joint efforts.

I don't remember ever hearing Mother complain about her life after the move to the Airport Farm in 1935. She took great pride in all that she and Dad were able to accomplish together. A good-natured person, she enjoyed her female friends, playing bridge, attending Grange gatherings, and occasionally accompanying Dad on a business trip. In 1939 Mother and Dad took an extended trip which included attending the New York World's Fair and stopping in Detroit to pick up and drive home a new dark blue Buick sedan. Before they left we all poured over Buick brochures. Orval had expressed strong feelings that the new car should be painted a bright yellow. I suspect Dad had dark blue in mind all the time, and it was a beautiful car. While they were gone, Dad's older sister Ruby stayed at the house. Aunt Ruby had a big heart; however, she was not as good a cook as Mother. All of my siblings and I were most anxious for our parents to return, although we tried to avoid doing or saying anything that would hurt Aunt Ruby's feelings.

Chapter 12

The Foursome

Mother really enjoyed playing bridge with her friends. She was a member of the so-called "Foursome," which consisted of Mother, Veva Jackson, Lottie Danner and Clara Jensen. They played on a regular basis, and always put a small amount of money on the corner of the table. The money would be accumulated for a year and then the wives would use the money to take their husbands out for dinner or to do something else they particularly enjoyed. Mother was also invited to join the VF Club, which was a larger group of women who met to play bridge one afternoon each month. The ladies would take turns hosting the bridge game at their respective homes. The club had been originally started by a group of Scandinavian housewives, mostly living in the New Sweden farming area west of Idaho Falls. Mother was a member of the VF Club for many years.

  I believe Mother was the only one of her many friends who did not drive a car, and generally, unless she was the hostess, one of her friends would pick her up and bring her back home. The ladies thoroughly enjoyed themselves. They loved the game, laughing at each other's jokes and sharing coffee and desserts. I enjoyed being around them when they gathered for bridge. They also were a great support group, always there when someone lost a family member, or experienced an illness or other adversity. Bridge gave these hard-working wives a social outlet, and they formed close relationships which lasted their entire lives.

  I was impressed with the fact that these women, who worked so hard, would really dress up for an afternoon of bridge. Hats were fashionable in those days, and Mother and many of the other ladies loved to wear them, often with veils. Normally, Mother dressed in what would be classified as her work clothes, but when she played bridge or went to town shopping, or out at night with Dad, she would dress up and always looked sharp. One time Mother went to Chicago with Dad on one of his business trips, and they went shopping at Marshall Fields. Dad was proud of Mother and liked her to look nice. Dad set up a

Marshall Fields charge account for Mother which she had for years. Occasionally ordering articles of clothing from Marshall Fields was one of her few indulgences.

Chapter 13

Holidays During the Great Depression

Christmas was a special time for our family. Our tree had many homemade decorations. We made popcorn, lots of fudge, and divinity candy. We each received a book for Christmas, which we picked out of the catalogue and ordered in time for the books to be received before Christmas. We always drew names around Thanksgiving, slips of paper in a hat, to find out the family member for whom we would buy a present. Mary often would prepare the names, and more than once she put her name on all the slips. The name we drew was supposed to be secret and so we wouldn't know until later in the day, when she would confess and then redo the drawing. The name gift was to be a serious gift, with a limit on its cost. In addition, we gave inexpensive and often silly gifts to one another.

    Our friends, the Jacksons, always opened their presents on Christmas Eve, even when the youngest one still believed in Santa Claus. Everyone, presumably except Mr. Jackson, left the living room on Christmas Eve and in their absence Santa came and left all the presents. Apparently, the Jacksons had a special relationship with Santa. My older siblings wanted us to open presents on Christmas Eve. However, Mother said until I stopped believing in Santa Claus, we would follow tradition and open presents on Christmas morning. At some point my older brothers sat me down and said, "You don't really still believe in Santa Claus, do you?" After a little more discussion along the same line, I decided that I probably no longer did, whereupon they so advised Mother and we started the tradition of opening our presents on Christmas Eve. I don't think I had been quite ready to give up the notion of Santa and the elves, but it was all pretty painless. It also simplified matters on Christmas morning. Those who wanted to sleep did so and those who chose to wake up early and play had that option.

    I never thought of our family as being poor. We lived much the same as all of our friends. And we always had a lot of fun. In later years Mother told us about one early Christmas season when we lived on the Airport Farm and she and Dad had absolutely no money for Christmas. To remedy the situation Dad sold a couple of loads of hay out of the stack, and he and Mother used the money for Christmas. I was surprised, as were all of the other kids, to learn how scarce money really had been during the Great Depression. Mother and Dad always made the holidays special. Dad in many ways was like a kid about Christmas. We all played a variety of board games, and it seems like we were always working on a difficult picture puzzle, a tradition that continues.

The same was true with the Fourth of July. Dad loved to celebrate Independence Day. He would order a variety of fireworks through the mail. Sometimes he would wake us up in the early morning by tossing a lit fire cracker under our beds. Some of the firecrackers were large and probably quite dangerous, but I don't recall anyone being hurt. The older boys made homemade bombs or rockets using pieces of metal pipe and all sorts of tin cans and other devices. One Fourth of July Orval made something, I don't recall what exactly, with a particularly large firecracker, placed it in an almost new round tin tub, filled the tub with water, and lit the fuse. When the device went off it blew the bottom out of the tub. Even Dad was upset over that. Mother was always a nervous wreck on the Fourth and couldn't wait for the day to end.

Chapter 14

Family Dynamics

I don't ever remember my parents having a serious argument. Later in life Mother assured me that they did have problems from time to time, but that they simply dealt with their differences in private. Our parents and our uncles were great role models. This was, of course, a blessing, but I believe there may also have been a down side. I did not really learn to deal well with conflict in relationships for many years. I would withdraw from, rather than attempt to deal with, conflict. It always bothered me greatly when I visited or stayed overnight with friends and heard serious arguing, parent to parent or parent to child. It took me awhile, years in fact, to accept the fact that this was more normal than a situation that seemed free of conflict. So much for that.

While all of us kids were "normal" kids with shifting moods and tempers, by and large we all got along quite well. The fact that we spent most of our time on the farm and had a lot of work to do no doubt helped a great deal. We did like to tease one another and did so often. When I was too young to do much more than serve as a water boy, I would spend time with my brothers when they were weeding potatoes, irrigating, or doing other field chores. They enjoyed teasing me. A favorite trick was to pull my pants off and throw me into the irrigation ditch. It made me furious and I often bawled, but I knew they were having fun and not intending to be mean to me. These experiences made me feel helpless and somewhat humiliated, but I soon got over it.

One time during a potato harvest, Farrel found a huge potato. He bet me a nickel that I could not eat the whole thing raw. I must have spent a good part of the day trying to finish it. Finally, after I had eaten most of the potato, I threw the rest away. I told Farrel I had eaten it all and he gave me the nickel. I felt justified because of a prior incident.

One day I had been fooling around in the potato field while the older boys were irrigating. I dammed up one end of a short section of the furrow between two rows of potatoes and made a long gradual slope of dirt at the other end. Then I let water run into that section of the furrow and watched the water level rise and move up the slope of dirt I had made. Having done this I went to Farrel and said I would bet him a nickel that I could make water run up hill. He wouldn't take the bet and told me emphatically that water would not run up hill. I tried hard to get him to bet, and or at least to come and see what I was doing, but he refused. I thought I was being very clever and I was quite disappointed and frustrated. I don't know if he was just being ornery or if he had already seen what I had done and was teasing me. Anyway, this incident made me feel justified in fibbing about having eaten the huge potato.

Chapter 15

Camping at the Yankee Fork

One very memorable event was a camping trip the entire family took to the Yankee Fork of the Salmon River. This was before much of the area was devastated by the huge gold dredge which destroyed miles of the beautiful Yankee Fork. The dredge, which was last owned and operated by J.R. Simplot, still exists as a museum open to the public at the exact spot where it was when mining operations stopped. Dad and several other local businessmen had invested in a gold mine and smelter some miles up the Yankee Fork from Sunbeam. We planned to camp nearby, and the outing served as a family vacation and gave Dad a chance to inspect the mining operations.

The trip was taken after the first crop of hay had been put up and the potato crop had been irrigated for the first time, which allowed us to take a break from farm work. We loaded up all our gear on the back of the farm truck which was equipped with a grain bed. We took extra clothes, lots of bedding, food and kitchen utensils, and some fishing gear. Mother and Dad rode in the cab, and some of the kids would take turns riding with them or riding in the back of the truck. The road trip was long; however we were all excited and even enjoyed the time on the road. We drove to Blackfoot and west to Arco, (the present Arco highway did not exist) north through Mackay to Challis and west along the Salmon River to Sunbeam and then north several miles along the Yankee Fork to the area where the mine and smelter were located.

The long ride was made longer by the fact that I experienced motion sickness. This meant we had to stop along the road several times to let me out. I was embarrassed and always felt guilty about slowing down our progress. Although my siblings were obviously impatient with me, I don't remember anyone saying anything. Once I was riding in the back of the truck after I had been sick a couple of times and my cap blew off. It was a New York Yankee baseball cap which Dad had given me as a present from one of his business trips back east. I had already delayed the trip several times because of my motion sickness, so I did not ask Dad to stop. Later Dad was visibly irritated when I told him what had happened.

We arrived at our camping spot late in the day. Dad had the younger kids gather pine boughs which we spread on the ground to serve as a mattress. On top of the boughs Dad laid a large canvass over which we spread our bedding. Nearby another large canvass was kept in case of rain.

All of our food was cooked over an open fire. It appeared that Mother worked as hard on the camping trip as she did at home, although we all pitched in and shared the chores. Dad did some of the cooking and took great delight in making his famous "Mulligan Stew," a mixture of potatoes and other vegetables, flour, and whatever meat and other ingredients were handy. The stew was always good. In fact, everything tastes wonderful when cooked and eaten out of doors, especially on a camping trip.

We camped at the same spot for several days. We inspected the mine and smelter, waded in the water, climbed the nearby hills and rolled rocks down the slope, which was always a favorite pastime for boys. We enjoyed fresh fish that Dad and the older kids caught. We did see a tiny amount of gold that had been smelted at the mill, although no mining operations took place while we were there. We were not allowed to go more than a few feet into the mine tunnel.

A short time after we returned home, the smelter burned down and was never rebuilt. That was the end of Dad's mining venture. When we were camping, the only other person at the mining operation was the fellow who had been hired as a night watchman, and as far as anyone knew, he was the only one around at the time of the fire. I believe he had been notified shortly before the fire that his employment was being terminated. Of course he was suspected of deliberately setting the fire. It was believed that he had returned to the state of Montana. He was never seen or heard from again. I have been to the dredge museum and Yankee Fork area several times. I am always reminded of our family camping trip, and how beautiful the river and valley had been at that time, but are no more.

Chapter 16

Early Trauma

One time when we lived on the Airport Farm, Dad brought home a small Boston Bull Terrier puppy. The pup was black and white and, of course, had a pug nose. He was perpetual motion and forever skipping across the floor and thus was given the name Skippy. Skippy was our first house dog. We had a farm dog, an outside dog named Jack, who helped bring the cows in from the pasture for milking. Everyone in the family loved and played with Skippy, including Mother and Dad. One day Skippy was found dead on the side of the gravel road in front of our house. He had been hit by a car and killed instantly. We were all devastated. No one saw it happen, and we never knew who hit Skippy. For some reason, I believed it to have been a deliberate act, but I never knew whom I should be angry with. It was my first experience dealing with death. We didn't have another house dog until we moved to the Osgood farm.

Probably the most traumatic experience I had in my pre-school years was the fire. Dad was at his office, and all the other kids were at school. Someone passing by stopped to tell Mother that a fire was burning in the area of the barn and corrals. When we first looked out the fire was not large; however, the wind was blowing and the fire was spreading quite fast. The barn, corrals and sheds were all made of wood that was very dry and there were stacks of dry hay and straw in the vicinity. Mother called Dad and he came racing home. I watched for his car as he raced toward home on the gravel road, and I remember seeing the great cloud of dust left behind. I thought that when Dad got home, he would know how to put the fire out and everything would be all right. The City of Idaho Falls fire trucks soon arrived, but the fire was totally out of control with flames one hundred to one-hundred fifty feet in the air. All the fire trucks could do was hose down the adjacent structures, mainly the shop, chicken coop and our house. I will never forget the noise and heat of the fire at its peak, nor the smell that remained after the fire had been put out. The barn, corrals and sheds were a total loss.

Neighbors came from everywhere to help. The animals had been turned loose, and I don't remember that we had any loss of livestock from the fire. One neighbor took the milk cows so they could be milked and cared for until we could make temporary arrangements at home. Other neighbors helped with the horses and pigs. The chicken coop and chicken run were a short distance from the fire. I don't believe any chickens were lost, although I am sure the egg production fell sharply for a while.

The cause of the fire was never determined for certain. There was some speculation that it started with a carelessly tossed cigarette, or was caused by faulty wiring. I think the consensus was faulty wiring. The main structures were old and had been expanded and wired for electricity. Birthing sheds for the sows had been built with lamps to provide warmth for the newborn pigs. Amateur electricians had done all of the wiring.

It was a major loss at the time; however, there was a positive side. New facilities were constructed that were a vast improvement over those destroyed by the fire. For years, whenever I saw a structure on fire or smelled the charred aftermath of a recent fire, I would get a sick feeling in the pit of my stomach and remember the farm fire. I guess I still do.

Chapter 17

From the Ashes

The next spring a new barn was built. W. O Shively was in charge of the construction. He was often accompanied by his young son, Ivan, who was a couple of years younger than I. Ivan often wet his pants and received a scolding from his dad. It seemed to me that the more Ivan was scolded the more he wet his pants. I was fascinated watching the new barn take shape and following the stages of construction until it was completed. It was a magnificent barn. W. O. Shively was the uncle of my longtime friends William, Jim and Jerry Shively. Jerry served in the State Legislature.

When the barn was finished, Mother and Dad had a huge barn dance to celebrate. The floor of the huge hayloft was fir which had been sanded down fairly smooth. The older kids put floor wax on the floor to make it danceable. The large crowd included all of our neighbors and friends from the New Sweden area, family friends from town, relatives, and many co-workers who worked with Dad at the Idaho Potato Growers. The music was live and included Claus Sealander, who played his accordion. I enjoyed watching the "older" folks dancing and having a good time. Many of the older kids also danced. Dances were a very popular social event in those days, and most of the adults were very good dancers. Mother and Dad danced well together. The dances included waltzes, polkas, the Schottische, and the Charleston.

Many more people smoked in those days than do now, and I remember being particularly afraid of another barn fire. Some folks stepped outside for a smoke, and there was also some drinking, although no one got out of hand. Mary and I were the self-appointed fire marshals. We spent the whole evening with flashlights, patrolling around and through the corrals and sheds. Our inspections included the various pens or cubicles on the first floor of the new barn, and also along the sides of the loft of the new barn where the dancing was taking place. We were on the lookout for any sign of a carelessly tossed cigarette or cigar. Fortunately, we did not find any. Later, when the City of Idaho Falls acquired the farm through condemnation proceedings for expansion of the Municipal Airport, the roof and loft portion of the new barn was moved to the present Osgood farm and placed on a new foundation with a new array of pens, stanchions and other facilities built as part of the first floor. It remains there today.

After listening to Mr. Sealander play his accordion, I very much wanted to have my own accordion and learn to play. I could not have even lifted one at the time. It never came to pass. I also remember Mother reading me a picture book about penguins, which prompted me to want a pet penguin. Mother tried to explain that a penguin could not live in our climate; however, I insisted I would keep it in a tub filled with cool water and would take very good care of it. I never did get an accordion, or a penguin, or a pet monkey like Nellie Lundgren had. I guess sometimes I just reached too high.

Chapter 18

School, at Last

On September 1, 1939, on orders from German Chancellor Adolph Hitler, Germany invaded Poland. Within a few days France and England declared war on Germany, and World War II was underway.

Also in September, 1939, I entered first grade. Finally, I also rushed frantically around in the morning, picked up my sack lunch, and stood in line with my older siblings to catch the school bus. I am sure everyone remembers his or her first grade teacher. Mine was Miss Floyd, who taught first grade at Eagle Rock Elementary School in Idaho Falls. The school was located south of the city business district along what is now South Capital and offered grades one through five. The school grounds were bounded on the north by Short Street and on the south by the Challenge Creamery and the freight offices of Garrett Freight lines, and on the west by South Capital Avenue, across and below which was the Snake River. Overall, the location was not exactly ideal for a grade school.

The principal was Mr. McVicker who, we were told, kept a piece of rubber hose in his office for use on any student who might leave the playground without permission or otherwise misbehave. I don't remember any student going down to the river bank. We lived in fear of the rubber hose. I am not sure if Mr. McVicker ever used the rubber hose to discipline a student; none of us was willing to take that chance.

I thoroughly enjoyed my first grade experience, once I became familiar with the routine and acquainted with the other students. Vonda Jackson and David Reed were two familiar faces. I soon met Jim Howard, Wilbur Collins, Jim and Bill Shively and others with whom I formed lifelong friendships. One of my best friends was Roland Wilson, son of a police officer. Roland married right after high school and started a family. One Christmas he was out of work and held up two Montana banks. His father, Captain Dan Wilson read the description of the suspected bank robber, recognized it was his son Roland, and arrested him. Roland was sent back to Montana, pled guilty and spent several years in the Montana State Prison at Deer Lodge. Roland later told me that he was out of work, had sick kids to care for, and was desperate. He is back in Idaho Falls working in printing, a trade he learned while in prison. I see Roland and his wife occasionally and respect them very much for the way they have handled themselves.

I liked everything about the first grade. Miss Floyd was a superb teacher. Learning to read was a wonderful experience for me, as was the opportunity to socialize with others kids my age. I think I was a pretty good student. As I mentioned, I was quite shy, and therefore I tended to be rather quiet, and I was eager to follow directions. The stories about Dick and Jane, Spot and Puff fascinated me. After school I was always anxious to bring Mother up to date on what we had done that particular day. Often I would bring home my work papers and read them to her.

Miss Floyd asked her first grade students if they would like to help set up a "grocery store" in one corner of the classroom. She thought it would be a lot of fun for us, and would teach us about money and buying and selling grocery items. We all thought it was great idea. Miss Floyd had a list of things we would need and asked if any of the students had any of the needed items at home. One item needed was a table, and I volunteered to bring a table. As it turned out we did not have an extra table at home that was the size needed. Uncle Glen heard me talking to Mother about the table, and said he thought he could build one, and he did. Miss Floyd was pleased, and I was proud when Glen delivered the table to the classroom.

I was extremely fond of Miss Floyd. When she was thanking Uncle Glen for the table, I remember thinking how nice it would be if they were to fall in love and get married. It was not to happen. Glen was dating Marjorie Lundgren, daughter of Nellie and Art Lundgren, who worked for a time as a secretary for Dad at the Idaho Potato Growers.

Chapter 19

Country Kid and School Daze

Many of the students who attended Eagle Rock School were bused in from the rural areas adjacent to Idaho Falls. Those of us who rode the bus to school always brought our sack lunches from home and ate at the school during the lunch hour. The students who lived in the neighborhood would generally walk to school and then walk home for lunch. In the early years, Mother always baked her own bread and she would make homemade sandwiches for us. The sandwiches tasted great; however, I was conscious of the difference between my sandwiches and those of some of the other kids that were made with bakery store bread.

I envied the kids who had sandwiches made with bakery bread. The bread slices were thinner and more uniform in thickness. Interestingly, some of the kids with bakery bread sandwiches envied those of us with homemade bread sandwiches, and we often traded. Every student received a half pint of milk at lunchtime. We paid a token amount for our milk, and those who couldn't afford to pay received the milk anyway, and were never identified. I believe the milk was part of a government program which was intended to provide nourishment for kids and financial support for farmers.

When I was a small boy, I always wore bib overalls at home, and for the first few years of school I wore bib overalls. The same was true of my older brothers. In the first, second and third grades most of the boys wore overalls, particularly those who lived in the rural areas. Over time more and more boys began wearing regular pants, and after a while I remember being self-conscious of my overalls. Riding the bus, sack lunches with homemade bread, and bib overalls marked us as "country" kids and tended to set us apart. I don't remember just when it occurred, perhaps in the third or fourth grade, but ultimately I began to wear regular pants. Mostly the pants were "cords" made of corduroy material, and some were "hand me downs." Levis were still a few years away.

One time several of us boys were playing softball on the school grounds and I stood too close to the batter, David Reed. When he took a swing at a pitched ball, the bat hit me squarely in the forehead. I was knocked out for a few minutes and the other kids thought I was dead. My head soon swelled to what seemed twice its regular size, although it probably wasn't. I was put on a couch in the principal's room, a school nurse came by and put cold packs on my forehead, and later I rode the school bus home. I returned to school the next day. I received lot of attention over the next few days, particularly when my face turned black and blue, although it did not hurt very much after the first afternoon.

We played with marbles at school, and also at home. Marbles and softball were our main activities. We also played the usual games of hide-and-seek and Red Rover. On the outside of the school house there was a fire escape for evacuating the second floor It was a large round metal tube about thirty-six inches in diameter. We had regular fire drills during school hours, and the fire escape was an attraction after school while waiting for the school bus to take us home. We kids would take off our shoes and climb up inside the tube and then slide down, over and over again. Fortunately, we never had to use it to escape a fire.

Chapter 20

Nearsightedness and the Joy of Reading

During the summer after I finished first grade, I was fitted with glasses. I remember being out in the field with Reed and Norman when several military planes flew over in formation. Reed and Norman were all excited and pointed at the planes. I could hear but was unable to see the planes. They were surprised and later reported the incident to Mother. As a consequence, Mother made an appointment for me to have my eyes examined by Dr. Scholler, an optometrist. I was nearsighted.

Over the intervening years my nearsightedness became progressively worse. Years later an ophthalmologist told me that my vision had been overcorrected when I was young, He believed that overcorrection when my eyes were still developing had probably caused increased nearsightedness. Beginning with second grade, glasses were a necessary part of my everyday life. A few years ago I had surgery to remove cataracts in both eyes. As a result my nearsightedness disappeared and I now enjoy 20-20 vision. I couldn't believe the difference it made to have good vision without glasses.

The pace of my life picked up after I started school. Because we rode the school bus to and back home from school, the school day was long. The customary chores left less free time for play. I enjoyed learning to read and started reading extra material at home. I tried to anyway; however, I often found words with which I needed help to understand and pronounce. Mother and Dad instilled in all of us kids a love of reading that we still have today.

As far back as I can remember Mother belonged to the Book of The Month Club, and her books were shared within the family. We also received magazines at home, including Life, The National Geographic, Colliers, and The Saturday Evening Post with the wonderful Norman Rockwell cover paintings. The magazines generally included a variety of short stories and cartoons, and new issues were passed around until we had thoroughly read them all.

When it was allowed, I would bring my school books home and read the stories over again, not because the reading was required but just for the enjoyment of reading. When I was in second grade, I enjoyed reading my school book, the *Elson-Gray Basic Reader Two,* so much so that I asked for a copy of the book for my birthday. I am sure Mother wondered about the request, but she bought it for me. I found it a few years ago, and have since given it to my son, Steve, who now teaches at McCall High School in McCall, Idaho. I am sure Steve will share the book with his siblings, as I shared books with mine. On the inside of the cover I had written "Johnny Hansen, Grade 2."

Chapter 21

Parent Days at Eagle Rock School

At Eagle Rock School we occasionally had cupcake sales to raise money or to celebrate a special occasion such as Valentine's Day or a class party. On these occasions, Mother never failed to bake and either bring or send to school a large number of decorated cupcakes. The school also occasionally had "Parent's Day," and parents would be invited to come to school for lunch and a program put on by students. I remember several occasions when both Mother and Dad came to Eagle Rock School to have lunch. I was extremely proud when they took time to attend our school functions, as not all of the parents would attend. Dad usually sat in a large desk chair in his office, or a large overstuffed chair at home, and it seemed funny to see him sit at a small desk at school. He was a large man, six feet tall and over 200 pounds, but he would somehow squeeze in and sit at a classroom desk and attached chair. Mary was two grades ahead of me, and we shared our parents on the days school events were held.

Dad had access to a 16-mm movie camera owned by the Idaho Potato Growers. He would often use the camera to take home movies when he traveled. I remember Mary and I invited Dad to come to school and show some of his movies. On these occasions, several classes would be combined for the events. I particularly remember Dad showing a movie he took of the newly constructed Grand Coulee Dam in the State of Washington. He also showed a home movie he took from a Washington DC hotel window, of the inaugural parade for President Franklin Roosevelt, following his election to a third term in 1940. Farrel Jr., as we called my oldest brother for many years, arranged to be excused from school and accompanied Dad on that particular trip. Whenever possible, Dad would take one of us kids along when he had a business trip. Dad always took time to give a brief narrative while showing the home movies. These events were attended and enjoyed by the teachers and Mr. McVicker, as well as by the students of Eagle Rock School.

Chapter 22

Observing the Field Work on the Airport Farm

Life at home on the Airport Farm was much the same when I was in the first, second and third grades. My chores were still mostly limited to bringing a supply of the coal and wood into the kitchen for Mother, gathering eggs and cleaning the chicken coop. As I became better at distinguishing weeds from newly emerging plants, hoeing in the garden during the summer became an added chore. When the garden vegetable plants had grown, of course, I had no excuse, and I did a lot of weeding in the garden. I also followed the bigger kids and uncles into the fields and watched their activities.

On the Airport Farm, the field work was all done with work horses. The alfalfa hay was cut with a horse-drawn mower. The mower had a sickle bar that extended out from the right side of the machine, and the cutting blades were moved back and forth by mechanical gears connected to the right wheel. The faster the mower went the faster the blades would move to cut the standing hay. The cut hay would fall directly behind the sickle bar as it was cut and remain on the ground until it was starting to dry. Then the hay was raked, first into windrows and then the windrows were raked into piles, both operations being done with a dump rake pulled by a single horse. It took a lot of skill to make a windrow with a dump rake. It took less skill to proceed down a windrow of hay and put the hay into piles.

When the hay was sufficiently "cured," that is sufficiently dried to prevent excessive heat and spoilage while in storage yet with enough moisture to be quality feed for livestock, the hay would be hauled to the stacking area. Horse drawn wagons were driven between the rows of hay piles in the hay field. As the wagon was moving, a person on each side would pitch the piles of hay onto the hay wagon, upon which another person would be positioned to receive and arrange the hay into a secure wagonload.

Before the wagons were loaded in the fields, two long chains were laid, front to back, along the bed of the wagon. When the wagon was half loaded, two more chains were similarly placed, front to back, across the hay already on the wagon. The fully loaded wagon was then driven to the stack yard. At the stack yard, the ends of the two chains under the top half of the load were hooked together and attached to a trip device. The chains were then attached to one end of a long cable that went straight up to a pulley fastened to the end of the large "boom" pole of the derrick. A long rope was attached to the pulley device, long enough to reach the ground when the load of hay was lifted to the top of the stack.

The cable went through two more pulleys attached to the derrick, one just below the cross beam at the top center and another at the center of the base of the derrick. The other end of the long cable was hooked onto a "singletree." or wooden bar attached to the back of the harness worn by the derrick horse. When all was ready, the person who rode, or sometimes lead, the derrick horse would start moving away from the derrick. This movement pulled the cable through all of the pulleys and the one-half wagonload of hay was rolled together in a large round bundle and lifted from the wagon

The derrick was an interesting structure that was constructed by hand. A derrick looked like a large toy. Large poles or wooden beams were used to make a square base, with as much as twenty-four feet on each side. Large poles went from the corners to a point high above and were secured to a cross piece consisting usually of a piece of beam about eight to ten inches square. A large pole, called the "boom pole" was attached to a pulley secured on the cross piece, at a point approximately in the middle of the boom pole. The boom pole could swing in an arc when the "sling" load of hay was lifted from the wagon, and be placed in a position above the point where a permanent haystack had been started or was to be started.

The sling load of hay would then be maneuvered by the person responsible for stacking the hay, the stacker, into just the right position. The stacker would yell "trip" and a person on the ground pulled the trip rope causing the chains to release and the sling load of hay to drop straight down. The process would be repeated and the lower half of the hay on the wagon would be lifted and placed on the haystack. An experienced "stacker" could maneuver the large swinging loads of hay such so that little pitchfork work was required to build a large, stable haystack that would not tip over.

In the morning, the stacker was lifted by the derrick cable to the top of the stack where he would stay until lifted down when the crew stopped for lunch. After lunch he was again lifted to the top of the haystack and stayed there until the crew stopped working about six o'clock. When a stack of hay became as high as the derrick could lift, it was topped out, that is given a dome-like shape. Then a team of horses would be hitched to the derrick to pull the large apparatus to a different location to start a new hay stack.

I enjoyed watching the operation, except for the occasional "runaway." The work horses were sometimes skittish, and if they were startled by anything they would often take off, pulling the wagon with them, and race off down a dirt farm road or across a field. These runaways often occurred in the field at the stacking area. After awhile the horses would become tired and slow down and be brought back. At times the wagon would be damaged and need to be repaired. It was frightening when the huge, powerful horses bolted and took off at full speed.

One time a team being handled by my Uncle Glen took off. He let them run until they started to become tired, and he was so angry he took his pitch fork and repeatedly poked the horses on the rump to make them continue running. He was either trying to teach the horses a lesson or just work off his anger; probably some of both. My only experience with the workhorses was when I was older and "rode" the derrick horse used to raise the hay onto the stack. I was a little apprehensive, but knew it was impossible for a derrick horse to run away. He was attached to the derrick by the cable, and also was usually the oldest and tamest of the big workhorses.

Chapter 23

The Grain Harvest

The grain harvest was another interesting farm operation. A horse-drawn grain binder cut the standing grain. A sickle bar cut the grain, much like the cutting of alfalfa hay; however, the grain fell back onto a moving canvas belt. The belt rolled the tall grain stalks into what we called grain "bundles," each one about ten to twelve inches in diameter. Twine was wrapped around each bundle and tied in a knot, mechanically, and the finished bundle was flipped to the ground. The binder was a rather intricate machine. It was operated by a person, seated on its center, who was able to watch to make sure everything was working properly. Others would follow the binder and put the grain bundles into a "shock." I often helped shock the grain.

A shock would consist of a number of individual bundles placed upright with the cut or butt end of the grain stalks on the ground, and with the heads, the ends containing the actual grain, above the ground. Several bundles were placed together, leaning toward the center, until a shock was completed. A field full of shocks of grain was a beautiful sight to see in the fall. When the shocked grain was determined to be sufficiently dry, horse-drawn wagons were driven between the rows of shocks and the individual bundles were tossed, using a pitchfork, preferably a light fork with three tines, onto the bed of a wagon. One person on the wagon would arrange the bundles on the load with the butt end of the bundle to the outside and the grain head end towards the middle of the load, to avoid losing grain which might shell out. The loaded wagons were then taken to the area near the corrals to be threshed; that is, the grain was shelled out and separated from the straw.

Large threshing machines and crews were often hired to complete the grain harvest, as few farmers had their own machines. Threshing machines were expensive and in use on a particular farm only a few days each year. A few farmers would purchase the machines to thresh their own grain and would then earn extra money by threshing grain for other farmers. The machines were huge and were operated by a large drive belt, perhaps twelve inches wide and sixteen or so feet in length, attached to a pulley of a large steam engine. In later years, the steam engine was replaced with a large tractor equipped with a power take off pulley. The loaded wagons were driven to a position along each side of the front or conveyer end of the threshing machine. Using the three tined forks, men tossed the bundles from the loaded wagons into the conveyor.

The conveyor carried the bundles into the inside of the threshing machine where they were shredded, and, through a rather complicated mechanical process, the grain was separated from the straw. The grain was then elevated by means of an auger to a large metal bin on top of the threshing machine. Periodically the bin would be emptied by putting the grain into burlap sacks. The sacks of grain were then taken to be stored in the barn to be used for livestock feed during the winter, or sold through a commercial grain elevator, or both.

The straw left over by the threshing operation was blown by a huge fan inside of the threshing machine, through a large metal tube attached to the rear of the machine. The tube was about twelve inches in diameter and could be extended up to about twenty-four feet. The tube was maneuvered as necessary to gradually build a cone-shaped straw stack. The straw was used for livestock bedding during the winter months. Threshing was a very dusty job, and many of the crew went swimming in the canal at the end of the day to cool off and get rid of the dust and dirt they had accumulated.

Chapter 24

Milk Cows Are Fulltime Work

I have mentioned that we always had milk cows, mostly Holsteins. Dad had a real interest in the dairy cows. He felt it was important to have quality cows and a quality purebred bull for breeding purposes, so that the bloodline of the herd would continually improve. The Holstein cows produced a larger quantity of milk than did others breeds, such as the Guernsey or Jersey cows, and the milk had butterfat content valuable for consumption or processing. We preferred Holsteins. I remember, however, that the owners of cows of other breeds would have friendly discussions about which breed was the best one, just as some vehicle owners would forever debate the relative worth of the Ford or Chevy car or truck. The arguments were usually based on which breed or make the person happened to own.

The cows at the Airport Farm were always milked by hand. The persons who milked the cows sat on wooden stools. Stools were generally made by nailing two short pieces of a two-by-four board together. The horizontal piece served as the seat and the vertical piece was a single leg to support the seat. There were few if any variations on the traditional "T" milking stool. The cows were usually milked in the barn, with their heads in a stanchion. This served to hold the cows in place, and allowed the cows to eat grain or hay placed in a trough, often called a manger, in front of the stanchions.

Most cows soon became accustomed to being milked. Some, however, were ill-tempered, and some were new mothers not used to the procedure. These animals could be a real challenge to the milker. The milker sat on the stool, leaned his head against the cow's flank and placed an open topped bucket below the cow's udder. The milker started to milk by gently squeezing two of the cow's teats, starting at the top and moving down the teat in a single motion, which forced the milk out of the tip of the teat.

The milker took hold of the back two or the front two teats simultaneously. Though a cow has four teats, obviously a milker can only manage two at a time. If the cow should kick, the milker had to react quickly to avoid being knocked over and also to hold the bucket to avoid any milk being spilled. When a cow had been completely milked, the milk in the bucket was poured into a large metal strainer, open at the top, which had been placed on top of a ten- or five-gallon milk can.

The strainer had a metal ring in the bottom that secured a thin cloth pad through which the milk was "strained." Periodically the cloth pad needed to be replaced with a clean one. During the hand-milking operation various things would fall into the open bucket. Such things as cow hair and manure which collected on the flanks of the cows would often be dislodged while the cow was being milked. In addition, there were always a number of barn cats in the area. Barn cats were not house pets, but really semi-feral cats that lived in the barn and farmyard area. They caught and ate live mice and lapped up any milk that was spilled.

The cats often became aggressive. They knew that milk was in the strainer, and they would leap from the ground and occasionally end up in the strainer. If that happened, the nearest person would immediately grab the cat, say a few cuss words, and throw the animal some considerable distance out the barn door. The cat, having been in the milk-filled strainer, had obviously contaminated the milk. Milk was occasionally re-strained; however, it was almost never thrown away. Our family drank the raw, un-pasteurized milk during all of the years we lived on the Airport Farm and several years after.

Dad enjoyed working with the livestock. Often when he was home on a Sunday afternoon, he enjoyed putting on his overalls and spending time with the livestock, especially the dairy animals. He would encourage us kids to join him, and I remember spending many a Sunday hauling and spreading fresh straw to make a clean bed for the livestock. We kids grumbled a bit to ourselves, never directly to Dad, because we felt we had been doing this kind of work every day while he was gone, and we preferred some free time on Sunday. It goes without saying, however, that caring for livestock is a full-time job. Animals have to be fed twice a day, and cows have to be milked twice a day, every day, seven days a week, and this includes Sundays, birthdays, Christmas, Thanksgiving and all other holidays, without exception.

Chapter 25

The Zenith Brings the News

At some point in time Dad purchased a Zenith radio housed in a large cabinet which was placed in the living room. Listening to the radio in the evenings became a family affair. We would listen to the evening news and a number of regular weekly programs. We listened to Fibber McGee and Molly, the Jack Benny Show, Amos and Andy, the Lux Radio Theatre Hour, and Inner Sanctum, the mystery program which opened and closed with the eerie sound of a creaking door. The living room was always quiet when our favorite programs were on, except during commercials, which incidentally were much shorter and less frequent than they are now. The Zenith had a shortwave band, and we kids would spend a lot of time trying to pick up foreign or shortwave stations, particularly as the war was spreading in Europe.

Dad's job as manager of the Idaho Potato Growers required that he travel a fair amount. When he was at home, he went to the office every morning and worked a full day. He generally also worked at the office on Saturdays and often went to the office on Sundays, for at least part of the day. I think I inherited this habit, perhaps to a fault. When quite small, some of the other kids and I would accompany Dad to his office on Sundays. While he worked in his office we would prowl around the office and the warehouse. The warehouse was a fun place for kids to play.

There were stacks of huge bundles of new burlap sacks, and a variety of handcarts used for moving hundred-pound sacks of potatoes from the potato sorters to railroad cars, which were always on the railroad tracks running along the side of the warehouse. During workdays, the warehouse was a beehive of activity, but on Sundays it was quiet and a great place to play. We played games and held races with the handcarts. Dad had a ticker tape in his office which gave him up-to-date potato prices in various markets in the United States, and sometimes breaking news, which I found fascinating to watch. These trips to Dad's office were fairly frequent and always a lot of fun for me.

On late Sunday morning, December 7, 1941, I accompanied Dad to his office. He and Mother had been listening to the Zenith in the living room, and they had been somber and quiet. As I look back, I am sure they were reflecting on the fact that Farrel, then seventeen years old, and Orval, then fifteen, could be called to serve in the military if the inevitable war lasted very long. They were well aware of the scope and duration of World War I, then known as The Great War.

On the way to his office Dad told me that our country would soon be at war. I immediately had a mental picture of two lines of artillery, each facing the other from a distance, with each side lobbing artillery shells at the other. I had no comprehension of Pearl Harbor and the Japanese aerial bombardment of the American warships crowded there. I think I had probably seen newsreels depicting war scenes in Europe and, perhaps, in the basement I had read articles in the *National Geographic* magazines which depicted similar scenes. I could not have begun to understand the significant impact the impending war would have on our family, and our friends and neighbors, not to mention the entire country and the world. However, I knew from Dad's demeanor something serious was happening.

Chapter 26

The B-17

One day during the following spring, we kids were returning home on the school bus. As we approached our house, the road was blocked. To our amazement, a B-17, then the largest four-engine bomber of the US Army Air Corps, (now the US Air Force) had crash landed at the end of the runway and skidded part way onto Airway Road. We had to take a circular route home through the neighbor's field to reach our house. The bomber was being guarded by members of the Idaho State Guard, and although the crash site was fairly close to our house, we were prevented from getting as close as we would have liked. Talk about excitement! I could hardly sleep that night. I could not wait to return to school the next day and tell the teachers and other students what we had practically in our back yard. I couldn't 'Show" but I really had something to "Tell"!

We knew that a B-17 bomber had landed at the airport earlier that winter, but the plane was kept at some distance north, closer to the Log Hanger. I don't remember paying much attention to it after the first day or so. Later, when I was serving in the Idaho State Senate and attended one of many receptions, I met the person who was the pilot of the B-17. I had mentioned that I was from Idaho Falls, and he laughed and mentioned the memorable occasion when he was also in Idaho Falls. He said he was piloting a B-17 bomber in bad weather, when the plane began to fill with smoke. He ordered the crew to bail out, and at the last minute, just before anyone had left the plane, he was amazed to see a large paved runway only a short distance away. This was the Idaho Falls runway. Instead of parachuting out of the plane, he circled right and made an uneventful landing at the Idaho Falls airport.

He said that the bomber needed to be repaired before it could be flown back to its base. The weather at Idaho Falls that winter was worse than anything he had ever experienced. He said the weather was so cold that the mechanics would stay in the log hangar to get warm before running out to the plane. When the mechanics became too cold to continue working, they raced back to the hangar to warm up again. Finally, in the spring when the repairs had been completed, an attempt was made for the bomber to take off and fly to Hill Air Force Base in Ogden, Utah.

    The pilot said he taxied the large plane to the north end of the runway, put the engines on full power, released the brakes and started his takeoff roll. During the take off roll he realized he did not have sufficient power for the plane to achieve lift off. He said he cut the throttles and hit the brakes as hard as he could. The landing gear of the B-17 collapsed and the plane skidded to a stop just off the end of the runway and partly across the road. I told him that I had lived in the house just west of where his plane crash landed, and how exciting it had been for me and my family. When I met him he was retired from the service. I believe his name was Colonel McNamara, although I cannot be certain. Meeting and talking with him was an interesting coincidence, one of several interesting coincidences that I have had in my lifetime.

Chapter 27

Introducing the Osgood Farm and Dad, the Pilot

In the summer of 1942 our family began the move from the Airport Farm to what we call the Osgood Farm, now operated by Bruce Hansen, a son of my brother Reed and his wife, Marilyn. Actually, the new farm, which was much larger, approximately 480 acres, was partly in New Sweden, partly in Osgood and adjacent to what is known as Oakland Valley. When we moved I had a choice of schools to attend. I could have attended the Osgood School, or the New Sweden School, or the Oakland Valley School which was a one-room schoolhouse. The Oakland Valley School was one of the last one-room schools in Idaho. I had been taking the school bus to Eagle Rock School in Idaho Falls, and all the other kids in the family were riding the bus into schools in town. I opted to continue attending Eagle Rock School. I did consider briefly how it would be to ride our pony to the one-room Oakland Valley School, but that was really not a serious consideration. I preferred going to school where I already knew all the students and teachers.

I remember the first time Dad took me to the location of the new farm. Most of the land was in sagebrush. Only about eighty acres of the land were then being farmed. This acreage was irrigated with water delivered through a wooden pipe or siphon connected to the Osgood Project, which was north of us. At that time the Osgood Project was owned by the Utah and Idaho Sugar Company, which was owned by the LDS Church. It consisted of small farms that were leased to individuals on a crop share basis. All of the renters were required to raise an allotment of the sugar beets the Utah and Idaho Sugar Company needed for making sugar at its factory east of Idaho Falls.

The wooden siphon was a large pipe, maybe thirty-six inches in diameter. It went down a hill, crossed under the county road, then back up the hill onto our land. It ended at a point that was slightly lower than where water entered the pipe back on the Osgood Project. The water, which flowed through

Chapter 27: Introducing the Osgood Farm and Dad, the Pilot | 59

the pipe, was discharged into and carried through an open irrigation ditch to the field where the water was needed.

We continued to receive water thru the wooden siphon pipe for the first year or two that we farmed the new place. It was made of tongue and groove boards held together by iron rods bent to the shape of the pipe. The rods were threaded at the end, and could be shortened with a wrench to hold the wooded boards tight to prevent excess water leakage. It would leak a lot when water was first put in the pipe in the spring. After a while the wooden slats became water soaked and swelled enough to seal most of the leaks. The wooden pipe was later taken apart and removed. Then the land that it had served was irrigated by the new system we had installed for the entire 480 acres. I was fascinated by the old siphon, and used to run on top of it, up and down its length on our side of the road, trying not to fall off.

When I first visited the new farm with Dad, I thought it was the most desolate land I had ever seen. There was little growing except weeds, sagebrush, dry grass, and the few acres of crops. At the Airport Farm there were a lot of large cottonwood and ash trees, and an orchard across the road. I always liked and enjoyed trees and still do. The only structure on the new farm was an old house on the land where Mother's round house was built years later. The house was then occupied by a Japanese family, and there were a few fairly large trees just north of the house. The trees are still there. I sensed Dad's enthusiasm, and I knew the new farm would blossom in time just as he said it would. My confidence in Dad really had no limits. I firmly believed in his ability to do anything he set out to do.

Shortly after we moved to the new farm, Dad decided he wanted to learn to fly and began taking lessons. Dad really enjoyed learning to fly and soon he soloed. To solo required that he take off and land in the plane three consecutive times without his instructor on board. He had flown several hours with the instructor who felt he was proficient enough to solo. Upon soloing he received a student pilot license which allowed him to fly alone or with an instructor, but did not permit him to take other passengers. A private pilot license required at least thirty-five total hours, with a specified number of hours flying cross-country, then passing a written and a flight test.

One Sunday Dad was going to the airport to practice and asked if I would like to go with him, and, of course, I did. Dad parked the car a short distance north of the log hangar. He said for me to wait until he checked a plane out and had taxied to a point opposite the car. He said for me to come to the plane when he gave me a wave of his hand. I did and climbed into the front seat of the Piper Cub, which had two tandem seats. Dad was sitting in the rear seat.

He took me for a ride around the area, which included flying over the farm. It was very exciting, and I did not get sick. Of course he had not as yet completed all of the requirements for his private pilot license. I am not sure if I was aware of this; however, I would not have cared. Dad was not one to take chances with his kids.

Chapter 28

Beginning a Year of Transition

World War II was raging in the summer of 1942, and not going well. Almost everything was rationed, including gasoline, rubber, building materials, meat, butter and a whole variety of other goods. Therefore, it was very difficult to get materials to build a house. The Airport Farm had been taken by condemnation proceedings for expansion of the Idaho Falls Airport. The amount of compensation for the taking had been set by a jury at the conclusion of the trial. It was an amount Dad never felt reflected the fair value of the farm and improvements.

As a result of the condemnation proceedings, we were left without a house in which to live. Under the circumstances, Dad received permission to purchase materials to provide a family home on the new farm, but only for a basement house. A basement house was not uncommon in those days because it was inexpensive to build. It was simply a basement with a flat roof over it, about three feet above ground level. Our basement had to be large enough to accommodate our family of eight. The basement house that was ultimately built had an entry, bathroom, kitchen, and living room on the south side and bedrooms on the north side. One bedroom was for Mother and Dad, another for all of the boys, and a smaller bedroom for Mary. The boy's bedroom often accommodated others who were not members of the family. We used to joke that you never knew who was sleeping in the boys' room unless you looked in.

The roof and loft of the new barn as well as the shop and chicken coop needed to be moved to the new farm. Dad talked with "Happy" Brothers, the most active house mover in the area, about moving the barn. Mr. Brothers said that it could not be done. A former employee of Mr. Brothers, Dave Lemons, who had gone into business for himself, heard that Dad wanted the barn moved.

Mr. Lemons looked the situation over and said he thought he could do it, and he did. It was an amazing feat to watch. He lifted the barn loft off the ground and arranged a variety of wheels and axels under it which were attached to a couple of large trucks. He then drove, with the barn in tow, across the fields, ours and our neighbors, in a northwest direction, to the Butte Highway at a point south of the new farm; then up the Butte Highway to the new location where the barn now stands. It took many days to complete the job because the movers had to remove and replace fences, fill in and reopen irrigation ditches, arrange for telephone and power lines to be temporarily taken down and put back up.

As an aside, "Happy" Brothers was the developer of "Happyville," which many will remember as a haphazard development on the west side of town, south of Broadway. The development consisted of several old houses which Mr. Brothers purchased and moved to parcels of ground that were covered with lava rock outcroppings. The development was not platted and did not have underground water or sewer lines, or street improvements. Some years later the development was annexed by the City of Idaho Falls and the necessary improvements were finally installed.

Moving the smaller buildings to the new farm was accomplished rather easily, compared to moving the barn. Also during the spring and summer new corrals were built at the new farm. Since the majority of the 480 acres were covered with sagebrush and native grasses and had never been farmed, the land had to be cleared. A machine was obtained which had multiple flanges that rotated at a fast speed under a large iron cover. This machine was driven over the ground to beat down and break off the growing sagebrush. This operation was only partially successful. Much of the broken sagebrush was piled and burned. Then the ground had to be plowed.

The clearing of brush and plowing had started as early in the spring as the weather permitted. Dad had acquired two Farmall M tractors by this time, and we also had an older Farmall H tractor. For plowing, the two International Farmall M tractors were used, each pulling a two-bottom "tumble" plow. As I remember one tractor and plow started on the south edge of the farm, and the other started on the north edge, then they gradually worked toward the middle of the main part of the farm. They plowed what seemed like an incredibly long distance. I recall watching the unplowed area becoming more and more narrow as the days went by. Finally, when the strip was quite narrow, an amazing amount of wildlife, including pheasants, grouse, sage hens, rabbits, a few coyotes, and even a couple of deer, emerged from the remaining cover and fled. Now they needed a home.

Chapter 29

Building the Westside Mutual Canal Company

Dad purchased several water rights of flow in the Snake River to provide irrigation water for the new farm which, except for the 80 acres or so served by the wooden siphon, had no water rights. Dad purchased a carrying right from the New Sweden Irrigation District, after much negotiation with its directors, to permit the newly purchased water to be transported from the Snake River, through the Great Western Canal, which ran along a portion of the east side of the new farm.

The water level in the canal was considerably lower than the new ground. We had neighbors adjoining us on the south who also had a considerable amount of undeveloped sagebrush covered land, about the same acreage as we were developing. Our neighbor's new land was also higher than the canal and thus could not be irrigated by gravity flow from the canal. These neighbors were Abner Snarr and his brother A.D. Snarr, and several of their sons. Another farmer, Bill Baxter, also had about 80 acres of land that was not being irrigated because it was at a higher elevation than the canal. All of the high ground owned by the Snarr family, the Hansen family, and by Bill Baxter—over 1,000 acres in total—was contiguous.

As a result of their common need, Dad and the others developed a plan for a pumping project that was quite unique for the times. After considerable planning, a large channel was dug from the bank of the Great Western Canal, across a portion of land owned by one of member of the Snarr family, to a location as far north as water could flow by gravity. The end of the channel was still approximately one half of a mile from the south boundary of our new farm, which was the highest point of all of the new acreage to be developed. At this location, a series of large electric motors and pumps were installed, and a pump house was constructed to enclose them.

A trench was dug from this area north and up the hill to the high point of our farm. A concrete pipe about thirty-six inches in diameter was laid in sections in the trench, then covered with dirt. The decreed water, owned by the participants in the new development, was to flow by gravity through the open channel from the canal to the pump house, then be pushed by the pump turbines up the hill through the pipeline to its terminus at the high point. The water would flow from the end of the pipeline into a concrete structure which we called the "water box" and sometimes the "outlet." From the outlet, the water flowed through three large head gates, in measured amounts, into newly built levies and ditches. This was to be the system to provide irrigation water for the 1,000 acres of new farm land being developed.

The water project, later formally incorporated as Westside Mutual Canal Company, was very ambitious for the times. Over one thousand acres of previously uncultivated land was under irrigation at one time. Irrigation water was lifted several hundred feet, higher than any other similar type of farming project at the time, I believe, in the state of Idaho.

Of note is that truckloads of the topsoil removed when the pipeline trench was dug were taken to the site of the LDS Temple on the east side of the Snake River in Idaho Falls. The Temple was under construction and the rich sandy loam soil was used to landscape the grounds when construction was completed. Mother often said proudly that the Temple was landscaped with topsoil from our farm. Technically, the soil came from the Snarr property across the fence; however, we never bothered to point that out to Mother!

Chapter 30

Cleaning the Pipe and Patrolling the Levies

When the construction of the project was completed and before water was put into the pipeline, several of us kids were asked to go inside the thirty-six-inch buried pipeline, and to navigate from the top end downhill to the pump house, a distance of one-half mile. Our job was to collect any rocks, pieces of concrete or mortar, or other debris left during the installation of the pipeline, thus preventing any such debris from backwashing into the pumps and causing damage to the pump turbines.

Reed, Norman, and I, and perhaps someone else, were involved in checking the pipeline. I had seen both ends of the pipeline just before we started and I knew it was not connected to the pumps. Still I was more than a little afraid during our journey down the inside of the pipeline. We each had a short length of a board, equipped with roller skates, on which, with gloved hands we propelled ourselves through the pipeline.

Once we had gone only a short distance, all light disappeared and we had to rely on flashlights. Our voices and the sounds made by the roller skates echoed and were almost deafening; the shadows from the flashlights were eerie, to say the least. I know I could not have done it by myself; perhaps none of us could have. Together we were able to complete the task, and we were helped by the fact that no one wanted to be the person who said, "Let's go back." We were all proud of our accomplishment and received congratulations from the grownups.

A short time later the pipeline was connected to the pump house and tested. All went well until a bolt of lightning shut off the pumps, as was supposed to happen. The weight of the water in the half-mile of thirty-six inch pipe was too great and it blew out the lower end of the pipeline. Experts decided that a large relief valve needed to be installed at the lower end of the pipeline, so that if the pumps shut off, for whatever reason, the water in the pipeline could rapidly escape back into the channel without causing damage to the facilities in the pump house.

From that point on the problems were minor. Because of the importance of the pumping system to crop irrigation at critical growing periods, and also a concern that vandalism might occur, a night watchman was hired. The night watchman stayed at the pump house throughout the night, ready to respond to any emergency. The pumping facility was impressive and unique, and many people came to inspect it, including some members of the US Army Corps of Engineers.

The water which reached the outlet at the high point, flowed in three different directions, north, east and west, through newly constructed levies and ditches. The soil from which the new levies were made was dry, powdery, and contained pieces of sagebrush roots and branches. As a result, when the first water was allowed to flow in the levies, and before the soil was soaked and had settled, leaks were frequent and difficult to contain.

We regularly patrolled the levies, but there were few people available to patrol and the levies were long and extended in different directions. Often our first indication of a washout was the fact that the water level in a levy had suddenly dropped. We would immediately run down the levy to find the place where the washout occurred, and attempt to plug the ever-enlarging hole in the levy bank. The remedy was to quickly shovel more dry powdery soil into the gap, which often took some time because the newly shoveled soil would also quickly wash away.

I have a vivid recollection of Dad coming from the office to watch the water being turned from the outlet into the levies. A washout occurred near the outlet, which took a large chunk of the bank of the levy, and we were having difficulty plugging the hole in the bank. Dad, dressed in a suit and tie, his normal office attire, jumped into the levy and stood in the middle of the gaping hole in the bank. He shouted for everyone to throw dirt and bags filled with dirt, against his legs, which we did, until the hole was filled. His suit was a mess; however, Dad was pleased. His quick action prevented an even larger section of the bank from washing away. A large uncontrollable washout necessitated that all of the pumps be shut off before the bank could be properly repaired. Shutting off the pumps, almost a mile away by road, and restarting them, was a major undertaking and one to be avoided if at all possible.

Problems with the banks of the levies occurred frequently. Pieces of sagebrush roots and branches were buried in the dry, powdery soil and water tended to follow these pieces through the bank. A small leak could quickly turn into a major washout. Leaks were also caused by mice and gophers burrowing holes into the banks through which the water would flow, resulting in washouts. The problems were gradually alleviated as the banks settled and were strengthened by the growth of grasses and other plants which held the soil together, but the problems with mice and gophers were ongoing.

Chapter 31

Farrel Goes to College

During the late summer and early fall, we made the final move from the Airport Farm. The family moved into the basement house, and the livestock was moved to the new facilities on the Osgood farm. Much of the machinery was also moved; however, some of the equipment was moved back and forth until all the crops on the Airport Farm were harvested. The potatoes harvested on the Airport Farm were trucked to a new cellar on the Osgood farm. As I said earlier, the year of transition was a hectic year for all of us. But we were in store for another change.

In the spring of 1942 Farrel had graduated from Idaho Falls High School and prepared to enter Washington University in St. Louis, Missouri, to begin his pre-med studies. I cannot remember when Farrel first decided that he wanted to be a doctor. I cannot remember when he was not going to be a doctor! Even when he was a young boy he talked about studying medicine, and his decision was understood and accepted. He was a good student, and serious about his studies. Once he received a chemistry set for Christmas, and he seemed to always be doing interesting experiments. His knowledge and experiments always impressed me, except when he made a gas that smelled like rotten eggs!

One time a barn cat had been stepped on by a cow and was injured. Fortunately, no bones were broken, but the cat had a large tear on its side and some of its intestines were exposed. Farrel put the cat under sedation by holding a piece of cotton soaked in chloroform against its nose. He cleaned out the wound and carefully put the intestines back inside the cat. After checking everything out, he sewed the wound with a needle and thread borrowed from Mother. I was very impressed with how he had handled the situation. The cat woke up after the procedure, and as far as I know, it survived and had a long and happy life.

Farrel worked on the farm throughout the summer of 1942 and left for St. Louis in the early fall. The Idaho Potato Growers had purchased a large semi truck that could carry the equivalent of a railroad carload of potatoes. The truck had refrigeration equipment and a sleeper compartment and was quite an impressive rig. Most of the potatoes that were sent to market were shipped by railroad cars owned and operated by the Union Pacific Railroad. The new truck was probably intended to give the railroad a little competition, although most of the potatoes continued to be shipped by rail. The semi could be driven directly to the customer who was generally in the middle of a large city, which eliminated a second handling of the potato shipment. Rail shipments always had to be picked up at the railroad siding and transported to the customer.

The semi was usually driven by Dib Otteson. Dib came to work for the Association when he was eighteen years old and continued working there his entire career. He was an amazing and talented man. I thought the new semi was pretty neat and often asked Mr. Otteson to tell me about the places to which he hauled potatoes. His destinations included Los Angeles, Chicago, Kansas City, New York City, and a variety of other large cities, mostly in the eastern part of the United States. I thought it would be fun to take a long road trip in the new truck, but I never did.

Well, Farrel did. He rode with Mr. Otteson to Washington University in St. Louis, Missouri. Dad had arranged for a truck load of potatoes to be delivered to Kansas City, at about the time Farrel needed to start his pre-med studies. The rest of us kids were very proud and excited when we saw him off on his journey. I believe that Mr. Ottesen drove the truck directly to the University campus where Farrel was deposited. Farrel was a student at Washington University for two semesters.

Chapter 32

The Unfortunate Tractor Escapade

From the time we had finished the move from the Airport Farm and had become settled on the Osgood place, life seemed to move at a very fast pace. Our dairy herd had increased, and by this time included many high quality purebred cows. I began to help with the cow milking, first by hand and later by milking machines. When we started using machines to milk, we started with a single machine. We understood that once we started milking the herd with a machine, we should no longer milk any of the cows by hand.

Reed and I were put in charge of milking with the machines. We started around 4:30 each morning and because of the size of the milking herd, we finished three to four hours later. It was terribly boring. We later realized that what we should have done was to milk some cows by hand while the single machine was used to milk others, and simply make sure that we hand milked and machine milked the same cows each day. We would have been less bored and finished in shorter time. It wasn't long, however, until we added a second machine, and later a third. Multiple machines kept us busier and shortened the time for doing the milking and related chores.

I was fairly large and strong for my age, and soon found I could do a variety of farm work. By now we were using tractors exclusively. I drove tractor to help disc and harrow the newly plowed ground prior to planting, and I became more and more involved in other field work. I particularly enjoyed working with tractors in the fields, and was eager to show others that I could do the work of a man, and I could. My judgment, however, was not always that of a grown man.

One day I was doing field work with a tractor which had been equipped with steel wheels with large metal lug cleats, instead of rubber tires. The metal lug cleats did not pack down the newly plowed soil as much as the wide rubber tires. I first pulled a disc across the newly plowed ground and then I hooked onto a harrow and pulled it across the same ground to prepare the field for planting. I was the only person in the field at that particular time. After I finished harrowing, I unhooked the tractor and started driving through a grassy swale along a cedar post fence at the bottom of the field. I decided to see if I could get the tractor to go in fifth gear, which was the "road" gear, something that was a challenge, and not recommended except for driving on a smooth road surface with rubber tires.

With the heavy lug wheels I had difficulty gaining enough speed so that the tractor could maintain the higher speed, but I was finally able to. I was driving in fairly tall grass with the fence off my left side, and was paying close attention to the wheels as I picked up speed. The smaller front wheels, which were connected to the steering wheel, struck a chunk of an old log or fence post lying hidden in the grass. The tractor swerved sharply to the left. The left rear wheel lugs caught the top of a fence post and the tractor flipped upside down, all in a split second.

I was knocked out temporarily, and when I came to, I was under the tractor, although not pinned down. One of the rear lugged wheels was still rotating, inches above my head. Gas was leaking out of the gasoline tank and the tractor had caught on fire. I reached up and shut off the ignition, crawled out from under the tractor and ran a short distance away. A man had been driving down the highway and saw the accident. He stopped his car, and seeing that I was apparently unhurt, he ran to the tractor and put the fire out with a fire extinguisher. It turned out that he was a fire extinguisher salesman! Talk about good fortune. If the man had not stopped, there was fresh dirt nearby which I probably could have used to smother the fire. I was somewhat in shock, however, and I am not sure I would have figured out what to do and have been able to react fast enough to put the fire out before the gas tank exploded.

The experience was very traumatic. The tractor was taken to the dealer for repairs and a new paint job. The new paint was red, however a slightly different shade from the original red, and from then on I could always tell which one of our several red tractors I had tipped over. Whenever I used that tractor, I would relive the experience and get a nauseous feeling in the pit of my stomach. Even though I had not used good judgment, neither Mother nor Dad scolded me. They were just relieved I had not been hurt. Farming is a dangerous occupation. Looking back, I am astounded that none of us had a really serious injury. All in all, we were a very lucky family.

Chapter 33

Holsteins and Guernseys and Bangs Disease

Not long after we had moved to the Osgood farm, Bangs disease was discovered in our dairy herd. Bangs disease can cause Brucellosis in humans, sometimes called Undulant Fever. The only solution to the problem was to sell the animals for slaughter. The meat was safe to eat; however, the milk could not be consumed. By this time we had quality, high producing purebred cows that, if disease-free, were much more valuable as milk cows than they were as meat. But we had no choice but to sell the animals for slaughter. This was a significant blow.

Shortly after Dad sold the Holstein herd, he purchased a herd of Guernsey milk cows and had them delivered to the farm. Reed and I had been hoping it would take Dad longer to find another herd, so we would have a break from milking. We were back in the dairy business, but we much preferred Holsteins over Guernseys. Guernsey cows were more difficult to milk and produced less milk. We had Guernseys for quite a while, but gradually we began acquiring Holsteins and ultimately all of the Guernsey cows were replaced with Holsteins. When the Bangs disease was discovered, we immediately bought a home pasteurizer. From then on, we drank only pasteurized milk!

Dad purchased a prize Holstein bull, a magnificent animal that was kept separate from the other animals in a small corral consisting of a large rectangular pole fence about eight feet high. This particular bull, named Pete, was exhibited at the Eastern Idaho State Fair in Blackfoot, and on more than one occasion received the Grand Champion award. One night after dark Dad came home from the office and checked on the bull. As I recall, he wanted to show the bull to a friend who was with him. Dad climbed into the enclosure and the bull charged and pinned him against the corral poles. The person with Dad distracted the bull and Dad was able to climb out over the fence. He sustained several broken ribs and was quite sore for several weeks. Dad took full responsibility for the incident, saying that since it was dark the bull felt threatened. Everyone was glad that only ribs were broken as he could have just as easily been killed. The bull weighed well over 2,000 pounds.

Some of our best Holstein cows were also exhibited at the fair and received a variety of ribbons. The older boys, Orval, Norman and Reed, all studied agriculture in high school and were members of the Future Farmers of America. For FFA projects they raised hogs or steers, animals that were often exhibited at the fair along with our dairy cows. The three brothers handled the stock at the fair. While he was in high school, Orval won the State FFA speech contest, and served one year as State FFA President. Later Reed was elected and served as State FFA president.

Taking animals to the fair was a lot of extra work. It was in addition to the usual chores at home, which included milking the cows twice a day and taking care of all the rest of the livestock. We had a fairly large number of sows which were bred and had litters of pigs that needed to be cared for. And we farmed 480 acres of pasture, alfalfa hay, grain and potatoes. Much more help was required for this farming operation than had been needed for the smaller 120-acre Airport Farm.

Chapter 34

Help Comes to the Osgood Farm

The four boys remaining on the farm in 1943 were still young, ranging in ages from seventeen down to ten. Farrel had left home, and Dad was busier than ever at the Idaho Potato Growers. The Association had begun to build and operate a processing plant capable of making a dehydrated potato granule product. The United States government had a great need for a dried potato product that would keep for long periods of time without refrigeration. Such a product could be shipped long distances and be easily reconstituted simply by adding water. The result was an edible potato product that could be mashed or fried and was served to servicemen stationed all over the world. It did not quite equal the taste of a fresh potato, but shipping and storing fresh potatoes overseas was simply out of the question.

The war compounded our labor problems. When we lived on the Airport Farm the Great Depression was still on, and labor was plentiful. When we moved to the Osgood farm, World War II was underway and labor was scarce. Many people were serving in the military and many more were working in factories and manufacturing plants producing materials for the war effort, including military equipment, airplanes, tanks, guns, munitions, and vehicles.

Dad purchased five older houses which were moved to locations across the highway from our basement house. The houses were fixed up to provide housing for the men who worked for us and their families.

About this time three young children were brought to the farm by their father and left to be raised by his daughter, Elizabeth Harris, who was the wife of one of the hired men. Their mother had died, and the father had remarried and was moving to Minneapolis. The kids were Lloyd Beal, who was a year older than I, Dorothy Beal who was just younger, and Ronald Beal, the youngest. They had an older brother, Ernest, who was the same age as Orval. He lived in town with another relative and went to high school with Orval and Norman. Lloyd and I become very close friends. At various times Lloyd stayed at our house. Ernest, or Ernie as he was called, worked summers on the farm and when he did, he stayed with us and slept in the boys' room in the basement house. Mother and Dad were surrogate parents to the Beal boys and encouraged them to work hard in school and to pursue a college education. All three of the boys did obtain college degrees. I am certain Mother and Dad not only gave them encouragement, but provided some financial help as well.

Ernie enlisted in the Navy in 1944, about the same time as Orval. After his time in the service, Ernie attended and graduated from the College of Agriculture at the University of Idaho. He later became an executive with a company that manufactured paper products. Ernie has since passed away.

Lloyd started college, but then joined the Navy and served in the submarine service after he graduated from high school in 1950. Upon discharge, he finished college and ultimately received a Doctor of Veterinary Medicine degree. He established a practice and an animal clinic in Sacramento, California. He recently retired and now lives in Utah. We keep in touch.

Ronald, the youngest, helped with our dairy animals for several years, and ultimately obtained a degree in Animal Husbandry from the University of Idaho. He managed several large dairy operations during his career, and also recently retired.

The Beal boys, particularly Ernie and Lloyd, were like members of our family. Their sister Dorothy did not live on the farm very long. Sadly, she was sexually assaulted by the husband of her sister, Elizabeth. He was prosecuted for statutory rape, at the insistence of his wife and was convicted. Elizabeth obtained a divorce and moved off the farm, taking Dorothy with her, but they stayed in the Idaho Falls area and I would often see them. Elizabeth contracted cancer and passed away a couple of years ago.

Back to the Osgood Farm, finding experienced help was becoming increasingly more difficult. Dad decided to rent the crop acres. He located and reached agreement with two brothers, Lester and Miles Hastings, who grew up in Teton County and had considerable farming experience. They rented the acreage, which had been planted to alfalfa, hay, grain and potatoes. Dad had always taken responsibility for making sure a proper crop rotation was followed, and for marketing the potatoes that were harvested, and he continued doing so. We boys took care of the dairy and other farm animals, and we also helped Lester and Miles Hastings with the farm work.

As the dairy herd grew, we constructed a new milking parlor and qualified for the Grade A milk program which enabled us to obtain a premium price for the milk we produced. As the dairy responsibilities grew and the number of Hansen boys still at home decreased, we found it necessary to hire a herdsman to be responsible for the dairy operations. One of the men hired by the Hasting Brothers was John Beal, the older brother of Ernie, Lloyd and Ronald. John ultimately became our herdsman and he did an excellent job. Lloyd stayed with his brother John much of the time; however, Lloyd and John's wife, Verla, often clashed. On several occasions, he moved in with our family for extended periods and shared my bedroom.

The new arrangement worked out very well. The Hasting brothers were excellent farmers. We boys and Dad were relieved of a lot of pressure. The boys were able to provide reliable help with the field work. The renters also hired additional fulltime help, all of whom had farming experience. These men and their families were very good neighbors.

Chapter 35

Calf Scramble at the War Bonnet Roundup

The War Bonnet Roundup rodeo was a fall tradition in the Idaho Falls area. It was held annually in the rodeo grounds located in Tautphaus Park, adjacent to what is now Rollandet Avenue. A large wooden grandstand made an arc around the east end of the arena. One year Lloyd Beal and I read that one of the rodeo events was to be a "calf scramble." A group of businessmen were donating young steer calves which were to be turned loose in the arena during a break in the rodeo competition. Young boys who signed up would try to catch the calves by hand. If a boy caught a calf, he would be allowed to take it home and feed and care for it. When the grown calf was sufficiently fattened for market, it would be sold through the local livestock auction. The market value of the captured calf when caught would then be deducted from the sale and the boy could keep the balance of the sale proceeds. The calf scramble program was intended to encourage young boys to start into the cattle business.

Lloyd and I decided to enter the scramble event. I practiced bulldogging on some of the young steers we had at the farm. Apparently I picked a young steer that was a bit too large, or maybe it was just my inexperience. In any event I grabbed hold of the animal by the head and tried to throw him to the ground, as I had seen cowboys do at previous rodeos. The young steer took off on the run, with me trying to hold on. I fell, and as I hit the ground I landed on my left arm and hand. My left index finger was bent at an odd angle and really hurt. I went to the house to have Mother take a look.

Mother suspected my finger was broken, so someone drove us to town to see the family doctor. Mother still had not learned to drive a car. I believe it was Dr. Cline who had his office above the bank at the southeast corner of Park and A Streets, now Inkley's Photo Shop. Dr. Cline asked me what had happened, and then examined and manipulated the finger, which caused even more pain. I asked him, "Is it busted?" and he started laughing. I didn't say anything but I was furious. Dr. Cline put a splint on the finger, wrapped it with tape, and Mother and I left. When we were back on the sidewalk, I asked Mother why in the world the doctor laughed. She said he was amused because of my poor English when I used the word "busted" rather than broken. I watched the calf scramble from the grandstand that fall. I don't remember whether or not Lloyd caught a calf.

Chapter 36

Vacation at Falconberry Ranch

In the summer of 1943 we took a family vacation, all members of the family, and also Ernie Beal, who was then working on the farm and living with us. Dad and a fairly large group of Idaho Falls businessmen had purchased the Falconberry Ranch located on Loon Creek in central Idaho. The Falconberry was essentially a dude ranch where owner/members and guests could go for rest and recreation, including hiking, fishing and hunting. The ranch had a manager, some part-time seasonal help, and a number of riding horses. Several acres of hay and grain were grown on the ranch, as well as a large vegetable garden. Crops were raised for the horses kept on the ranch, and for sale to the US Forest Service. The ranch was less than two hundred acres, a narrow strip of land which ran along the west bank of Loon creek, between the creek and a range of mountains. An airstrip on what amounted to pastureland had been laid out on the ranch. The only other access to the ranch at that time was a horse trail about ten miles long that ran from the end of a vehicle road running north along the Yankee Fork of the Salmon River.

I am sure one of motivations for the trip in the summer of 1943 was the fact that Farrel would soon be going into the military service, and Orval and Ernie Beal would likely be entering the service the following year. Mother and Dad believed this might be the last time all of us would be able to take a trip together as a family. In fact, it was. We loaded up the farm truck with all of our gear, food and supplies and started our journey. We drove to the end of the road where we were met by men from the ranch who had brought a number of horses, one for each of us to ride, and a few with pack saddles to haul the gear we brought. Mother was always nervous when she was near a horse; however, she was a good sport and got right into the spirit of the occasion. In fact, Mother had ridden on a number of occasions when she was a young woman. All of us kids occasionally rode the ponies we kept on the farm. I think we were fairly at ease, although none of us were expert horsemen.

The scenery along the trail was beautiful, as was the weather as we started down the trail to the ranch. I was riding a mare. I guess someone thought that since I was the youngest, then ten years old, she would be about right for me. Wrong! The mare was nervous and fidgety. I learned later that she had recently given birth to a colt that was back at the ranch. After we had ridden some distance, the mare worked the bridle bit out of her mouth and took off running. The horse jumped water, brushed tree branches and kept on running. All I could do was hold on to the reins and the saddle horn and try to keep from falling off. Without the bit in her mouth I could not control her with the reins, and she did not stop until we reached the ranch corral, a distance of several miles.

I arrived long before any of the other riders. When I disappeared ahead of them on the trail, the others assumed I was having a great time and were unconcerned. After all, there was only one trail and I was going in the right direction.

On arrival at the ranch, still running fast, the mare headed straight for an open loafing shed. The shed was not much higher than the horse was tall and had several large upright poles supporting the roof. I really became frightened at this point. I ducked my head as she entered the shed and was certain that if I didn't hit my head on the roof beams, I would hit one of the upright posts and break a leg, or perhaps both. Fortunately, neither happened. My horse came to a dead stop inside the shed, and I jumped off. The mare was soaking wet and covered with sweaty foam. I was very, very saddle sore. I dropped my jeans to inspect the damage, and found that most of the skin on the insides of my thighs had been rubbed off. I was hardly able to walk. I waited at the shed until the others arrived. The rest of the riders had a pleasant ride and had received a "guided" tour of the ranch. Later Mother had me apply salve on the insides of my thighs, and in a day or two I recovered.

We had a fabulous time at the Falconberry Ranch. One day we followed Dad along Loon Creek and sat on a large boulder while he tried unsuccessfully to catch salmon with a large three-pronged hook attached to a rope. We could see the huge, beautiful fish at the bottom of a couple of deep pools. Another day Reed and I were fishing in Loon Creek, without much success. We spotted a large fish in the shallow water near the bank. It was the largest "trout" we had ever seen. We waded into the water, chased the big fish toward the side of the creek, and then we scooped the fish out of the water and onto the bank.

We ran back to the main ranch house to show off our catch. We learned that our catch was not a "trout"; it was a salmon. The salmon we caught had spawned, that is, laid her eggs and covered them with gravel. When we spotted her, she was weak and simply waiting to die, as female salmon do after their arduous journey from the ocean up river to the tributary in which they had hatched out years before. We also learned that the salmon was not edible and would have to be thrown away.

    We took horse rides and did a fair amount of hiking and exploring, and in the evenings we enjoyed listening to tales about the history of the area. I enjoyed being with and watching Mother and Dad when we were on one of our rare family vacations. They were both totally relaxed, particularly Dad. When we were at home, as I have mentioned, Dad worked long hours. Even when he was home, I am not sure he was ever totally relaxed, at least to the extent that he would relax while on an extended vacation. On these occasions, he would laugh, joke, tell stories, and have fun helping with the cooking. One could almost see the boy in him come out. All and all it was a great time. In due course, we rode horses back down the trail to the end of the road where the truck had been parked, and we drove back to the farm and our usual routines. In the fall I entered the fifth grade at Eagle Rock School. Farrell Jr. entered the United States Navy.

Chapter 37

Farrel, Jr. Joins the Navy

Farrel worked on the farm during the summer of 1943, after which he enlisted in the US Navy and was sent to the Farragut Naval Training Station in north Idaho for basic training. Having an older brother entering military service at a time when the war was not going well for the United States was traumatic for our family. I remember the day he left. Dad was talking to Farrel in a quiet tone of voice and gave him a big hug. Tears came to Dad's eyes and he started to break down, and then got himself back under control. This was the second time I had seen Dad express such deep emotion. To see Dad, who was always a take-charge, under-control person, break down, made a lasting impression on me.

At Christmastime, 1943, when Farrel was stationed at the Farragut Naval Training Station, he was unable to be home for Christmas. This was the first time that any family member had been away from home at Christmastime. We went ahead as usual, decorated the tree, shopped for presents, ordered books, and made the customary candy. Mother always did extra baking. We had drawn names for presents, as was always done. Someone had drawn for Farrel and sent a letter telling him who was to be the recipient of his gift. Everything proceeded in the customary fashion until we started passing out the wrapped presents under the tree on Christmas Eve. Our practice was to pass out all the presents, and then we would each take turns opening one present and keep going around until all the presents were opened.

On this occasion all the presents were passed out; however, before any present was opened, someone, I am not sure who, started to cry, and then almost as if by signal, we all started to cry. We put all of the presents back under the tree, still wrapped. We knew there was a chance Farrel would be able to get a leave from his base, and that he would try to come home. We decided to postpone our Christmas and wait to see what might happen. Farrel did get a leave, and by hitchhiking, as I remember, he arrived home a few days after

Chapter 37: Farrel, Jr. Joins the Navy | 83

Christmas. When he was home, we all relaxed, opened our presents, and had a most enjoyable holiday. Farrel seemed surprised; however, I am sure was pleased that we had waited for his arrival.

After his leave, Farrel returned to Farragut and finished his basic training. While awaiting orders for his next assignment, he applied for admission to the V-12 program to further his medical career. Certain professions, including medicine and dentistry, were considered to be uniquely important to the war effort. Farrel was selected for the program and assigned to the Long Beach Naval hospital in the Los Angeles area. Still a member of the US Navy, he enrolled at UCLA and finished his pre-med studies.

The period from his admission into the V-12 program through his completion of the surgical residency spanned the years from 1943 until 1955. They were years well spent.

Chapter 38

Supporting the War Effort

By 1943 the war economy was in full swing, and the war news was getting somewhat better. The Allied forces had landed on the shores of North Africa late in l942, and, after a rough start, were making progress. Key targets in Europe were being pounded by bombers flown out of England. The bombing was causing extensive damage, but we later learned that the axis powers were incurring huge losses of planes and crewmen. There was beginning to be some optimism that the tide was also turning in our favor in the war raging in the Pacific.

Almost everyone had a family member, relative, or neighbor or friend serving in the military service. As a consequence, we wanted to do what we could to help the war effort, hoping that what we did would shorten the war.

We school kids regularly bought US Savings stamps at school. The stamps were put into booklets and when filled, the booklets were exchanged for a US savings bond. The purchase of the stamps and bonds helped fund the war effort and made us kids feel that we were playing an important part. It also provided a great incentive to save and invest. I remember seeing publications which indicated exactly how many savings bonds of a certain denomination were required to purchase a jeep, or a truck, or a tank or a particular airplane. We knew exactly where our money was going, and we felt very patriotic and proud of our contribution to the war effort. Classes and schools competed to see which one could raise the most money.

Scrap drives were organized. Kids helped collect scrap iron, aluminum, tin foil, rubber and other materials that were vitally needed by the government. There were areas throughout the county, including on the new farm, where over the years people had dumped a variety of items, including old automobiles, farm wagons, machinery, appliances, buckets, cans and bottles. One time in school I mentioned the junk that had been dumped on the far end of our farm. The following Saturday a truck with several men and boys arrived at the house. Some of us boys rode with them to the location and helped load the items deemed usable. The scrap drives provided an added bonus: in addition to salvaging needed materials, a lot of junk was cleaned up.

Casualties were regularly reported in the local newspaper, and by this time, young men whom we knew were listed as killed or wounded. The first one I remember being killed was Doyle Stewart. His father farmed and also drove the Osgood school bus. Doyle helped us in the potato harvest before entering the service. Many additional servicemen from our area were killed and wounded before the war finally ended.

At this time, Uncle Glen was in the US Army. He had attended Utah State University on and off for a number of years. He would stay out of school to earn money, then return to school and stay until he ran out of money, and so forth. Utah State University is a Land Grant College, and as such required that students take two years of ROTC, Reserve Officers Training Corp. ROTC students were issued uniforms, which helped with expenses. A student could elect to take two additional years of ROTC, and receive a monthly stipend, which also helped with expenses. Upon graduation, the student received a commission as a Second Lieutenant in the US army, and was committed to active duty service. Glen received a commission as an infantry officer, regarded as one of the most, if not the most vulnerable position during combat.

We all knew that Uncle Glen was in Europe, although we did not know where he was or exactly what he was doing at any given time. I wrote to him often, as did other family members. We used what was called V-Mail, a single sheet of thin, tissue like paper, which folded into an envelope for mailing. Glen often wrote back, and as with all of the servicemen in combat, his letters were heavily censored to avoid inadvertently disclosing any information useful to the enemy should the letter be intercepted.

Glen's younger brother, Grant, was in the US Army Air Corps, training to be a fighter pilot. He had enlisted in October, 1942 and spent the next twenty-six months in basic and advanced pilot training. He ultimately qualified to fly a P-51 fighter, the newest and fastest fighter plane in service. He received orders to go overseas in February, 1945, and after a furlough he was sent to the Pacific Theatre where he was stationed at an airfield in New Guinea. He was assigned a P-51, which he regularly flew on combat missions.

Grant came to visit us on his last furlough before going overseas. While he was with us the annual meeting of the Idaho Potato Growers was held in Idaho Falls. As general manager, Dad had the primary responsibility for the event and presided over the evening meeting. Uncle Grant and several of our family attended. Uncle Grant wore his uniform, complete with the gold wings he earned when he had completed his flight training, and the gold bars that signified his rank of Second Lieutenant. He was very handsome and we were all extremely proud to be identified with him.

I had a lot of cousins who were in the service. Uncle Heber had four sons in the service. His oldest son, Dean, was a navigator on a B-17 bomber and flew bombing missions throughout Europe. Max Hansen was in the Army, and served in the Aleutian Islands when the Japanese landed troops on the island of Attu. He said the weather on Attu was the worst he had ever experienced. Later, after the Japanese troops withdrew, Max was transferred to and served in the European Theatre of Operations.

It was common to see a small flag hung inside a front window of a house to signify that a member of that family was in the military service. Each flag had a star, silver in color, for each family member in the service. If a person serving had been killed, it was customary to hang a flag with a gold star attached. As the war progressed we saw more and more such flags, with both silver and gold stars. The war seemed to touch about everyone.

In the summer of 2006, Farrel and I drove to Twin Falls to visit briefly with our cousins Joy Staples, Dean, Glen, Harold, and Jim Hansen, the offspring of Uncle Heber and Myrtle Hansen. Dean told us he had been able to access the official records and reports of all of the bombing missions flown by the B-17 on which he was the navigator, including "the time our plane blew up." Dean then started talking about something else. I told him I had to hear the full details of the incident. He said they were taking off from an airfield in England for a bombing mission over Europe, with full gas tanks and the maximum load of bombs. The regular pilot was unable to fly that day and a former fighter pilot was assigned as a substitute.

The new pilot was "hot dogging" down the runway, doing sort of a side-to-side sashay. As a result, the plane did not reach sufficient speed to lift off at the usual point. As the end of the runway neared the landing gear was raised. The plane stayed aloft, gained a few feet of altitude, and then crashed onto a farm field. He said the entire crew scrambled out of the plane and ran away as far as possible. When they had gone about 300 yards, the plane blew up, and a large piece of the fuselage blew up and over their heads. Dean had never related the incident before, even to his family. I am certain many war experiences remain untold.

In the fall of 1943, I entered fifth grade, the highest grade offered at Eagle Rock School. Early in June the following year I was sick and stayed home from school. I was in bed, listening to the radio, when suddenly the radio program was interrupted to announce that the long-awaited invasion of Europe had begun with an Allied landing on the beaches of Normandy in Northern France. It was D-Day, June 6, 1944. Throughout the day I was glued to the radio, listening to news accounts about the landing and its progress. Though the information that first day was sketchy, it was obvious that the fighting was fierce and the casualties were high.

Chapter 39

Sixth Grade at Riverside Elementary

In the fall of 1944 I entered sixth grade at Hawthorne Elementary School on South Boulevard. I was anxious to start at Hawthorne, where most if not all of my siblings had gone. All who went to school there were fond of the principal, Doyle Ellison. As it turned out, I attended only a week or so and then transferred to Riverside Elementary School, located a few blocks north of downtown Idaho Falls. Hawthorne was overcrowded, and those students who rode a school bus were transferred to schools with additional room for students. At first I was disappointed. I did not know anyone except my friends whom I rode with on the bus. The school was located in a poorer section of the city. Many came from what we used to call Duttonville, located a few blocks north of the school, and close to the "city dump," an area where trash and garbage were taken to be dumped and burned.

In time, I became acquainted with the other students, many of whom became lifelong friends. The principal was A.H. Bush. He was a tall, thin man with reddish hair, and he spoke in a nasal tone. He had a ruddy complexion as the result of allergy problems with which he always seemed to be afflicted. I look back on my year at Riverside and count it one of my best years of school. I rate Mr. Bush as one of the best, if not the very best, teacher I ever had. In and out of the classroom he made his students feel important, and in his quiet way was able to get his students to try harder and to achieve more than they would otherwise have thought possible.

Mr. Bush was frequently on the playground before school, during recess, lunch break, and after school. He was not there as a school authority to keep order; he was organizing the students into all types of sports, including softball, basketball, tag, foot races, tugs of war and so on. Mr. Bush would often be right in the middle of the activity as a participant. He didn't have to worry about keeping order. The students loved and respected him. I later became a close friend and colleague of his son Eugene Bush who became a lawyer and practiced law in Idaho Falls.

During sixth grade one of the teachers, Reva Clark, taught music in addition to her regular classroom duties and was in charge of musical events held at school. At some point early in the school year she decided to put together a small boys' choir. She invited six boys, the three Reed brothers Leroy, David and Larry, Wilbur Collins, Glen Robertson and me to form a sextet. We practiced regularly after school. Larry Reed and Wilbur Collins had excellent voices, and the rest of us had good voices which blended in. We learned a variety of songs, including "Blue Skies" and "Hawaiian War Chant."

We performed often at school, and Miss Clark arranged for us to be invited to perform at other locations, including O.E. Bell Jr. High and the Idaho Falls High School. Miss Clark worked us pretty hard. I enjoyed singing as long I was a part of a larger group. I was still quite shy, not comfortable singing a solo in public. For example, once we were preparing to sing as a part of a school Christmas program and Miss Clark assigned parts to "We Three Kings." She asked me to sing the part of the king who brought myrrh as a gift to Baby Jesus, newly born in a manger. I was petrified. Even though I practiced in private, I just could not make it happen and begged off. I wanted to sing the part, and I had a suitable voice, but when I sang alone my voice tightened and nothing came out right. Someone else sang that part.

Over the years, I have had fun telling my kids and some of our friends that I used to regularly sing on the radio. I don't believe many believed me, but I was telling the truth. Our sextet was invited to sing on a Saturday morning show on KID radio. After we had performed, we were asked back, and ultimately we sang the opening and closing number each week. The one-hour radio program featured local amateur talent every Saturday morning. One more person who frequently appeared and performed was a local man known as Tumbleweed Tom who sang and played his guitar. He really had a wonderful voice, similar to Hank Snow and Eddie Arnold. People said he could have made it to the big time, but sadly he had a problem with alcohol. He performed regularly in several of the local bars until he died years later from the effects of a lifetime of drinking.

A black girl, then called a Negro, attended Riverside School when I went there. Her name was Darlene Lewis. It was not easy to be black in a school or community which had so few blacks. She was a nice person, and I admired how she handled herself in often-difficult situations. I made a point of spending time visiting and befriending Darlene. She ultimately graduated from Idaho Falls High School, also in 1951, and she attended most of our class reunions.

Later when I was practicing law, Darlene came to my office to see me. She said she had a cancer that was untreatable and was expected to live for less than a year. I gave her some legal advice and helped get her affairs in order to protect the interests of her young children. At that time, Darlene was a single mom. A short time later she brought her three children to the office. She told her kids that if they ever needed help that I was a trusted friend and that they should come to see me. Her three kids, who ranged from ten to fourteen years of age, were delightful children. A couple of times I went to see Darlene in the hospital just before she died. I went as her lawyer and also as a friend. I saw the children a few times later on; however, I have not had any contact for a long time. I often wonder where they are and what they are doing. I would enjoy visiting with them again.

Chapter 40

The Potato Harvest

The harvesting of the potato crop on the Osgood farm was similar to the operations on the Airport Farm, with some exceptions. We raised many more potatoes than before, now close to 200 acres each year. We no longer used horses, only tractors and mechanized equipment. The equipment was large. We now used a two-row digger, larger trucks to haul the potatoes, and potato conveyers that were larger and more moveable. There were two large cellars for storage. The new conveyers made it possible to pile the stored potatoes higher than before. Although we often sold some of the potatoes directly out of the field, our cellars were usually full when the harvest was completed.

Potato harvest could not begin until ten or so days after a hard frost had "killed" the potato vines. During this waiting period the outer skin of the "spuds," as we called potatoes, would firm up and be less likely to be skinned or bruised during the harvest operations. The harvest had to be completed before the weather turned really cold and the freeze hard enough to damage the potatoes still in the ground. On average, we could not start harvesting until around the 25th of September, and as a rule of thumb, tried to be finished by the 10th of October. Some years we were able to start a little earlier and continue for a little longer, but if we waited beyond mid-October, the risk of a damaging field frost rose significantly. To complicate matters, we could only harvest a given number of acres on a good day when the weather was favorable and we had no major equipment breakdowns. In reality, the weather often did not cooperate and breakdowns occurred. Everyone felt a lot of pressure during the potato harvest.

The labor shortage for the potato harvest was alleviated by the adoption of the "spud harvest vacation." Senior high schools and most junior high schools closed for two weeks to allow the kids to work in the harvest, mostly picking potatoes. Letting the kids out of school was helpful in getting the crop out of the ground. It also allowed the kids to earn extra money. The kids worked hard and seemed to have a good time picking potatoes. The harvest break was also a social event in many ways. Many of the young women who came to our farm to help in the harvest were in school with, and some were being dated by, my older brothers. I was very conscious of what appeared to be romances in progress.

When we moved onto the new farm, I was still in grade school and therefore my role in the harvest was somewhat limited. The potatoes were dug with a two-row digger which simply lifted the potatoes out of the ground and onto a chain made of small iron rods, or links. The chain links carried the potatoes, vines and dirt, a distance of several feet and dropped them back onto the ground. The chain had a series of sprockets which caused the chain to bounce and most of the dirt to fall between the links. The pickers would then move along the rows, bending over to pick up spuds and put them in wire baskets.

One of my early jobs was to sit on the potato digger with a large pile of burlap sacks. I dropped the sacks at intervals so that an empty sack would be within easy reach of the picker as needed for emptying the baskets. I estimated the interval I thought would be appropriate by the quantity of potatoes being dug. The yield of potatoes would vary from field to field and also within a field. It was always better to have a few extra sacks, which the buckers could pick up, than to require a picker to hunt for a sack.

One day my older brothers and some of their high school friends helping in the harvest had decided to have a big "chicken fry." Much like today, it was simply an excuse for kids to have a party. They decided how many chickens they would need, and I and someone else were given a few hours off and told to "find" chickens. We were well aware that our job was to steal chickens from some place in the neighborhood, and we did. I can't remember which neighbors made the "contribution." The practice of stealing chickens and having a party was often called a "chickaree." We drove around looking for small farm flocks, preferably flocks located some distance from a farm house and the farm dog. Ultimately, we were able to catch the required number of chickens. We put them into burlap sacks and returned to the potato field.

We gave the live chickens to the organizers of the "chickaree." The older boys killed, plucked and cleaned the chickens, and gave them to a group of the older girls. I believe that some of the older girls took the chickens home where they fried them and brought them back the next day. I am sure Mother was well aware of what was being planned and may have even helped fry the chickens. Some of the girls brought different side dishes, including potato salad, and a variety of beverages. I remember being given a couple of pieces of chicken;

however, only the older kids helping in the harvest were included in the party. The party was held in the evening at an old gravel pit on West River Road, which was filled with water and frequently used by kids for swimming and partying. I believe it was called the "Mode Lagoon."

Chapter 41

1945 Brings Distinction and Tragedy

As we entered 1945, optimism was in the air. The gains being made by the Allies, in both the European and Pacific areas, were significant. I was aware that the European operations were set back by the fierce fighting in Battle of the Bulge around Christmas, but the German counter offensive had been stopped, and the Allies were on the march toward Berlin again. At the same time, the forces of the Soviet Union were advancing from the east. Allied forces were on the move in the Pacific, hopping from island to island. The tide was turning; however, the war was not over and the casualties continued to be heavy.

Orval had gone into the Navy in the summer of 1944. Following boot camp at the San Diego Naval Base and a period of additional training, he was assigned to the USS Saratoga, an aircraft carrier operating in the Pacific. Previously the carrier had been in several major battles, was badly damaged, and subsequently repaired and returned to serve in the Pacific. I believe the carrier was primarily used to transport war materials from the west coast to the Pacific Theater.

My cousin George Stoddard, the son of Dad's sister Stella and William Stoddard, was a First Lieutenant in the U.S. Marine Corps. His unit was in the first wave of amphibious craft which landed on the island of Iwo Jima and was assigned to capture the high point on the island, which they did after fierce fighting and horrific losses. George was seriously wounded during the second day of fighting and evacuated to a hospital ship stationed off shore. He is mentioned in *Flags of Our Fathers* by James Bradley, a best seller on the invasion and the lives of the six men who raised the flag on Mt. Suribachi, captured in the famous photograph taken by combat photographer Rosenthal. I highly recommend the book.

I mentioned earlier that I wrote to Uncle Glen when he was serving overseas. Once I asked if he could send me a war souvenir. Kids my age were really into the war and were forever playing war games. One day when I came home from school I had received a large box. I opened it and found a German steel helmet, a German officer's cap, a German bayonet and blanket. Mother was surprised. I told her about my request, and that I was thinking of something small. I was overwhelmed and slightly embarrassed by his generosity.

I took the box and all of its contents to school the next day to show to the students in my class, all of whom were greatly impressed. I was reminded of the time Uncle Glen had made the table for our classroom store in first grade. Uncle Glen was always very good to me, and probably would have done anything I asked, within reason. I put the souvenirs in the original shipping box in the attic of the farmhouse when I left for college. Over the years it was discovered and scattered around. I did find and retrieve the helmet which I now have at home. The rest of the items have disappeared.

Uncle Glen was awarded the Silver Star, the second highest military award, while in combat in Germany in the spring of 1945. The official citation reads, in part, as follows:

"For gallantry in action. On 21 March 1945, during an attack by Company "C" of enemy fortifications near * * * * *, Germany, an intense concentration of enemy artillery and mortar fire pinned our forces to the ground. LIEUTENANT Wahlquist, moved among his men, urging them forward, and when the second platoon lost its commander, he took over and organizing both platoons, continued the advance. Personally knocking out an enemy 88 millimeter gun with hand grenades he enabled the entire command and regiment to succeed in its mission. LIEUTENANT Wahlquist's superb coolness, fearlessness and leadership under fire reflected the highest traditions of the military service."

We understand that his commander, who witnessed the action taken by Uncle Glen, recommended that he receive the Congressional Medal of Honor, the highest military award. The large German 88 millimeter battery and its crew were positioned high up on the point of a hill which provided an excellent view of the entire US regiment. The large gun battery had stopped the US Army advance and was inflicting severe casualties. Uncle Glen crawled up the hill with a Thompson machine and a supply of hand grenades, and single handedly destroyed the gun battery and its crew.

On March 27, 1945, the Commanding General of the Division signed the order that Glen be awarded the Silver Star and ordered that Glen also be promoted to the rank of First Lieutenant. The award and promotion took place in the battlefield, and his unit continued on without let up until the war in Europe was over. I hope to research the official records some day and learn the exact location referred to in Uncle Glen's citation. Someday I would like very much to visit the area where the events took place.

V-E Day, as it was called, ending hostilities in Europe, occurred on May 8, 1945. We later learned that a few days earlier Adolph Hitler, who was ensconced in a deep underground bunker in Berlin, had married his long-time mistress, Eva Braun, following which the two of them committed suicide. In the meantime, hostilities in the Pacific Theater continued with the invasion of the Island of Okinawa, and an invasion of mainland Japan was being planned.

Uncle Grant Wahlquist was flying his P-51 fighter plane on combat missions from a field somewhere in New Guinea. On May 3, 1945, he flew on a combat mission from which he did not return. Mother received a telegram from the War Department which stated that Grant was "missing in action." I remember Mother called her brother, Brent Wahlquist, who came to the house right away. They were both confident that Grant was still alive and would return. Mother said, "I know that someday he will come walking right through that door" and pointed to the front door to our basement house. Uncle Brent agreed. They were convinced that somehow Grant would have figured out a way to survive.

Later the War Department declared that Uncle Grant's plane had crashed and he was officially declared dead. Neither his body nor the wreckage of his plane was ever found. The details of his death are not known for certain. Later there had been an indication that a fellow airman who was flying some distance away, reported that he thought he had seen Uncle Grant's plane going down. He did not see a parachute. Then he lost sight of the plane and did not see the end of its descent. Losing her younger brother was very difficult for Mother. Grant's mother, Grandma Wahlquist, was devastated.

Chapter 42

Grandma Wahlquist, a.k.a. Aunt Mattis

Mother's natural mother died when Mother was only five or six years old. Her father, Andrew Wahlquist, had three small children: Mother, Anna, and Uncle Carl. Ultimately Andrew married Matilda. She had come from Sweden as a convert to the LDS faith when she was a young woman. Matilda and Andrew had four sons, Glen, Brent, Clyde and Grant, and a daughter Jean. Jean died of an eating disorder when she was a teenager. Mother, Anna, and Carl called their stepmother Aunt Mattis.

Mother and her brother Carl and sister Anna, the children of Andrew's first marriage, had lived in Murray, Utah, where their father and his brother owned and operated a lumberyard. Sometime after Andrew and Matilda were married, they sold the lumberyard and moved to a small farm in Roosevelt, Utah, where they raised their second family. Uncles Glen, Brent, and Grant were living at home in Roosevelt when they began to spend time helping Dad and Mother on the Airport farm.

Life was difficult on the Roosevelt farm and Andrew had health problems that limited his activities. I remember Uncle Glen telling us how hard his mother worked, raising the kids and handling all the household chores and also doing the equivalent work of a fulltime man. He told us of his mother standing in the corral, knee-deep in wet manure, with a pitchfork in her hands, and pitching manure onto a wagon. Then she went with the wagon pulled by horses out to the field where, using a pitchfork, she helped scatter the manure as fertilizer for the crops. She worked hard, hours on end, without any complaint. He greatly respected and admired his mother for the role she fulfilled on the farm. He said everyone worked hard; however, no one worked any harder than his mother.

Grandma Wahlquist was widowed in 1936. At first she remained in Roosevelt. However, years later she started spending time with us and also with her son Brent. She took care of us kids at times when Mother and Dad were traveling. She was a grand lady, always neat as a pin, and she was an excellent cook. We enjoyed her Swedish cooking, and I particularly remember her sugar cookies and Swedish pancakes, which were very thin and more like a crepe. She had a wonderful Swedish brogue. When I was attending high school, Grandma Wahlquist had a small apartment across the street from the school grounds. I would stop by to visit with her, and she always gave me a couple of freshly baked sugar cookies.

Chapter 43

The War Ends and Junior High School Begins

In late July 1945, an atomic bomb, known as the A Bomb, was successfully tested in the Nevada desert. Within days a similar bomb was dropped on Hiroshima, Japan, followed a few days later with yet another bomb dropped on Nagasaki. V-J Day arrived, formally ending hostilities in the Pacific when Japanese officials signed unconditional surrender documents on board the USS Missouri on September 2, 1945. World War II was finally over. I remember V-J Day quite vividly. Glen Robertson, with whom I became acquainted in sixth grade, had ridden his bike to the farm from his home in town. Word of the official end of World War II came over the radio.

We took off on our bikes and rode up and down the Butte Highway, US 91, and we flagged down oncoming vehicles to spread the good news. The drivers started honking their horns as they continued on. It was a happy time and, of course, a great relief to Mother and Dad. Orval, along with many friends and relatives, was still serving in the Pacific. Many servicemen were in the process of being transferred from Europe to the Pacific Theater and were awaiting orders for the expected invasion of Japan. While it would be months before most servicemen would be able to return home, at least the hostilities were over.

In September I entered seventh grade at O.E. Bell Jr. High School located on Elm Street in Idaho Falls. O.E. Bell was much different from previous schools I had attended. It included seventh, eighth, and ninth grades. The high school included tenth, eleventh, and twelfth grades. Ninth graders were considered high school freshmen, although they completed the year at the junior high. While I was going to school there were several elementary schools, however only one junior high and one senior high in Idaho Falls.

When I was in sixth grade we were the "big" kids. When I entered seventh grade we were the "little" kids again. We were led to believe that we would be hazed and tormented by the eighth and ninth grade students. In fact, very little happened. The enrollment in junior high was close to one thousand students, and it took us new seventh graders time to adjust to the new surroundings. Fortunately, most all of my sixth grade friends from Riverside School were there.

I reconnected with others I had known at Eagle Rock School. I soon made many additional friends, including Don Burtenshaw, who farms in the Mud Lake area and later served with me in the Idaho State Senate. Ossian Packer, Walter Boltz, and I became close lifelong friends. As seventh graders are prone to do, we soon thought we were pretty important, particularly when we were around younger kids. I liked my classes and teachers, and the experience was good. Actually, I always enjoyed school, and when I applied myself, I was a pretty good student.

When I attended O.E. Bell, I rode the school bus to school in the mornings. After school the bus I rode first took a load of students on another route. To make things more difficult our house was almost the last stop at the end of a long route. As a result, when I rode the bus back home I had a long wait at school and arrived home quite late. So after school I started walking through downtown and across the Broadway Bridge over the Snake River, and when I reached the edge of town I started hitchhiking. Hitchhiking was a fairly common means of transportation in those days, and particularly during the war years. Gasoline and rubber tires were rationed, and many people simply did not have cars. Also, many servicemen were hitching rides to save money, and to give a ride to a serviceman was considered a very patriotic thing to do.

Rides were easy to get, and I usually had one within minutes after I put my thumb in the air. I knew some of the persons who picked me up; however, many I did not know. I was never apprehensive when hitchhiking home, and I was alone most of the time. Sometimes, my first ride would be continuing west and I would be dropped off at Reeds' Corner. From there I would start walking north on the Butte Highway and catch another ride. Other times I would catch a single ride to the farm. Frankly, I enjoyed thumbing a ride home, provided the weather was good, and I would always be home long before the school bus. Since we always had a lot of chores to do after school, I found that being able to arrive home early was a real advantage.

On my way home I would occasionally stop at Dad's office at the Idaho Potato Growers Association to say hello. Even though the visits were short, I enjoyed having a chance to talk with Dad one-on-one. He was always pleasant and we had adult conversations. He never talked down to me and always seemed interested in what I was doing at school and at home after school. He would often tell me of some of the things he was considering doing. This would include

Chapter 43: The War Ends and Junior High School Begins | 101

expansion projects at the potato facilities, upcoming trips and business ventures he had in mind. Dad always had a lot of "irons in the fire." If he was busy when I stopped by, I would say hello to some of the staff and continue on my way.

Dad's office was equipped with a radio microphone that would enable him to connect with KID radio and give market reports. His program was aired during the noon hour to catch the listeners, mostly farmers and ranchers, when they were having lunch. In addition to the market reports he would cover other topics of interest and often would interview someone who was visiting his office. Dad had a good voice and was an excellent speaker. One day I was in the office when he was going to do the regular reports and also interview a man who was beginning to make a name for himself in agricultural circles: Jack Simplot. Dad and Jack Simplot were both active in the potato industry; Mr. Simplot was also into phosphate mining and fertilizer. They became pretty good friends.

Dad gave the usual market news and then introduced his guest for a few remarks, after which Dad and Mr. Simplot engaged in conversation. Dad was used to speaking into a microphone; however, Mr. Simplot seemed ill at ease when it was his turn to talk. When the program was finished, Dad gave KID the signoff signal, saying "Well that's the market news for today" or something similar. As soon as Dad stopped talking Jack Simplot let out a string of foul swear words, cussing himself for what he felt was his poor performance. Dad grabbed the microphone and turned it off.

Harry Truman, a Democrat, had been vice president and became president when President Roosevelt died on April 12, 1945. In 1948 President Truman was running for a full four-year term, challenged by the Republican nominee, Governor Thomas E. Dewey from New York. The Democratic Party was deeply split, primarily over issues of civil rights. Several of the southern states broke away from the Democratic Party and formed a third party which nominated as its presidential candidate Sen. Strom Thurman, from South Carolina. A Fourth party, the Progressive Party was also formed. Its presidential nominee was Henry Wallace, who had served as Vice President during President Franklin Roosevelt's third term. The Progressive Party nominee for Vice President was US Senator Glen Taylor, a Democrat from Idaho. The year 1948 was a wild political one, to say the least.

Under the circumstances, it was widely believed that Governor Dewey would be elected, and the polls showed that he had a substantial lead. Dad had been traveling extensively during the summer and fall of 1948. Although he was a strong supporter of the Republican Party nominee, as the campaign progressed he became convinced that President Truman was going to be reelected and told

Jack Simplot of his prediction. Jack Simplot, a staunch Republican, bet Dad a new suit that Governor Dewey would win. Dad won the bet and the new suit.

Chapter 44

Advancing from Cub Scout to Boy Scout

I was quite active in scouting, and had been involved in the Cub Scout program. Lorene Shively, wife of W.O. Shively who supervised the building of the new barn on the Airport Farm, was Den Mother of our Cub Scout troop. I went through the ranks, which included Bear, Wolf, Lion, and Webelos. My older brothers had also been involved in the Boy Scout program, and they owned various pieces of the official scout uniform. I was anxious for the day to arrive when I turned twelve and could join the Boy Scouts of America. Some of my friends attended Trinity Methodist Church, which sponsored Boy Scout Troop 6. Several of us, including David and Leroy Reed, Jim and Bill Shively, and Wilbur Collins were interested in becoming members of Troop 6. One of the older boys, Henry Rigby, was already an active member.

When I turned twelve I arranged to go to the next scheduled troop meeting to officially join. I dressed up in a scout uniform, consisting of articles of uniforms Farrel and Orval had outgrown, and I went to the meeting. Someone, I think it might have been Henry Rigby, told me that since I was not yet a member, I was not yet entitled to wear the official scout uniform. I was embarrassed. I gathered up the application. As I remember, the paper work had to be taken to the Boy Scout office a day or two later for me to become an official member. I still remember how proud I had been when I walked into that scout meeting, and how crestfallen I was when told I had breached Boy Scout etiquette.

I enjoyed my scouting experience. I took it seriously and advanced rapidly. I wanted to become an Eagle Scout. We learned all the usual skills, including knot tying, semaphore code, camping, cooking, and first aid. We also learned to start a fire by striking a spark into combustible material and also by rapidly spinning a hardwood stick, by hand or with a bow and string. We went on overnight camping trips in the summer and also in winter, and on these occasions, we practiced the skills we had learned. I attended scout camp for a week each of three successive summers.

The camp, called Treasure Mountain, was located in east Teton County. We practiced water safety in the small lake, took hikes, and learned to identify a number of trees, bushes, and plants. We took turns helping with the cooking and cleaning chores. We always had a great time at camp. The routine was for first-year campers to take the hike up Lightning Mountain, and for second-year campers to climb to the top of Table Rock, both of which were long day hikes. Third-year campers were eligible to take the overnight hike to Inspiration Point overlooking Jenny Lake and the Jackson Hole area.

After completing the overnight hike and passing several tests, a scout was eligible to receive the rank of Chief. This involved a moving ceremony after which the scout was "branded" and given his Chief name by Vernon Strong, our Scout Executive. We were led to believe that the brand would be hot and leave a burn mark. Fortunately it was a cold brand that had been pressed on a large inkpad. I was given the name Chief Alpine Fir. I was very proud, although I had been hoping for an animal name. The new rank allowed the scout to climb on top of Chief Rock.

Each night during scout camp a large fire was built and after dinner we gathered at the base of the large rock to sing songs and get information about the next day's activities. Toward the end of the evening, Scout Executive Vernon Strong, dressed in an Indian costume with a full chief headdress made with real eagle feathers, climbed onto Chief Rock. Ceremoniously, in his booming voice, he told Indian lore stories. It was a great experience. Incidentally, the rock was six to eight feet high and the size of a medium sized room at its base. When I first climbed Chief Rock, it was during the day. I found it was not as impressive in daylight as it was at night with the light from a large bonfire illuminating Mr. Strong, dressed in his full Indian regalia.

I was active in the Boy Scout program during my three years at O.E. Bell. I was a Life Scout and working on becoming an Eagle Scout. I had earned all of the merit badges that were required for Eagle Scout and had finished all of the other requirements. By this time, all of my close friends had dropped out of scouting and I began moving on to other activities. At some point, someone asked me if I was going to come back and finish the last requirements, which were simply making application, writing an essay and going before the Scout Board for an interview. I said I thought I would, but I never did. At the time it did not seem that important; however, today I regret that I did not follow through and receive the award that had always been my goal.

When I came back to Idaho Falls to practice law, I became involved in scouting once again. I was asked to serve as the District Commissioner for the entire Teton Peaks Council territory. At the time I checked to see if my scouting records still existed, thinking perhaps I could finally finish my goal. The records were gone, and the requirements for the rank of Eagle Scout had changed significantly, and that was that. There is a lesson to be learned here.

Chapter 45

Dad, the Potato Man

Dad was flying more and more. The Idaho Potato Growers had, on Dad's recommendation I am sure, purchased a used airplane, a Piper Super-Cruiser. It was similar to the Piper Cub Dad had first flown, although larger, and its engine had considerably more horsepower. The pilot sat in the single seat in front and there was a rear seat wide enough for two people, if they were not too large. Reed and I could fit in the rear seat just fine. Dad often flew this plane to visit branch offices as well as to make business trips to Salt Lake City, Boise, and other locations in southern Idaho. I am sure he saved time by flying, but I am sure he also flew because he enjoyed flying.

I often flew with Dad; if he asked me to ride with him I always said I would. Then I would begin worrying whether I would become air sick. I think the problem was as much in my head as my stomach. Winter was a much more comfortable time to fly, as the colder air is heavier, and generally there is less wind than in the summer. In the summer, the early morning is usually the best time to fly when the air is cooler and thus more stable. Later on during the day the ground and air will heat up causing thermals, which can really bounce a light plane around. I can remember flying with Dad to Boise in the early morning and all would be well. When we returned in the afternoon, however, the turbulence would have increased significantly, particularly over the desert and lava areas of southern Idaho. Sometimes I would not do well on the return flight.

Dad liked to drive a nice car. The Association furnished him a business car. When we lived on the Airport Farm he had a business car; however, I don't remember the make or model. Later on his business car was an 1941 Packard four-door sedan which he used throughout the war. When the war was over, the 1941 Packard was traded in on a 1946 Packard. The Packard cars were beautiful, very comfortable, and quiet on the road. I liked riding in these cars, and it was obvious that Dad took great pleasure in driving them. With the exception of a few 1942 cars which came out early, no new automobiles were manufactured for civilian use from 1941 until 1946. All of the automobile plants were converted to the production of airplanes, tanks, trucks, jeeps and various other vehicles needed in the war effort.

The Idaho Potato Growers expanded rapidly during the years Dad served as General Manager, and its operations were quite successful. Dad worked extremely hard for the Association and its directors treated him well. Dad helped to establish grade and marketing standards to promote the Russet potato variety. The famous Idaho Russet had developed a national reputation and market as the premium baking potato. In those days Idaho was the only area in the nation where Russet potatoes could be successfully grown in commercial quantities. Other states, including Maine which produced a lot of potatoes, were much closer to the big population centers in the east, however. It obviously cost much more to ship a carload of potatoes from Idaho to the eastern markets.

Fortunately, the Russet potato produced in Idaho was truly of a high quality and brought a premium price in the market. Much work was done by a lot of people, including Dad, to promote and protect the national market for Idaho Russets. Dad occasionally interacted with the Idaho Legislature. One time he was invited to speak to a special joint meeting of the House and Senate Agricultural Committees. He urged that higher grade standards be adopted by the State of Idaho for potatoes to be shipped out of the state. Shortly thereafter the recommended standards were passed by the Legislature and signed into law.

Dad was active in the Idaho Cooperative Council when Ezra Taft Benson was its Executive Secretary. Dad was also active in the National Association for Cooperatives. He often traveled to Washington D.C. to attend and speak at various meetings and conventions. During the war, he was appointed to and served on an advisory committee which regularly made recommendations on agricultural production matters to the National War Production Board.

Because of Dad's demonstrated abilities and experience in the food industry, he had several attractive employment offers. In 1938, Dad was contacted by the National Council of Farm Cooperatives and asked to serve as its Executive Secretary. After he and Mother discussed the offer which would have required that they leave the farm and move the family to Washington D.C., they decided against it. In January 1939 Ezra Taft Benson was offered and accepted the same position. He later served as Secretary of Agriculture in President Eisenhower's cabinet.

Mother told me Dad was also offered a job in Chicago that would have involved a significant increase in his compensation. Dad turned down the offer without hesitation. The two of them had discussed it and Mother fully agreed with the decision. They believed that the farm in Idaho Falls was a far better place to raise six kids, than Chicago or Washington D.C. Upon hearing this, I remember thinking Dad had made the wrong decision. I imagined it would have been exciting to have lived in a major city.

The directors of the Idaho Potato Growers Association were pleased with Dad's performance as General Manager and were well aware that he had other options. The Board compensated him well, and did not hesitate to approve the purchase of a Packard automobile as a business car, and an airplane for Dad's business and personal use.

Chapter 46

An Eighth Grader's Dream Trip

In the fall of 1946 I entered eighth grade at O.E. Bell. From the time I was born until I entered eighth grade, I was called Johnny by everyone. There was a popular song "Oh Johnny, Oh Johnny" which the girls at Eagle Rock sang to me on a fairly regular basis, just to tease me. The lyrics included "Oh Johnny, Oh Johnny, how you can love, Oh Johnny, Oh Johnny, heavens above…" I was bashful and I would always blush when they started singing, although I have to admit I did somewhat enjoy the attention.

When I was registering at O.E. Bell Jr. High, Mrs. Owen, who was the regular attendance clerk, was helping with registration. When I filled out the registration form, I wrote my name as Johnny Hansen. She looked at me and said, "Don't you think you are a little old to be called Johnny?" I hesitated a moment and then erased Johnny and wrote in John. I have been John ever since. I liked Mrs. Owen, and if she thought John fit better that was okay with me. I am surprised that I didn't ask Mother or my older siblings whether I should change my name. The name change was painless, as had been my abandonment of the idea that Santa Claus was real!

Dad was planning a business trip to Chicago and asked me if I would like to go with him. Obviously I did, and Dad arranged for me to be excused from school. It was a fabulous opportunity for a boy my age. This was my first trip that required me to pack a suitcase, and I was really excited. On the morning we left, Dad and I were picked up by Bill Metcalf, who also worked at the potato growers. Mr. Metcalf drove us to Pocatello to catch the train for Chicago.

Dad loved good cigars and often smoked them at his office and on road trips. He seldom smoked at home, never in the house, and only in the plane or car if family members were not along. I am sure this was a courtesy to Mother and us kids. Anyway, Mr. Metcalf had a fairly small car, so we put the luggage in the back seat and the three of us sat in the front seat, me in the middle. As soon as we were on the highway to Pocatello, both Dad and Mr. Metcalf lit cigars and started talking. I thought I would die from the cigar smoke. I think they were so wrapped up in their conversation about the business that they were oblivious to me sitting in the middle. Mr. Metcalf had a reputation for lighting his cigar in the morning and then letting it go out and then chewing on the unlit cigar most of the day. He was seldom seen without an unlit cigar stuck in the side of his mouth, even while he was talking.

Dad and I were dropped off at the passenger terminal to await our departure. The place was filled with people and luggage. At the time, air travel was quite uncommon. Civilian air travel was just developing; however, it had been sharply curtailed during the war, and was just coming back. In 1946 almost everyone who traveled long distances did so by train. Train travel was a truly elegant way to travel, especially when traveling on the new diesel powered Union Pacific Streamliner, as we did on this trip. The engines were huge and beautiful, and I took numerous pictures of the front of the train when it pulled into the station. I had only seen and heard the older trains before, ones that were pulled by steam engines. I still have some of the pictures I took of the train we rode on, along with points of interest in Chicago, in my memorabilia box. This large cardboard box is in filled with a variety of stuff I have accumulated over the years, and which I regularly promise myself I will sort through and organize. Maybe some day I will.

Dad and I shared a small compartment which had bunk beds and a small bathroom facility. Everything was new and shiny and sparkling clean. The passenger crew was made up mostly of African-American men who were helpful and friendly. Dad put his shoes outside our door at night, and the shoes were shined and returned to the same spot in the early morning. We ate in the dining car on white table linen with matching napkins, and more silverware, dishes and glasses than I knew what to do with. Dad did not always travel first class, as we were doing, but I knew he loved to travel and I began to understand why.

I also believe he wanted this trip to be special for me, and it was. Also when he and Mother traveled together, I am sure he wanted the trips to be special for her. Mother and Dad traveled together on combined business trips, to San Francisco, Chicago, New York City and St. Louis, always traveling first class and staying and dining at nice places. Mother often talked about how much she enjoyed staying at the Sir Francis Drake Hotel in San Francisco and the Palmer House in Chicago.

During the day Dad and I spent most of the time in the train club car. Dad would open his brief case and review data relevant to the business purposes of the trip. I believe we spent three days getting to Chicago, which included at

Chapter 46: An Eighth Grader's Dream Trip | 111

least two nights. It seemed like a long time. I enjoyed sitting in the club car with Dad, and I spent the time sightseeing out the window, playing cards, reading and talking with Dad and other passengers. I saw no other kids on the train. Of course school was in session at the time, and as far as I know, few kids traveled by train. I was very fortunate to be able to take this trip with Dad.

When we arrived in Chicago, I could not believe the number of railroad tracks leading to the terminal, the size of the passenger terminal, the number of people, the noise and overall confusion. Dad seemed to know exactly what to do, and I just followed, staying as close to him as possible for fear of getting lost. Dad hailed a taxicab and we rode to the hotel in downtown Chicago. I don't remember the name of the hotel, but it was in the Loop and was a very grand hotel. Our room was unlike anything I had ever stayed in before. As I think about it, I probably had never stayed in a hotel prior to this trip, except maybe once in Salt Lake City. We stayed at the hotel about a week.

Each morning after getting up, showering, shaving in the case of Dad, and dressing, we went to the dining room for breakfast. Dad had meetings and other commitments during the days. During breakfast Dad would mark on a city map the places he suggested I visit that particular day. Dad gave me money for cab fare to and from the hotel and for my lunch. He would then hail a taxi for me, tell the driver where to take me, and he would leave. I was on my own for the entire day, a fourteen-year-old farm kid from Idaho, alone in Chicago, Illinois! I am still amazed when I think about it. I really was not overly concerned, at least after the first day. Dad seemed to be confident that I could handle the challenge and his confidence in me in turn gave me the confidence I needed to proceed on my own.

One day I went to the Chicago Museum of Natural History. On another day I went to the Chicago Museum of Science and Industry. I spent a full day at the Chicago Art Museum and another at the Chicago Planetarium. In each case I took a cab in the morning following breakfast, and spent an entire day there. I may have gone to the Museum of Science and Industry on two separate days. I was overwhelmed. I had not seen anything like this before. I am not even sure I have since seen anything more fascinating.

I enjoyed the Chicago Art Museum very much; however, I enjoyed the others even more. The Museum of Natural History had several skeletons of a variety of large mammals, dinosaurs, dinosaur eggs and a fascinating collection of other animal and plant species found in all parts of the world. There were thousands of other exhibits. After going through this museum, I thought I would someday be an archeologist. The Museum of Science and Industry was magnificent, with its full-sized trains, steam engines, and a working mine I could enter and watch men extracting ore. They even had a dramatic simulated mine explosion.

After spending the day out, I would find a cab to return to our hotel and give Dad a full run down on what I had seen and done. One day I thought I knew how to get back to the hotel and decided to walk and save the cab fare. I had paid fairly close attention to the route we took that morning. I walked for some time in what I was pretty sure was the right direction, but when I reached downtown Chicago, with all of its tall buildings, I became lost. I walked up to a parked taxi and gave the driver the name of the hotel that was written on a card Dad had given me. The cab driver motioned for me to get in, made a U turn and stopped in front of the hotel about a half block down the street. I paid him the fare, and wondered why he hadn't simply pointed out the hotel to me. I guess the driver had to make a living, too.

On a Sunday toward the end of the trip, a potato broker with whom Dad had done business invited us to his home for dinner. We had dinner with the broker, his wife and very attractive teenage daughter who was a high school sophomore. They had a lovely home and were very gracious. During dinner, the daughter asked me if I had ever been to Chicago before. I replied, "No, this is my first trip to the East." Though they were polite and didn't want to hurt my feelings, there were a few chuckles and the young girl explained to me that they did not really consider Chicago to be in the East, rather it was in the mid-West, and in fact they considered themselves Westerners.

Shortly after our Sunday visit, we caught the same train, the Union Pacific Railroad Streamliner, and headed back to Pocatello and home. By now I was a seasoned traveler, or so I thought. I couldn't wait to get home and tell everyone what I had done and what I had seen, and to show them all the pictures I had taken. This trip to Chicago with Dad was one of the most memorable I have ever taken. And I am still amazed that Dad placed such confidence in me while we were there. I have often wondered whether I would have been able do the same with my own kids when they were fourteen years old. I am certain that the trust and confidence Dad had placed in me then, and on other occasions, has helped me to undertake with confidence some of the travels I have been privileged to experience in later years.

Chapter 47

At Last, the Dream House

Following the trip, I settled into my classes in eighth grade. One of my teachers was Catherine Nelson. I liked her very much and I believe that my friend Reese Goodwin and I were her "pets." Mrs. Nelson would routinely have us both excused from study hall in the afternoons and we would return to her classroom and help her with whatever she needed. We spent a lot of time just visiting. She had recently graduated from college, and this was her first year of teaching. Her husband, Gordon, was an officer in the US Army and was serving in North Africa. She would read his letters to us, at least parts of them. Catherine Nelson has been a good friend over the years. I still see her fairly often, and sometimes kid her about being my eighth grade teacher. Today anyone who saw us together would think we were about the same age.

After the war ended and materials and labor were more plentiful, Dad and Mother started building a new house on the farm. An architect had drawn up plans to build on top of our basement house. The farmhouse is the one currently occupied by my nephew Bruce Hansen and his wife and family. Because we had a large family at the time we moved to the Osgood farm, the basement house needed to be quite large, and it was. The size of the basement in turn dictated the size of the new house to be built on top of it.

During construction of the new house we continued to live in the basement. We were busy with field work and caring for the livestock; however, we also helped with some of the construction activities. We helped put asbestos around the hot water pipes of the heating system. We helped to install, sand, and varnish the oak flooring which was laid in all of the rooms on both the first and second floors. And we helped with the cleanup and much of the backfilling of dirt around the foundation. Most of the subcontractors had no problem with our help. It speeded up the construction, and they appreciated the fact that we were trying to hold down expenses as much as possible.

This was not true, however, of the bricklayers. Normally the brick masons would lay brick until sometime late in the afternoon, and then clean the brick laid that day with a diluted sulfuric acid solution, for which they received their regular fairly high hourly rate. Dad had suggested that we kids could clean the brick in the evenings, and we did. The brick masons, including the foreman, did not openly object; however, they were not happy to have their work shortened by us kids.

As the bricklaying progressed, the brick masons became less careful in the use of wet concrete mortar when laying the bricks. We were not always even with them in cleaning brick, and by the time we reached some of the higher bricks, we found many places where wet mortar had been left on the side of the brick, and had hardened. It was difficult to clean; we never were able to completely remove some of the concrete. I can still see some of these splotches on those bricks. Their worst work came the last few days, and the bricklayers were gone by the time we realized how slipshod their work had been.

The problem with the bricks did not in any way lessen our enthusiasm for the new house or our excitement as we watched the construction progress. The polished oak floors were beautiful. Mother decided not to cover any of them with carpeting; instead she used throw rugs. Waxing and polishing the floors was a lot of work and we all pitched in and helped. We had a considerable amount of wind and the soil was light at the Osgood farm. No matter how tight the doors and windows were, dust always seemed to penetrate. This problem diminished as the lawn and shrubs were planted and grew.

New furniture was gradually purchased for the new house. We kids were allowed to choose the wallpaper, and also to have a say in the selection of furniture for our respective bedrooms. I picked out yellow plaid wallpaper for my room and also helped Mother pick out the furniture. My bedroom set was made of pine that was finished to look like maple, and consisted of a bed, dresser and bedside table. I thought my room looked great, and it really did. When I was married, Mother gave me the bedroom set. It has been moved several times and is now used to furnish a spare bedroom in our present home.

The new house had two bedrooms, a large living room, dining room, kitchen and bath on the main floor, and four bedrooms and a large bathroom on the second floor. The basement stayed pretty much as it was when we lived there. The boys had the upstairs bedrooms, and Mary occupied one on the main floor and Dad and Mother the other. As often happens with large families, I suppose, by the time we were able and could afford to build the new house, kids were starting to leave the nest and scatter.

Farrel was pursuing his medical studies full time and no longer lived at home. Orval came back from the Navy and enrolled at the University of Idaho in the fall of 1946, and thereafter spent only a limited amount of time at home. Norman graduated from high school in the spring of 1946 and also attended the University of Idaho in the fall. By the time the house was completed Reed, Mary and I were the only kids living at home. Reed graduated from high school in the spring of 1947 and left for the University that fall. We never fully utilized the house, except on certain holidays and during the summer months. One of the four upstairs bedrooms was never furnished, simply used for storage. The room Orval had selected was occupied only a short amount of time.

In a perfect world perhaps Dad and Mother would have revisited their long drawn house plans and reduced the size of the new home. To continue with the original plan obviously seemed to them to have been the right course of action. I don't think there were any second thoughts. It is a wonderful, well-built home, one we all longed and planned for during those years we were crowded together in the basement house.

Chapter 48

Swimming and Hunting

I first learned to swim after we moved to the Osgood farm. The Great Western Canal ran past part of our farm and in front of the barn, corrals and potato cellars. The current was fairly swift, and when I was first starting to swim I would pick out a spot on the opposite bank, enter the water, and paddle as hard as I could to the other side. When I reached the other side, I would check to see how far downstream I had been carried by the current.

As I became bigger and stronger, I would note the progress, and ultimately I was able to swim directly across the canal without being carried downstream by the current. Because of the proximity of the canal, we would often take a brief swim several times during the day. At the end of the day, it was common for almost everyone who worked on the farm to gather at the canal near the highway bridge and spend time diving and swimming. This was refreshing and also enabled us to wash off the dirt and dust collected while working in the fields. Most of us routinely used a bar of soap and had a cold bath during the swim. It became a social event which brought the young kids and adults together for a little fun. Often, we were joined by neighbors and friends from town.

When I was on the Airport Farm, we had BB guns which we shot at birds, targets, tin cans, and sometimes at each other. We had a rule that we could not shoot each other above the waist, and since we always wore denim pants or overalls, the pellets would not really hurt, only sting a bit. At the new farm, I started using a .22 rifle owned by my older brothers. There were literally hundreds of ground squirrels we called gophers, which were always digging their holes in the canal and ditch banks. This caused leaks. We spent hours, particularly in the evenings and on Sundays, shooting at the gophers with our .22 rifles. Gophers were very difficult to kill because they have such small heads, and they were generally standing at the opening to the hole when we took aim. Many times, I suspect, a gopher was hit and fatally wounded and yet darted down the hole. We never knew for sure if the gophers we shot had died down in the hole or had escaped unharmed.

We also hunted ducks and pheasants. I received a double-barreled 410 gauge shotgun as my first real gun, and I hunted with it a lot. The only problem with the gun was the fact it had two hammers, one for each barrel; they were hard to pull back into the cocked position. At first, I was in the habit of pulling the hammers back while I was walking, rather than waiting until I had an opportunity to shoot. I soon discovered that this practice was dangerous if I was hunting with someone else. Once while I was walking down a canal bank, my gun accidentally discharged. Fortunately, the gun was pointed toward the ground. Nonetheless it frightened me, and thereafter I would not pull the hammers back until a bird flew. I missed a few opportunities to shoot because I had to put the gun across my leg and really press hard to pull the hammers back to cock the gun, but it was a much safer practice.

When I was a little older, I ordered a 12 gauge single shot shotgun through the Montgomery Ward catalogue. I remember the gun cost just over fourteen dollars. It was a great gun which I kept until it was stolen out of my house in the early 1980s. The shotgun had a long barrel and a long range. I found that having only one shot at a bird forced me to take more time to aim carefully. As a result I became fairly successful knocking down the bird at which I was aiming. I discovered I could hold an extra shotgun shell in my right hand, fire the shell in the chamber, quickly "break" the gun to eject the used shell, insert the new shell and get off a second shot at the same target. I was proud of my skill with that old single shot 12 gauge shot gun. It became my favorite.

Reed had a 16 gauge Ithaca pump shotgun that he used and shared with other members of the family. Reed and I often hunted for pheasants in the ground cover along ditch banks and near the willow patches when we used gravity irrigation. We watched the pheasants hatch their eggs and raise their young while we were involved in fieldwork during the summer. We knew the best places to hunt for birds in the fall when the season opened. If we waited too long, other hunters would shoot the birds first. We also did a lot of duck hunting along the canal when duck season opened in the fall.

At that time the irrigation company kept some water in the canals during the winter months to accommodate many of the area cattle which depended on canal water for drinking. During the hunting season Reed and I would often walk along and sneak up on the bank to look for ducks. When we spotted ducks, we would quietly back down the bank and move closer. When we were closer to the ducks, we would again sneak up the bank, jump up and scare the ducks off the water and take a shot or two.

We hunted ducks along the canal almost every evening during the regular season. One time when it was late in the hunting season, there was ice on the edges of the water in the canal. We jumped a couple of ducks and Reed shot one which landed in the water on the other side of the canal. Rather than walk a long distance to the bridge and then back on the other bank to fetch the duck, Reed took off his clothes and swam across, grabbed the duck and swam back. He almost froze to death, but he got the duck, a large Mallard drake. He was extremely proud to be able to shoot and also to retrieve the bird.

Deer and elk hunting were also popular. All during the potato harvest the older brothers and their friends would plan a deer or elk hunt. It became almost an annual ritual to drive into the hills, set up a hunting camp and hunt for several days after the harvest was finished. I was too young to go on these trips, and also I had to return to my classes and catch up with the other students. The hunters sometimes brought game home, but not always. They played a lot of poker, drank a few beers and otherwise enjoyed each other's company. Those of us who stayed behind used to kid the hunters by accusing them of taking their sport coats instead of hunting rifles. We knew that they did go to hunt, but in fact, hunting was not the only purpose. They went to relax, do some bonding, and have a good time, all of which they deserved after working hard in the harvest. For some of the fellows it was a last outing before entering the military service.

Dad liked to hunt; however, he seldom had time to do much hunting. He had an old 12 gauge pump action shotgun. I accompanied Dad and Ernest Jackson on a day trip when they hunted for sage grouse. They bagged several large birds, which they brought home to be cooked. They also talked in low tones and laughed a lot. I was pretty sure they were exchanging ribald jokes. Dad purchased a beautiful rifle equipped with a high-power scope, which he used for some big game hunting, mostly in the areas around the Falconberry Ranch on Loon Creek.

Chapter 49

The Stinson

Dad occasionally flew to the Falconberry Ranch, which we simply referred to as Loon Creek after the creek that ran along the side of the ranch property. At first Dad flew with a more experienced pilot. After he had some instruction and practice using the airstrip on the ranch, he started taking his own plane. At this time Dad still had the Piper Super Cruiser, which was a good short landing and takeoff mountain plane. The airstrip on the ranch was short and could only be approached from one direction, and therefore was tricky to use. The canyon in which it was located was narrow and deep, with high mountains on both sides and across one end of the canyon.

Once a pilot was on his final landing approach to the ranch airstrip, he was committed to complete the landing. At other locations a pilot usually has the option to apply full power and make another approach if weather conditions, alignment, altitude on approach, or other conditions suggest that another try would be prudent. The Loon Creek Ranch landing strip was different. Once you reached a certain point in the landing approach, you were committed. Because of a high mountain further up the canyon, there simply was not enough distance to allow a plane to reach sufficient altitude to fly back out of the canyon. After a plane landed on the strip, it could only take off by going in the opposite direction from which the pilot flew when approaching for a landing.

One fall day, Dad and Norman flew into Loon Creek to hunt big game. Dad flew over the strip and ranch house to alert the foreman that he was planning to land. There were horses grazing on and around the airstrip. The foreman chased the horses away and then went back into the house. Dad flew around and when he reached the point in his final landing approach that required him to land, some of the horses had wandered back onto the airstrip. Dad tried to crowd the edge of the strip area and encountered some rocks, resulting in a very rough landing and damage to the airplane. No one was injured, although Dad did receive a bump on his head.

After the landing accident with the Super Cruiser, the hunting trip continued and several deer were taken. In addition, Norman was successful in killing a mountain goat, which he had really wanted to do. Mountain goats are found in rocky areas high above the timberline. Goats are seldom seen and hard to hunt, in part because their coats turn white in winter and they are difficult to spot. If one is spotted, it is difficult to get close enough for a shot without alerting and causing the animal to take flight. Norman was persistent and after several days, he successfully bagged his goat. He brought the head and hide home, had the head mounted and the hide made into a beautiful floor rug. Norman proudly hung the trophy head on the wall at home. The goat was named Bedilia. I have no idea why.

Because of the damage sustained on landing, Dad could not fly the plane out. At the end of the hunting trip, the wings were removed and the plane was towed by a small tractor down the trail to the end of the road coming from the Yankee Fork of the Snake River. This was the same trail we used when the family rode horses into the ranch just a few years earlier. From the end of the road the plane was hauled by truck back to Idaho Falls for repairs and was later sold.

Dad started looking for another airplane for the Association. He considered several different planes and finally settled on a new four place Stinson Station Wagon with a 165 horsepower Franklin engine. He and Glen Thorne went back to the Stinson Aircraft Factory in Michigan to check out the new plane and fly it back to Idaho Falls. I believe it was during December of 1947 or January of 1948. Glen Thorne had been a Navy pilot during the war.

Years later Glen told me about the trip to pick up the Stinson. When they arrived at the Stinson Factory, they were given instruction on the characteristics of the airplane and spent a few hours of practice flying around the area. The Stinson was a beautiful plane and handled well. On the way back, however, they encountered a blizzard and zero visibility. Glen said they became lost, had trouble controlling the plane in the violent winds, and were unable to contact any airport facilities by radio. Dad never did say much about the trip, but Glen said he was scared to death, more so than at any time during his military flying career. He said he really did not think they were going to survive. They were barely able to keep the plane aloft. After what Mr. Thorne said seemed like an eternity, they lifted above the storm. They were then able to get their bearings, make radio contact with an airport in the vicinity, and land. They stayed overnight and continued on the next morning. Glen said the rest of the trip was uneventful.

Chapter 49: The Stinson

I loved the Stinson. It was dark blue with metal wheel covers and was quiet and comfortable in flight. The inside was upholstered and had simulated wood trim. Dad flew it often, and I flew with him as often as I could. Mother and others also rode with Dad in the Stinson. When Dad terminated his employment at the Association, the directors gave him the almost-new Stinson as a bonus.

Chapter 50

Hansen-Allen, Inc. Starts Selling Fords

One time I was riding in the car with Dad when he drove to a point on the west side of the Snake River across from downtown Idaho Falls. I believe I was still in the eighth grade. He told me that he and three others, Bill Gourley, Anton Poitevin and a Mr. Lindsey, were purchasing the large parcel of land that ran from the Snake River Equipment Company just north of Broadway, north to the John Hole Bridge over the Snake River. The parcel extended west from the river, to and across what is now Lindsay Boulevard, and back south to Broadway and included some frontage on Broadway. At the time there were a few existing businesses on the north side of Broadway, including Wackerli Buick, Walt Langseth's bait and tackle shop, and Feltman's gas station. The parcel being purchased was covered with dry grass, lava rock and sagebrush right down to the river. Some of the land had been used by many as a place to dump trash. Dad explained to me that someday the land along the west side of the river would be the location for several motels. While I had difficulty envisioning such development, I was confident Dad could make it happen if anyone could.

Dad had great foresight and vision and was willing to take a risk. He loved investing in land and seeing it develop. With the exception of the gold mine on the Yankee Fork, his business judgments were generally sound. I do not believe that the gold mine investment was necessarily a reflection on Dad's judgment. After all, the mine smelter facility had burned down shortly after it was constructed, and the government had fixed the price of gold at $35 an ounce, You cannot win them all!

The newly-purchased acreage was surveyed and platted into lots. Dad acquired a couple of the lots on West Broadway and built a large truck garage on the property in 1946. He acquired a truck franchise, and the business, for a time, was managed by Mr. Lindsey, one of the partners in the land purchase. Business was slow and did not generate enough cash flow to service the debt incurred in the lot and building, but Dad saw it as a long-term investment. I believe the idea of ultimately acquiring an automobile agency and locating it in the new truck facility had already occurred to Dad.

In 1946 rumors were heard that the Ford Motor Company was going to terminate the dealer franchise held by the owners of Bonneville Auto Company, located in downtown Idaho Falls. Ford Motor Company did not deem the location and facilities to be adequate. The owners, who had been in business for many years, were nearing retirement and apparently were reluctant to invest the money necessary to make the changes suggested by Ford Motor Company officials.

New automobiles and trucks for civilian use were only recently being manufactured and sold in large quantities. With the war now over, the demand for new vehicles was high, and more people were financially better able to afford them than ever before. Everyone expected new models would be coming out soon. Dad saw this opportunity and was making plans to apply for the Ford franchise. After all, he had control of a large new garage facility at an ideal location, fronting on Broadway just west of downtown Idaho Falls.

For several years Johnny Allen had been serving as sales manager in charge of the sale of all fresh and processed potatoes shipped by the Idaho Potato Growers Association. Mr. Allen also had other experience in business and sales. Dad knew Johnny Allen well, and they and their wives often socialized together. Dad talked to Mr. Allen about acquiring a Ford dealership, and he was very interested, but he did not have much capital to invest in the venture. Dad and Johnny Allen had the understanding that Dad would put in most of the initial capital. More would be borrowed by the new corporation and Mother and Dad. They agreed verbally that Mr. Allen's contribution would be his forgoing a portion of his compensation for the first few years until the capital accounts were evened out and the loans were substantially paid down. The understanding was based on personal trust.

Knowing that competition for the Ford franchise would be strong, I believe Dad felt the combination of business management and sales experience he and Mr. Allen had, plus the new truck garage facility on West Broadway, would give them an advantage. They incorporated as Hansen-Allen, Inc. and started the application process. Ultimately, they were successful, and in early 1947 they both resigned from the Idaho Potato Growers. They remodeled the facility on West Broadway to meet the requirements of the Ford Motor Company, and Hansen-Allen, Inc. opened for business. (This facility, after some remodeling, now houses Broadway Ford.)

Life was not dull in the years after the war. The new farm, with its irrigation system, was developed. The dairy herd was expanded. Tractors and mechanized equipment for the farm were acquired. The older kids were being helped with college expenses. The property along the Snake River was purchased. A truck garage was built on West Broadway and later remodeled for the new Ford franchise. All of this required that Mother and Dad borrow a considerable amount of money, secured by mortgages on the various properties. Dad was forty-five years old, in his prime, and things were going well.

Chapter 51

Ninth Grade at O.E. Bell

In the fall of 1947 I entered ninth grade at O.E. Bell Junior High. I had played football the previous year and did so again. I played on the line, usually left tackle, because I was large for my age. Also, without glasses my vision was not good. As Orval, Norman, and Reed before me, I signed up for a class in agriculture and became active in Future Farmers of America. I also signed up for algebra and Latin, among other courses.

Soon after school started, the high school closed for the harvest vacation. However, the junior high school did not. Because I was needed in the harvest, I received permission to be out of school for two or three weeks. When I returned to school I was far behind, particularly in algebra and Latin, and I struggled to catch up. I asked permission to drop Latin, but my teacher, Zuma Hale, would not allow it. She was a very good teacher and a tough taskmaster.

For a while I decided that if I did not do well in her class, Mrs. Hale would understand that she should have let me drop the Latin class. When I finally decided to apply myself, I had waited too long and received a D. I had never received a D grade before. I liked school and generally did well without putting forth a great deal of effort. I was embarrassed by my grade and vowed not to be that bullheaded in the future. I did better second semester and took another year of Latin the following year. Latin may be a "dead" language, but the classes I took benefited me throughout the rest of my schooling and continue to benefit me today.

I became somewhat high-spirited during ninth grade. During the year I was suspended from school on three different occasions. One day a few of us left school following lunch, to see a cartoon playing at the Paramount Theater. A couple of friends who declined to go knew of our whereabouts. During the movie someone came down the aisle looking for Walt Boltz. Walt left and then came back to tell us that he had to go home; he had just been told that his father had died. Our mood quickly changed, and we returned to school. Our principal,

Mr. Elmer Crowley, told us we were suspended and would not be readmitted unless one of our parents came to school with us. Dad went to school with me the next morning. I apologized to Mr. Crowley and was sent back to class.

On another day a few of us were walking along the sidewalk across from school and someone spotted a ten dollar bill in the leaves. Someone had a car, and we decided to go to Heise Hot Springs for the day. Later in the afternoon we returned to school. We were met by Mr. Crowley, who sternly told us we were suspended. The next morning Dad went back to school with me and I again was sent back to class. Dad was not happy, but he didn't scold or punish me. If I knew I had disappointed Dad or Mother, I felt terrible. Further punishment was probably not needed. I believe Dad and Mother appreciated the fact that all of us kids worked hard on the farm, were usually very respectful, and did well in school. As a consequence, I think they cut us a little more slack than we probably deserved.

The third time occurred in my agriculture class. It was right after lunch. Some of the kids in class were accused of something, I have since forgotten what. The accusation was false and I tried to defend the group. I alone was dismissed. The instructor, Angus Pond, said I could not return to class without permission from the school principal. I was furious. I walked across town to Dad's office at Hansen-Allen to tell him what had happened. I started cooling down as I came closer to his office, mindful of the two prior incidents for which I had had no excuse whatsoever.

I sat down in Dad's office and explained to him exactly what had happened. I never shaded the truth when talking to Dad. He listened, sat quietly for a moment, and then he told me that I had done the right thing, or at least what I had tried to do was the right thing. I remember that a wave of emotion and relief came over me. Dad was always fair with me. The next morning Dad and I went to school and we once again met with Mr. Crowley. Actually, Dad and Mr. Crowley were well acquainted, and I believe they enjoyed visiting even when the occasions involved my questionable behavior. I was allowed to return to class the next day. This gave the instructor time to cool down as well. Nothing further was said about the matter.

One additional incident in ninth grade warrants mention. I took a social science class from Mrs. Roche. She was a teacher I liked and respected very much, and she seemed pleased to have me in her class. I worked hard in her class and did well. Most of the classes at junior high were large, and Mrs. Roche's class was particularly large. One day in late spring, the room was quite warm, and I'm sure Mrs. Roche was more than a little frazzled.

The class was noisy, and she was trying to emphasize a point. I raised my hand and said that what she was saying was "like asking if someone had stopped beating his wife." She whirled around, glared at me, pointed at the classroom door and said, "Get out of here, right now." I felt terrible and left the room; however, I stayed in the hall until the bell rang and her class was dismissed. I went back in and apologized, and all was fine. A few days later, at the end of school, she motioned for me to stay after class was dismissed and said she wanted me to consider becoming a lawyer. A seed was planted.

Chapter 52

Gus

One summer day after I had completed ninth grade at O.E. Bell Junior High School, Dad asked me if I would drive a truck to Salt Lake City for him. I was comfortable driving the trucks and pickups on the farm, and had even mastered the "double" clutch maneuver without grinding the gears, a major accomplishment among farm boys. Dad said he would follow and bring me back. I was excited when I saw the truck. It had been stripped down to the frame and axles in order for some type of special body to be installed at a truck garage in Salt Lake. It was equipped with air brakes and was larger and had more gears and axles than any truck I had driven before. I told Dad I thought I could handle it, and I took off. Dad followed for a while and then led the way in his Packard sedan.

Once I got used to the air brakes, the drive was uneventful. We reached the truck garage and Dad made arrangements for the truck modifications and we drove away. Dad had some stops to make while we were in the city. When we had lunch, Dad picked up a newspaper and began reading the want ads. He asked me what I thought about buying a puppy as a birthday present for my sister Mary.

After lunch, we drove into a residential section of Salt Lake City and found the house identified in the paper as having puppies for sale. In short order we picked out a Cocker Spaniel male puppy. Dad paid for the puppy, had its tail "docked," or cut off short, and we left for home. When we arrived home, Dad put the puppy in his felt hat, and, with a big grin on his face, he carried it into the house and gave it to Mary. Mary recalls that the puppy peed in Dad's hat. She named the pup Gus, short for August which was her birthday month. Mary was a senior in high school and a year later left for the University of Idaho. Gus, who became a family pet, stayed at home.

Unfortunately, a few years later Gus was hit by a car and one of his back legs was broken. He was taken to the veterinarian we used for our farm animals.

He put a heavy full-leg cast on Gus. Afterwards Gus did not do well at all. He lost weight and appeared to be in constant pain, so Norman took him to another animal clinic for a second opinion. An X-ray showed that Gus's fracture was even with the top of the cast. The weight of the cast was pulling the fracture apart and preventing the bone from healing. The cast was removed, and the fractured leg bone was pinned. Gus recovered, however his leg was always tender, and over time he developed arthritis in the hip. As a consequence, he became a bit cranky and occasionally bit strangers who attempted to pet or play with him. We all loved Gus. He stayed with us until he died of old age.

Chapter 53

Lloyd Beal and I: Future Farmers

At the beginning of the school year, those of us who enrolled in agriculture at school and were active in FFA were asked to select a farm project. This required that we keep careful records on the project as a part of our classroom work. Most students either had a livestock project or raised a crop on a certain number of acres. The most common project was to raise and fatten yearling steers, lambs or pigs, which were exhibited and sold at the annual spring FFA Fat Stock Show. The show was always held at the Idaho Livestock Auction facilities on North Yellowstone in Idaho Falls.

The Fat Stock Show was a big event for FFA and 4-H kids. The sale was well supported by local ranchers, businessmen, and buyers from the large meat packing businesses. The prices paid for the livestock raised by the kids were generally higher than the market price. During the auction the ranchers and businessmen would sometimes make the highest bid and then donate the animal back to be resold. This amounted to a donation and extra money for the kid who owned the animal. It was fun, exciting, and often profitable.

My good friend Lloyd Beal and I were partners on three different projects. Our first project was to purchase yearling Hereford steers from a rancher in Montana who was a friend and former employer of Lloyd's older brother, John Beal. After potato harvest was finished, Dad lent Lloyd and me the money, and John Beal arranged to buy seventeen steers from the Montana rancher. He used a farm truck to haul the steers from the ranch back to the farm. They had been on summer range, and as I recall we paid sixteen cents per pound.

We put the steers in one of the corrals on the farm, built a hay bunker, and installed an insulated water trough that was heated in cold weather. We researched the merits of various feeds and selected Purina Steer Chow which we supplemented with dried beet pulp and ground corn. We ordered a quantity of shelled corn which was shipped by rail from the Midwest. Lloyd and I scooped the corn out of the rail car onto a truck and hauled it home. Based on a formula we were using, we ground the corn and included it in the grain mix we were using as steer feed. We had also borrowed the money for the corn from Dad. We kept accurate records of all our expenses, which included rent for the use of the farm corral and equipment based on a formula used by the government.

Looking back, I am surprised at all we did with our first FFA project. We were proud of what we were doing and took extra care to make sure the animals had ample clean straw and adequate feed and water. One of the steers was a "runt," and we knew this one would not fit with the others at the show. I can't remember for sure if the small one died or was butchered for meat, but we were left with sixteen head for our project. The steers did well through the winter and spring. By the time of the Fat Stock Show the following spring, they had gained considerable weight and were in excellent shape for the show and sale.

Lloyd and I took the sixteen steers to the auction yard the day before the event started. The animals were judged and most received the highest grade, Prime; the rest received the next highest, Choice. The night of the sale was exciting. When it was over, all of the steers had been sold at an average price of just over forty-two cents per pound. After we settled with Dad for the initial loan to purchase the steers and all the rental fees and other expenses, Lloyd and I split the balance. We had done very well. My half of the profits went directly into a savings account at First Security Bank.

One day during the Fat Stock Show and just before the sale, I drove my car to the livestock yards during the school lunch break. Several of us kids were in the car, which was parked near the Pavilion at the bottom of a hill. I was in the back seat and we were just goofing around. Suddenly Walt Boltz said that a large cattle truck was starting to move down the hill toward us and that no one was in the truck. The large, driverless truck was heading straight for our parked car. We didn't have time to do anything. Part way down the hill one of the truck's front wheels struck a rock outcropping which caused it to change direction. It just barely missed the car and then crashed into the livestock facilities, cutting a swath through the holding pens. Apparently the brakes had somehow released, allowing the semi to roll down the hill.

Lloyd and I were bullish. The next summer, for an FFA class project we asked Dad if we could rent the hog pasture to plant seed potatoes. This was the field just north of where Mother later built her "round house." The three-and-one-half acre field had been used for several years as a summer pasture for our hogs, but was now due to be rotated into potatoes. Dad agreed, and we arrived at a fair amount to pay for rent.

To be a class project, it was important that rent be at the going rate for comparable ground, and all other expenses be the same as that paid by area farmers and ranchers. This was part of our learning experience. We talked with Rex Blodgett who worked for the Idaho Potato Growers Association and was in charge of its certified seed potato program. Mr. Blodgett looked at the field we were planning to rent. He liked the fact that the field had never been planted to commercial potatoes and that commercial potatoes had not previously been grown on the adjacent fields. He believed the soil would likely be free of disease organisms and be a good location to grow certified seed potatoes.

Mr. Blodgett offered to help us locate a quality potato seed to plant, and he helped to supervise the required farming practices during the growing season. He also agreed to help us with roguing the young potato plants, a critical part of raising certified seed. Roguing consists of walking down every row of the growing crop to check for weak or diseased plants. Any such plants must be pulled from the ground and removed from the field. We had raised certified seed on other parts of the farm, and I had some experience with roguing.

With Mr. Blodgett's help, we purchased the seed. The ground was plowed and prepared for planting. All of the equipment, including the potato planter, was cleaned and sprayed with disinfectant before being used on the field. Special care was taken to disinfect and treat the potato seed while it was being cut into pieces and while it was hauled to the field to be planted. The project was meant to be a meaningful learning experience, and it was.

When the planting was completed, we cleaned out the ditch at the top of the field so that it would carry the necessary irrigation water. When the new potato plants had sufficiently emerged, we cultivated the rows. This made furrows for irrigation, removed weeds, and provided extra soil around the base of the plants. At the appropriate time, which depended on the soil moisture, we set out plastic siphon tubes to move the water from the open ditch to the furrows. During the growing season, it is important that the potatoes receive adequate water. This involves checking the soil moisture on a regular basis by putting your hand or a shovel in the ground to see how much moisture is present below the surface. If the potatoes get too dry, rough potatoes are likely to result. If the potatoes receive too much water, the roots can become water soaked and result in spotty potatoes and plants and potatoes more susceptible to rot and disease.

Lloyd and I were involved fulltime in other work on the farm; however, we found time to keep close watch on our crop of potatoes. The soil was rich and fertile as a result of being used as a hog pasture for many years. We also selected and applied additional fertilizer. The growing crop was really beautiful. People who periodically examined the field were impressed. As the small potatoes were starting to form on the roots, we would periodically check a plant and count the number of potatoes under it. Mr. Blodgett checked the field several times and helped with the roguing, as did representatives of the Idaho Crop Improvement Association. The field passed its field inspections, the first step in the certification process.

Ultimately the potato crop was ready to be harvested. Special care was taken to clean and disinfect the potato digger and wire baskets, and the baskets of potatoes were dumped into brand new sacks. The potatoes were placed in storage, in a disinfected area separated from the other harvested potatoes. The yield was outstanding. I believe more potatoes were harvested per acre on this small field than had ever been grown on the farm, and the quality of the crop was excellent. The next stage for certification involved having representatives of the Idaho Crop Improvement Association select a sample of the potatoes in storage and send the samples to a location in California. There, the sample potatoes are cut into pieces and planted, and the new plants carefully observed for any signs of disease.

The Idaho Crop Improvement Association is the official state agency responsible for the certification of all seeds grown in Idaho. They later notified us that the harvested crop was eligible for certification and could be sold as Blue Tag seed, the highest grade of certification. This was important news because Blue Tag grade potatoes brought the top market price for certified seed. There were lower grades of certification, Red and White, which reflected lower degrees of quality and brought a correspondingly lower price on the seed market. The market price for seed potatoes depended on supply and demand and varied from year to year. The market price was unusually high for Blue Tag when, with the help of Mr. Blodgett, we marketed the crop. Our potatoes had become a valuable crop.

The proceeds of the crop grown on that small three-and-one-half acre field, after we had settled with Dad for expenses (land rent, labor, the use of equipment, and the costs of the certification process), exceeded our wildest expectations. My half of the profits went directly into the bank. The total of the profits from my share of the sixteen steers and the potato crop later covered the cost of my first two years of college.

Lloyd and I were pretty cocky. Twice we had done surprisingly well. We thought we knew how to make money farming, unappreciative of how lucky we had been. We even talked about renting a forty or sixty acre farm, borrowing or renting equipment, and thought we could make a pretty good living. Fortunately, we put off doing what we thought would be a sure thing.

The next fall we again purchased steers, this time Angus steers. The steers were larger and cost more than the Herefords we had bought the year before, and had already put on considerable weight. Nonetheless, we were enthusiastic. We again arranged to rent corral space and utilize our knowledge of the optimum diet to maximize weight gain during the winter months. The Angus steers looked good and showed and graded well at the Fat Stock Show the following May. The prices we received were pretty good, but the spread between what we paid for the steers and the sale price was much less than the previous year.

I can't remember the exact figures, but after all expenses were paid and accounted for, we either made or lost about $30. It was a good lesson. At least we had not lost our shirts. Probably the overall experience helped persuade Lloyd to become a veterinarian and me to become a lawyer!

Chapter 54

Time Speeds by in High School

I was a saver by nature. I liked the feeling of having a little money in the bank. I would contemplate what I could buy with what I had saved, but I did not want to spend it. I would regularly check and keep track of the interest earned. This became a habit that I still follow today with savings and investments. I soon learned that if I had money in my pocket, I was more likely to spend it; also, that it was easier to take money out of than to put money into savings. These were good lessons.

There was one exception to all this talk about thrift. I decided I wanted a car. Actually, I rationalized that I could save time going to and from school, and thus be able to spend more time on the farm before and after school. I bought my first car, a 1941 Ford coupe, from Dad at the Ford agency during the spring I finished ninth grade. The car had low mileage, excellent metal, glass, and upholstery. I was told it had been owned by an elderly lady who drove very little. It sounded like a real buy. I soon discovered the car had serious clutch and engine problems. It turns out the lady always "rode" the clutch and almost never had the oil changed or the car serviced. Dad took the car back and sold me a 1947 Ford two-door sedan, with low mileage. It was a great car which I took excellent care of and drove for several years.

I enjoyed the FFA projects and activities that we engaged in when I took agricultural classes in my ninth, tenth, and eleventh years. The activities included week-long trips to Boise in the spring to attend State FFA conventions. We always stayed at the Idanha Hotel and always had a lot of fun, sometimes too much fun. Orval had been active in FFA, won the State FFA speech contest, and served as State President. Reed also served as State FFA President. I achieved State Farmer rank and served as our local chapter president.

One year, along with Reed, Lloyd Beal, and other local members, I attended the National FFA Convention in Kansas City, Missouri. We took the Greyhound bus from Idaho Falls to the convention site. It was quite an experience. One night we had professional entertainment, which included Roy Rogers of cowboy movie fame, and Judy Canova, a well-known movie star and comedienne. Lloyd Beal and I decided to go backstage to try to get autographs. When we were quite close to Judy Canova, she was apparently very angry with someone and let out a string of gross swear words. I was not a stranger to swear words, but I had never heard a woman swear before, and some of the words she used were even new to me. Lloyd and I abandoned our plan to pursue the autographs.

I had intended to continue playing football when I went on to high school for my sophomore year; however, at the last minute I decided not to. That fall Reed and Norman were attending the University of Idaho, and I was the only boy left at home. We still had the field work, putting up the last crop of hay, and harvesting the potatoes. And although we now had hired a person to be responsible for the dairy cows and manage the Grade A operations, he needed help and had to be relieved, or given a break, from time to time. And Lloyd Beal and I had our FFA steer project to manage. I had a lot on my plate and the time sped by.

Chapter 55

A Sad Ending to a Partnership

Several months after Hansen-Allen opened for business, problems began to surface. Johnny Allen started drinking heavily. He was in the habit of going out for long lunch breaks, which included having several drinks. His excessive drinking was noticeable to others in the business, including customers, and it affected his performance in the afternoon. He became increasingly difficult to work with. He also began demanding that he be able to draw more money out of the business than the informal agreement called for. Mr. Allen was unwilling to forgo a portion of his compensation to allow the substantial business loans to be paid down, which was the basis on which he and Dad had formed the partnership.

Johnny Allen, for the first time in his life, had his name on a business, was driving a new company car, and wanted a higher lifestyle. He was unwilling to plow money back into the business to build it up. Dad was deeply disappointed with Johnny Allen, and with the fact that he had so misjudged him. They had worked very well together in the potato business, and their talents seemed to complement each other. The opportunity to go into business together had seemed a reasonable step for them to take. Opening up an automobile agency shortly after the war was a once in a lifetime opportunity that they began with excitement and enthusiasm.

The problems at business weighed heavily on Dad. One afternoon he came home early. He spoke briefly to Mother and then they each packed a bag. Dad said they were going to West Yellowstone for a couple of days. He said little else and I really didn't know what was going on, but obviously Mother did. When they returned they had jointly decided that the Hansen-Allen partnership had to be terminated. During their time away Mother and Dad had reviewed their finances and analyzed the value of the automobile business. They arrived at a figure which they believed to be fair, for a one-half interest in the net assets of the business.

Dad met with Mr. Allen and presented him with a proposal to either purchase the interest of Mother and Dad or to sell his interest, at the same price. Although Mr. Allen himself had few assets, it might have been possible for him to associate with others who could have helped him acquire the business. Many people would have seen the potential long-term value of a well-run exclusive Ford car and truck agency in eastern Idaho. Johnny Allen accepted Dad's offer to buy out his interest. However, he wanted to be paid in full right away.

Angus Pond was working for the garage in new car sales. He told Dad that his father, the founder and owner of Ponds Lodge in Island Park, might be able to provide the money on a personal short-term loan. They drove to Ponds Lodge where Dad met Angus's father for the first time. Dad later said he explained how much money he needed and what it was for. The old gentlemen went into the next room and returned with a small box which he opened and then counted out the amount of the request, in cash, either $20,000 or $25,000. Dad wrote out and signed a paper acknowledging the loan, shook his hand, and left. Dad loved to tell of this event, proud that business could be done in such an informal way based on trust and reputation. Shortly thereafter, Dad did some refinancing and repaid the older Mr. Pond, with interest.

The termination of the partnership was accomplished without bitterness; however, it really was a sad outcome. Given the right circumstances the business could have provided a very good income and a comfortable future for both families. The Allen family returned to Salt Lake City after the partnership was dissolved.

Years later when I was serving in the Idaho State Senate and walking to the Capitol in Boise I was hailed by a fellow pedestrian on the other side of the street. It was the younger Allen son. I had not seen him in about forty years. He was working in Boise and had recognized me from news reports on the Idaho Legislature. He said he had been hoping we would have a chance to meet. We spent several enjoyable minutes getting reacquainted and bringing each other up to date on our respective families. The members of the Allen family were fine people. I have often thought about what might have been. Under different circumstances, the youngest Allen boy and I might have taken over the business our fathers started, who knows.

Chapter 56

More Time with Dad

I spent a lot of time with Dad, at home, at the garage, and when he flew the Stinson. One Sunday I went with Dad to his office. He often wanted to check things out and make sure all was in order for the next business day. He shared with me some of the financial details of the Ford agency. Dad seemed to me to be more relaxed and confident about the future. He and Mother carried a lot of debt; however, he could see that within a relatively short time he would have it paid down substantially.

The business and the farm were both doing well. Dad had been covered with a large life insurance policy to provide protection from the large indebtedness that he and Mother had incurred in recent years to develop the automobile business and the Osgood farm. It was a rather expensive policy; and he decided to let the policy lapse.

At this point in time Dad began to relax and seemed to be really enjoying life. He had confidence in the employees at the garage. He began taking time off once in a while, something he almost never had done before. When he flew the Stinson, he mostly did so for pleasure, and he enjoyed having company when he flew. Mother started flying with him more often. Several times they flew to Salt Lake to meet with Ford Motor Company officials. They flew to Moscow, Idaho, to visit kids attending the University. He and Mother attended state automobile dealer meetings and conventions at places like the new Shore Lodge at McCall and the Lodge at Sun Valley.

One time Dad, Mother and I drove to Moscow to attend an annual Dad's Day event at the University and to visit the kids who were then in school. We drove a brand new Ford convertible Dad borrowed from the garage. Dad let me drive most of the way up and back. At times I exceeded the speed limit; however, Dad didn't say anything. We all had a great time, and Dad and Mother were in good humor and thoroughly enjoyed themselves. On the drive back from Moscow they began talking about the traveling they hoped to do someday, including overseas trips. Mother said that at an earlier time in their lives they had talked about taking trips to Europe, Africa and China. She said at that time the prospects for travel seemed more like a dream. Now they were beginning to believe they were actually going to be able to take some of those trips.

I particularly enjoyed my opportunities to spend quality time with Dad when I was in the ninth and tenth grades. During those years my older brothers were away from home and attending college. In a way this period of time reminded me of the days on the Airport Farm, when all of the other kids rode the school bus and I was home alone with Mother. It was a special time for me with Mother then, as it was with Dad now. I believe Dad enjoyed it as well. He was always interested in what I was doing, and in what I planned to do after finishing high school. He took time to explain what was happening at the garage, and to share some of his future plans. I believe Mary also enjoyed being able to spend more time with Dad. He was at home more, and when Mary was a junior and senior in high school, she worked part time at the Ford garage.

Farrel married Alice Kissner on August 20, 1947. This was a real milestone, the first of the six kids to be married. Farrel and Alice were married in the Holy Rosary Catholic Church in Idaho Falls following a large wedding breakfast at the Bonneville Hotel. Dad was in a festive mood, as I am sure we all were. After the wedding ceremony, when they left the church, Farrel and Alice saw their wedding present from Mother and Dad: a brand new Ford automobile which we kids had appropriately decorated. I remember wondering if receiving a new car as a wedding present would become a family tradition. It was not to be.

Orval was discharged from the U.S. Navy in 1946, and Norman graduated from high school in the spring of 1946. In the fall of 1946 they both enrolled at the University of Idaho in the College of Agriculture. Norman came home from school in the spring of 1947 without having finished the second semester. He returned to the University in the fall and again enrolled, and then returned for good in the spring of 1948. He decided to commit himself to farming. Norman was restless in college; however he was a good farmer and an excellent mechanic.

Norman married Marjean Davies on June 24, 1948. Marjean was nicknamed "Clem" and has been called "Clem" by most of us since they were married. I was told that Farrel first came up with the nickname "Clem." Marjean had very small feet, unlike the "number nines" of the Clementine in the song "Oh my darling, Oh my darling Clementine…." I was told this inspired Farrel, as a joke, to start calling her Clem when he and Alice and Norman and Clem were double dating. After they were married, Norman and

Chapter 56: More Time with Dad | 141

Clem did some remodeling of the basement of the new house on the farm and moved in.

Reed graduated from high school in the spring of 1947 and in the fall enrolled at the University of Idaho in the College of Agriculture. In the fall of 1948 he returned for his second year, and Orval, who had changed his major to political science, returned for his third year of college. Reed helped on the farm during the summers. Orval was available to help on the farm if needed; however, he primarily worked part-time at the Ford garage and also part-time at the KID radio station in town. In the fall of 1948 Mary entered her senior year at Idaho Falls High School, and I enrolled in my sophomore year.

Chapter 57

The Infamous Winter of '48

The winter of 1948-49 was memorable. We experienced one of our most severe winters ever recorded. The storms dropped record amounts of snow, not just in our area, but throughout the western and midwestern states. A national state of emergency was declared, and the military was brought in to help rescue people who were stranded, often without food or heat. US Air Force cargo planes dropped food and emergency supplies to isolated farms and ranches and small towns. The cargo planes also dropped bales of hay for herds of stranded livestock that were starving. It was amazing to me just how quickly a large area of the country and millions of inhabitants could be placed in real jeopardy by a sudden record snowfall and low temperatures. Many roads, including major highways, were impassable for weeks.

We were snowed in at the farm for over two weeks. Dad was unable to drive back and forth and stayed in town to be able to attend to the needs of the business. There were ironies. I was unable to go to school for a couple of weeks. On the other hand, we had a fairly large herd of milk cows that needed to be milked twice a day. At the same time, the milk could not be delivered to town because the roads were blocked. We filled every milk can and container we could find. We even filled a bathtub with milk. Finally we had to dump much of the milk in order to have a container to hold the fresh milk. I remember saying, in jest, that if we couldn't deliver the milk to town, we should be excused from having to get up in the morning to milk the cows. Life doesn't work that way.

One day we received a call from the trucker who regularly hauled the milk cans to town. He said that the plows had been working on the highway, and he was going to try to reach our place to pick up milk. He asked if we could meet him part way. We loaded full cans of milk onto a farm wagon hooked to a tractor. Another tractor with a front-end loader to scoop snow was in the lead. A small crew of us worked for several hours and we were able to go about a half-mile toward town where we met the hauler. The cans were quickly transferred.

We made it back to the farm and the hauler was able to reach town; however, a blizzard started up quickly and closed the highway again. That was the only time during the ordeal that we were able to send milk to town. The rest of the time we simply dumped it.

One time a Greyhound bus filled with passengers was stopped by drifts about a quarter of a mile north of our house. The whole busload of passengers trudged through the snow to our house for food and warmth and stayed until the Greyhound Company was able to rescue them that evening. Several times our mail and newspapers were dropped by a small airplane. I am not sure if this was a widespread practice or if Dad had arranged for the drops. Each time, we received a call that a plane was going to make an attempt to deliver; we watched for the plane to fly over and then ran through the deep snow to locate the items dropped. Flying conditions were poor most of the time. We had a series of severe blizzards and fierce winds throughout the two weeks of our isolation, and the snow continued to pile up.

All in all, it was a great adventure and provided us with a lot of fun. Sometimes the power was off for extended periods of time, leaving us without lights or heat. We kept a fire going in the fireplace and even did some cooking over the fire in the fireplace. When we were not milking or caring for animals, we played cards and board games for hours on end, often by candlelight. We did a lot of reading and talking. The hired men who lived across the road had families, and we all kept close track of each other to make certain everyone had food and was safe. Fortunately, we did not have any medical emergencies or major illnesses.

All of the main roads in the Intermountain West were blocked when the storm ended. The highway past our house, US 91, was the main highway from Salt Lake City to Butte, Montana and points beyond. We kept waiting for snowplows to come up US 91 from Idaho Falls. In fact, the highway adjacent to our farm was finally plowed out from the north by two large State of Montana snowplows!

Chapter 58

1949: Looking to the Future

Mother and Dad observed their 25th wedding anniversary on January 9, 1949. Because of the severe weather conditions, the actual "silver" wedding anniversary celebration was deferred until sometime in the early spring. All of the six kids contributed to the purchase of a sterling silver dinnerware service for twelve as our anniversary present to them. The silverware was purchased from Don Leymaster, who owned and operated Leymaster jewelry on Park Avenue in downtown Idaho Falls. Mr. and Mrs. Leymaster helped us select the set. We had purchased Mother and Dad a sterling silver serving tray and accessories the previous Christmas. All items had matching patterns.

Mary graduated from high school in the spring of 1949. During the summer, she continued to work for Dad at the garage, and to help Mother at home when needed. When he finished college, Reed planned to return home and run the farm with Norman. I had not really given much serious thought to my future at that time. I did enjoy the time I spent at the Ford garage and my talks with Dad about the automobile business.

I knew and liked all of the key employees. Grant Orme was in charge of the body shop and his chief mechanic was Lloyd Mori. Bruce Lundgren, the oldest son of our former neighbors, at one time was the new car sales manager. He later acquired his own Ford dealership in Bountiful, Utah. Dad hired Roy Van Houghten, who had been a flight instructor at the Idaho Falls Airport, to work in car sales. He later owned the Ford dealership in Gooding, Idaho. I began to think, more and more, that I might end up in the automobile business someday. I later learned that both Orval and Mary were entertaining thoughts along the same line.

Chapter 59

Watering Potatoes and Chopping Hay

Extra help for irrigating was needed when the new potato crop was first watered. Prior to planting, the soil had been plowed, disked and harrowed and was loose. Many of our fields had a fair slope. It was important that the right amount of water be put into the furrows between the rows of planted potatoes. If too little was put in the furrows, the water would not reach and properly soak up the lower half of the rows. If too much water was used, the water would wash the soil down the row, causing deep ruts.

To accomplish the first irrigation of a potato crop, a new ditch was made along the top of the field, parallel to the main ditch. Water was diverted from the main ditch into the new smaller ditch from where the water would flow into the individual furrows. Until the new ditch became soaked and had settled from a couple of irrigations, washouts were common. A great deal of skill was required to properly irrigate crops on the new farm; the consequences of under watering and over watering were serious.

Sometime after the war we started a different method of harvesting hay. We started field chopping the hay from the windrows made with a side rake. Dad felt that by feeding the cows chopped hay rather than the long stalks in the stack, more of the hay would be efficiently utilized. The tops of the hay stalks were more tender than the butt ends and the dairy cows left much of the more coarse parts of the hay stalks uneaten. By chopping the hay, the hay stalk was cut into small pieces and mixed in with the rest.

We had to make new equipment for the chopped hay operation. We made several wagons with screens on the upper half of the sides. A false front was placed inside of each of the wagons, with small cables attached which ran to a roller on the back of the wagon. The hay chopper blew the chopped hay into the wagons. When a wagon was full, it was taken to the stack yard adjacent to the corrals and backed in between two large wooden panels, about sixteen feet high and fourteen to sixteen feet apart. The roller was turned by a power takeoff which pulled the false front from the front of the inside of the wagon, and thus pulled the load of chopped hay back. The chopped hay dropped into a conveyer which carried it to the top of the stack face.

We later discovered two drawbacks to field chopping our hay crop. We had many acres of alfalfa hay. When we started cutting, we often had a lot of hay cut and curing in windrows at the same time. When conditions were just right the quality of the chopped hay was vastly superior. Unfortunately, if we had rain, we had to suspend operations until the windrows of hay had dried sufficiently. When we resumed haying operations, all of the hay that was in the windrows would dry out at about the same time. As a result, some of the hay would be drier than was ideal and most of the leaves would be shattered into a fine hay dust. We would try to remedy the excess dryness by starting our haying operations as early as four o'clock in the mornings, when there was dew on the hay, and then work until the rising temperature made the hay too dry to chop. We started early also to avoid strong winds, which often increased in the afternoons. It was a very dusty job.

There was another drawback we didn't discover until we had been field chopping our hay for several years. The field chopper cut the hay and anything else that the side rake had picked up when the hay was put into a windrow. This included small pieces of wire, nails, and fence staples. The person operating the chopper would occasionally hear a "zing" as a piece of metal went thru it. This didn't happen often and was not really considered a serious problem at the time. I also believe that the longer we chopped our hay, the problem tended to subside, because less metal debris remained in the fields.

A few years later, however, a few of the cows started looking poorly, and began to lose weight. The veterinarian discovered that the bits of metal, eaten along with the hay, had been deposited in a particular low part of one of the cow's four stomachs instead of passing through its intestinal system. There the metal remained and over time corroded rust produced an acid which caused a hole in the cow's stomach. This allowed partially digested feed to escape from the stomach and caused internal infection to develop. Surgery was performed on several cows to remove the metal and close the hole in the stomach. Usually the cow survived following surgery, but it seldom returned to full milk production. We lost our prize bull, "Pete," to what we called the "hardware disease."

Chapter 60

Trauma and a Camping Trip

Early in the summer Dad began talking with Reed and me about a summer trip into the Falconberry Ranch, otherwise known as the Loon Creek Ranch. We had been working hard and the plan was to fly in for a few days of fishing, hiking, and relaxation. After the first crop of hay had been chopped and put into the stack and we had irrigated the new potato crop a couple of times, Dad, Reed and I set a date for departure.

At the scheduled time, we packed our fishing gear and sufficient clothing for a week or so, and made ready for the trip. At the last minute I also packed my .22 caliber Remington rifle, although I am not sure what I expected to shoot. Dad had the mechanics at the Idaho Falls airport give the Stinson the required annual inspection and a thorough engine check. We loaded the car, which was a new Ford station wagon, drove to the airport, moved the Stinson from the hangar, and transferred the items we had packed from the station wagon to the plane.

It was early in the morning. For safety reasons, Dad wanted to arrive at the airstrip at Loon Creek early while it was still cool and the air was heavy. He filed a flight plan with the FAA and airport authorities, as was his practice. We boarded the plane and Dad taxied to the end of the runway. I was seated in the back and Reed was in front with Dad. Dad revved the engine, checked the instruments, and made radio contact with the control tower. He spent more time than usual listening to the engine, decided it sounded all right, and we took off. We headed in a westerly direction, but after about 15 minutes Dad was not satisfied with the sound of the engine. Dad notified the tower that we were returning and then turned the plane around. He was disappointed because the engine should have been in tip-top running condition, but it was not. It was running rough.

The plane was able to maintain altitude and the return to the airport seemed routine except for the sound of the engine. As we approached the airport

Dad entered the flight pattern, flew in the direction of the south end of the runway, and made his final turn. He lined up with the runway and pulled the throttle back to reduce power and began his final glide. As he pulled the throttle back, the engine stopped, totally. Suddenly everything was quiet. We were too far south of the airport to glide to the end of the runway for a routine landing. Dad told Reed and me to tighten our seat and shoulder belts and prepare for impact. We could see that without engine power, our glide path would put our point of impact in a farm field south of the runway. In fact, we could see the exact spot we would hit the ground.

The glide seemed to take forever, although it could have taken only a matter of seconds. For a while we just seemed to float. As we neared the ground, I became more aware of the speed of the plane. Then all hell broke loose. The noise was horrific. The propeller hit the ground and shattered, and then the plane began bouncing out of control. It struck a fence and flipped. After hitting the fence, the plane vaulted through the air and onto the end of the runway, upside down. Sparks were flying everywhere. The windshield was broken out and gasoline was pouring from the wing tanks. I still cannot believe that with the sparks and the leaking gasoline the plane did not immediately catch on fire.

We unhooked our seat and shoulder belts and dropped out through the broken windshield, one at a time. We then ran a short distance away from the plane. We checked each other over and were relieved to find that none of us was injured, although Dad did have a small gash on his forehead. Dad asked me to run to the control tower which was halfway down the runway and notify the persons on duty that we had crashed on the end of the runway. He was concerned that the morning commercial flight from Salt Lake City was due to land shortly.

I will never forget the next few minutes. I was sixteen years old. We had just survived an accident that could have been fatal for all of us. I was pleased to have something to do that Dad considered to be important. I started running and promptly fell down. I stood up and started running again, and again I fell down. I couldn't understand what my problem was. I was still near Dad and Reed, although I don't know if they saw me fall. Twice again I started running and two more times I fell down. I was embarrassed. My legs were like rubber. Finally I stood up, didn't move right away, and then I started walking very slowly. After several steps, I picked up the pace and started walking a little faster. Finally, I started to run, slowly at first and then I increased my speed.

I realized later that I had been in a state of shock. I finally reached the airport control tower and notified the officials of the accident, and then ran back. When they considered the fire danger had passed, Dad and Reed unloaded the plane. The airplane was extensively damaged. The Stinson was structurally strong. Later someone said if we had been in a Cessna, we would all have been killed. Dad called the Ford garage and asked someone to bring a wrecker and pull the plane off the end of the runway, which was done. Then we drove home.

Mother couldn't believe what had happened. I guess we couldn't either. Dad made a quick decision that he, Reed, and I needed to get away, to try to get over what had just happened. I think we were all in a state of shock from the close call. We had a quick bite to eat, and since the station wagon was still loaded, we headed north to Montana. Very little was said as we drove. I think we were all absorbed with our own thoughts. We drove through Salmon, Idaho and over the Lost Trail Pass to Darby, Montana. We ate at the Tin Cup Café in Darby and then backtracked a few miles to Conner, Montana, where we found a motel and spent the night. For obvious reasons, the Tin Cup Café was a regular stop for me over the next several decades, until it was destroyed by fire. The following morning we drove west on an unpaved road in the direction of the Magruder Ranger Station, picked a site, and set up our camp.

We spent several enjoyable days at our camp. We caught and cooked fish. We also shot, cleaned and cooked a species of grouse that we called "Pine hens." Dad was our "chief" cook and seemed to thoroughly enjoy it. At one point a soldier on leave, driving a jeep, came into our camp. He was on a thirty-day leave and had driven from Grangeville, Idaho, camping along the way. The road was not listed on the official maps as passable. From then on, I planned to someday follow the route he had taken; however, I never have, at least not yet. He joined us for supper, camped nearby, and left the next morning.

This was a special trip for a lot of reasons. We never discussed the accident. The experience was simply too "fresh," and our emotions were too "raw" for us to grapple with the subject at that time. I know that each of us quietly gazed at the others, conscious of the fact that we were very, very lucky to be alive. Frankly we didn't really discuss the accident after we returned home, either. We didn't need to, I guess.

While we were on this trip, we drove around and explored the area. We drove west to the top of the Nez Perce Pass. At this point I took a picture of Reed and Dad, and Reed took a picture of Dad and me standing by the forest service sign at the top of the pass. Later I found the pictures and had one framed for Reed and one for me, which I have hung on the wall at home. This picture of Dad and me is one of my favorite pictures. As far as I know these are the last pictures taken of Dad. After the camping trip in the summer of 1949, Dad, Reed, and I returned home and went back to our regular routines.

Years later my son Steve and I took a camping trip through parts of Idaho and Montana, retracing parts of the trek of Chief Joseph and the Nez Perce Indian tribe as it tried, unsuccessfully, to escape to Canada. We retraced part of the trip Dad, Reed and I had taken, and Steve and I took our pictures by the sign marking the top of Nez Perce Pass. The experience was emotional for me, to say the least.

Chapter 61

An Arrival and a Devastating Departure

The rest of the summer went rapidly. In September Orval, Reed, and Mary drove north to the University of Idaho. Orval enrolled in his senior year, Reed in his junior year, and Mary in her first year. I was sixteen years old and enrolled as a junior in the Idaho Falls High School. Norman and Clem were living in the remodeled basement. Clem was expecting a baby in October, the first grandchild for Mother and Dad. The baby was born in October, 1949, a healthy boy. His parents named him David Ray Hansen. Dad was very proud to be a grandfather and appeared both proud and tender when he held the baby.

The house seemed particularly quiet after the three older kids left for the University. Norman and Clem were adjusting to their new life in the basement. Only Mother, Dad and I were left in the new house, and the house suddenly seemed large. I occupied my bedroom on the second floor and had the upstairs bathroom all to myself. Mother and Dad occupied their first-floor bedroom. Now that Dad was in the automobile business, he did less traveling than before and was home much more in the evenings for meals and conversation. All three of us enjoyed this opportunity for a closer, more normal family relationship. I felt fortunate to be able to spend more time with Dad and get to know him better than was the case when I was younger.

I remember several times in the early fall of 1949 that Dad was lying on the couch in the living room when I arrived home from school. This was really unusual. He was experiencing severe headaches much like severe migraine headaches. Dad also had high blood pressure and tried to watch his weight and eliminate sweets. He always put saccharine tablets in his coffee, in place of sugar. I believe the headaches were assumed to be related to his blood pressure. However, in retrospect, I do not believe the headaches were related to blood pressure. As an aside, in later life most of Dad's kids have developed some degree of elevated blood pressure, for which modern medicines have been routinely and successfully used. Our tendency for high blood pressure is probably an inherited characteristic.

The headaches that Dad experienced that fall were quite disabling. When they were the most severe, Dad would simply leave work and come home. He would lie on the couch with a cold, wet towel over his forehead and pretty much tough it out until the pain subsided. Standing in the doorway to the living room, I would hear him audibly moan. Both Dad and Mother were concerned, and Dad saw a couple of doctors to try to find relief. Sadly, in 1949, we had access to some fine old family doctors in Idaho Falls, but there were very few diagnostic tools available, and the skill and experience of the local family doctors to understand and treat relatively unusual problems was quite limited.

On Sunday, October 13, l949, Dad was home all day. He was relaxed and seemed to enjoy the day. He was free from the severe headaches. My friend, Walt Boltz, came out to the farm to spend the afternoon with me. Walt was the kid who skipped school in ninth grade to see the movie at the Paramount Theatre, when his father died unexpectedly. He was a very close friend. We spent the afternoon mostly goofing around. Late in the afternoon Mother asked if I wanted to invite Walt to stay for Sunday dinner; he accepted the invitation. Dad liked Walt and engaged him in light conversation during the late afternoon. At dinner time the four of us sat down at the dining room table. Mother had prepared a typical Sunday meal: a pork roast, applesauce, mashed potatoes and gravy. I am not sure why I remember the menu but I do. The events of the 13th of October will forever stay with me.

Before we sat down to eat, Dad had started a fire in the living room fireplace. All of us loved having a "real" fire in the fireplace. The sound and smell of a wood fire was intoxicating. And it still is for me. Halfway through the meal he went into the living room, adjacent to the dining room, to put pieces of split logs on the fire. A large supply of logs was stacked on the left side of the fireplace, so that we could enjoy a fire throughout the evening without going outside for more logs.

Mother, Walt and I heard a loud "thud." Mother and I rushed to the living room and found Dad on his knees. He had dropped an armload of wood. He seemed confused. Dad was a large man, so Mother and I were unable to lift him to his feet. I ran to the basement to get Norman, and with his help we were able to help Dad to his feet to the living room couch. We helped him to lie down.

Dad was alert and said, "Something serious has happened—this is really serious." Mother called for the family doctor, who was spending the evening at the Elks Club. She explained the problem and had reason to believe the doctor was on his way. At this point, Walt Boltz realized something serious was happening and he could be of no help, so he left for his home in town.

Dad said he had to go to the bathroom. Norman and I helped him to his feet, and with one on each side, helped him walk to the bathroom where he did, in fact, urinate. He seemed alert and mentioned again that something very serious was happening. Norman and I helped him walk back, through the hall, his bedroom, and into the living room. We helped him to get back on the couch in the living room. He became less alert and spoke very little. Mother became alarmed with what she was seeing and called the doctor again and asked him to come to our house. The doctor suggested we have an ambulance take Dad into the Sacred Heart Hospital and he would meet us there.

In 1949 we had no ambulance service in Idaho Falls. The function of an ambulance service was performed by the local funeral homes, on a rotation basis to ensure that no funeral home had an advantage over another. I suppose most of the persons they picked up on an emergency basis ended up not at one of our two hospitals, but at one of the local mortuaries. The funeral home personnel did their best; however, they were not trained in first aid procedures. I do not want to imply, however, that having funeral home personnel transport Dad to the hospital had anything to do with his ultimate death.

In later years Farrel was instrumental in helping Idaho Falls set up a professional ambulance service with trained EMTs. He also helped set up emergency programs at both hospitals. His efforts have undoubtedly helped save countless lives.

Dad was transported by Wood Funeral Home to the Sacred Heart Hospital. Mr. Jack Wood, Sr., the founder of the Wood Funeral Home, had grown up in the Murray, Utah, area, and had gone to school with Mother. He came with the funeral home vehicle and an assistant and helped move Dad into the vehicle and to the hospital. He did so with compassion and dignity.

We followed the funeral home vehicle to the hospital. We spent the rest of the evening in Dad's room at the Sacred Heart Hospital. Dad never regained consciousness. When the doctor examined Dad, he stated that Dad had suffered a serious cerebral hemorrhage, a rupture of an artery in the brain, an aneurism. The burst artery was causing swelling in the brain cavity. There was no way to relieve the resulting pressure.

The doctor said that Dad would probably not survive through the night and that if he somehow did survive, he would be severely limited in cognitive and physical capabilities. In other words, the doctor was saying Dad would be better off if he quietly passed away. Mother, Norman, and I were reeling from the doctor's comments. We had hoped and expected that something could and would be done to improve his condition.

About five o'clock in the morning on October 14, 1949, Dad passed away. Mother, Norman and I were escorted into a side room and served very strong coffee, while we tried to adjust to the fact that Dad was actually gone. After a short period of time, we drove home. Just after we arrived home, the rest of the bridge group, the "Foursome"—Veva Jackson, Lottie Danner, and Evelyn Jensen—arrived at the house. How they had received the word of Dad's illness and passing I do not know. When the three ladies arrived, they took over the kitchen, put on a large pot of strong coffee, and started cooking. This is what they knew how to do best. They seemed to ignore us and simply went about their task of providing what they knew would be needed.

Mother, Norman and I were in shock. Clem came upstairs to join us for a short time; however, she had David Ray to tend to. I saw John Beal, who was helping us with the Grade A dairy operations, walk past the house on his way to the milking parlor. I walked out into the yard and told him that Dad had passed away. It was hard for both of us. I wanted John to tell the others who lived and worked on the farm so that I would not have to.

Shortly thereafter Orval, Reed and Mary drove into the yard. They were hoping to hear that Dad was doing all right and that they could visit him in the hospital. They were devastated to learn that he had passed away a couple of hours before. They broke down and that caused the rest of us to break down. Up to that time we had been pretty stoic dealing with the reality of Dad's death. Maybe we needed this opportunity to just let go. It was a sad and difficult few hours. Orval seemed to have the most difficulty dealing with Dad's passing. I had never seen Orval completely break down emotionally. He spent some time in his room on the second floor of the house; I could hear him sobbing when I was downstairs. These memories are etched in my memory.

Later I was struck with a few comments Farrel made when he returned home. I had the impression that Farrel believed steps might have been taken in response to the cranial swelling and to deal with the aneurism. I remember a couple of years later an actress, Patricia Neal, had a cerebral hemorrhage, was operated on and not only survived but returned to her normal state and level of activities. She obviously benefited from medical technology and experience not then available in Idaho Falls. In fairness, the procedure which was used in treating Patricia Neal was, even then, in an experimental stage. That is just the way it was.

Chapter 62

Arrangements Must Be Made

The next few days were blurry. Many people stopped by the house to pay their respects; some I knew and some I did not know. Arrangements had to be made for the funeral, and the family was totally unprepared for what had to be done. However, we managed. I remember all of the kids accompanied Mother to Wood Funeral Home to select a casket. I particularly remember going from one area to another in the basement of the funeral home, looking at the selection. We were escorted first to the lower priced caskets, and then to the next price level and finally to the most expensive. Mr. Wood commented on what a great fellow Dad had been and that he deserved to be buried in one of the finest coffins.

I know Mother was numb, as all of us kids were, and susceptible to the suggestion that Dad's character and accomplishments warranted the very best, which happened to be the most expensive. The casket selected was covered with a metal, either a layer of bronze or copper. A vault was also selected. Later I reflected on the cost of the casket and realized that Mother had agreed to pay too much, and that with the purchase of a vault, the materials the casket was made of were of no importance. At the time we all concurred that the selection was appropriate.

Later as a lawyer helping family members dealing with estate administration, I always inquired as to the cost of the funeral. I advised people to make funeral arrangements in advance, and to negotiate the price rather than deal with the matter after a death had occurred. Substantial savings can and do occur. I remembered how easily people are persuaded to spend more than they can afford, or at least more than is necessary. Funerals do not have to cost a lot of money.

Dad's funeral service was to be held at the LDS Tabernacle which was, at the time, on E Street. A large crowd was expected, and therefore the Tabernacle, which was larger than the average LDS Church, was deemed appropriate. Dad had been quite active in civic affairs, including the Elks Lodge and the Idaho Falls Chamber of Commerce, and served on the committee responsible for selecting the site of the new high school to be built on Holmes Avenue. The mayor of Idaho Falls had issued a declaration that the city offices be closed for the funeral, to allow employees to attend the service.

Tony Naegle was asked to be the main speaker at the service. I had never met him and was never clear why he was asked; however, his remarks were appropriate. Mr. Naegle was a local realtor, and later served in the Idaho State Senate. I became better acquainted with him when I returned to Idaho Falls to practice law.

I remember talking with him years later, and he indicated he was pleased, but surprised, to be asked to speak at the funeral, as he really did not know Dad very well. I always wondered why a few of Dad's closest friends were not asked to speak. Maybe this again emphasizes the importance of doing advanced planning of funeral service matters. Doing so will avoid a lot of pressure on the immediate family, particularly when death occurs suddenly.

I did not have clothes that were appropriate for a funeral. I seldom dressed up. I did have a suit which was a hand me down from Norman, a brown suit, which had been tailored to fit me, and which I wore to school dances in junior high school. When I was sixteen however, the suit was too small. Mother took me to Blocks Men's Store on Park Avenue in downtown Idaho Falls. I was outfitted in a formal blue, double-breasted suit, a shirt and tie, and black shoes, my attire for the funeral. I kept this suit and the shoes for years thereafter. I wore it on several formal occasions. I tend not to throw things away, even when worn out, and I may still have the shoes, a reminder of the time, my emotions, and the circumstances of Dad's funeral.

The day before the service, officials at Wood Funeral Home brought the casket and Dad to our home on the farm. The casket was placed in the living room, was opened, and stayed there until just before the service. It seemed reasonable at the time, I guess. I had not had much experience with funerals before, having attended only two. I don't know how common the practice was; in fact I do not recall another instance where this occurred. Many relatives and friends of Mother and Dad came to the house to pay their respects.

Almost all of the people who came to the house praised Dad and his many accomplishments. Their comments were consistent with my own opinion. I thought Dad was the greatest, most capable person that ever existed, and that he could do almost anything. I remember the comments of one person, however, who stated that Dad's real strength and success was not so much what he was able to do by himself, but was his ability to identify and attract capable people, to give them the support, incentive, and encouragement that enabled these persons to achieve more than they might have otherwise felt possible. He said that the combined efforts of Dad and those he surrounded himself with were the real reason for Dad's success.

When I heard the person make the comments, I was a bit disappointed. I wanted Dad to receive all the credit for what he had accomplished. Later, I came to appreciate that what was said was absolutely true, and the qualities he attributed to Dad were the real measure of his success. I wish I could remember who made those remarks.

The church was crowded and I felt very self-conscious; however, I remember little else about the service. I was conscious of people on the sidewalk watching the funeral procession as we drove from the Tabernacle to Fielding Memorial where Dad was buried. I wished they would look away, rather than at the vehicles in the funeral procession. I have thought of this over the succeeding years, and make a habit of looking at the ground or pulling my car over and averting my eyes when a funeral procession passes, as a gesture of respect to the family members. Dad's sudden death and the immediate aftermath had an enormous effect on me.

Chapter 63

Life Goes on and Mother Manages

At an appropriate time after the service had been held and we had gathered as a family, Orval, Reed, and Mary returned to the University of Idaho. Reed decided to finish his fall semester and then withdraw from school to return to help Norman run the farm. I returned to high school to continue my junior year.

Everyone came home for the Christmas holidays. It was a difficult time, our first Christmas without Dad. But we managed. I don't remember much about the rest of the school year. I came home right after school every day and helped with the chores and some of the farm work. I do remember how quiet the house was, with only Mother and me living in the large new house, together with our dog Gus.

Mother started spending time at the Ford garage, and soon was going in on a daily basis. She felt it was important that she have a presence, to make sure things continued to go smoothly. I know she felt inadequate, but in fact she did a remarkable job of managing the operation. She had been manager of the farm for many years, handling much of the hiring and firing, and all of the banking and payroll. In addition, Mother was a real working partner with Dad. The major decisions were joint decisions.

Dad was more of a risk taker and had great vision in business matters; however, he valued Mother's judgment and sought her opinions and advice on a regular basis. Mother was a quiet, unassuming person, and many friends and acquaintances were not fully aware of the extent to which Mother and Dad collaborated on business decisions. The employees respected Mother, and the new arrangement worked well. The longer she was involved, the more confidence she gained; however, Mother knew her limitations.

Later, with the help of officials of the Ford Motor Company, Mother was able to hire Clarence Rodgers to take over much of the management of the Ford agency. Mr. Rodgers had been a successful John Deere farm equipment dealer in the Midwest. He had retired; however, he was persuaded to move to Idaho Falls to assist Mother in managing the garage. He was a remarkable find, and he and his family became close friends of our family. Mother had been officially informed by the Ford Motor Company that company policy did not permit a woman to own a Ford franchise. She would be allowed to operate the agency for a limited period of time, and the Ford Motor Company would help her find a suitable buyer. It seems odd now, but was simply accepted at the time. Mr. Rogers was to help her keep the business running until it could be sold.

Shortly after Dad passed away, Mother brought me a form to fill out and sign. It was an application for Social Security Survivor Benefits. I was sixteen years old and was told that I was entitled to a monthly payment until I reached twenty-one years of age. It didn't make sense to me at all, and I felt uncomfortable equating a monthly benefit payment with the loss of Dad. Nonetheless I signed the application and started receiving $18.00 per month, which ultimately increased to $22.00 a month.

I never wanted to cash the checks, and I simply deposited the money into my checking account. I reasoned that if I wrote a check, I was spending other money in the account, not the proceeds from the social security checks. It was just a mind game I played with myself. I am sure that Mary also received a monthly check until she reached twenty-one years of age.

Chapter 64

Summary Morphs into Senior Year

When school was out in the late spring of 1950, Mary was finishing her freshman year at the University. She apparently needed, or wanted a ride home from Moscow, and I offered to go pick her up. My friend Bill Shively rode with me. When I picked Bill up at his house, he wanted to bring a new rifle he had just purchased. When we were driving in the vicinity of Leadore, he asked me to stop. He raised his rifle, took aim and shot an antelope a considerable distance away.

The hunting season was closed, and I asked him what in the world he was going to do with the animal. Bill said he was just going to leave it, and he put his gun away and got back into the car. I was really upset with him, and surprised that he was so cavalier about the incident. I liked to hunt; however, we were always careful to limit our hunting to the regular hunting season and not to waste anything we shot, except gophers, sparrows and magpies, of course.

Many of the students had already gone home when we reached the University, and Bill and I were able to stay overnight at the Sigma Chi Fraternity house. Both Orval and Reed were members of the fraternity, and Dad had belonged to the same fraternity during the one year he attended the University. We picked up Mary and her personal belongings the following day and returned home. The trip overall was enjoyable, except for the antelope incident. I have always enjoyed driving, particularly in the spring. I find it very relaxing, and it gives me an opportunity to engage in "deep" thinking.

There was a lot to do on the farm and the summer of 1950 seemed to go by quickly. In the fall I started my senior year in high school. I was the local FFA Chapter President. I still resented the class time required for the Ag classes and the fact that I had less class time for other electives. Most of my close friends were taking the classes and also involved in FFA activities, so I hung in. While I had fun, I believe I should have dropped out of the Ag program after the first two years, but I didn't.

Chapter 64: Summer Morphs into Senior Year

The main school project of the Ag kids was to sponsor the Harvest Ball in the fall of the year. We always decorated the gym with bales of hay and straw, and with pumpkins and squash and stalks of corn. We would even have a few small animals, including a calf or two, lambs, rabbits and chickens in pens on the gym floor. They always had live music, and the dress was informal. The Harvest Ball was a popular, well attended event. The chapter president had the privilege of crowning the queen and giving her the traditional kiss during the halftime ceremonies. My senior year we selected Vonda Jackson as queen of the Ball. Everyone liked Vonda and she was a great sport. We had gone to school together from first grade at Eagle Rock.

My routine during the last semester of my junior year and during my senior year of high school was pretty much to drive to school in the mornings and back home immediately after school, to help with the chores. I became less involved in school activities. Mother was still adjusting to the death of Dad, and I am sure I was also. I did a lot of reading. I had really enjoyed my freshman and sophomore years, and had been active and engaged in school. After Dad died, however, I guess I sort of pulled back or withdrew.

I remember some of my friends saying that high school, particularly the last couple of years, were the best years of their lives. That was certainly not the case for me. I was anxious for my high school experience to finish. I was a bit bored and was ready to move on, without knowing what that would lead to. The Korean War was not going well, and perhaps the prospect of being drafted and entering the military service was part of what I was going through.

I had enjoyed the experiences I had with FFA projects and activities. However, after three years I began to lose interest. I was planning to attend college and in retrospect I would have been better off to take electives that would have helped prepare me for college, such as chemistry, more advanced algebra, world history, and similar courses. I did take physics, and a word derivation course that was excellent. One day the typing teacher, Mrs. Holmgren, asked me if I was going to college and I replied that I was. She said, "Sign up for my typing class." I was one of the few boys in the class. I felt a little silly at the beginning, but soon realized how helpful learning to type would be. From then on I typed almost everything, including class notes. The only down side was that the quality of my penmanship went downhill.

When I drove back and forth to school, I could not pass by anyone along the road who had a "thumb in the air." I had done quite a lot of hitchhiking before I owned a car, and even did some later on. One day when I was driving home from school, I picked up a young fellow from Australia. We started talking and he told me he was on a trip around the world. Whenever possible he would hitchhike to save money. He was a year older than me and very bright and articulate.

I was fascinated to hear him tell about the places he had been and the things he had seen since leaving his home in Australia. He would occasionally stay in one place long enough to earn additional money, and then resume his journey. He said he planned to spend at least a year traveling. I invited him to come into the house for a bite to eat, and Mother told him he was welcome to stay overnight. I really wanted to talk with him and learn more about his travels. After an early supper, however, he left. He said he was trying to maintain a schedule and hoped to reach Butte, Montana, that night, a distance of 200 miles. I went with him to the highway in front of our house, the main highway to Butte. We were still talking, when he caught a ride and was again on his way.

That encounter really fired up my enthusiasm for travel, an enthusiasm that has been with me all of my life. I was fascinated by the articles and pictures in the National Geographic magazine, and for years I had one of their world maps on my bedroom wall. Travel wasn't always possible, due to the demands of a young family and the law practice, but I have had the good fortune to do a fair amount of traveling.

Chapter 65

Future Farmers Gone AWOL

In June of 1950 North Korea had crossed the border and invaded South Korea. President Harry Truman ordered US military forces in the area to resist the attack. An emergency session of the United Nations was convened, and a resolution was passed authorizing a multi-national force to enter South Korea and repel the attack. The US draft was reinstated, and kids were being called into the active military service.

In the spring of 1951 several of us who were involved in FFA were excused from school for an entire week to attend the State FFA convention in Boise. I had attended a couple of times before and decided to go again. It was attended by students from all over the state and was always fun and worthwhile. The weather was beautiful, and I really looked forward to having a break from school.

I drove my car, the 1947 Ford 2 door sedan, and headed for Boise with three friends: Walt Boltz, Ossian Packer, and LaVerle Noreen. When we left Idaho Falls we were all in high spirits. Passing through Twin Falls, we saw a sign with an arrow pointing to the left, indicating the highway to Elko, Nevada. Someone in the car said, "Hey, let's go to Nevada!" As a joke I turned left on the intersecting highway and started driving south a short distance. I planned to turn around, but I waited for someone else to suggest that we turn around and continue on to Boise. No one did, and I continued south, slowly at first, and then began to drive a little faster. Someone, I think it was Walt Boltz, said, "Hey, let's go to San Diego and see Lloyd Beal!"

That is exactly what we did. We discussed the idea and no one could think of a good reason not to go visit Lloyd Beal. We were excused from school for a whole week, and we were not expected at home until the weekend. We each had a suitcase with enough clothes for the week, and some spending money. We were confident that we could pool our money and would get along just fine. We were in high spirits. We didn't dwell on what the others would think when we failed to arrive in Boise and check in at the Idanha Hotel. I think we were satisfied they would simply think we had decided at the last minute not to make the trip to Boise.

Lloyd had enrolled at the University of Idaho in the fall, and may have finished the semester, I am not certain. He then enlisted in the US Navy and had been sent to the San Diego Naval Training Station for his basic training. I am sure we were aware that some or all of us would likely end up in the service in the next year or two, unless the Korean War ended in the meantime

This may have contributed to what seemed like a wild fling on our part. I am not sure we really expected to be able to connect with Lloyd, but the possibility gave the trip a purpose with a patriotic flavor. This probably helped us justify our decision, although we didn't spend much time dwelling on it; we just went. When we reached Elko, theoretically we could have retraced our steps and returned to Boise. By this time, however, we were committed, and excited at the prospect of our new adventure.

I believe we drove all the way to Reno, Nevada our first day on the road. We spent the night there, wandering through the casinos. Nobody objected to our being in the casinos and playing the slot machines, which we did sparingly because of our limited finances. I did have a checking account so I could have written a check in an emergency, but I did not want to. I have never been much of a gambler; my limit was nickel slot machines and penny, nickel, dime poker. If the truth were known, some of us had a beer or two as well. But we were very careful. We did not want to get into any trouble, and we had a long way to go before returning home.

From Elko we headed over Donner Pass to San Francisco. We were seeing places none of us had ever been to, and we were really having fun and in high spirits. The weather was beautiful and the hills were green. We drove across the Golden Gate Bridge and around other parts of the city, including Fisherman's Wharf, and later headed south on Highway 101, the route along the coast. We made numerous stops along the trip down the coast and walked down to the beach and took pictures. We stopped at San Louis Obispo one night and then headed for Los Angeles.

I don't remember all the places we stayed overnight, but I remember that we drove long distances. I was mindful that we wanted to reach San Diego and try to make contact with Lloyd Beal, and then return home by the time we were expected. We drove through Los Angeles, which was an adventure for us because of the size of the city and the amount of traffic we encountered. We had specific things we wanted to see, including Sunset Boulevard and Hollywood.

Chapter 65: Future Farmers Gone AWOL

We drove past the Paramount and MGM movie studios. We then located the highway to San Diego and continued on our way.

On arrival in San Diego we asked for directions to the US Naval Training Station. The base was huge, and a large number of vehicles were entering and leaving the facilities through several heavily guarded checkpoints. It was obvious that only authorized persons could enter, and that no one could enter without a gate pass. I pulled out of the lane of traffic, parked, and a couple of us walked up to the guard at the nearest gate. I was starting to feel foolish at how naïve we were in believing we could actually locate and visit with Lloyd. We explained to the guard that we were from Idaho Falls and that we had driven to San Diego to visit our friend Lloyd Beal who was receiving his basic training. The guard asked if we knew Lloyd's serial number, or the unit he had been assigned to, or when he had arrived at the base. Of course we didn't know the answer to any of his questions.

The guard then told us how many thousands of sailors were at the base receiving basic training. I fully expected him to tell us to get the hell out of there and to quit wasting his time. He was a nice guy, and must have believed we were sincere. We were obviously tired from the trip and appeared to be "country boys." He said for us to wait in our car. He said he would continue to check vehicles entering and leaving the base at his gate, and then he would see what he could do. We waited for over an hour, although it seemed like six hours. We fully expected that the military police would check us out and tell us to leave the area. Then our friend Lloyd Beal appeared at the gate.

Lloyd had been told that someone was at the gate who wanted to see him, but he didn't know who. When he saw us he knew right away that we were on an unauthorized trip. He left and when he returned, he had a twenty-four-hour pass.

Lloyd jumped into the car, we had a bite to eat, and then Lloyd gave us directions to Tijuana, Mexico, and off we went. On the way to Tijuana we told Lloyd what we were doing and why we were in San Diego. He was incredulous. When we arrived in Tijuana, Lloyd seemed to know where we were going; we had the impression that he had been there before. We were only there during the day, which was probably fortunate.

We stopped in a few places, most of which were quite seedy to say the least. Women were everywhere, both young and old, and were willing to sell you almost anything. I am proud to say that we observed, but nothing else. We did buy a few porno comic books which we took back home, but that was all. Collectively we had the good sense to maintain our cool and avoid problems. We really were "rubes" from Idaho.

Later we took Lloyd Beal back to the base, bid him goodbye, and headed back to Idaho. I cannot remember when we left San Diego but I know we were cutting it close and had to push hard to get back in time. I did most of the driving on the entire trip; however, on the way back I finally reached my limit. I could hardly stay awake.

Walt drove awhile and then he became too tired to continue. I drove a little longer and then I had to stop. Ossian Packer said he was able to drive, so I turned the wheel over to him and fell asleep. Suddenly I heard a loud blast from the air horn of a semi truck. I woke up and asked, "What was that?" Ossian replied that we had just passed an oncoming semi truck. Walt Boltz said, "That's right, but we passed him on the wrong side." I realized that Ossian had dozed off and had in fact drifted over to the left and the oncoming semi had passed my car on the right side! I was suddenly wide awake and told Ossian to stop the car. I took over the driving for the rest of the trip home. I had then and still have the ability to drive for long periods of time. I don't know if this is a blessing or a curse.

Finally, we arrived in Idaho Falls. I dropped my travel companions off at their respective homes and then drove to the farm. When I entered the house, Mother asked me how the trip went. I told her what had happened. When I finished, she simply said, "Well, when you go to school in the morning, you need to tell the principal exactly what you did and accept the consequences." That was it. She did not berate me, did not scold me, but simply told me to accept the consequences of my decision.

I almost wished she would give me hell, ground me, or inflict some type of punishment. She didn't and never had. The quiet disappointment she displayed had a greater impact on me than any other punishment she could have inflicted. This occurred on more than one occasion. She always surprised me with her ability to underreact.

When I arrived at school the next day, I went to the attendance clerk, Mrs. McCowan. She was a wonderful lady. She gave me a white slip, an excused absence, and told me to go to class. I tried to tell her that I had skipped school. I said that I had not gone to the FFA convention in Boise, but rather had gone south to California and also to Tijuana, Mexico. She just laughed and pushed the white slip toward me and told me to go to class. Remembering what Mother had told me, I insisted that she give me a pink slip, indicating an unexcused absence. Mrs. McCowan was accustomed to our joking with her and simply did not believe me. While we were bantering back and forth, the principal, Mr. Clair Gale, come out of his office. He understood what I was saying, and told me I was expelled from school.

I left the school building. Walt Bolts, Ossian Packer and LaVerle Noreen were also expelled. This was our senior year. We did not know for sure what expulsion meant. Would we be allowed back in school to finish our senior year? Would we be allowed to graduate and receive our diplomas? We stayed out of school for a few days, and later came back. We were allowed back into our classes to finish our course work, and, in fact, were able to go through commencement and receive our diplomas.

It may be wrong to say this, but I have never regretted our decision to head for California to see our friend Lloyd Beal. Taking the trip was the wrong thing to do, of course, but it was also a wonderful experience. I am glad we went and thankful that we suffered no misfortune during the trip that would have caused it to have been a huge, perhaps even a tragic, mistake.

Many years later, when my son Steve was in high school, his mother and I had given him permission to go to Boise to participate in an activity, the exact nature of which I don't recall. When he returned, he told me that he and several friends had driven from Boise to Portland, Oregon, to attend a concert, I believe. They had driven throughout the night to attend the venue in Portland and return to Boise before they were missed.

I was quite upset, and lectured Steve on the dangers of driving all night when he was tired, and on exceeding the permission granted in allowing him to go to Boise. Steve said, quietly, "Didn't you go to Tijuana, Mexico, when were you about my age, when you were supposed to be attending a convention in Boise?" I paused for a few seconds, and said, "Yes, I guess I did, but I was more mature when I was your age than you are now." We both laughed and that was the end of that. I wondered how he had found out about my escapade in the spring of 1951, and he said he had heard the story many times. Kids catch more of our grownup conversations that we often realize.

Chapter 66

The Summer Before College

I graduated from Idaho Falls High School in early June of 1951. Life on the farm was much the same. We were always busy with the usual fieldwork and with caring for the livestock. Our Grade A dairy herd was increasing, both in number and quality. There was little time to be bored. I assumed that I would go to the University of Idaho in the fall and would probably enroll in the College of Agriculture; however, I had no real goal in mind. Upon turning eighteen I had registered for the draft, and there was the possibility I would be drafted.

In the fall of 1950 following graduation from the University, Orval had gone to Washington D.C. He started working for then Congressman, later Senator, Henry Dworshak from Idaho. Orval worked on Capitol Hill during the day and enrolled in night classes at George Washington University College of Law. In early summer of 1951 Orval called to say he planned to drive home for the summer. He asked if I would be interested in flying back to Washington. D.C., to help drive back. He was anxious to get started as soon as possible. I jumped at the chance.

I called the airlines to arrange for the flight and discovered that on such short notice I could only be confirmed to Denver, through Salt Lake City, and would be on standby the rest of the way. I said that would be fine and purchased a one-way ticket to Washington D.C. I wasn't concerned about layovers or delays. I was ready for a little adventure. I packed a small bag which I carried instead of checking through, just in case I was unable to catch flights all the way. I left in the afternoon and arrived in Denver after dark. Within a very short time I was fortunate enough to catch an overnight flight to Chicago, and by the time I arrived in Chicago, I had been cleared with flights all the way to Washington, D.C.

Orval picked me up at the airport and drove to his apartment. We did some brief sightseeing, and Orval pointed out the major places of interest in the area. Our time in the Capitol was limited, however, and we were soon on the way to Idaho. The routine was to stop for meals and gas, when needed, and continue driving. Orval did most of the driving. When he became too tired to drive, I took over while he slept in the back seat. I don't remember that we actually stopped overnight at a motel. I don't believe we did. I remember a lot of all-night driving.

At one point, somewhere in the Midwest, I took over driving after dark. Orval showed me on the map the route that we were to take and went to sleep. I drove most of the night, however I ran into a detour due to a bridge being out, and had to take a different road north, then took another to the west a distance, and then back to the south to get back on the main highway. This took most of the night, and when I became too tired to continue I woke Orval up and asked him to take over. It turned out that in spite of the number of hours I had driven, we were only about 100 to150 miles further west that when I had taken over the driving. Apparently at some point I had missed the detour route and ended up driving a much larger loop before returning to the main highway.

I enjoyed the drive home, although I am aware that others might have thought it grueling. I liked to drive and to be able to see new country. I drove through cities and states that I had never been in before. When we stopped we always picked up a local newspaper which I enjoyed reading. I believe Orval also enjoyed driving long distances. The trip gave us a chance to visit and also time to quietly reflect on anything and everything. I don't believe I was ever bored while on a road trip. I'm sure Orval made a point of selecting a route that would take us through interesting country, even if it added a few extra miles to the trip. Because we took turns driving we made good time, in spite of my problem with the detour.

The summer went by fast, and I began to get ready to leave for the University. Mother helped me shop for school clothes. In high school I usually wore Levi pants, a Levi jacket, and logger boots, occasionally oxfords. I really did not need much of a wardrobe in those days. I had the double-breasted suit Mother bought me to wear to Dad's funeral, but it was much too formal. I called it my "wedding and funeral" suit. But at the end of summer, 1951, I wasn't expecting to go to many weddings or funerals. I was college-bound!

Married in 1924, Farrel and Lily Hansen built success out of hard work and vision, values they passed on to their children. Lily served as Farrel's "silent partner" throughout their marriage, and he relied on her good judgment and business acumen in making many decisions that had far-reaching effects.

Things were hard for the family in the Depression years, but John remembered no signs of hardship: food was plentiful and life was good. This 1933 picture was probably taken at the Firth farm that Farrel owned with his brother, Heber. Mary is up front and Baby John is in Lily's arms next to Farrel, as Reed, Orval, Farrel Jr, and Norman line up in the middle row.

In 1943, World War II was in full swing as the family transitioned from John's beloved Airport Farm to the much larger Osgood Farm. Overalls morph into "city attire" for this family portrait with Reed, Norman, Farrel Jr, Orval, and Mary standing behind their parents and young John.

Let the Record Show by John D. Hansen

The airfield bordering the east side of the Airport Farm was a constant source of fascination to the young John--including the mysterious appearance of a B-17 during WWII. The outbuildings and the barn were moved onto the Osgood Farm after the city took the Airport Farm to expand the airport.

Farm work was second nature to John (on the right) by the time he was old enough to operate the big equipment. But he was glad that mechanized farm equipment had replaced horses by that time.

Lily (above on the left) worked tirelessly to manage the family and the farm work, but she found time to play Bridge every week with Veva Jackson, Lottie Danner, and Clara Jensen, "The Foursome." The hard-working ladies shed their everyday attire to dress up and enjoy an afternoon together.

John and Lloyd Beal, shown left, became successful entrepreneurs as they partnered up on Future Farmers of America projects.

Photo Gallery 1

At sixteen, John began to question where his future would lead him.

Uncle Glen Wahlquist, Lily's brother, was a positive influence in John's life.

Big brother, Farrel Jr. was the first to "sign up," enlisting in the Navy in 1943.

John, second from the left in front, and his FFA compatriots show no sign of the rebels they would become when they went AWOL from the FFA convention in Boise to drive to San Diego to visit Lloyd Beal in boot camp.

Let the Record Show by John D. Hansen

LET THE RECORD SHOW

Part II:
The College Years

Chapter 67

College Classes and Sigma Chi

In the fall of 1951 Mary and I packed our bags, loaded up my car, and drove to Moscow, Idaho, where I enrolled as a freshman and Mary registered for her junior year at the University of Idaho. Mary was a member of the Delta Delta Delta Sorority, having pledged in the fall of 1949. I stayed at the Sigma Chi Fraternity as a guest and prepared for "Rush Week." Rush is a process during which fraternities and sororities recruit potential new members. Rush gives new students a chance to visit with several fraternities and get oriented with college life and gives the fraternity members the opportunity to meet prospective pledges.

At the end of Pledge Week the fraternity and sorority members decide whom they wish to invite to pledge or join that particular fraternity or sorority. Some new students received more than one invitation and a few did not receive any. And new students did not always receive an invitation from the living group that they preferred. The process involved a matter of matching student preferences and fraternity invitations.

I was a "legacy" of the Sigma Chi Fraternity which simply meant that I had a relative or relatives who had previously belonged to that fraternity; Dad, Orval and Reed had been members. Being a legacy meant that I would be given preference. In other words, unless I really screwed up or was a total loser, I was practically guaranteed that I would be invited to pledge Sigma Chi.

The rush process was somewhat stiff and formal, but also it was a good experience for me. I soon met a large number of students and interacted with many fellows from my high school graduating class who were also going through rush. I knew what I was going to do in any event, so I didn't really feel any pressure. Orval and Reed had lived with many of the members of the Sigma Chi house and they were both liked and respected. I was confident that I would be asked to pledge, and I was and readily accepted. Bill Whitman and Merlin "Duke" Powell also pledged Sigma Chi.

Bill Whitman had lived in Idaho Falls and attended O. E. Bell Junior High for a couple of years, and we had been good friends then. Bill's father, Gene Whitman, was connected with the Extension Service of the College of Agriculture at the University. He and his wife Marlys had been friends with Mother and Dad. I was acquainted with Duke Powell when we both attended high school; however, we did not move in the same circles. While at the University, however, Bill, Duke, and I spent a lot of time together and became very close friends. Incidentally, Vonda Jackson pledged the Alpha Phi house, I believe, and Jim Howard pledged the Phi Delta house. Vonda and Jim and I attended first grade at Eagle Rock Elementary School and graduated together from Idaho Falls High School.

I liked the members of the Sigma Chi house and benefited greatly by the experience of living there. The older students mentored the pledges. We had regular study periods in the evenings, housekeeping responsibilities which included working in the kitchen and serving at meal times, cleaning our rooms, making our beds and doing our own laundry. I was not particularly experienced at doing laundry and soon discovered that it was unwise to put a red sweatshirt in with a load of whites. For years I had T-shirts, shorts and handkerchiefs that were bright pink. I had excellent supervision and at the same time I felt a great deal of independence. We had some great times as well. Life was not just classes, studying and work, particularly on Friday and Saturday nights. I made many friendships that have lasted for my entire life.

I enrolled in the College of Agriculture, almost by default, and with no specific goal in mind. That was my background and it was a comfortable place to start. The classes were interesting, although I did at times feel that I had been there before, having studied agriculture in high school. I liked all of my professors. My courses included ROTC, Physical Education, and Chemistry. The class in chemistry was given in the College of Letters and Science primarily for premedical and predental students. The professor had little time or patience with "Aggies," and we were often made to feel as though we really didn't belong.

Most of the other chemistry students had taken at least one year and in many cases two years, of chemistry in high school and the course work was geared to them. I had not taken chemistry, and although I thought the subject was fascinating, I was soon in over my head. A couple of times I went in to see the professor to see how I could get extra help and he seemed totally uninterested in my dilemma. Fortunately the fraternity included premed and predental students and others who helped me. In retrospect I should have sought more help, but I was fairly independent and was satisfied with getting by rather than trying to excel. Also, I was not particularly fond of the professor. I have since wondered why I didn't really apply myself and get a top grade just to show him that I could. At the time, I guess, that didn't seem terribly important to me.

The University of Idaho is a land grant university and so required that all male students take classes in ROTC during their freshman and sophomore years. This involved military training: classwork and marching on the parade grounds. The students could choose Army, Air Force or Navy ROTC. The main benefit we enjoyed was to receive a uniform of the branch of service we chose, including pants, jackets, shoes, socks, shirts and ties. The quality of the clothing was excellent and greatly saved on our clothing expense. We wore the uniform only on the days we drilled or attended ROTC classes. I chose the Air Force.

ROTC students could elect to take military classes for a full four years. Upon graduation, these students received a commission as a Second Lieutenant in the regular Army or Air Force, or as an Ensign in the regular Navy, with the obligation to serve at least two years in active military service. Students who elected to go beyond the required two years received a monthly stipend. In addition, students of a land grant university were required to take two years of physical education classes. I heartily approved of both the ROTC program and the requirement for P.E. classes, and I still do.

Bruce Sweeney was the house manager during my freshman year. Bruce and I later served together in the Idaho State Senate. Bruce and others were focused on paying off the balance on the mortgage against the Sigma Chi house and were cutting costs wherever possible. The meals were adequate, however not fancy. We pretty much helped ourselves at breakfast time to what had been set out by the morning kitchen crew. One of the savings measures was to serve powdered milk, rather than fresh milk. This was a bit difficult for me, having grown up on a farm with a herd of Holstein cows. I was assigned the task of mixing large quantities of the powdered milk in the evening so that it would be chilled and drinkable by morning. I never did think it was very good; however, better than no milk at all. The powdered milk assignment gave me unlimited access to the kitchen and I became good friends with our regular cook, which I used to my advantage.

Lunches at the fraternity generally consisted of soups and a variety of sandwiches. Dinners were full meals. We would all be called to dinner and were expected to conduct ourselves a bit more formally. Sunday dinner was the most formal meal at the fraternity. Our housemother, Mrs. Edith Magnuson, came each Sunday in the early afternoon and stayed through dinner. The house was always meticulously cleaned the day before. On Sunday, we were on our best behavior; we were expected to dress up for dinner, and we all did.

There was no evening meal on Fridays, as this was our cook's day off. We had the option of fixing ourselves a meal from leftovers; however, almost everyone went out to eat. A favorite place was the Plantation, located south of the city of Moscow. They had music, food which was relatively inexpensive, and excellent cold beer that was sold by the pitcher. My usual meal at the Plantation was chicken fried steak, salad with blue cheese dressing, and beer.

Group singing was a big thing at the fraternity. We had some members with marvelous voices and the whole group would practice regularly. Because of the number of fine voices, the rest of us were able to be carried along. All in all, the results were quite good and always a lot of fun. We had a quartet which often sang around campus as well as in the house. Bruce Sweeny had an excellent tenor voice and was part of the quartet. We also had a larger group of house members called the "Singing Sigs," who also performed elsewhere on campus.

Many of our members were members of the university choir and they took the singing quite seriously. Occasionally during the first semester, one or two pledges would be called upon during the weekly evening meal and asked to sing or recite something to entertain the rest of the fellows. I didn't totally enjoy these times, but it was all in good fun and all of us wanted to be good sports. In the evenings the entire membership would occasionally serenade some of the sororities and other fraternities. On some occasions during the week, we would open all of our dining room windows and serenade the nearby fraternities, most frequently the Beta house which was just below us. We had some favorite Beta songs which they detested. I still remember some of the lyrics, which I will not burden this narrative with. The other groups often reciprocated, with equally interesting lyrics.

Playing bridge was a frequent pastime at the house. I had learned to play bridge from Mother. Many of the house members were excellent bridge players, and there were always a couple of bridge games going after lunch and before the next class, and in the late afternoon. We played fast games and the frequent playing sharpened my bridge game considerably. I still enjoy playing the game; however, I believe I played my best bridge during my college days.

Pledges were encouraged, almost required, to take part in extracurricular activities. One of our members was editor of the Argonaut, the University paper, which came out weekly. I was persuaded to join the staff as a reporter. I had no previous experience in journalism; however, I volunteered and rather enjoyed the experience of interviewing people and writing stories. Mary was a reporter at the same time. Bill Whitman and I also served on the University elections committee which had the responsibility to plan for, conduct, and monitor the results of the elections for school officers and student council members.

We worked closely with Charles "Chuck" McDevitt and Mike Callahan. Chuck was a Sigma Chi, graduated from law school, and later served on the Idaho Supreme Court. Mike was a military veteran who had lost his lower leg in combat. He was elected U of I student body president, and later served two terms as governor of the State of Nevada.

Chapter 68

Home Cooking and Winter Casualties

The time went fast and soon Thanksgiving was approaching. We did not get an official vacation; however, we usually had a light day of classes on the Wednesday before and on the Friday after Thanksgiving. We loaded the car and drove home on Wednesday and returned the following Sunday evening. It was good to be home to visit with Mother and to enjoy her home cooked meals. I always had a full car, with Mary and often Vonda Jackson and whoever else needed a ride to Idaho Falls. The ride was long; however, we always had a good time along the way. All too soon we were back in Moscow, mindful that Christmas vacation was only a month away.

The time from Thanksgiving to Christmas vacation went very fast. Winter came early and a lot of snow fell in Moscow. We had a toboggan at the Sigma Chi house which would hold ten to twelve persons. In the evening we would load up the toboggan and head to the bottom of the hill which was a tee intersection in front of the Alpha Phi Sorority. With all the weight of a full toboggan the end of the sled run was always interesting. One time we had a collision and several of the riders ended up in the infirmary for first aid, namely stitches. Somewhere I have a picture of the "walking wounded" which reminds me of some of the pictures of Civil War wounded.

Just before Christmas vacation started, I went out to my car to put something in the trunk. The trunk lid was frozen shut. I pulled hard on the trunk handle and it broke off, and in the process the broken handle sliced the inside of the index finger of my right hand leaving an ugly open wound. Bill Whitman and Duke Powell took me to the infirmary. The doctor on duty prepped me for stitches. He asked Duke to hold the lamp, which allowed the doctor to have a good view of the injury. As the doctor was starting to put stitches into my finger, the light suddenly disappeared. Duke, who played varsity football on the Idaho Vandal team, had passed out and fallen onto the floor.

Someone else grabbed the light and the stitching was completed. We kidded Duke a lot about that incident.

Chapter 69

The Christmas Special

When the Christmas vacation started the snowfall had been unusually high. Mary and I and several others started out for home. We usually drove through north Idaho and Montana; however, the highway was closed due to the adverse weather. We started down Highway 95 to Boise, the longer route home, but we were unable to go over Winchester Hill because of an ongoing blizzard, so we returned to Moscow. Because of the extreme weather and blocked roads, the Union Pacific Railroad had put together a special passenger train to take students south to Boise and then east to Pocatello. We called it the "Christmas Special." That seemed to be our best bet to make it home for the holidays, so we parked the car, bought tickets, and boarded the train. It was a wild trip.

The train was packed with students anxious to get home. No one had a compartment; we either sat in Pullman chairs or on the floor. The train had very little food service. The lavatories were used to capacity and beyond! Most of us brought some food and beverages on board, but not enough for the entire trip. We hoped to be able to purchase additional supplies along the way, and we did whenever possible and everyone shared. It was a great time, with lots of singing and partying by the passengers, all of whom were students from the University; however, after the first full day and night, people started to wear down. It was difficult to sleep for any extended period of time. Even college students need a rest break once in a while.

I cannot remember just how long the trip took, but it seemed like a long time. When we approached the Nampa, Caldwell, and Boise area a number of the students disembarked which left more room for the rest of us. The train continued across southern Idaho. When we approached Glenns Ferry, it came to a stop. A couple of the students left the train and raced to a store near the tracks, bought a couple of cases of beer, and started running back to the train. The train started moving and we all cheered them on. I suspect the engineer was having a little fun with them, and with a little more effort the students reached the moving train. The students and the needed supplies were taken on board. By the time we reached Pocatello, Idaho, we were all worn out. Mary and I and others from Idaho Falls were picked up at the Pocatello terminal and driven home for a much-needed rest.

The fall semester ended in the latter part of January, and as a consequence all of the course final exams came in the two to three weeks following our return from enjoying the Christmas holidays. Students routinely took school work home during the holiday break with the intention of studying for the semester exams. Most of the students, however, me included, found it practically impossible to do any meaningful studying while at home. As a result, during the trip back to school, panic would set in and upon our arrival back on campus serious cramming for exams would begin.

Chapter 70

Serious Studying and College Dances

The atmosphere at the Sigma Chi house and elsewhere on campus was always much different after the Christmas holidays. There was more tension and much less fun and games. Without question most students were aware that their main purpose was to get decent grades, graduate in four years, find a job, and get on with life. The weather helped, since January was just another winter month. The first snow during November or December always set a festive tone; however, after the holidays it became more monotonous and so it was easier to stay indoors and study.

I was impressed with the fellows with whom I lived. They were boisterous and full of fun on certain occasions and yet they were very serious about their studies and future careers. Many of these students were veterans, and thus older and more mature than most other students, but their attitude seemed to prevail among all of us. I know I buckled down and took my school work more seriously because of this peer influence.

We had regular study hours Monday through Thursday. Upper classmen mentored and monitored the younger students. The overall grade average of the pledge class and the entire fraternity was regularly calculated, and good averages were applauded. Even a slight drop in the grade average resulted in individual help where warranted, and an increase in the amount of time set aside for evening study.

After final exams and registration for the spring semester, the atmosphere was relaxed. When the opportunities arose we always found ways to have a good time, some of which was spontaneous and some more structured. The fraternity held several formal dances each year and everyone was encouraged to participate. These dances were usually held off campus and involved decorating beforehand and cleaning up afterwards. We were all expected to have dates and attend. When we had the annual Sweet Heart of Sigma Chi Ball and crowned the queen for that year, we were required to wear a tuxedo which was an entirely new experience for me. We also occasionally held a "mixer" which involved inviting another living group, usually a sorority, to the house for dinner and conversation. If I had lived in a less structured living group or in an apartment, I know I would have avoided many of these experiences and it would have been my loss.

Chapter 71

Spring Fever and Sports

Winters in Moscow were generally milder than at home in eastern Idaho. We often had a fair amount of snow, but less wind and warmer temperatures. Also the winters were shorter, followed by a "real" spring season. In Idaho Falls the winters were much longer and we seldom experienced a distinct spring, but instead went from winter through a "blah" period into summer. Springs in north Idaho can be quite beautiful, and often led to an outbreak of "spring fever." My close friend Bill Whitman was on the University golf team and practiced often at the University golf course. In the spring of 1952 I started going out with Bill to keep him company. He let me use his clubs and gave me tips on the game of golf.

Duke Powell went out for football and was on the varsity squad which took up a lot of his spare time. Duke was a pretty good football player; however, he was smaller than most, and I believe he was "red shirted" his freshman year to preserve a year of eligibility. We had several excellent football players in the house and we attended all of the home games. Unfortunately, at that time the University was part of the old Pacific Coast Conference, which included the University of Washington, Washington State, the University of Oregon, Oregon State, Stanford, UCLA, and the University of Southern California.

The University of Idaho really didn't belong in the Pacific Coast Conference. That, however, had been the tradition going back to a time when there was not such a great disparity in the size of the various conference member schools. The winner of the Pacific Coast Conference always played in the Rose Bowl on New Year's Day, and as a member of the league the University of Idaho received a share of the Rose Bowl revenue. In football, the University still played the conference teams in Washington and Oregon, however not the California teams. On occasion, we also played other large teams, including the University of Texas.

The University had some excellent players, but lacked depth, and as a result we always played a strong first half and then often fell behind in the second half. Jerry Kramer and Wayne Walker played when I was at school. They were both Idaho boys who went on to have great careers in professional football; Jerry Kramer was with the Green Bay Packers and Wayne Walker with the Detroit Lions. There were other players as well who had distinguished careers in professional football. The University was more competitive in conference basketball and track and field.

Bill Whitman, Duke Powell and I had a reputation for being quite high spirited during our pledge year. The use of a wooden paddle was a common sport at the fraternity, mainly on pledges for almost any real or imagined infraction. Being paddled without complaining or showing symptoms of pain was considered a sign of manhood. Almost all of the upper classmen had paddles, usually with holes bored through, and some were experts in the use of their paddles. It was all in the spirit of seeing what a person could handle, and there were never any hard feelings.

Chapter 72

Pranksters

One night in the early spring Bill, Duke and I got the idea of gathering up and hiding all the razors in the fraternity. In those days everyone shaved each morning; no one grew a beard. We found a pillowcase, and after everyone was asleep in the top floor dormitories we went into each room, removed the razors, put them in the pillowcase and put them in the sub-basement of the house.

We didn't intend to carry the prank on very long. However, the next morning the reaction of some of the members was stronger than we had expected and by the second day even stronger. At first we thought we would simply confess and return the razors and it would be treated as a clever joke, but it soon ceased to be a humorous matter. There was a general belief that someone from outside the house had been the culprit and several wanted to involve the local police department. We were anxious to return the razors but did not want to be recognized as the ones responsible. We worried that we might be expelled from the fraternity if caught, which was the last thing we wanted to happen. The matter had gotten out of hand.

We decided to sneak the pillowcase from the sub-basement and put it in a central place in the house to be "discovered." Some house activities as well as persons studying late at night complicated our efforts for another day or so. Finally, one night we went to the sleeping dorm, and after we thought everyone was asleep we retrieved the pillowcase, placed it on one of the dining room tables, and started back upstairs to return to the dorm. We were spotted by one of the upperclassmen who was still up. He ran up to the sleeping dorms and sounded the alarm among the other house members. All hell broke loose, or so it seemed for the next few minutes. Almost everyone who had been sleeping came running down and chased us throughout the house.

We tried everything we could think of to avoid being caught. We had no idea what the ultimate punishment would amount to. In a panic I did a stupid thing. I ran into a room on the second floor on the back side of the house, and with several persons chasing me, I jumped out an open window and grabbed hold of a steel bar on the outside fire escape. Somehow I managed to hold on; otherwise I would have fallen to the ground three stories below. It was obvious that the three of us had been identified and were going to be subdued despite our best efforts, so I stopped resisting.

The three of us were taken down to the hallway on the second floor of the house and while we were being physically restrained, several house members held a brief conference to decide what should be the appropriate punishment for us. It soon became obvious, fortunately for the three of us, that the rest of the fellows in the house were relieved to solve the razor mystery and were now beginning to enjoy themselves. Someone suggested that since razors were the subject of the prank, razors should be involved in our punishment.

A couple of straight razors were retrieved from the pillowcase while the three of us were stripped of our clothing. Soon the razors came out along with shaving soap and all of our pubic hair was quickly removed. Rest assured we remained very still during the whole procedure. At least they did not remove the hair on our heads. By this time everyone was having a good laugh. It was obvious that no one harbored any ill will and that we were back in good graces. All in all, we were relieved to have the ordeal behind us. Over the succeeding years, I have occasionally encountered a fraternity member who lived in the house at the time and we have had a good laugh recalling the incident.

Chapter 73

A Character in the House

We had a lot of great fellows in the house, and I became close friends with most of them. One was Bill Bradburn from Spokane who was a real character. He had a realistic tight-fitting rubber mask of a very old man, a disheveled wig, tattered clothes and a pair of worn out shoes. He explained a prank he and friends used to pull in his high school days. We repeated it several times in downtown Moscow. We would drop him off at a quiet spot on Main Street and then drive away. He would shuffle slowly down the sidewalk with the aid of an old stick he used as a crutch, with his head down and turned to one side, moaning and in obvious pain. He reminded me of Igor, the lab assistant who helped the doctor who created Frankenstein.

It was always fun to watch Bill go through his act. Soon he would attract the attention of others on the sidewalk who were both intrigued by and a little frightened of the old man as he shuffled along. After he had attracted a small crowd, I would drive back down the street to Bill and bring the car to a quick stop. At least four persons wearing dark overcoats would jump out of the car, run over to the "old man," knock him to the sidewalk and start beating on him with their fists as the poor soul screamed for someone to help him.

I remember once seeing the look of horror on the faces of a couple of elderly ladies nearby, and I was afraid the incident might cause one of them to have a heart attack as it was so realistic. Then those who were administering the "beating" picked up the old man and threw him into the back seat of the car. Then they jumped in and we all sped away. It all happened fast, no one ever tried to stop us. We repeated the incident on several occasions in different locations.

When Bill Bradburn graduated, he had completed four years of ROTC and received a commission as Second Lieutenant in the Marines, went to flight school and became a jet fighter pilot. Shortly before he was due to be discharged, he was practicing dive bombing maneuvers over the Atlantic Ocean off the east coast. He pulled out of his dive a split second too late, crashed and was killed instantly.

Chapter 74

Spring Leads to an Initiation

The spring semester went fast. I was pursuing a Bachelor of Science degree which required close to 140 credits. As a result, it was necessary to successfully take 17 or 18 credit hours each semester in order to graduate in four years, which most students were committed to doing. Eighteen credit hours was a full class load which required a fair amount of time and effort. While I had a good time and thoroughly enjoyed my university experience, I was mindful that my primary purpose was to get an education resulting in a degree and to do so in four years.

Although we did not get an official Easter break, I and others drove home for the Easter weekend. The drive home was about twelve hours. It was not uncommon for us to leave Moscow in the late afternoon after classes and drive straight home, and then drive back to the University in a couple days or so. I usually did all of the driving, not because I didn't trust others to drive my car, but because I really enjoyed driving long distances. I have always believed I do my best thinking while on a long drive.

In the spring, several of us drove to Spokane to see a performance of the musical "Mr. Roberts," which was a Broadway play on tour from New York City. I had previously only seen high school plays and movies, and I was really impressed. From that time on I have tried to take advantage of the opportunity to see similar performances whenever possible.

After Easter the pledges at the Sigma Chi house took the traditional "pledge sneak." We went to Spokane for the weekend and stayed at the Davenport Hotel, then and now, a magnificent hotel. A little while later, we pledges went through initiation week, which involved a certain amount of somber formality followed by a celebration by the entire fraternity when we were accepted as members. Membership entitled us to purchase our own official paddles, among other things, for use on the pledge classes to follow! Alfred "Bud" Hagen was our pledge class advisor and worked with us through our freshman year to prepare us for formal membership. I did not take the ritual as seriously as some. Bud was an extremely fine person who did take it seriously. Bud took everything seriously.

Bud was in law school when I was an underclassman and was a mentor to me while I was at the fraternity and also after he graduated. He encouraged me to enter law school after I received my Bachelor of Science degree and helped me find my first job with a law firm in Boise. Bud was a successful lawyer in Boise, became an outstanding State District Court Judge and later was appointed as a Federal Bankruptcy Court Judge. His career was cut short a few years ago when he died following a lengthy bout with cancer.

Chapter 75

More Hijinks

During the spring the ROTC students had regular early morning drills to practice various marching maneuvers as an entire group. The marching, which was to culminate in a parade review of the group to be attended by a few military "big wigs" from bases in the region, was very important to our ROTC Commander, Colonel Mossman. When the weather was nice, which was most of the time, it was actually kind of fun. We were served an early breakfast and benefited from the fresh air and exercise before classes started.

One night a couple of fellows, including Chuck McDevitt, came up with a scheme to force cancellation of the drill to be held the next morning, shortly before the scheduled final parade review. Chuck McDevitt had a voice that sounded much like Col. Mossman and he called all the fraternities and male housing units to announce that tomorrows drill had been cancelled. Only a handful of ROTC students showed up on the parade grounds. Colonel Mossman was furious. He vowed to find the culprit but never did.

There were other hijinks. It was an annual tradition in the Sigma Chi house for the pledges to subdue, blindfold, and transport to the top of Moscow Mountain the current house manager and turn him loose to find his way back, a distance of several miles. This was always done after dark and the person was left wearing only shorts. Bruce Sweeney was the house manager my pledge year. I really felt a bit sorry for Bruce because the nights, even in spring, can be a bit chilly. He showed up the next morning. I suspect some of his friends may have rescued him.

Whenever a house member gave his pin to a girlfriend, considered a pre-engagement, it was the duty of the pledges to subdue the member and place him in wooden stocks in front of the house. While locked in the stocks the member was smeared with eggs and other unpleasant things including feathers. The girl friend was notified and after a period of time was given the key to release him.

Later in the evening the house members serenaded the "pinned" woman and her living group.

In addition, pledges were supposed to subdue and "tub" each of the graduating seniors. This was not always an easy task, depending on the size and strength of the graduating senior. These and other activities including pranks in the sleeping dorms such as "short sheeting" or scattering corn flakes in someone's bed were always carried out in the spirit of good fun and gave a needed break from the pressure of final exams.

Chapter 76

A Momentous Decision

The second semester went by quickly and soon it was time to pack up and drive home. I usually drove through Montana because it was shorter. My sister Mary and others from Idaho Falls were often looking for a ride home. In the spring of 1952, however, Mary was involved in sorority matters and needed to stay in Moscow an extra week. My friend Bill Whitman asked if I could give him a ride to Boise and invited me to stay overnight at his home. I knew his folks well and I said I would be delighted to drive home via Boise. I didn't realize it at the time, but this was a momentous decision, actually a life altering decision.

Bill's father, Gene, had been for many years a part of the extension service program of the College of Agriculture at the University of Idaho. During dinner, Mr. Whitman explained to Bill that he had taken a two-year assignment with the Point Four program of the US State Department. This government program was dedicated to helping countries develop or improve their agricultural practices, thereby increasing the production of food for consumption or for export, or both. The program was very successful in helping improve the standard of living of many countries. The experience of World War II illustrated that an adequate food supply and an improved economy were very important to the cause of peace. My Uncle Glen Wahlquist spent five years in Iran with the Point Four program.

Mr. Whitman told Bill that he and Bill's mother, Marlys, would be moving to Amman, Jordan, in late summer. They very much wanted Bill to take advantage of the opportunity to live abroad for two years and accompany them. Bill could attend the American University of Beirut in Beirut, Lebanon, which was the nearest university that offered classes taught in English. Bill was excited at the prospect of traveling and attending university classes overseas.

Mr. Whitman turned to me and said "Why don't you come along for at least a year? You and Bill could room together at the American University and spend vacations with us in Amman." Marlys and Bill quickly reinforced the suggestion.

Maps were laid out and the countries of the Middle East were located. I had never heard of Lebanon. I had heard of Jordan, Syria, Iraq, Saudi Arabia and Egypt but knew little about the countries or the area. We talked until late in the evening and I caught myself becoming excited at the prospect, but deep down I knew the trip would be impossible. Dad had been gone only a little over two-and-a-half years and I was sure that I would be needed on the farm that summer.

Before I left Boise I told Bill and his parents that I would talk to Mother and see how things were when I arrived home. Mr. and Mrs. Whitman offered to talk with Mother if she had any questions. Mother and Dad had known and liked Gene and Marlys Whitman and had been acquainted Bill. I knew she would be comfortable with my being under their supervision; however, I still was sure the whole idea would be beyond my reach.

The next morning I left for home and while driving by myself I had a lot of time to contemplate the prospect of a year studying and traveling abroad. After I arrived home and unpacked, I told Mother about the conversation at the Whitman home the night before. She was quiet for a moment or two, and then she asked me if such an experience was something I really wanted to do. I said that it was and she said, "Well, let's see what we can do." I was elated. I called Bill Whitman and obtained the address for the Registrar at the American University of Beirut, AUB for short.

Chapter 77

Plans Come Together

I wrote to the AUB registrar to inquire about the possibility of enrolling in the fall. I knew that I needed to be able to continue my schooling and that completion of the equivalent of my full sophomore year would be critical to my being able to go. If the trip came together, this would allow me to return to the University of Idaho as a member of the junior class and stay on track to graduate in four years.

In a few days I received a reply, including a catalogue of courses and a variety of forms I needed to fill out and send back. I arranged for a transcript of my classes and grades to be sent directly to the registrar. In the meantime, I studied the AUB catalogue and felt confident that if accepted for enrollment, I could select courses that would allow me to complete a full year of credits that would transfer back to the University of Idaho and count toward a Bachelor of Science degree.

I started to become more confident that perhaps things just might fall into place; however, I was almost afraid to become overconfident. I learned that the cost of attending AUB would be slightly less than a year school year at Moscow, exclusive of travel expenses. I had paid for my first year of college with money I had saved from the FFA projects. I was pretty sure I could cover the cost of my sophomore year as well. Finances were tight at home and I would not have been comfortable going overseas for a year and being unavailable to help on the farm the following summer if I had to depend on Mother for the necessary finances. By this time it was clear that my trip overseas, if it occurred at all, would be for just one year.

I soon learned that AUB was a highly-regarded University. It had been founded in 1866 as a private, independent, non-sectarian institution of higher learning based on the American model of higher learning. Its founding was directed by the American Board of Commissioners for Foreign Missions then involved in the Middle East, however with the directive that it be funded separately and administered independently from the Mission. Its initial charter was issued under the name of the Syrian Protestant College by the State of New York. In 1920 the Board of Regents of the State University of New York changed the name of the institution to the American University of Beirut. Its mission is "…to enhance education, primarily of the peoples of the Middle East, to serve society through its educational functions, and to participate in the advancement of knowledge."

Over the years the school had grown into a full university. A School of Medicine was established in 1867 and the American University Hospital in 1905. The University had a School of Nursing, Dentistry, Agriculture, Engineering and Architecture, and Public Health. When I applied for admission, the President of AUB was Doctor Stephen Penrose who had previously been President of Whitman College in Walla Walla, Washington. Dr. Penrose had served as president for a number of years and was highly respected in academic circles throughout the world. Because the mission of AUB was to provide an opportunity for higher education primarily for qualified and deserving students living in the Middle East and in northern Africa, its enrollment was limited.

In due course I had a reply from the registrar at AUB advising me that I would be accepted for enrollment as a "special" student, not as a regular student. The letter further stated that as a "special" student I would be allowed to enroll and take classes for credit so long as I agreed that I would not seek a degree at the University. Enrollment for degree-seeking students was at capacity; allowing me to enroll as a "special student" would not deny admission to a student living in the Middle East. I was elated. By this time, I already knew that I could take a full load of courses that would transfer back to the University of Idaho and fulfill the requirements of my sophomore year.

I began to think that all the pieces just might fall into place. Much more remained to be done; the summer was slipping away and time was of the essence. The registrar had stressed the importance of my being at the University when classes started. I began looking into travel options. Orval planned to drive back to Washington D.C. at the end of the summer so that part of the trip would be simple. Bill and his father were scheduled to fly all the way from Boise to Beirut, Lebanon, with a stopover of several days in Washington D.C. where Mr. Whitman was scheduled for a briefing by State Department officials. Marlys Whitman was to follow at a later date to coincide with the arrival in Amman, Jordan, of the shipment of their car and household goods. The airline tickets for the Whitman family were furnished by the US government. A similar ticket would cost more than my budget allowed and I started exploring other ways to get from the east coast to Lebanon. I knew I could get to Beirut; however, I wanted to do so as inexpensively as possible.

In the meantime, I began taking the shots required for travel to countries in the Middle East. I also made application for a passport and the necessary visas. Since I was driving to Washington D.C. with Orval and would be staying with him at his apartment for a few weeks, I decided the various travel plans I was considering could more easily be explored and finalized while I was there.

I also checked with the draft board. After I registered for the draft when I turned eighteen, I received a student deferment for my first year of college. I wanted to make sure that I could also receive a student deferment for another year of college study at a university overseas. If not I would be required to wait for a draft call, or enlist, and either way a year long trip abroad would be impossible. At the draft board office, I presented a copy of the transcript of my first year at college and explained what I hoped to be able to do for my sophomore year. I was assured that I was eligible for and would receive a student deferment for another school year.

Summer sped by quickly. In addition to everything else, I was busy helping on the farm. Everything was falling into place. It was no longer if I would go, but when and how. I did some last-minute shopping for clothes; however, I assumed that what I wore during my freshman year, minus the winter clothing, would be adequate in Beirut. I was really getting excited.

Over the summer I had been reading as much as possible about the region I was going to, particularly Lebanon, Syria, and Jordan. I read several books, including *The Syrian Yankee* about a young Arab boy who immigrated to the United States. I learned that Lebanon had for years been part of Syria. I reread *The Arabian Nights*. I checked several encyclopedia sets and searched back issues of the *National Geographic* for information on the region. I tried to familiarize myself with the new country of Israel which came into being in 1948, just four years earlier. I knew that the creation of Israel was related to the Holocaust during which millions of Jewish people were exterminated in death camps by Nazi Germany during World War II. My knowledge of all these events at the time, however, was sketchy at best.

Chapter 78

First Stop, Washington D.C.

After we had packed and loaded Orval's car and said our goodbyes, he and I started on the trip to Washington D.C. around Labor Day. We stopped at Salt Lake City to visit with Farrel and Alice for a few hours. Farrel gave me a short course on photography and loaned me a variety of camera equipment. I really appreciated his efforts, but I was thoroughly confused. I had previously only used a very simple camera; Farrel was a real expert on the subject and had more sophisticated equipment.

Farrel and Alice treated us to a smorgasbord dinner. Orval took a short nap and we left Salt Lake City shortly after midnight, and we drove straight to Washington D.C. without an overnight stop. As we had done when I flew back and helped Orval drive home, we simply took turns driving, and only stopped for gasoline and to eat. We took a different route this time, which included a swing south, through Arkansas and then north through the Allegheny and Blue Ridge Mountains and on to Washington D.C. This route gave me a chance to see several additional states and I was starting to keep track of all the states I had been through. Shortly, I would start keeping track of countries I visited.

When we arrived in Washington D.C. I found the heat and humidity almost unbearable; however, over time I became acclimated. I was with Orval three to four weeks before departing for Beirut. I toured extensively in Washington D.C., spending time at the Capitol, visiting the monuments in the mall area, the Smithsonian, Mount Vernon and Arlington Cemetery. I met Louise Shadduck, a wonderful woman who was from Idaho and, along with Orval, worked in the Congressional Office of Idaho Congressman Henry Dworshak. Louise was later Director of the Idaho Department of Commerce when Robert Smylie served as Governor of Idaho. She later headed Orval's office staff when he served three terms in the US House of Representatives from 1968 to 1974.

In the summer of 1952 General Eisenhower received the Republican Party nomination for President at the National Convention. Senator Robert A. Taft of Ohio had been the runner up. General Eisenhower selected Senator Richard M. Nixon of California as his running made. In late summer a scandal of sorts developed when it was discovered Senator Nixon had maintained a "slush fund" consisting of private donations of money which he used for certain personal expenses. It was widely believed that he would be removed as the vice-presidential candidate, and I understand General Eisenhower was close to doing so. Ultimately "Ike" as he was called, decided to await the public reaction to a speech Senator Nixon had scheduled to deliver on nationwide television.

I watched the speech on a television set Louise Shadduck had in her apartment, along with Louise, Orval and Calvin Dworshak, son of the congressman. This was the first time I had ever seen a television broadcast. We were all impressed with what has become known as "The Checkers Speech." Senator Nixon talked about his modest means, wife's cloth coat, and his dog named Checkers. Polls taken after the speech were surprisingly favorable and Ike kept him on the ticket. The rest is history, I guess.

I also had an opportunity to attend a small gathering of Republican Party workers held at the Washington Hotel at which both General Eisenhower and Richard Nixon appeared and spoke. A secretary in Congressman Dworshak's office was able to arrange for her and me to attend the event. I thought General Eisenhower looked much younger and more vigorous that he appeared on television or on film, both of which were then only in black and white. Eisenhower and Nixon literally ran into the room, and after their remarks, ran out of the room. They were obviously on a very tight schedule.

While I was walking in downtown D.C. I passed a camera store and went inside to look around. I had spent time trying to figure out how to use Farrel's camera equipment, without much success. I knew that taking photos overseas would be important for me and for others back home, and I didn't want anything to complicate my ability to take a lot of pictures. On the limited budget I had set for myself, I figured that pictures would be my souvenirs. I ended up purchasing an Argus C3 and an inexpensive light meter. The camera had a good lens, was easy to operate, and relatively inexpensive. It was a very good investment. During the trip I took lots of pictures with the idea I could always throw some away. I never threw any pictures away! I took mostly color slides, all of which I have since scanned onto a CD, with each slide identified with a caption.

Everyone I met while staying with Orval was impressed that I was going to go to college for a year in Beirut. Many had travel suggestions which I found useful, and some had specific knowledge of the Middle East and suggestions on places to go and things to see. By this time I had finalized my travel plans. I was to travel on the USS Independence from New York City to Naples, Italy, and then catch a train to Rome where I would spend a day, and then take a night flight to Beirut on Pan American airlines.

Shortly before I was to leave, Orval and I drove through the New England states as far north as Maine. We stopped in New York City where Orval met a friend from his days at the University of Idaho, and we toured around some. I saw the Broadway play, *South Pacific*, which was wonderful. We went to Lindy's Restaurant and had some of its famous cheesecake. This was my first taste of cheesecake.

We then stopped in Boston and visited with Alvin "Al" Denman Jr. and his wife, Donna. Donna had been a year behind me at Idaho Falls High School. Al had a law degree, but was attending seminary in Boston. While in Boston we had dinner at Durgin Park, a famous restaurant located adjacent to the Boston harbor. Wonderful meals were served family style, on long tables covered with red and white checkered tablecloths. The portions were huge and the food was delicious. I had prime rib as an entrée and Indian Head pudding for dessert. Ever since that experience whenever I talk with someone who is going to Boston, I suggest they stop and eat at the Durgin Park Restaurant and that they have Indian Head pudding for dessert. [Editor's note: Durgin Park Restaurant closed in 2019, after 200 years.]

From Boston, we drove north with a brief stop at Plymouth Rock and on through Connecticut, Rhode Island, Vermont, New Hampshire and Maine. The trees were starting to turn a variety of colors, and though it was still early for the full color display, it was beautiful. I now had several more states I could claim I had been to! I felt like a seasoned traveler and wasn't a bit homesick, at least not yet. Of course, I was still staying with Orval.

Chapter 79

The Adventure Begins

Shortly after our return to Washington D.C. I did my final packing and Orval drove me to New York City where I was to board the SS Independence. Bill Whitman and his father were also in New York City preparing to fly to Beirut. They came with me to the pier where the ship was docked. Bill helped me carry my luggage on board and place all my things in the common room I had been assigned to. Bill and I explored the ship and chatted until it was announced that all except ticketed passengers should disembark.

Bill and his dad planned to arrive in Beirut approximately ten days before me. In fact, I would arrive one day after the official deadline for enrolling at the University; the AUB registrar had been so notified. The SS Independence and its sister ship, the SS Constitution, had recently been built and put into service. They were each about 26-28,000 tons as I recall, which was considered a large ship in those days. I found the SS Independence to be quite fancy although I had nothing to compare it with as I had never been on any type of ship before. I was soon to learn, however, that there were significant differences between the Tourist, Second Class and First Class accommodations.

I stood by the railing overlooking the pier and spotted Orval and Bill and his dad who remained on the pier until the ship was well underway. The ship carried a full load of passengers, many of whom were also by the railing waving goodbye to friends and family members. I didn't know a single person on the ship. All of a sudden I felt the enormity of what I was doing. The previous weeks had been fun and exciting; suddenly I was entirely on my own. I remember feeling a bit of panic as I realized that if something significant happened at home during the coming year, such as a serious illness or a death, I would in all likelihood be unable to return. I found myself feeling alone and homesick for the first time since leaving home. All of these feelings were mixed with the excitement I felt about the experiences I would have during the next twelve months.

Chapter 79: The Adventure Begins

The ship slowly left New York City harbor and as we passed the Statue of Liberty I felt a lump in my throat about the size of an orange. With all of the emotions I was feeling, I have to confess that tears welled up in my eyes. I began taking a lot of pictures which helped to divert my attention. I really felt alone. About this time someone spoke to me and I turned around to see a fellow who was close to me in age. He asked if I was a medical student on my way to Rome, Italy. We introduced ourselves, shook hands and I explained who I was and where I was going. He explained that aboard the ship were several American medical students who were returning to Rome.

Within a few minutes I had met a couple more medical students, and after chatting briefly, we all went to dinner. They were also traveling in tourist class; however, they had accommodations that were more private than mine. My new friends had traveled on the ship before and helped me learn my way around and also gave me several helpful hints.

Over dinner they explained how difficult it was to get into a medical school in the United States. Preference was routinely given to relatives of practicing physicians, and otherwise to those with the highest grades. Enrollment in US medical schools were restricted, which my friends felt was kept artificially low for the economic benefit of the medical profession. They said that qualified American premed students were often unable to pursue the medical profession unless they attended an institution in a foreign country, usually in Europe. They explained that the medical school in Rome was considered one of the best in Europe, and that after finishing medical school and a year of internship, a young doctor would likely be able to return to the United States and be admitted to the practice.

That evening I discovered that many students who were planning to study at various places overseas were on board, as well as many young servicemen and tourists. I soon was acquainted with a number of people with whom I felt very comfortable. Before the evening was over, several of my new friends had given me a complete tour of the tourist section of the ship. The lump in my throat had disappeared and I began to feel right at home by the time I returned to my room. I discovered that my roommates were considerably older than I, none were students, and many of them spoke little, if any, English.

My choice of accommodations was based strictly on cost, and I had selected the least expensive accommodations on the ship. Ten men shared a common room, several levels below the main deck and on the inside of the vessel. We each had an iron bunk, some single and some double bunks, with a small cabinet in which to put our luggage and personal belongings. A toilet and shower facility was a short distance down an inside passageway.

At first I was concerned about security in the room; however, I soon decided not to worry. I never did get to know my roommates very well, but everyone turned out to be compatible and friendly, although communication was limited. In any event, I did not spend much time in the room. I usually was up early and left the room after showering, shaving and dressing and I seldom returned until late in the evening. I seldom saw any of my roommates outside of the room.

The main meals we had were very good and compared favorably with the food we had at the Sigma Chi house. In addition, food and beverages were available day and night. Those of us in tourist class were unable to enter the first class section of the ship at any time. In fact, first class was closed off by a steel mesh gate that we could see through but not enter. The exception would be during life boat drills, which occurred fairly often. During those drills, some of us would wander into first class and look around, but never for long as we were usually quickly spotted by members of the crew and asked to leave.

I discovered that the food available in first class was much fancier and more plentiful. The crew kept a close watch on us and several times we were gently asked to return to our section. The tourist class and second class passengers were able to intermingle except during meal times. I took full advantage of this because second class was noticeably a step above tourist class, which I jokingly called "steerage." In truth, the accommodations in tourist class were more than adequate, and most of the young persons I spent time with were in the tourist section. I would not hesitate to again travel tourist class, although with a smaller room and fewer roommates. For a farm kid from Idaho, I was actually traveling pretty "high on the hog" which was a common expression of the times.

After a fairly uneventful first day on board the ship, the weather changed and the ocean became quite rough for a couple of days. The ship rolled and "groaned" as we went through large swells. I occasionally spent time at the rail to get fresh air and I was struck by the extent of the rise and fall of the ship. The ship would dip down and I would almost be on a level with the water, and then the ship would rise and I would be far above normal height. In calm water the rail seemed quite high above the water.

Although I had always been prone to motion sickness, I remained fairly comfortable and never did become seasick. I don't think I missed eating a meal. Once when the sea was particularly rough I attended a movie in the ship theater. The theater was located in the middle of the ship and several decks below and as a result the movement of the ship was less.

One night a member of the ship's crew, who was about the same age as I, invited several of us to inspect the working parts of the ship. We spent a few pleasant hours in a room adjacent to the engine room in the lowest level of the ship. We listened to 45 rpm records of Broadway musical shows and sipped scotch provided by our new friend. I believe his title was Assistant Purser. I am sure these diversions helped me weather the storm, so to speak. After a couple of rough sea days the weather cleared and we had good weather and calm seas for the rest of the trip to Naples, Italy.

On the way across the Atlantic we passed through the group of islands comprising the Azores. This was our first sighting of land since leaving New York City. The ship did not head into port, nor did it stop as far as I know. The water seemed to be a lighter color, more bluish, and the vegetation on the islands, some distance away, was green and quite pretty. We heard that a ship wreck had occurred a few days before in the area of the Islands and that some survivors had just been picked up the day before. We didn't see anything of the incident and never knew exactly what had happened. Our next stop would be Gibraltar. I was interested in finding out if the Rock of Gibraltar looked the same as pictures I had seen. It did.

Among the group of friends who did things together on the ship, was a lady from Morocco and her younger sister. The lady had met and married an American soldier serving in North Africa during World War II and had gone to live with him in the States. She was returning to Casablanca, Morocco, to visit with her family. She was accompanied by a younger sister who had been visiting in the States and who was also returning home. I never understood whether her trip home was for a routine visit or whether the marriage had failed. Several of us had dinner together the night before arriving at Gibraltar, and we met again the next morning to see the two women off. We all exchanged addresses and agreed to keep in touch; however, as is often the case, we never did.

The ship did not enter port but stopped in the harbor. Those wishing to leave the ship or come on board did so by harbor boats, some operating out of Gibraltar and some out of a port on the African side of the strait. The Straits of Gibraltar are quite narrow, and the coast of Africa was visible from our position in the harbor. While we were stopped, a number of small boats came close to our ship in an effort by boat merchants to sell a variety of items to passengers. The crew of our ship used fire hoses in a successful attempt to keep the boats at bay. Apparently similar boats had in the past been used to deliver drugs to passengers, which had resulted in substantial fines being levied against the ship line owners. Some trinkets were tossed onto the deck of the ship which crew members would intercept and the angry merchants would throw metal dominos at them. I took a number of pictures of the frantic activity.

While we were at anchor, a US Navy cruiser circled our ship. All of the crew members were dressed in dress blues and the ship's band played for us. The cruiser was part of the US Sixth Fleet which the United States maintained in the Mediterranean Sea at the time. After a few hours we left Gibraltar and headed north toward our next stop at Cannes, France. On the way to Cannes we passed the Islands of Corsica and Sardinia at some distance. As with Gibraltar the ship did not dock at Cannes. Some passengers left and a few came on board via a harbor boat. We were stopped only for a short time. We had an excellent view of Cannes while in the harbor area. I was conscious for the first time of the beautiful architecture of the buildings and villas, particularly the many red tiled roofs which are a trademark of cities on the coast of the Mediterranean Sea.

Our next stop was Genoa, Italy, also a very picturesque coastal city. Again we simply anchored in the harbor; however, this time we were scheduled to remain at anchor for at least six hours. As a consequence, several of us went ashore by harbor boat for a look around. This was the first time we had been on land since leaving New York Harbor. We took a bus tour of the city and visited a cemetery filled with marble statuary, at least one of which, we were told, had been carved by Michelangelo. Those buried in the cemetery were only allowed internment there for a limited period of time, following which their remains would be removed to make room for others. Most of my companions in Genoa were American medical students who spoke fluent Italian which added to the experience, and also reminded me that I could speak only English. One of the students with whom I became acquainted on the ship decided to disembark at Genoa to visit friends and then continue to Rome by train.

Chapter 80

Glitches

In retrospect, I didn't plan very well for my departure at Naples, our last stop, or for the journey to Rome. I had made a reservation to fly to Beirut from Rome on Pan American Airlines. I assumed I would just tag along with a couple of the medical students going to Rome, and that they would take care of me. The person who disembarked at Genoa was one I had spent a lot of time with on the ship. Another medical student I came to know quite well decided at the last minute to stop in Naples for a few days. Being naïve, I still wasn't concerned and assumed I would run into a couple of other medical students as we prepared to disembark. Wrong. I was not prepared for the huge number of passengers who were on board and rushed to disembark at the same time. They all seemed to know what they were doing and where they were going. I didn't see a friendly face among the crowd.

I declined the help of a small horde of porters who suddenly appeared on the dock. I couldn't understand what they were saying and didn't know how to tell them where I wanted to go. I did manage to get through customs, all the while struggling with my luggage. I managed to find a carriage which took me to the train station. "Train Station" and "Rome" seemed to be enough to communicate what I wanted to do. I had opted not to exchange some dollars into lira before leaving the ship, as someone had suggested. I assumed I could get along with US dollars and wanted to avoid having extra lira when I left for Beirut. On arriving at the railroad station, I again was greeted by a horde of people who were shouting in Italian. Obviously they wanted to help with luggage or otherwise, for a fee and tips, but again I could not understand a word they were saying. In such a crowd of people I was afraid some of my luggage would be stolen if I wasn't careful, something I had been warned about while still on the ship.

I continued to look for someone I had known on the ship. No success. A young man, really a boy younger than I, who spoke limited English, approached me. I told him I wanted to take the train to Rome. I only had US dollars and the smallest denomination was a ten-dollar bill which I gave him, wondering if I would ever see him again. He returned with a ticket. I asked him for the change and he said it was his tip. I had a porter help me take my luggage to the train soon to leave for Rome. I tried to tip him with American coins which he would not accept. I ran to a place where I could exchange dollars for lira to cover the tip, and back to the train which I finally boarded only minutes before its departure. I was a basket case by now.

When I sat down, I was joined by an American student I had met on the ship and calmed down a bit. I asked him how much my ticket to Rome had cost and, as I remember, it was the equivalent of one or two American dollars. My "friend" at the railroad station in Naples had secured a nice tip for himself. Ten dollars was a lot of money and I was really pinching my pennies so I was both upset and embarrassed about being "taken" and frustrated that it had really been my own fault. After arriving in Beirut, in my first letter to Mother, I neglected to mention the ten-dollar incident. It bothered me for some time; however, I eventually decided it was my just punishment for being so unprepared and cavalier about my arrival at Naples.

Meanwhile, back on the train to Rome, I explained to my companion who spoke fluent Italian that I needed to go directly to the office of Pan American Airlines. I had to confirm my flight to Beirut and also double check the name of the hotel where I was to stay in Rome. Bill Whitman had made me a reservation with a hotel where he and his father had stayed.. I had been told the name of the hotel but wasn't sure what it was. Fortunately, Bill had left the information at the office of Pan American Airlines. On our arrival at the Rome railroad station my new friend helped me with my luggage, arranged for a taxi to take me to the airline office, and explained to the taxi driver that I did not speak Italian. Things seemed to be going smoothly now.

When we arrived at the Pan Am building, I got out of the taxi, paid the driver and started to leave. He was speaking to me in Italian, which I did not understand. Finally, I walked away and to the building only to discover that it was closed. I knew it was Sunday; however, I had naively assumed the office would be open. Fortunately, the taxi driver waited for me to return. I thought I remembered the name of the hotel as being the Hotel Mediterraneo. I mentioned the name to the taxi driver who nodded his head and took me to the hotel. He had been most kind and helpful, and I think he was glad to finally be finished with me.

The clerk at the desk spoke some English and told me they could not give me a room unless I had a reservation. I explained that I had a reservation somewhere but wouldn't be able to find out the details until the next day when the airline office opened. He checked in his register and found my name! I went to my room and collapsed on the bed. I don't think I have ever had a more frustrating day in my life. Adding to the frustration was the knowledge that most of the trauma could have been avoided. I had learned a valuable lesson. It took me a couple hours to calm down, following which I went downstairs for a cold beer and a bite to eat, and my life began to improve.

The next morning I went back to the airline office and confirmed my flight reservation for a direct flight to Beirut leaving late that same evening. On the way back to the hotel I ran into an American medical student I had become acquainted with on the SS Independence. He offered to give me a quick tour of some of the significant sights in the old City of Rome, including the Colosseum, Parthenon, parts of the old Roman aqueduct, and several churches and cathedrals, including St. Peter's Cathedral.

The tourist season had ended and the streets and attractions were not crowded. We walked a good pace and rode street cars to cover as much ground as possible. My friend was a devout Catholic and very knowledgeable about the history of ancient Rome. The tour was very interesting. Life was looking up again. I had learned quickly that being in a strange country without knowing the language and without a traveling companion can be stressful to say the least. I was anxious to get to Beirut, reconnect with Bill Whitman, and enroll at the American University of Beirut.

Chapter 81

Meeting Beirut and AUB

It was raining when we left Rome, and stormy for a part of the flight. The plane was a Boeing Stratoliner which had two levels connected by a narrow circular stairway. My seatmate was a Pan Am official who had an office in Beirut. He told me quite a bit about the city and area. He gave me his card and extended an open invitation to visit him. After my recent experience in Italy, it was reassuring to meet someone I could contact if a problem arose.

In the early morning of October 7, 1952, we landed at the Beirut Airport where I was met by Bill Whitman. The heat seemed almost unbearable. The area around the Beirut Airport was mostly sand with little vegetation, and the glare of the sun on the sand was quite intense. I found the sounds and smells to be overwhelming and unpleasant. My cultural shock was just beginning. I collected my luggage and we headed for downtown Beirut and the American University of Beirut.

I had been concerned that I was arriving at the University a day or so later than had been specified when I was granted admission. I assumed that classes would have already started; however, that was not the case. Registration for the fall semester would not occur until October 10th. I may have missed some orientation activities, but little else. Bill had been at the University for a few days, had arranged for us to room together, and had secured a room in West Hall, a men's dormitory. On the taxi ride from the airport, Bill said he was anxious to see my reaction to our living accommodations. I had not slept much on the flight from Rome and was tired. The heat and smells made me feel a bit queasy, and I just wanted to deposit my luggage in our room and rest a bit.

West Hall was an old stone building. Our room was on the main floor and was about twelve by sixteen feet, with high walls and no mopboards. The walls had been painted yellow sometime in the past and now were badly chipped. There were small windows with iron bars too high for us to see out of, although the windows did let some light into the room. We each had an iron bed, a study table and chair, and a portable wooden closet. There were no other furnishings in the room.

The main floor of our hall had community bathroom facilities, which consisted of one shower, three toilets and four sinks. The dorm toilet was simply a bowl without a seat. I was to find out that a common toilet was simply a long open pit about twelve to fourteen inches wide and about six inches deep with water running through the pit on a good day. We soon were used to the toilets, and frankly, they were probably more sanitary without than with a seat. The bathroom had an odor and was not as clean as we were used to; however, it was functional and, of course, it was all we had. I was beginning to wonder what I had gotten myself into. Bill and I were the only American students housed in West Hall.

Bill took me on a tour of the campus. The University overlooked the Mediterranean Sea, and consisted of a number of old stone buildings and others of more modern architecture. There was an interesting variety of tropical trees, shrubs, flowers, and stone walkways, grassy areas for playing softball and soccer, and a beautiful beach along the edge of the sea. The campus was surrounded by a high rock wall along the top of which broken glass had been set in mortar to discourage anyone from crawling over.

The only entrances were gated with guards on duty at all hours. The gates and also the dormitory doors were locked at ten p.m. on weekdays and at midnight on weekends. We were late coming in one night and after identifying ourselves as students we were allowed through the gate only after giving our student booklet/pass to the guard. This required us to go to the office of the Dean of Men the next morning to retrieve our student identification booklet where he would again make sure we understood all of the rules. A student proctor had to be awakened to unlock the door and allow us to enter. This only happened once or twice. It was just too complicated to gain entrance to the campus and dormitory after hours.

At first I was uncomfortable with being locked into the dormitory at night; however, the structure was made entirely of stone and concrete, had no central heating and limited electrical wiring, and therefore was completely fireproof. The high ceilings and high windows helped keep the room cool in hot weather, but it was barely tolerable in the winter. Without any central heating, during the winter the temperature in the room was quite low and the air was more humid than I was used to. In the beginning the University seemed like a prison; however, we soon realized that the walls and gates were not really to keep the students inside the campus so much as to provide for our security.

We finally registered for classes. Registration seemed disorganized and chaotic, at least as compared to registration at the University of Idaho. In fairness, everything was new to us at the time, and the vast majority of the students and most of the faculty who were involved in the process were from the Middle East and Africa and speaking their native languages. In addition, much of the signage was in Arabic, and it was hard to distinguish the lines to stand in as most students were simply milling around in a group.

While almost all of the classes at AUB were taught in English, most of the faculty members were from non-English speaking countries and English was a second or third, and in some cases. a fourth language for them. While the students and faculty members all spoke English quite well, they spoke with an accent, and the accent was quite different depending on the person's native language. It took a number of months for my "ear" to adjust to the various accents I heard on campus. An Arab who spoke English had a particular accent, and if that person also spoke fluent French, as many in Beirut did, the accent was somewhat different sounding.

This was all quite fascinating; however, I was always a little embarrassed to have difficulty understanding someone who spoke English well, however with a heavy foreign accent. I worried that the person speaking was embarrassed about not being understood. After a few months I had no difficulty. Today when I hear someone speaking English with an Arabic accent I try to make a point of visiting with that person. I was pretty good at being able to tell the country that person was from after my year in the Middle East. I can still distinguish the person's native country.

Registration was finally complete and I had signed up for sixteen credit hours. My classes included Economics, French, and Political Geography, History of the Near East, and Survey of Modern Europe and the Near East. I was excited about the two history courses which I hoped would help me achieve a better understanding of the part of the world in which I was now living. I remember thinking that sixteen credit hours was a "light" load compared to what I had taken at the U of I. I considered adding another class; however, decided to wait until I had a better feel for the requirements of the classes I had already selected.

During registration Bill and I met some of the other students who were also "foreigners," that is, who also spoke English as a first language. These students were mostly from the United States, but also from Great Britain and Australia. Out of a total student body of between 2,000 and 2,500 only about fifteen or sixteen spoke English as a first language. We were an interesting group of students, with several young women included. The parents of one fellow were living in Nairobi, Kenya, where his father was with the US State Department. The parents of another fellow lived in Tripoli, Tunisia, where his father was stationed with the US Air Force. The same thing was true of a few others, whose parents were in that part of the world, some with an oil company, some with an agency of the US Government or in the military; AUB was an excellent alternative to returning to the United States for college studies.

There were a few students pursuing graduate studies in subjects relating to the Middle East. They were interested in becoming more proficient in the Arabic language as a stepping stone to State Department careers. One undergraduate with whom I became quite close, Richard Shaheen, was the son of parents born in Lebanon who had moved to the States. The parents wanted their son to spend time in Lebanon to learn to read, write and speak Arabic, and to be immersed in the Middle East culture. We all became fairly well acquainted and some of us made a point of getting together socially from time to time.

Most of the students were serious about pursuing their academic goals. Being able to attend the University was deemed a privilege by almost everyone, especially students from countries in the Middle East and North Africa. They worked hard and were tough class competitors. The University was filled to capacity, with a waiting list of additional students who wanted to attend. Two of our new American friends slacked off in their studies and did poorly on some of their exams during the school year. They were called into the Dean's office, given a warning, and later when their performance had not sufficiently improved, to their surprise, they were summarily dismissed from the University and told they would not be allowed to return the following year. They had above average abilities and had not been in any trouble or broken any University rules. They simply fell short academically and were taking up space.

Chapter 82

School Starts

Shortly after classes started, Bill and I went apartment hunting. Our room in West Hall seemed depressing. We found a small apartment near the University which would cost only a small amount more than our dormitory on campus. Permission of the Dean of Students was required for a student to live off campus; permission was denied. In retrospect, I am glad we were required to stay on campus. We went shopping and found a six by ten-foot colorful cotton rug to cover a part of the concrete floor, something to hang on the wall, a cheap hot plate and a coffee pot with which to make coffee and heat up soup occasionally. We settled into our surroundings and started getting acquainted with the other students.

After the first week of school, I decided to stay with sixteen credit hours for the first semester. The classes were interesting and the instructors were excellent. And demanding! Four days each week I started a class at 7:30 am. Political Geography was taught by a British professor from London. French was taught by a French professor from France. He spoke rapid fire French and only limited English. An Arab professor taught the course on Economics. I loved the course and the field of economics and later obtained my BS in Agricultural Economics. I seriously considered pursuing economics at the graduate school level. I credit the AUB professor with sparking my serious interest in the subject. An Arab professor, originally from Turkey, who was considered one of the very best experts on Middle East history in this part of the world, was the main lecturer in both history classes. His lectures were truly outstanding. During the year when I felt I knew him better, I looked for opportunities to visit with him outside of class time. He was generous with his time and seemed pleased when a student showed a particular interest in some facet of Arab history and culture.

Many of the students in the language class had already taken up to four years of French, and simply wanted a 'brush up" experience with a highly regarded French professor, in order to try to speak French correctly. A few others had no prior French instruction, including myself and Bill Whitman. The professor would shout your name and you were expected to stand up and face him. He would then shout a question to you in his difficult-to-understand English and demand an answer. It was very traumatic, particularly at first. Many students, myself included, spent a lot of time studying the lessons; however, the classroom experience was still difficult, principally because the professor spoke so rapidly and his ability to speak English was so limited.

The fall of 1952 was the first time this French professor had been out of France. We finally made it through the first semester and I actually felt I was learning more French that I had expected. The professor had a wife and a couple of small children in France. Sometime into the second semester he became quite smitten with an attractive young American woman who was taking the class. He began spending more time chatting with her during class time and less time with the rest of the students. This continued for the balance of the semester. The professor became much less demanding. As a consequence, my French did not progress as much as I now wish it had. We all liked the young woman who was distracting the professor. Although toward the end of the semester he did occasionally take her out in the evening, we were confident that she was simply playing along, and we applauded her success in reducing the pressure in the class room.

All students at AUB were required to attend Chapel at 8:30 am on Monday, Wednesday and Friday of each week. Attendance was strictly monitored; only three unexcused absences were permitted each semester. I was not very excited about a requirement to attend a Chapel service; however, after the first time I changed my mind and became an enthusiastic attendee. Each service was routinely opened by a prayer given by member of a different faith or religion. Then we would listen to a speaker on an interesting, non-religious topic.

Our first speaker was AUB President Stephen Penrose. He was an impressive and able speaker. He told of a humorous incident when he first came to Beirut and spoke to a group at the University. He explained where he came from and the audience roared. He was told that the term "Walla Walla" in Arabic means something like "bullshit."

Chapel helped me quickly gain insight into the complex political, economic, religious and cultural mix of that part of the world. Most of the speakers presented serious topics that had been well prepared and were often delivered with a mixture of good humor. I looked forward to attending Chapel, even though it meant delaying my first cup of coffee and a bite to eat. The audience included most, if not all, of the different races and religions, and many of the nationalities of the world, and consisted of individuals of all economic levels. There seemed to be a complete absence of prejudice. Chapel service was a good way to start the day.

Chapter 83

Dealing with Culture Shock

I really experienced culture shock when I first arrived in Beirut and for some time thereafter. I had never been in a foreign country, and while I expected life to be different in the Middle East, and I looked forward to the experience of living in a different cultural environment, I was not prepared for the dramatic change. In the beginning I was not quite sure what I had gotten myself into.

I've already mentioned the heat on arrival, the intensity of the sunlight on sand, and the limited vegetation in some areas. In addition, the odors seemed rather unpleasant. The new smells were a mixture of raw sewage, public toilets, a different level of hygiene, open air markets with wonderful spices and row upon row of freshly slaughtered animals, mostly sheep, goats and chickens hanging in the hot open air and often covered with flies, and the exhaust fumes from thousands of motor vehicles, just to mention a few.

Even the background sounds were different. The music at first seemed loud and harsh and the traffic noise in and around the city never seemed to let up. During the summer before I left home, I had read an article in a magazine that reported Mexico City and Beirut to be the two most traffic-congested cities in the world. The article rated Beirut the worst, with limited traffic control, drivers who used their horns more than their brakes, and taxi drivers who always seemed to be racing with their competitors along congested streets. I think the observation was quite accurate.

In addition, the main streets of Beirut had numerous trams which ran on double tracks laid in the center of the street, and the old-fashioned trams which were usually jammed with passengers, seemed to run constantly. Ras Tanura was a main street with double tracks which ran along the south side of the Campus, just outside the stone wall. The wall blocked only some of the street noise. At least some of the sounds were pleasant, such as the Muslim call to prayer and the bells and chimes of churches of various denominations.

Sand storms were not infrequent, and the major sand storms brought clouds of sand from a considerable distance, some from parts of the Middle East and much of it from parts of Africa. Although the campus was quite beautiful and covered with colorful trees, shrubs and flowers, we were not immune from the sand storms. When they occurred they seemed to last for days. The fine sand permeated everything, including our rooms in the dormitory and of course our clothes and our beds.

Adding to the culture shock was the fact that the food was much different from what I was used to eating, although I never was a fussy eater. Persons who spoke English as a first language were few in number. All of those who were native to the area spoke Arabic and the signs, billboards, posters, newspapers and magazines were written in Arabic. We gradually located a newspaper printed in English, The Beirut Daily Star, and a few international newspapers and magazines. However, those published in the US or the UK were expensive and beyond our budget. I read the Beirut Daily Star each day. Since it is now available on the internet, I continue to read it, almost on a daily basis.

Dress customs were different. There were some, particularly in the larger cities such as Beirut, who dressed in "western" clothes. Many more, however, wore clothes more traditional to their particular culture, tribe, or religion. The variations, colors and contrasts were remarkable. All of the above would be seen in almost any street scene in downtown Beirut. In the smaller cities and villages the only difference would be that fewer people were wearing western clothing. We gradually were able to identify nationalities and tribal groups by their style and color of clothing or by what they wore on their heads, or both.

In the first few weeks I remember feeling that I had been dropped on a planet somewhere in outer space, and while my new life was fascinating and exciting, there were times I felt it was just coming at me too fast. I wanted to take a break; that is, experience life back home for a few days and then return. The emotions I am trying to express were real; however, they gradually subsided over time. Several things helped. Bill and I were close and we both were reacting in much the same way, so we could share our feelings and frustrations, and often did so with humor. We gradually started making friends with some of the students who were from the United States or otherwise spoke English as a first language.

Chapter 84

Making the Adjustment

Many of our new friends had been in the Middle East before or for a longer time and their experience and knowledge were helpful to our adjustment. Also, we became acquainted with some of the staff at the American Embassy, including some of the young Marines who guarded the compound. We learned that American movies were shown certain evenings and that an occasional reception was held at the Embassy for Americans living in the region.

We attended several receptions and became acquainted with a few more Americans. I think every American had had similar experiences to those Bill and I were experiencing during our first few weeks in Beirut. They gave us helpful tips on what to do and not to do, and ways to avoid or at least minimize the risk of becoming ill. We enjoyed an occasional evening at the Embassy; however, outside of a few movies or two or three Embassy receptions, we really had very little contact otherwise with the persons we met there. Knowing that they were there and that they were ready, able and willing to be of help was reassuring and eased some of our early anxieties.

Gradually my "ears" adjusted to the different accents and verbal communication became easier and more relaxing. I began to acquire a taste for the food we were getting at the University cafeteria. The fruits and juices were excellent, and the variations of rice, lamb, goat and curry were tasty. We could get ice cream which was good, although less creamy than our ice cream at home. I tried to drink milk as often as I could. The milk was pasteurized although diluted with water. And gradually the music seemed less harsh and the odors less objectionable.

I missed eating salads which we had been warned to stay away from. There were nice restaurants in the luxury hotels in Beirut that served wonderful meals comparable to anything that could be obtained in the United States; however, the prices were exorbitant. I think I went to a nice restaurant only a couple of times; once in the fall as a guest of Mr. and Mrs. Whitman and once in the spring with Donna at the invitation of her parents, Harry and Hazel Lebsock.

There was a restaurant called Uncle Sam's across the street from the University where we often sought refuge. The owner, who was Lebanese, proclaimed that he served authentic American food. That was somewhat of an overstatement. The restaurant had a good atmosphere, was air conditioned and the food was generally good although slightly more costly than the University cafeteria. We generally went there for a coke or a snack, and occasionally treated ourselves to a meal on Sunday.

A lot of the students we were acquainted with, and some new friends we made were regulars at Uncle Sam's. We spent a fair amount of time there occupying space, but not a great deal of money, a fact that the owner would occasionally mention. He was very friendly and had a good sense of humor and I know he enjoyed having us stop by. Our presence confirmed that his place served "authentic" American food, and many of his local clientele enjoyed associating with Americans. Simply put, I believe he felt we were good for business.

Bill and I ate most of our meals at the cafeteria on the University campus, for about one US dollar per day. The food was basic, but nourishing and tasty. We had a variety of meats, mostly mutton and goat, and some beef and pork. The food was generally served with a curry and a bit more spice than I was used to eating. Vegetables were commonly served, and we ate rice and beans at almost every meal. Occasionally we received a serving of squash, carrots, small potatoes, or peas. Fresh Arabic bread was served with every meal, and French bread was also available at a nominal extra cost. A carafe of olive oil was on each table in the cafeteria.

The Arabic bread was similar to the pita bread we eat today. At first I found the Arabic bread somewhat tasteless, at least as compared with French bread. Over time however, I became very fond of the Arabic bread. As the year progressed we became familiar with when and where the breads were baked and would enjoy an afternoon snack of fresh warm Arabic bread, hummus and olive oil. Of course we avoided salads, and instead substituted fruits that could be peeled, such as bananas, oranges, and tangerines all of which were excellent. I particularly liked the bananas, which were smaller than the ones we had at home, and very tasty. I drank a lot of diluted pasteurized milk. We often topped off the evening meal with a scoop of "local" ice cream, which was similar to ice milk.

We had been warned about dysentery. Most of the "foreigners" whom we met had had one or more bouts of dysentery while living in the Middle East. I paid careful attention to matters of personal hygiene and tried to heed the advice of others as to what to avoid eating, particularly from street vendors, no matter how good it looked. I never did experience dysentery; however, I did have an "extended" problem with constipation during the first weeks I was in Beirut. I think my problem was a combination of the dramatic change in diet and an aversion to the public toilet facilities which took me a while to adjust to.

The toilet facility in the building which housed the cafeteria was in the basement and consisted simply of a fairly large room with a cement floor and several "troughs," each about a foot wide and five or six inches deep, running the width of the room. The "troughs," which the user straddled, were parallel and about six feet apart, and each had a trickle of water running through. The facility would accommodate a number of people at the same time and afforded absolutely no privacy. I could provide a description of the sounds and smells; however, I will spare you that bit of detail. This facility was fairly typical of the ones we experienced, varying only in room size and the amount of water trickling through the "troughs."

Chapter 85

Learning the Arab Perspective on Israel

We soon were getting settled into the new routine. The classes were very interesting and the food began to taste better. We began getting acquainted with Arab students. Often in the evening we would get a knock at the door to our room and find we were being visited by a group of Arab students who also lived in West Hall and wanted to get better acquainted with us.

I was struck by how knowledgeable the Arab students were about the United States, particularly its politics and history, from the Revolutionary War to the present. Generally, they were friendly toward Americans; however, they were very upset with fact that United States had formally recognized the new State of Israel. Israel was created by United Nations mandate in 1948 which partitioned part of the area known as Palestine. The United States was one of the first nations to formally recognize the new country.

Immediately after the UN resolution was adopted, the War of 1948 ensued, resulting in a larger part of Palestine being claimed by Israel. The mandate and expansion of territory by the new nation of Israel resulted in the displacement of large numbers of Palestinians citizens being driven from their homeland. They were housed "temporarily" in refugee camps established by the United Nations while efforts commenced to reach a solution to the refugee problem. There was general expectation that the Palestinians would be allowed to return to their homes and lands, the so- called "Right of Return," where possible and would be compensated where return was not possible or practical. Keep in mind, I was in Beirut in 1952, only a short four years later.

When I arrived in Beirut my knowledge of the events that led up to the creation of Israel was sketchy at best. Like everyone else I had been horrified to learn of the Holocaust and the extermination of millions of people, mostly Jews, by Nazi Germany during World War II. I had read *The Rise and Fall of the Third Reich* by William L. Shirer and other accounts of the persecutions the

Jewish people had been subjected to for centuries. I had become familiar with their passionate desire for a "homeland" and I was sympathetic to their cause. Mother and Dad had Jewish friends and business acquaintances, all of whom were very fine people. In Beirut I learned the "rest of the story" as it related to Palestine and the impact of the creation of Israel upon millions of Palestinians.

Arabs are emotional and excitable people, and nothing arouses their passions as much as the Arab-Israeli issue and the plight of the Palestinian refugees. Some of the students at AUB were Palestinian refugees. Many of them had friends and family members who had been killed or driven out of their cities, villages and farms as a result of the conflict in 1948. We had some very interesting and emotional discussions with our fellow students. Fortunately, although both Bill and I were "weak" on the issue, we realized how truly sensitive the issue was among the Arabs and we had sense enough to do more listening than talking in our early discussions. Our fellow students soon understood how little we really knew about the issues, something which they were quick to attribute, with some truth, to the powerful influence of the Zionist movement in the United States.

Bill and I were both struck by the intensity of the feelings of our fellow students over Arab-Israeli issues. Initially, we were concerned that as Americans we would be unwelcome on campus and that our experience at AUB, which we were adjusting to and beginning to enjoy, would be adversely affected. We expressed our concerns to others. We conferred with some of the University faculty members and staff at the US Embassy.

We gradually gained a much better understanding of what had taken place and the plight of the Palestinian people, including, but not limited to, the war refugees. We became much more knowledgeable about and were genuinely sympathetic to the Palestinian cause. Clearly the Jewish people deserved to live in an environment without persecution, and perhaps to have a separate homeland, but the killing of thousands and the dislocation of large numbers of Palestinians from their homeland to accomplish the goal was tragically wrong. We Americans were almost universally ignorant of the full story of the tragedy at the time, and most still are today.

Fortunately, we were generally accepted by almost all of the Arab students and made many friends. We found that most of them liked Americans, however strongly they disagreed with the policy of the US government. We avoided discussing the Arab-Israeli issues as much as possible. From what we had heard and what we had seen of the conditions of the many UN refugee camps in Lebanon, and would later see in Jordan, we concluded a tragedy had indeed occurred. We hoped, as did many of the Arabs, that the major powers operating within the framework of the United Nations would soon find a better solution satisfactory to both the survivors of the Holocaust and the Palestinians, and that the refugees would be able to return to their former homeland.

We had occasion to drive through several of the refugee camps in Lebanon, and later some of the camps in Jordan. The camps were tent cities, crowded with young and old alike living in hot, dry conditions without electricity or running water and without adequate toilet facilities. Much of the food the refugees received was provided by the United Nations. I believe most people believed that the refugee camps would only be a temporary measure.

These "temporary" refugee camps still exist today. The tents have been replaced by poorly constructed slum dwellings. The population has dramatically increased over the years and the residents experience continued poverty and high rates of unemployment. The inevitable hopelessness and despair have resulted in increased numbers of militants and extremists. After more than fifty years the situation is largely overlooked or ignored by the rest of the world. Sadly, the situation of the Palestinians is still the major obstacle to achieving a stable political environment in the Middle East.

Many books have been written, some of which are good and many of which are simply propaganda, emotional rhetoric really. One of the best is *Palestine: Peace Not Apartheid* by former US President Jimmy Carter. Another I would suggest is *From Beirut to Jerusalem* by Thomas Friedman.

Chapter 86

Day Trips and Intrigue

Early in the fall semester the students of AUB held a reception for students who did not live in the countries of the Middle East or North Africa. Most of the relatively few American students and other "foreign" students attended, as did a fair number of Arab faculty and students. There was no program and there were no speeches. We were served refreshments and had the opportunity to engage in conversations with small groups of students. I had the impression the event was an annual affair that was encouraged and perhaps required by the University administration.

Other than participating in and watching some sporting events, mainly soccer and softball, there was little organized activity among the students. The Arab students rarely dated because their culture required the young woman to be chaperoned. The life on campus at AUB was much different and more subdued than that at the University of Idaho. The students were on campus to get an education and get on with their careers. They knew how fortunate they were to be able to obtain access to a college education at the American University of Beirut. They were well aware that if they didn't achieve academically they would be asked to leave and that there were many other young men and women eager to take their places.

At AUB most classes were taught in English and used English textbooks. This was an added burden for the Arab students, and frankly, an advantage for Bill Whitman and me. Some of the students came to the University quite well prepared for college level courses, and others, many of whom came from small towns and villages, were less prepared. The University had a strong program for mentoring and tutoring students and many availed themselves of the program. They knew that earning a University degree would provide them with almost unlimited opportunities and much prestige. Even as students, many were looked up to and had considerable influence in their villages and cities.

Once during an evening discussion in our room at West Hall, one of the Arab students made critical comments about a high official in his country. He dropped his voice and said that the official would soon be assassinated. Bill and I weren't sure whether the student was simply trying to impress us with his bravado or might have knowledge of some conspiracy. The next day after class, we looked for an opportunity to visit with our history professor with whom we often conferred and highly respected. We related the conversation to the professor and asked whether he thought the comments should be taken seriously.

He explained that a number of the students were some of the most educated in the regions they were from, and as such were actually regarded as leaders by many people in spite of their young ages. In addition, he said most young men were involved in politics at various levels in their respective countries, and the Professor said in all likelihood this particular student had received information of a planned assassination.

He also said that the Middle East was full of political intrigue, and that more assassinations were planned or seriously talked about than were successfully carried out. He finished by saying that we should take very seriously what the students said; however, that we should never get involved by trying to do anything with information we were given. We also related the incident to a member of the staff of the US Embassy who agreed with the Professor. For a couple of years, I remembered the name and citizenship of the person who was supposed to be assassinated and I carefully monitored the news from the Middle East. I have long since forgotten those details.

At the reception for American and other "foreign" students, Bill and I had learned that for a nominal cost the University arranged for weekend trips to places of interest, usually for a single long day trip. We signed up for the next trip which was to see a Crusader Castle in northern Syria. Bill and I were the only Americans who took the trip. We rode in older school buses. The students were friendly and made us feel right at home. We had purchased some food to take with us as had all of the others. We shared food, conversed, and sang songs. The students loved to sing "rounds" and wanted us to teach them some American songs that were sung in the "round," which we did. We remembered "Row, Row, Row Your Boat" and a couple of others, and they taught us some of their songs. It was a great way to get everyone on the same level so to speak.

This trip was our first trip across the Syrian border and we had neglected to get a visa to enter the country. We may have assumed that a visa would not be necessary for a school trip of one day, particularly as there were Syrian students in our group. We were stopped at the border and told that all non-Syrians had to have a valid visa to enter Syria. However, we could purchase one at the checkpoint for what seemed to us a ridiculously high price. Many in the group of students were non-Syrians. We declined the offer to pay the high price for a visa and began getting ready to board a bus to return to AUB. Several of the Arab students began protesting and negotiating the charge for a visa. Ultimately, we were able to obtain visas at a much more reasonable cost and continued the trip.

The scene at the border was repeated often during the year I spent abroad. The police and military personnel in countries of the Middle East were very creative in devising ways to extract extra money from foreigners. They were poorly paid and lived in a cultural environment which not only tolerated but in fact encouraged such practices as a means of supplementing their income. We became accustomed to the various practices. We soon learned that you could avoid being shaken down "too hard" by saying no and being prepared to spend a lot of time waiting. The longer you waited the lower the ultimate fee or charge would be.

Sometimes after a length of time the fee would even be waived. At times, but not always, it would help to demand to talk to a superior officer. It was just a way of life. The amount you would be asked to pay was not large in US dollars, but we resented the principle and we were on a tight budget. I have since wondered if we should have been more tolerant of the system and a bit more generous. In many ways it was almost like a game.

Another University day trip we took was to the ancient Roman city of Baalbek which is located high in the mountainous area of Lebanon and reached by taking the main road to Damascus, Syria. Baalbek reputedly has the most beautiful Roman ruins and the finest examples of Roman architecture in the world. The ride into the higher elevations through a variety of small farms, orchards, villages and forested areas was really beautiful. The weather was sunny and warm and a large number of students made the trip. Beirut, of course, is at sea level. There were lots of banana and orange trees and tropical flowers of all kinds. In Damascas the highway climbs steadily and in a rather short time we passed through many different elevations, each with its unique vegetation. We were told that during the drive from Beirut to the pass many of the different varieties of vegetation found elsewhere in the world can be seen.

The pass is quite high, and considerable snow accumulates in winter. Not far from the pass a first-class ski resort has been developed in the area known as the Cedars of Lebanon. The area contains groves of old growth cedars, which is the national tree of Lebanon, and which once covered much of Lebanon and other parts of the Middle East. The large cedar trees were prized for the lumber used principally in shipbuilding because of its hardness and its resistance to rot and decay. Sadly, over time, the forests were over-harvested to the point that only a few protected old growth trees now remain. The loss of the cedar forests has changed the character of the land and also changed the climate in some respects to more of a desert-like condition. We made a couple of trips to the Cedars and the ski resort. We did not ski, but we did ride the ski lift to the top and enjoyed the view. It almost seemed like we were back in Idaho.

Chapter 87

Snapping Shots in Beirut

One Saturday, Bill and I rented bicycles and rode around the outskirts of Beirut. It felt good to stretch our legs and get out of the heavy traffic and the noise of the inner city. We stopped at a creamery and upon showing interest, we were invited to go on a tour of the facilities. This also reminded me of home, although the buildings and equipment were not as modern as facilities I had seen back in Idaho. We were relieved to find that the milk was pasteurized before being bottled, and the equipment although somewhat old was keep relatively clean.

Shortly after visiting the creamery, we noticed a formation of Lebanese soldiers and a military band marching down the road. We took pictures of both and then started riding away on our bikes. We heard shouting and turned to see a group of the soldiers hurrying in our direction. For a moment we couldn't figure out where they were hurrying to. It soon became obvious that they were hurrying to us, and suddenly we were surrounded. We couldn't understand a thing they were saying to us; however, they made it known that we should follow them back to what turned out to be their headquarters a short distance down the road. There we were met by an officer who spoke only Lebanese and later another officer was summoned who spoke only a little broken English.

We were told that we were under arrest for taking pictures in a military area. The officer demanded to know who we were and why we were taking pictures. He also asked for our cameras. We showed them our passports and AUB booklets and explained that we were American students who were simply taking a bike ride. We had taken some good pictures earlier during our ride and we were afraid the soldiers would open our cameras and either take or ruin the film.

At first the soldiers we encountered seemed quite upset with us, even angry. As time went on, however, and they had a chance to observe us closely, they seemed to relax. The student booklets and the fact that Bill carried a

Diplomatic passport because of his father's position with the US State Department helped us, I am sure. By the time we were allowed to go many of them seemed somewhat amused by the whole incident, and we were given our cameras back, unopened. We were learning not to take pictures of military installations, personnel, or equipment.

On this ride, we also learned that most in the Arab world did not like to have their pictures taken. For some, it was because of their religious beliefs. We were fascinated by the people we encountered, and their different styles of dress. It ranged from western style clothing to that commonly worn by Bedouins, by different tribes and ethnic groups. There were beautiful robes and kaffiyehs or head bands worn by the men with some prominence, and the different uniforms and kaffiyahs worn by men in the various branches of the military.

Almost everything we saw would have made a unique picture. However, people often became angry with us if they thought we had taken or were about to take their picture. This was frustrating for me because I wanted to record the colorful uniqueness of this part of the world to take back home, and yet at the same time I did not intend to be disrespectful. At first I would try to be discreet in my picture taking; however, I soon learned that those who did not want to be photographed also assumed that I would try to do so on the sly, and it seldom worked. Finally, I did the right thing and refrained from taking photographs unless prior permission had been granted, which often came with a small fee attached.

Chapter 88

Beggars and Bargaining

Beirut was commonly known as the Paris of the Middle East. This was because it had first class hotels, restaurants, and shops which catered to the very wealthy who lived in Lebanon and who also came from surrounding countries. The wealthy class was quite small, the middle class fairly significant, and the people living in poverty were considerable in number. There was no real separation of the various economic and social classes in Beirut. On almost any street you would encounter a mixture of people from the wealthy dressed in western clothes of the latest fashion to the poorest of the poor, clothed in rags and begging for alms. Many of the beggars were nomad women and children who were often physically disfigured. We were told that sometimes very poor parents who were unable to support all members of the family would intentionally disfigure or inflict blindness on a small infant or child to render the child more likely to be pitied and given alms. I came to believe that this in fact did occur, although I did not know how common the practice was. We did see many blind persons who were begging; however, we were told that eye diseases resulting in blindness were not uncommon among the poor. Often the scene was pretty pathetic.

On the positive side, I was struck by the generosity of the Lebanese people and their willingness to help their unfortunate fellow citizens. There were a few young boys near the campus who sold small packets of Chicklets, small pieces of gum coated with a candy shell. We bought a lot of their gum. We were advised to be careful about giving to beggars. We soon found out why. If an American gave money to someone on a busy street, that person would immediately be surrounded by a number of other aggressive and persistent beggars. We made sure that when we gave, we were unnoticed by other beggars in the vicinity.

Local goods and services were quite inexpensive. We could take the tram from in front of AUB to central Beirut, see a movie, and ride back on the tram for a total cost equivalent to about 18 cents each. A shave and a haircut cost about 45 cents. I had never had a barbershop shave before arriving in Beirut, and usually had a shave each time I had a haircut since the extra cost was nominal. As I remember when I first had a haircut, the barber shaved me without asking. He assumed most fellows wanted both. While in Beirut I grew a goatee and mustache and soon discovered that the barber did a much better job of trimming my facial hair than I would.

Anything imported from the United States or European countries was generally quite expensive, while goods from Arab and African countries and India were very inexpensive. It was customary to bargain or haggle, regardless of the marked or asking price. We were told in fact that it was considered impolite not to bargain. Bargaining was expected and appreciated. It took me a long time to become comfortable with this and overcome the feeling I was somehow insulting the shopkeeper. I finally got used to it and actually had fun bargaining, even though it often took considerable time to complete a purchase. Often, I would counter with a price and when my offer was rejected would walk away. If the item was something I really wanted, I would come back and wait for the new price and then counter to it. When the price was agreed upon and the purchase completed, we were always invited to sit and have a cup of coffee.

It was not uncommon to be offered coffee before you even expressed interest in a purchase. I never encountered a merchant who was unpleasant to deal with. Of course, I didn't buy a lot of items. One Saturday I bought a camel skin duffle bag which was priced at thirty-four or thirty-six Lebanese pounds. After several hours, I was able to buy the bag for less than 10 Lebanese pounds. Afterwards we shook hands and had another cup of coffee. I felt like a real pro.

Chapter 89

Fall Happenings

In the fall Bill and I received an invitation to dinner at the Lebanese home of the Iliya family in Beirut. Farrel was acquainted with a Dr. Al Iliya who was in the residency program at the University of Utah Medical School. Dr. Iliya was from Beirut and when Farrel mentioned that I was attending the American University of Beirut, Dr. Iliya notified his family. We had a most enjoyable evening with Dr. Iliya's parents and his brother who was attending medical school at AUB.

The home consisted of a large, elegantly furnished apartment in an upscale Beirut neighborhood. The food, all Lebanese dishes, consisted of numerous courses served over several hours. Mrs. Iliya took great delight in explaining the various foods we were being served and in describing how the foods were prepared. Bill and I tried everything, and not knowing how many courses remained to be served, I am sure we ate more than we were used to eating. Mrs. Iliya showed me a cookbook of Lebanese dishes she thought my mother would enjoy; however, it was written in Arabic. I later found an English version of the same cookbook. I bought two copies and sent one to Mother and one to Louise Shadduck for Christmas.

In early November, we received the news that General Dwight Eisenhower had been elected President by a landslide over Adlai Stevenson, former Governor of Illinois. Orval had predicted the landslide earlier, although I thought the vote would be closer. Harry Truman was President but had chosen not to run for another term. At the time his popularity had dropped considerably. It is interesting that his popularity has risen dramatically in subsequent years. I had voted for General Eisenhower by absentee ballot and was pleased with the election results. During the campaign he had pledged to go to Korea if elected. There was high public expectation that General Eisenhower would be able to find a way to end the Korean War hostilities, which ultimately occurred early in his first term as President.

In early November Bill and I received an unexpected visit from his mother, Marlys Whitman. She accompanied her husband to Beirut where he was checked into the University Hospital. Mrs. Whitman returned to Amman, Jordan, after a few days; however, Mr. Whitman remained in the hospital for about two weeks. Bill and I visited with Mr. Whitman while he was in the hospital. It turned out that he had picked up a bad case of amoebic dysentery; following excellent treatment and rest, he was once again in good health and returned to Amman. On his last night in Beirut Mr. Whitman took Bill and me out for a nice dinner. He loved his assignment with the Point Four Program, and after the two-year commitment in Jordan, he went on to a similar assignment in Turkey for another two-year stint.

On Thanksgiving Day we had turkey and pumpkin pie at the University cafeteria. It wasn't bad, though not like Thanksgiving dinner at home. It was the first Thanksgiving I had spent away from home.

By this time we were pretty well adjusted to life at the University and in Beirut. The weather turned cool, which at first was a relief from the summer heat and while it never did get really cold by Idaho standards, we were often in fact cold. There was no central heating system in West Hall or in any of the classroom buildings. The humidity was still fairly high due to the breezes off the Mediterranean Sea.

We started wearing warmer clothing and putting on an extra blanket at night. When the stone walls and floors of the buildings cooled down, they stayed cold. The cafeteria did have some heat, mostly from the kitchen area, and Uncle Sam's had a source of heat, so we spent more time in those two places. I particularly noticed the cold when studying in our room during the evenings after dinner and would often simply give up and climb into bed. Often the outside air was warmer than the air indoors.

The United States Sixth Fleet stopped in Beirut for several days and over 6,000 US sailors were given shore leave. The Sixth Fleet principally sailed within the Mediterranean Sea at that time. When the fleet arrived, the carrier planes buzzed the city and put on quite an air show. The flagship of the fleet was the USS Franklin D. Roosevelt, an aircraft carrier. Bill and I arranged to have a tour of the carrier. Most of the crew members were about our age, away from home for the first time, and about as homesick as we were. It was nice to be around so many people who spoke English and we had a good time. The opportunity to swap stories was good therapy all around. Some of the sailors came by the University, however they spent most of their time touring, shopping, and barhopping.

Chapter 90

Street Demonstrations

The Arabs are an emotional and passionate people, and demonstrations were an accepted way for the average person to express anger and frustration. Several of these events occurred during the school year. Mother was particularly concerned about my safety.

Occasionally we would be called and given the word by US Embassy staff that a street demonstration was to occur on a certain day and advised to stay indoors and out of sight. Of course, when this happened, we always positioned ourselves so that we could watch the events. We often watched the demonstrations and would later read about them in a US newspaper. The news accounts always seemed to exaggerate what actually took place. One demonstration we watched was noisy, boisterous and a bit wild, but not violent. And yet the *New York Times* reported a number of people were injured and killed.

The amount of caution we would exercise would depend on the purpose of the demonstration. One of the first was a protest of the displacement of the Palestinians in the new State of Israel. The marchers were to march down the street in front of the University and we had a call from the Embassy warning us to stay away. We stood in front of Uncle Sam's restaurant just across the street from the main gate of the University. The demonstrators filled the entire street and were shouting anti-American slogans and waving signs with similar messages.

The marchers worked themselves into a fevered pitch and it became scary, even for a nineteen-year-old farm kid. A young man whom I recognized as a student in one of my classes spit on me as he went past. He was so enraged I actually felt sorry for him. I believe his anger was not directed at me personally but rather at the policies of my country. I saw him regularly thereafter, and although he never apologized or made reference to the incident, he was friendly. I decided to cut him a little slack.

Demonstrations were prompted by a variety of causes. One protested the continued French control of what was then called French Morocco. It was followed by a demonstration protesting the way France handled riots which broke out in Morocco protesting the French occupation. Another demonstration involved support for student riots in Iraq and was followed by a contingent of Lebanese soldiers coming on campus to make sure the Iraqi students on the AUB campus did not riot. The presence of armed soldiers on campus in turn caused a protest from the University students who believed the campus should be off limits for the soldiers.

Sometimes the University was shut down for the day when a demonstration was held and at other times it remained open. Depending on the purpose some of the demonstrations were peaceful and entertaining, somewhat like a football rally back home, while others had to be taken more seriously. We became pretty good at predicting the tone of a coming demonstration by the cause that was to be supported or protested.

Chapter 91

Christmas Vacation in Amman

As the Christmas vacation approached, remembering the problems we had on the school trip to Syria, I made sure I had a valid Jordanian visa. We left for Jordan by "service" (pronounced serveese) which was simply an automobile used as a taxi which loaded up passengers until it was full. These vehicles constantly roamed the city and were a very common way to travel, less money than a tram or streetcar or a regular taxi. For cross country travel the service would generally leave from a fixed location. There you would find one that was going to Damascus or Amman or Aleppo, for example, and settle on a price by briefly haggling, and when the automobile was filled, you departed.

Damascus, Syria, is on the main road to Amman, Jordan and Bill and I planned to stop in Damascus and spend a night or two to see the city and then proceed on to Jordan. When we arrived in Damascus, a heavy rain was coming down and gave no sign of letting up. We decided to continue on to Amman and to see Damascus later. We had three passengers on the leg to Damascus, but we had a total of seven passengers with luggage plus the driver crammed into our vehicle for the drive to Amman.

Our vehicle stopped at about ten checkpoints between Beirut and Amman and the trip took a total of seven hours. On the first part of the trip, the countryside was green with lots of orchards and small farms. Most of the drive was familiar to us as we had taken much of the same road to visit the Roman ruins of Baalbek. After leaving Damascus, the countryside was bare and rocky, primarily grazing land for goats and sheep. There was very little farming, not unlike parts of southern Idaho.

We arrived in Amman at about eight o'clock in the evening. Bill's parents had no idea when we would arrive and we did not have their address or phone number. Bill was finally able to get in touch with someone at the US Embassy to obtain their telephone number. They picked us up and took us to their home for a late snack. We had hardly eaten anything since leaving Beirut. There I met

Esau, a Jordanian who was hired to work full time for Mr. and Mrs. Whitman. Esau helped with the household chores and the shopping, acted as a chauffeur and guide, and did anything else that was needed. He was a great person, with a wife and two small children who lived in Madaba, a village some distance from Amman. Esau would periodically go back home to spend a day or two with his family. Mr. and Mrs. Whitman were very fond of Esau and his family, and later helped them move to the United States and become US citizens.

The Whitman home was new and largely constructed with marble, which was quarried on the outskirts of Amman. The marble was inexpensive but very beautiful, particularly when polished. The floors were all marble, with colorful marble inlays, and the mop boards, counter tops and fireplace were marble as well. The house was modern in all respects, had central heating, and western style modern bathrooms. We were very comfortable and we ate a lot of good "western" food and played many hours of bridge. We put on a few pounds and overall had a pleasant stay.

Mrs. Whitman was determined that we would all take advantage of the unique opportunity to be in the Holy Land during the Christmas holidays. She had read extensively and had considerable knowledge about the history of the region and the various religions and cultures it contained. She had laid out an ambitious agenda. The four of us and Esau went together. Marlys was our "tour" guide and Esau, being the only one who spoke Arabic, was invaluable as our interpreter and as the person who helped us avoid getting lost or in trouble.

The first morning in Amman we went with Marlys Whitman and Esau to the native market to do some food shopping. The contrast with Beirut was striking. I was fascinated with the selection of foods and the many people we encountered as well as camels, goats, sheep, and donkeys. Some of the animals were loose while others were hitched to carts or wagons and shared the road with a variety of motor vehicles. It was quite a sight. We had to be careful not to be knocked down, stepped on, or run over.

The weather was wet, near freezing and many of the people were scantily clad. I saw young children walking barefoot. There were few Americans in Amman at the time; we were considered an oddity and received a lot of attention. Everyone seemed friendly. Later in the day Mr. Whitman took us to visit a Jordanian experimental farm and also a reforestation project, both of which Mr. Whitman had been involved with as a part of his Point Four assignment.

The evening after we arrived in Amman, we attended a church service conducted in English and Arabic, with speakers alternating languages. A choir sang Christmas songs in Arabic. The group of about 200 people attending the service was an interesting mix, including the U.S. Ambassador to Jordan, the Commanding General of the Arab Legion of Jordan, and a variety of young and old, many of whom were obviously quite poor. Except for a few small kerosene heaters placed in the aisles, there was no heat in the church. It was quite cold during the service; however, everyone seemed to have a good time.

The following day was Christmas Eve. We left early in the morning to visit the holy sites in Jerusalem, including the Church of the Holy Sepulcher, the Church of All Nations, the Garden of Gethsemane, and the most holy site for Muslims, the Dome of the Rock. We also visited the Damascus Gate, one of the main entrances in the Old Wall of Jerusalem which surrounded the original city. We went through the ancient streets in the old part of the city which were lined with shops selling everything imaginable. The crowds were huge, and it was difficult to move about.

We were warned of the danger of pickpockets. Fortunately, none of us experienced a problem. Without Esau we would have been lost. Later we went to Bethlehem, which is a much smaller city, where we visited the Church of the Nativity, believed to be built on the spot where Jesus was born. The crowds in Bethlehem were also huge; however, we saw very few other foreign tourists in either city. The color and pageantry of people representing the various religious dominations was beautiful to see.

We then visited Shepherds' Field, where the angels were supposed to have appeared to announce the birth of Jesus. And finally, a midnight mass in Bethlehem. We reached the Whitman home in Amman just before sunrise and slept much of Christmas day. We had had a very strenuous, but a very remarkable day. I had difficulty believing that I was really in the Holy Land and at perhaps the holiest time of the year. After Christmas Day, Bill and I went back to Jerusalem and Bethlehem for a couple of days and spent the night in Ramallah. There were fewer people then and we visited most of the same places. We were better oriented this time, and without the huge crowds, we had little difficulty finding our way around.

I was surprised to find out the relatively small size of the old walled City of Jerusalem and the older part of the City of Bethlehem, and also to discover the relatively small distance that separates them. It is only a few kilometers from one to the other, and the same is true of the distance between Shepherds' Field and Bethlehem. When I was small and first heard Christmas and Easter stories, I imagined the distances to have been hundreds if not thousands of miles.

I still find it remarkable that I was in the Holy Land for two weeks over Christmas in 1952 and later for two weeks during the Easter celebrations. My attempts to describe the experiences and the events do not and cannot do them justice. Fortunately, I have recorded the two weeks I spent in the Holy Land over the Christmas and Easter holidays with many color pictures which, along with all of the other pictures I took during my year abroad, are scanned onto a CD. And, of course, I will always have all of my wonderful memories.

The day following our return to Amman, Mr. and Mrs. Whitman, Bill, Esau, and I drove to the small village of Madeba where Esau's wife and small son and daughter lived. Esau and some of his family and friends prepared a "mansaf" for the Whitman family and me. A mansaf, I learned, was a "village feast" especially prepared for some noteworthy occasion and in this case the special occasion was our visit.

A sheep had been roasted on a spit over an open fire. When cooked to the desired stage, the meat was separated from the carcass and mixed with a large quantity of cooked rice and a variety of nuts and served on a large communal tray. The sheep skull was placed on top of the mound of food. After everyone had washed their hands under an outdoor faucet, all of the men sat around the tray of food and commenced to eat. The men ate first, and the women and children ate only after the men were finished. Marlys Whitman was allowed to eat with the men since she was one of the honored guests. Marlys was a very liberated woman and I know she would not have tolerated being told to defer to the men.

We had no eating utensils. Everyone ate only with the right hand which was in keeping with tribal custom. In many areas, the left hand was used for bodily functions and considered "unclean" and therefore not fit to use in eating. In some Middle Eastern countries punishment for stealing was, and still is, the complete severance of the thief's right hand, condemning the thief thereafter to eating with the "unclean" hand.

We were given a lesson on the protocol for eating without utensils. The men demonstrated, and then instructed Bill and me how to reach our right hand into the mound of food and obtain a small hand full of food without fingers. They showed us how to slowly work the food into a round ball, still only using the same right hand and, using the thumb of the right hand, to propel the ball of food into your mouth. The eldest in the group was the first to start eating; the guests were next. Early in the meal there seemed to be a respectful rotation among the men, each taking a turn; however, I did not understand the rotation, and it may have been more a matter of patience and good manners to eat in an unhurried manner.

Mr. Whitman told Bill and me earlier that certain parts of the sheep were considered delicacies and that if they were offered, we must accept the offer to avoid offending our hosts. With his prior experience attending a "mensef", he seemed to be looking forward to this part of the ritual. I later suspected that he had encouraged the host to single me out for some of the "special parts." One of the men pulled the tongue out of the head of the sheep and handed it to me. I ate the tongue without difficulty. When I was a boy we often did our own butchering on the farm and I had grown up enjoying sliced tongue sandwiches. We were also offered to partake of the brains extracted from the skull. Again, I was no stranger to brains as food and took a small taste.

My father loved a breakfast of brains and scrambled eggs. Since he was fond of the dish, I as a small boy, was, too. I have to say that eating brains mixed with scrambled eggs is easier to handle. Next I was offered one of the eyes of the sheep. This was a new experience; however, remembering Mr. Whitman's admonition, I took the eye and quickly swallowed it whole, trying not to think about what I was doing. I recently reread one of my letters to Mother written shortly after this event. I mentioned the tongue and brains, but fudged on telling her about swallowing the eye, fearing she would be nauseated.

We also had a variety of other side dishes along with the main course. We were treated well, and our willingness to eat in the style of the hosts was appreciated by the hosts and all of the guests. Mr. Whitman had a great sense of humor and he obviously enjoyed watching my reaction as I was "tested," and I believe he was relieved that I handled the challenges without gagging. Bill Whitman was squeamish about certain foods and somewhat of a picky eater. He was not put in the same predicament as I was. I think his dad had something to do with that as well.

After the meal was finished, we again washed our hands and Bill and I were dressed in traditional tribal clothing and had our pictures taken. I have some great pictures of the "mensef" and our short stay in Madeba, which remains one of my fond memories.

We were invited to a New Year's Eve party while we were in Amman, which was attended by several other Americans, some of whom were about my age. I remember becoming a bit nostalgic. Up until then everything we saw or did or ate was so unusual it was almost surreal, and since it did not remind me of home I don't think I really felt homesick. Being with mostly Americans, who talked of home, sang the traditional songs, and toasted the New Year as we always did back home, started to make me homesick. Also, reflecting on the previous two weeks caused me to actually feel guilty. I saw and did things I would never have dreamed of seeing and doing six months before. I wished that Mother and other family members could have the experiences I was having. I decided all I could do was try to help them share my experiences through the letters I wrote and the many pictures I was taking.

Chapter 92

A Close Call and a Good Lesson

Upon returning to the University we learned that over the holidays a French passenger liner, the Champollion, while approaching the Beirut harbor, had been driven onto rocks by a severe storm and had overturned and broken up. There had been a frantic rescue operation and many passengers were saved; however, quite a number had drowned. The overturned ship was visible and lay half submerged a short distance west of one of the most popular beaches in Beirut.

That spring a friend from the University, Dick Engan, and I were at the beach and decided to swim out to the shipwreck. Dick hailed from Montana and we had become pretty good friends. We thought of ourselves as good swimmers. The sea was calm and the ship did not seem too far away; in reality it was further than we had estimated. The sea seemed calm when we left the shore; however the further we went, the heavier the swells became. Soon we began having difficulty staying oriented with the location of the shipwreck. I was strong but had no experience swimming under these conditions. I remember coming up above the crest of the swells and finding I was going in the wrong direction. Occasionally a wave would pass over me and I would swallow sea water.

I realized that I was getting tired and we still had a fair distance to reach the ship. I was young and healthy, and I was reluctant to admit that there were limits to what I could do. I was hoping Dick would suggest we go back but he did not. We were becoming separated in the rough water. I finally realized that I might not be able to make it and I remember thinking that I could actually drown out there. For a moment I reflected on how such news would be received back home. I began to feel quite apprehensive and swam toward Dick. Finally, when I was close enough, I shouted that I thought we should turn back and he agreed.

By the time we reached the point on the beach from where we started, we were both totally exhausted. Dick admitted that he also had wanted to turn back but didn't want to be the one to suggest it. So much for the male ego! As I was catching my breath on shore, I realized this is just how people exceed their limits and get into trouble. I don't remember any other persons being on the beach in the area where we were. We were very close to being in serious trouble and we would have been entirely on our own. In truth, I am convinced that if I had delayed the decision to return to shore for even a few minutes longer, I would have drowned. When Mother gave permission for me to go to Beirut, I made a vow to myself to not do anything that would reflect poorly on my judgment or cause Mother to regret her decision. I had learned a good lesson that day.

Chapter 93

The Iranian Connection

After classes resumed, the Dean of Students at the University asked Bill and me if we would be willing to move in with a group of male Iranian students for the first half of the semester. Some of the Iranian students were having difficulty with the English language and the dean thought it would help them to be able to interact with us and practice their English. The students occupied an upper floor of the International House, a high-rise apartment building located a few blocks from the AUB campus. We checked out the facilities and found they were quite modern compared to West Hall. We also met a few of the students, who were very friendly, and decided to accept the invitation to move in with them.

At the time my Uncle Glen Wahlquist was in Tehran, Iran, with the Point Four Program of the US State Department and teaching at the University of Tehran. I had hoped to be able to visit Uncle Glen in Tehran before I returned home, and I thought the experience of living with Iranians would give me some exposure to their language and culture.

All in all, the experience of living in the International House was positive. We found the students to be friendly, however they were quite reserved. Unlike the students in West Hall who loved to discuss politics, it was impossible to engage the Iranian students in political discussions. They simply would not discuss politics and seemed to be uncomfortable when I would ask questions of a political nature. This was unlike almost all of the Arab students at the University who seemed to live and breathe politics. I remember mentioning my surprise in finding this difference during a conversation with one of the University faculty members.

The faculty member told me that the expenses of the Iranian students were paid by the government of Iran which was controlled by the Shah who had a vast secret service network. He said that there likely were one or more students who were members of the network living with in the International House. The students would be aware of this, and aware that any political comments they made could be interpreted as critical of the Shah or the current government of Iran. This would result in the student's immediate expulsion from the University, a mandatory return to Iran, and likely further punishment.

I found this a little hard to believe. After all, the Shah was a close ally of the United States and looked upon most favorably by our government and most of our citizens. Later, after the Shah was overthrown during the 1979 revolution that was strongly supported by students and religious leaders, we all came to learn a lot about the ruthless nature of the Shah's regime, including his extensive use of a secret service network that operated outside of the law. The analysis given me by the AUB Professor was most likely correct.

Through our visits to the American Embassy we became fairly well acquainted with a few of the State Department employees who were on the Embassy staff. One approached Bill and me in the winter of 1953 and asked if we would be willing to attend a World Communist Youth conference to be held soon in Sophia, Bulgaria. He was trying to persuade his superiors of the wisdom of having someone not connected with the US government attend the conference and provide a firsthand report of the activities of the group. We were told that the expense of our travel and accommodations would be covered. Bill and I were mindful of the Cold War anti-communism hysteria and paranoia of that time.

The US was in the middle of the Joe McCarthy witch hunt era. Also current was the fall of the Iron Curtain in eastern Europe, the Mao Tse-tung led communist revolution in China, and testimony of Whittaker Chambers before a Congressional Committee that Alger Hiss, a high State Department official was a spy for the Soviet Union. Sen. McCarthy, then at the height of his popularity, claimed the State Department was riddled with Soviet spies and much of the country feared he might be right. Careers were ruined by rumor and baseless allegations that led to a person being "blacklisted" and thus denied his or her means of livelihood. Today it is hard to imagine the atmosphere of hysteria that prevailed at the time, but it was real.

We considered the fact that the experience could be harmful to us in the future. Frankly, we were excited about the unique opportunity and its intrigue, and quickly discounted the downside risks. The next day we went to the Embassy staffer and told him that we were ready and willing to attend the conference in Sofia. The conference was to last four to five days and included a weekend so that we would only miss a couple days of class time. We had been studying hard and our grades were good. We never heard back and can only assume that the Embassy staffer's plan for our attendance at the conference did not receive approval from his superiors.

Chapter 94

The Egyptian Adventure

Registration for the second semester occurred just before we started taking first semester final exams, which made January a busy month. I signed up for a heavier course load, adding college math and statistics, both required courses at the University of Idaho. Based on the experience of the first semester, I was confident I could handle the extra work and knew that doing so would keep me on track to finish my bachelor's degree in four years as planned.

Soon after second semester registration was completed, we began taking final exams. Bill and I learned we would have a little over a week from our last exam until the start of second semester classes and decided to take a trip to Egypt. We went to the Embassy to get information on any travel concerns and suggestions on how we could best structure a trip in the time we had. As usual the staff at the Embassy was very helpful. They gave us maps and suggested we go directly to the US Embassy in Cairo to obtain any last-minute travel alerts and suggestions on where to stay and what to avoid.

We obtained our visas and purchased a round trip ticket to fly from Beirut to Cairo and back on Middle East Airlines. The airlines gave a reduced fare for students and our roundtrip tickets cost $30 each. As soon as we finished our last exams, we finished packing and left for the Beirut airport. We flew on a DC-3 which had not been cleaned for some time. I remember that I found spoiled fruit and other debris in the front pocket of my seat. We were excited about our new adventure, however, and enjoyed the flight. I was struck by the size of the Suez Canal, really not much bigger than a large irrigation canal and located in the middle of flat sandy desert terrain.

We were met at the Cairo airport by a friend from AUB who helped us go directly to the US Embassy where we met with the young woman on the staff recommended by our friend at the Embassy in Beirut. She was very helpful. Actually, I was favorably impressed with the embassy personnel wherever we traveled. It was our practice to visit the US Embassy when we traveled, for tips on what to do and how to conduct ourselves.

Anti-American sentiment existed in many parts of the Middle East, including Egypt. In addition, the anti-British sentiment was even higher. Demonstrations against the United States were common. The demonstrations were primarily over the US support for the creation of Israel, but also its support of dictatorships in the Middle East. Anti-British sentiment was high when we visited Egypt, driven primarily by the growing desire of Egyptians to take ownership and control of the Suez Canal operations from the British government. Demonstrations against the British government were common and often spontaneous. We were advised by our new friend at the Embassy that we would have less trouble if we avoided being identified as British citizens. On two or three occasions while walking around the city of Cairo, we were approached and asked, somewhat accusingly, if we were British and we quickly exhibited our US passports.

In fact, as we left the Embassy, a young man who appeared to be of high school age fell in step with us. He was pleasant, spoke English pretty well, and started pointing out some of the sites. In about fifteen minutes or so he was claiming to be our guide and asking for money. We refused to pay him anything and kept moving away. He followed us and began shouting that we were British spies. A number of people in the area started toward us. I know it sounds corny, but we were suddenly in the middle of a small crowd of Egyptians who were attracted by our "guide" in an isolated area on the outskirts of Cairo.

We circled back in the direction of the Embassy, and although we did not want to appear frightened, we began moving faster. As we neared the Embassy, the young man and the crowd he had attracted fell back. This was a ploy we had encountered before and we should have known better. On the other hand, we were strangers in the country and the young man was pleasant and seemed to want us to feel welcome. Sometimes the line between being friendly and being conned was hard to distinguish.

We located the accommodations that had been recommended and found a place to eat. Afterward we spent the rest of the afternoon and evening in the Egyptian National Museum. The museum was absolutely packed with priceless artifacts, works of art, obelisks, rows of mummies propped along one wall, and everything else imaginable. Many items were simply in opened boxes or on the floor of cavernous rooms, but not otherwise displayed, identified or catalogued.

The work of establishing a museum was just getting underway. The Egyptian government was short of funds for such purposes and because of the unrest in Egypt, international funds were not readily forthcoming. I believe I could have spent days inside the museum and not seen it all. I would love to go back to Cairo and see the new National Museum, said to be one of the finest in the world.

Back in our small hotel the first night in Cairo we were sitting on the balcony of our room when General Muhammad Naguib and his entourage drove by. At this time, General Naguib was President of Egypt, as well as Prime Minister and Commander in Chief of the Egyptian army. Some historical perspective seems in order. Bill and I were in Egypt in February of 1953. The previous year, 1952, General Naguib and a group of young military officers undertook a coup which ousted Egyptian King Farouk. One of the junior officers in the movement was Major Gamal Nasser, who is credited by many as having been the mastermind of the coup. Nasser became the leader of the ruling military junta, which served loosely as a cabinet under General Naguib.

The following year, 1954, Colonel Nasser orchestrated a coup d'etat which ousted General Naguib, who in turn was replaced by Colonel Nasser. Many historians believe Colonel Nasser intended to become the head of state after the 1952 coup, but that he was astute enough to realize that the stature of the better known General Naguib was a necessary link in his own transition to power. Nasser negotiated an agreement by which Britain agreed to give up ownership and control of the Suez Canal in two years, which ended over seventy years of British occupation.

King Farouk had assumed the throne in 1936 at the age of sixteen upon the death of his father. Later that year the Kingdom of Egypt entered into a treaty with Great Britain which gave Britain control over Sudan and allowed the presence of a large garrison of British troops in the Suez Canal Zone. For years King Farouk was perceived as someone the British Empire could manipulate, and events would seem to bear this out. In 1951, under populist pressure, Egypt announced plans to eject Britain from the Suez Canal, and in response Britain sent a fleet of warships to Port Said, Egypt's main port on the Mediterranean coast. In 1952 widespread anti-Britain riots broke out in many parts of Egypt. King Farouk put the country under martial law and suspended parliament. This caused the military to feel threatened, which gave rise to the coup led by General Naguib.

This may help to explain the anti-British sentiment Bill and I experienced in Egypt in February of 1953. This was truly an historic time and certainly an exciting experience for me. Anyone who is a student of history would enjoy reading the history of Egypt and the rest of the Middle East during this time. Much of the history of these years is very relevant to the dramatic events unfolding in the Middle East today.

The following day we got up early, had a light breakfast, and followed the suggestion of the young woman at the embassy for a low budget tour of the Sphinx and the Great Pyramids. We caught an antiquated, street car which after a long, slow, and interesting ride ended up at the pyramids. An Egyptian approached us and asked if we wanted to climb the Grand Pyramid. We negotiated a reasonable price and started up.

The stone building blocks were huge, and no distinguishable path was evident, at least to us. Our guide knew the way and after much time and effort we did indeed reach the top. The view was magnificent. Our guide took a picture of Bill and me on top of the Grand Pyramid, one of my favorite pictures of the trip to Egypt. From our vantage point we could see the Nile River and just how narrow the Nile Valley really was. I had heard about the annual flooding of the Nile River and how the overflow helped keep the adjacent land fertile and productive. The scene from on top was dramatic proof. On each side of the river was a relatively narrow green band of crop vegetation beyond which was barren sand which seemed to stretch forever on either side. While we caught our breath on the top of the Grand Pyramid, General Naguib and his large convoy arrived at the area just in front of the pyramid. By the time we descended they had left.

While we were there, in 1953, the Aswan Dam was being constructed further up the Nile River. The massive dam was intended to control the Nile's annual spring flooding by drastically reducing the annual flow of the river, resulting in the rejuvenation of the land adjacent to the river. Initially, the United States government had offered to help the Egyptian government fund the construction of the Aswan Dam; however, recent political events and the current upheaval in Egypt persuaded the US government to pull back from its commitment. The Soviet Union took full advantage of the opening and committed to underwrite the expense of constructing of the dam. Egypt forged other political and trade relationships and alliances with the USSR, much to the chagrin of the United States.

After we descended the Grand Pyramid we spent several more hours touring the area, including an active archeological dig being supervised by British scientists. There were several small pyramids, most of which were in various states of disrepair. We were told that a significant number of pyramids had been constructed in a fairly large area adjacent to the three large better-known pyramids. Often the stones of smaller, lesser-known structures were taken for use in building others. In due course, we walked to the tram line and caught the street car back to Cairo. We had a fascinating day and to our surprise had encountered hardly any other visitors.

That evening we walked around the older section of Cairo and took in the sights, including a variety of mosques, bazaars, and an outdoor military museum. While Bill and I were standing at a fence surrounding the exhibits, an older Egyptian gentleman "engaged" me in conversation. He was speaking Arabic in a friendly conversational tone, and I didn't understand a word he was saying. I was still sporting a moustache and goatee. In addition, my wardrobe had gradually changed over the period of time we were in Beirut.

We had been advised to avoid advertising the fact that we were Americans, particularly while traveling around the Middle East outside of Beirut; however, we still dressed "western." Rather than "button down" shirts and bright colored clothing, though, we wore darker and undistinguished articles. Also, since we had been in the Middle East, we had learned many of the head, hand, face and shoulder motions that were commonly used to communicate a variety of messages.

One common and effective gesture, for example, was a sharp tipping of the head upwards simultaneous with a distinctive sound made with the tongue pulling away from the roof of the mouth, all done without any facial expression whatsoever or eye contact. This was a firm but not rude method to indicate to beggars, shopkeepers, or whomever that you did not want to be bothered by to "bug off." After much practice, we were able to use these gestures like a native. Anyway, I was pleased that my Egyptian "friend" took me for a native, or at least someone for whom Arabic was a first language. It was evening and we were in an area that was dimly lit. We were only a couple feet apart, yet I could tell by the inflection in his voice when he was simply making a comment or when he was posing a question. The latter was more difficult, but I would shrug my shoulders and turn my hands outward and it seemed to satisfy him and he would return to a commentary.

Suddenly I remembered that the Americans and British were extremely unpopular, and realized that my efforts would only last so long before it would become obvious that I didn't speak Arabic. At that point I became concerned that my "friend" would be insulted and feel I was making fun of him. I could tell Bill was also becoming nervous for the same reasons. I gave my "friend" a traditional gesture that was a combination of "Peace be with you and Allah is great," shook his hand, and we quickly left.

The next morning we boarded a train for a twelve-hour journey up the Nile River Valley to the small city of Luxor, Egypt, where we stayed for three days and nights. We made arrangements for the trip to Luxor through a travel agency. When we arrived, we discovered that the place for which we had reservations had been closed. Fortunately, the travel agency arranged for us to stay at a much nicer place at no extra charge. Behind the hotel was a large area covered with a variety of tropical ferns, orchids, and palm trees. It was also filled with a variety of colorful birds. The vegetation and birds provided pleasant aromas and bird calls, night and day. Our beds were large and enclosed in mosquito netting, although we saw very few flies or insects.

At the hotel, we gathered up a variety of local maps of the areas that we hoped to cover in our visit. We were staying on the east side of the Nile River. Located across the river was the Valley of the Kings and Queens where the ancient city of Thebes had been built. Thebes was the capital of Egypt 3,000 to 3,500 years ago when the majority of the construction in the area had occurred, much of it undertaken by King Ramses II.

Just north of Luxor was the Karnak Temple Complex which contained the largest temple ever constructed in Egypt. The road leading north to the Complex was a street called "a dromos" which had a row of sphinx sculptures lying on large blocks of granite on each side leading to the Complex. When we were there, the road had not been fully excavated and the road and sphinx sculptures would go on for some distance and then disappear into a sand hill, and later reappear some distance further north. Ultimately the "a dromos" extended for about one and a half miles to the Complex. The whole area is vast and filled with early Egyptian history. It is often referred to as the largest open-air museum in the world.

We found very few tourists in Luxor when we visited. We were told that most of the tourists had traditionally come from European countries and due to tensions related to the recent turmoil in Egypt, tourism had dropped off dramatically. We had been advised to avoid hiring a guide for our entire stay, but simply to follow the routes we had tentatively lined out and occasionally negotiate for the services of short-term guides along the way. The first morning we walked with another guest of the hotel to the east bank of the Nile River and located a man with a small boat. We negotiated a price and headed across the river to the Valley of Kings and Queens, a complex of amazing temples which had been built as tombs for deceased Kings and Queens and members of the royal families.

The boat had a small sail and rudder and the boatman at times used a long pole to help move us along. Once on the other side, using our local maps and guide book, we started off. The structures were so vast and covered such a large area that we soon accepted an offer for guide services from a local Egyptian who spoke English. The size of the columns, stone statutes and obelisks and the beautiful stone reliefs of hieroglyphics were overwhelming and difficult to describe. Fortunately, I took a lot of color slides. We spent the entire day on the west side of the river. Late in the afternoon we found another boat to take us back across the river to our hotel where we planned our next day's excursion.

The next day we wandered around numerous excavation sites on the east side of the river, mostly in the direction of the Karnak Temple Complex. Many of the structures had been identified, however they were not totally uncovered. At the time of our visit, there was very little archeological activity. The political turmoil discouraged foreign governments, universities, and foundations from contributing money or sending teams with the knowledge and expertise to continue the archeological digs, and the Egyptian government lacked necessary financial and manpower resources. Fortunately, the Egyptians understood the importance of the sites and did take care to ensure that they were protected.

The next day we went back across the Nile River to the Valley of the Kings and Queens. Even two days was not adequate to do the area justice. We saw King Tut's Tomb, which had been discovered untouched. One of our guides showed us some of the ways the original builders of a tomb had constructed elaborate and complex false tunnels and passageways they hoped would make entry to the inner chambers by looters impossible. In spite of this, most of the tombs had long since been plundered.

The valuable contents of the tombs were such that long extensive searches were apparently deemed warranted; not all of the inner chambers had been found and looted. Bill and I were fascinated with the scale of the architecture of the tombs, temples, and of the statuary. Sometimes we found a massive stone statue in the middle of a field; sometimes a pair of statues located a considerable distance from other ruins. It was a very moving experience to be there and to try to imagine what life was like in Thebes when it was the cultural and political center of Egypt. It must have been something to behold.

That night we caught the train, which regularly ran between Cairo and Khartoum, and returned to Cairo. The next day we walked around Cairo. Poverty was a much bigger problem in Cairo than we had seen elsewhere in the Middle East, and we had seen quite a lot of poverty. Large sections of the city consisted of slums full of litter. There was a grey or brown appearance that lacked color and vibrancy. The living conditions were poorer than anything I had witnessed before or since, and there was little evidence of a means by which many of the residents could earn even a meager a living.

I was struck by the contrast of these conditions in large sections of Egypt as compared with the civilization that had existed thousands of years before. The knowledge that had existed in ancient Egypt was truly amazing: in literature, architecture, agriculture, construction, mathematics, medicine, and dentistry to name a few. Obviously, the ancient Egyptians had reached a sufficiently high standard of living to have achieved these levels of knowledge and to have allowed them to flourish. This was also true in other Middle East countries including Persia, now Iran, Iraq, and Syria which then included Lebanon, and Turkey. Why these early civilizations declined rather than continued to advance and benefit from their remarkable accomplishments is difficult to comprehend. I remember wondering if a similar decline could ever occur in the United States and if so, what would be the cause.

We visited the site where the Shepheard Hotel had been blown up the year before, resulting in a large loss of life. The hotel had been the headquarters of the British military and government officials who were charged by the United Nations with the management and oversight of the Palestinian Protectorate. In that capacity, the British authorities resisted the unauthorized immigration to an expansion of Israel beyond that authorized in 1948. We now know that the "terrorists" who blew up the hotel were Israeli and included some individuals who later became prominent elected officials in the Israeli government.

On our way to the airport, which was a considerable distance outside of Cairo we were able to briefly stop close to the Suez Canal. There we watched ships taking advantage of this short route between the Mediterranean Sea and the Red Sea. The Suez Canal allowed ship passage to India and Asia and eliminated the need to sail the much longer distance around the Horn of Africa. No vegetation exists in the area and the canal has a high sand bank on either side created from sand excavated when the canal was dug. It was an interesting sight to observe only the top halves of large ocean-going vessels slowly moving across the desert. Then we caught the airplane for the flight back to Beirut.

Chapter 95

Settling into Second Semester

Bill and I confirmed that we were very compatible traveling companions. Our interests were similar, we had no difficulty agreeing on what to see and where to go, and we were able to navigate a lot of territory in a relatively few days. We both enjoyed the "adventure" involved in exploring a country and its culture on our own, and we gained the personal confidence that we could tackle almost anything if we kept our wits about us. After our experience in Egypt, we were much more confident that we could get along on an extended trip throughout the Middle East and up into Europe, and we began to seriously discuss the prospects of such a trip. But first, we had a whole semester to navigate.

When we returned to Beirut, Bill went on to Amman to spend a few days with his parents. I stayed in Beirut to get ready for my classes. By this time, I had really developed a fondness for the study of economics and decided I would change my major when I returned to the University of Idaho. I mentioned this in a letter to my sister Mary and she suggested that if possible I get the required courses in college math and statistics out of the way in my sophomore year. I remembered some of the upper classmen at the Sigma Chi house saying that statistics and upper level college math were difficult and required a good background in courses such as algebra and calculus. I had not taken any math since my sophomore year in high school, but decided to give it a go.

Bill and I had both appreciated the experience of living in the International House with the Iranian students; however, there were drawbacks. The noise level was high. Many of the students played Iranian music almost constantly. Bill and I each shared a room with several Iranian students, some of whom stayed up quite late. We found it almost impossible to study at night and the only places we could study were back on campus. We finally decided to discuss the situation with the Dean of Students who had asked us to make the move to the

International House in the first place. He took into account the additional courses I was taking and authorized us to move.

Our room in West Hall on campus had been filled, so the Dean said he would approve of our living off campus if we could find suitable accommodations. We rented an inexpensive room a short distance from campus. Our room had no heat and no facilities for cooking so we continued to take most of our meals on campus. Warmer weather was coming, we hoped, and at least our new place was quiet. As luck would have it, we had a period of extreme cold weather right after we moved in. We nearly froze.

My classes started at 7:30 a.m., so each day I got up early and headed for the University. After class I went to the University cafeteria for a bite of breakfast and to check the post office for mail. Sometimes I would spend most of the day on campus. Occasionally Bill and I would get together and buy something for lunch which we would take back to our room for a change of pace. My favorite lunch consisted of a couple of loaves of freshly baked French bread from the nearby bakery, slices of Dutch cheese, and a bottle of cold Lebanese beer.

About this time, we had some excitement in Beirut. Riots had broken out in an outlying area of Lebanon. I can't remember now for sure what triggered the outbreak, some tribal rivalry I believe, but several people were killed and more were injured. A couple of days later accusations were being thrown back and forth by some deputies in the Lebanese Parliament and a real brawl ensued, complete with fists, knives and guns. Fortunately, none of the deputies were injured, however the Lebanese army was called in and Parliament was shut down.

The afternoon it happened, Bill and I went downtown to an airline office which was across the street from the Parliament building and found that the entire block, including the airline office, was cordoned off by soldiers. After we explained our purpose we were allowed to proceed. Of much greater concern at this time was the turmoil resulting from recent developments in Iran which were dominating the news.

On March 1, 1953 I celebrated my twentieth birthday. This was a busy time for me and I took little note of the benchmark. School was taking a lot of my time and the schedule for exams had been posted for later in the month, following which we would have an Easter break. Bill and I hoped to spend time in Amman and the Holy Land during the break. On March 5, 1953, we received the news that Joseph Stalin had died. Stalin had served from 1922 until his death as the leader of the Soviet Union. His death was met with mixed feelings in the US and in many parts of the world. Many were pleased that the dictator was gone and at the same time apprehensive about who and what would follow.

Chapter 96

Classmates to Remember

We met some very interesting individuals who were attending AUB. Ankie Schuller's father was a high official in the diplomatic corps of the Netherlands who was stationed in Beirut. The entire family had been in the Dutch East Indies at the outbreak of World War II. Ankie, along with her Mother and siblings, were interned in a Japanese prison camp, and her father was held in a separate camp for the duration of the war. All of them suffered greatly. Ankie invited me to her eighteenth birthday party which was hosted by her parents at their home in an upscale section of Beirut. I knew only a few people; however, her folks and their friends were very gracious and I had a good time. After the party, Ankie suggested we go swimming in the Mediterranean Sea below the AUB campus. We walked for over an hour only to find that all accesses to the beach were locked, so we returned to her home. I arrived at my room about four o'clock in the morning, totally exhausted. After I had finished law school and had returned to Idaho Falls Donna and I, by a remarkable coincidence, came in contact with Ankie and her new husband Wes Foel. More about that later.

Another interesting person was Sammy, a young Chinese student who was attending the AUB medical school. He was a few years older than we were, spoke almost perfect English, and liked to associate with American students. He was extremely busy with his medical studies but we managed to have meals together on a fairly regular basis. Sammy came from a well-to-do Chinese family. He told us about his literally walking south across most of China ahead of the Great March of Mao Tse-tung. Mao Tse-tung successfully overthrew the corrupt Kuomintang government of Chiang Kai-shek who fled with his followers to the island of Taiwan in 1949.

Sammy crossed into Southeast Asia, ultimately made his way to Beirut, and enrolled at AUB. During his several months of walking across China with thousands of others, he heard no one speak his native dialect. He was unable to communicate with any of his fellow travelers. One day he was resting under a tree when he suddenly realized that someone was speaking his dialect., a person from his home town in northern China. I had assumed that everyone in China spoke the same language, however Sammy explained that at that time there were hundreds of totally different dialects. Most Chinese could only speak or understand their own dialect. Much of that has changed now, with Mandarin being the predominant dialect.

One day Sammy and a group of us were having lunch in the University cafeteria. Sammy went downstairs to the post office to check for mail and brought back a small gift-wrapped package. He mentioned that it was his birthday and opened the package. The package, which did not identify a sender, contained the penis of a cadaver from the AUB Medical School, obviously a prank by one of his fellow medical students. We were all highly amused with Sammy's gift and our loud laughter attracted the waitress to come to our table to find out what was going on. Someone handed her the box which she examined carefully. When she realized what was in the box she shrieked, threw the box containing the penis high in the air and when it landed the penis rolled halfway across the cafeteria floor. Sammy was very concerned because he said anyone found to be responsible for the prank would face immediate expulsion from medical school. I am not sure what Sammy did with his gift; however, I assume he returned it to the cadaver.

Another student we spent time with was Jose Abbuzaid, from Mexico City. Jose's mother was Mexican and his father was Lebanese and they were living in Mexico City when his father died. The family had considerable property interests in Beirut, and Jose and his mother had moved to Beirut to manage the property, mostly real estate holdings. Jose was a friendly, carefree person and a good student. He began to spend some of his free time with our small group and was well-liked. He joined us on a trip to the Cedars in mountainous Lebanon.

Dick Shaheen had borrowed a car and was driving us to the Cedars. Dick, who lived in Ohio, was of Lebanese descent. His Lebanese parents sent Dick to Lebanon to learn the language and experience Arabic culture. He took special classes and received extra tutoring to learn to read and write Arabic. To me, he seemed to speak the language well. Dick often served as our interpreter.

Along the way, Dick was unsure whether we were on the right road and he stopped to asked directions from a couple of men. We were about to resume our trip when Jose cut loose with a long and loud streak of angry sounding Arabic directed at the two men and engaged them in further heated conversation. We had known Jose for many months and were unaware he spoke any Arabic, let alone was able to speak it fluently.

When we resumed the drive, Jose calmed down and explained that the men had deliberately given Dick the wrong directions and were joking to each other about misdirecting the "foreign" college kids. Jose went on to say that he in fact was fluent in Arabic but asked us not to tell anyone. He said he seldom spoke the language and preferred that people believe he did not speak any Arabic at all. He found this particularly useful when he and his mother were around people with whom they had business dealings. He said he found it very helpful to listen to what people said when they had no idea he could understand them. This carefree Mexican with a heavy almost musical accent was smart as a whip and deadly serious.

Chapter 97

Easter in the Holy Land

After midterm exams were finished, Bill and I went to Amman for spring break. Again, we went by "serveese." Again we went via Damascas, Syria, and again we negotiated one price in Beirut, and then had to renegotiate in Damascas for the ride on to Amman. Some things seemed never to change, but we were more experienced and up to the challenge; we held to the agreed price and all went well. Actually, the countryside we drove through at Christmas and had described as "god forsaken" was quite beautiful, the result of considerable moisture and warmer weather and perhaps a change of attitude on our part. The crops looked good; the hills were covered with green grass, resulting in lush looking pasture for the herds of sheep and goats.

When I first arrived in the Middle East, I was extremely conscious of all the differences and the strangeness. Things that seemed strange then, we now accepted as normal. I was seeing many things in a different and less critical light. I was undergoing a pleasant transition. I have since decided that it is often a mistake to lock onto first impressions when visiting a different country and culture.

Unfortunately, we are seldom able to spend extended time in places we visit. The opportunity I had to spend almost a full year in the Middle East was unique. The experience made me better able to appreciate the positive aspects of another culture and to avoid focusing on the differences from our own culture which are too often interpreted as negatives. In all of the travels I have been privileged to undertake since that wonderful year, I can truthfully say I have not had a bad experience; challenges and adventures yes, but never a bad experience. I have not undertaken a trip I would not repeat, if given the opportunity.

The Easter pageantry was beautiful, as much so as the Christmas pageantry in Damascas had been. Shortly after we arrived it was Palm Sunday and, as part of the Whitman party, we had been invited by Jordanian officials to watch the parade from the grounds of Russian Church of Mary Magdalena. This was a choice location. The parade passed within ten feet of us as it proceeded along its historic route of the Stations of the Cross from Bethany to the Church of the Holy Sepulcher in Jerusalem. The pageantry, color, dress, and emotion of the groups of people taking part in the multi-cultural and multi-religious procession were overpowering and are difficult to describe. Fortunately, I took many color photographs.

Many highlights of the Easter ceremonies occurred at the same locations we had visited at Christmastime. We attended the Holy Fire Service held in the Church of the Holy Sepulcher in Jerusalem. We arrived early because a huge crowd was expected. Long before the service, we were in the middle of a large throng of people jostling for a good position to watch the event. Mrs. Whitman was not feeling well and became tired of being pushed around and wanted to leave. Bill and I went with her to another location where she could rest, and then Bill and I returned to the church which now was absolutely packed.

The church was being renovated and there was a lot of internal scaffolding in the area adjacent to the main entrance. We noticed some people had climbed the scaffolding and we decided to do the same thing. It was either climb or we would miss the ceremony. As we started up several Jordanian soldiers motioned for us to come down. As there were others already positioned on the scaffolding we ignored them and continued our climb. Ultimately, we reached a great position from which to watch the ceremony.

 Unfortunately, as we made our climb we kicked an accumulation of dust onto some of the spectators standing below, but they seemed to tolerate the situation. When the ceremony began a large number of people representing different religions started marching in a circle, each holding a lighted candle or torch. There was much jostling among the participants and a fight broke out among some of them. They appeared to be religious figures intent on getting into a prime position in the processional. I took several pictures, but it was dark and required a time exposure which was very difficult since I was hanging on the scaffolding. I did not then and still do not fully understand the significance of the Holy Fire Service, but aside from that, the spectacle was exciting to watch.

During the Easter break, we also had the opportunity to drive down a precipitous road into the Jordan Valley and on to the city of Jericho, the Jordan River and the Dead Sea. On the way down to the Jordan Valley we stopped for a picnic at an area famous for its springs; the flowing water was believed to have healing powers. It was an area annually frequented by pilgrims seeking cures to a variety of ills and we were told the springs had been a favorite place for King Herod who had visited them frequently. We saw only a very few other people there, but we were told that within days, many thousands of pilgrims would arrive and camp in and around the springs. Near our picnic area we saw an old man who had been there for several weeks awaiting the pilgrimage. Esau talked with him and learned he had nothing to eat, and in fact was eating grass. When we were finished with our meal, we gave the man all of the food we had left over.

On the way back to Amman, we became engulfed by a huge swarm of migrating locusts about the size of a large hummingbird or half the size of an English sparrow. We stopped the car to watch them pass. At one point the flying locusts were so thick that the sun was obscured, and the buzzing noise made by the locusts was almost deafening. Mrs. Whitman, who was our trip "biblical scholar," was delighted that we had had this experience during our visit to the Holy Land and told us some of the Bible stories of the devastating locust infestations that occurred in biblical times.

Another highlight was a second trip to the small village of Madaba, the home of Esau and his wife, where we had enjoyed the memorable "mansaf" at Christmastime. We had a fine meal; this time there were no special parts of the sheep to be concerned with! The event was much lower key. Later we again went back to Madeba and spent the day with Esau's family and friends. We had hoped to go to Petra, an ancient city on the Red Sea, but weather and other complications made the trip to Petra impossible.

On another occasion, we returned for a picnic on the Mount of Olives on the outskirts of Jerusalem, located near the Garden of Gethsemane and the beautiful Church of All Nations. We also returned to the central part of Jerusalem to revisit the Dome of the Rock and other historical sites. The Dome of the Rock is one of the most revered sites for Muslims and was constructed to house a large rock that reputedly has the foot print of Allah. Again, all of the historic cities and sites are so relatively close together, Amman included, that it was quite easy for us to go back and forth a number of times.

One day Mr. and Mrs. Whitman gave us a tour of a marble quarry and a marble factory on the outskirts of Amman. Another day Mr. Whitman took us out in the country to visit a Point 4 water project which he had been involved in developing. The project consisted of a series of dikes arranged to maximize the spread of natural rainfall. We arrived shortly after a heavy downpour and could see how the dikes directed the water to provide coverage of large tracts of land producing the lush grasses twelve to eighteen inches high.

Mr. Whitman explained that rainfall was the only moisture in this area. The plant growth was strictly native plants and grasses. The seed was naturally in the soil and only needed water and sunshine to sprout and grow. The project was impressive. The construction of simple dikes and nothing else resulted in a thirty-fold increase in plant food production. This particular project had been visited by Jordanian King Hussein. On that occasion, Mr. Whitman had had his picture taken with the King.

On the way back to Amman, we saw King Hussein's entourage traveling the palace complex. His official coronation would occur in Amman on May 2, 1953. Coronation decorations had been put up all over Jordan and the coronation was to be a yearlong celebration. Mr. and Mrs. Whitman had been invited to attend the ceremony at the King's palace. Mr. Whitman was confident he could obtain an invitation for Bill and me; however, we knew it would be impossible for us to arrange to attend.

King Hussein, known as the "Boy King," was sixteen years old when his grandfather, King Abdullah, was assassinated in 1951. At the time, he and his grandfather were in a mosque in Jerusalem where they regularly attended prayers on Friday. The young Hussein narrowly escaped assassination himself. Reputedly, he was saved by a large medal he wore which was given to him by his grandfather.

At the time of the assassination, young Hussein was attending the Royal Military Academy Sandhurst in England. King Abdullah's son, Talal, became king in the fall of 1951. King Talal served for about one year at which time his son, Hussein, was proclaimed King of the Hashemite Kingdom of Jordan. A regency Council was appointed to assist and guide the young King until May 2, 1953, his eighteenth birthday and the date of his official coronation. King Hussein served as king until his death from cancer in 1999. He was a remarkable leader and is considered the founder of modern Jordan.

Bill and I, by this time, had seen thousands of camels during our travels in the Middle East. During the drive from the Point 4 irrigation project back to Amman, we saw a man plowing his field with a camel hitched to a crude wooden plow. We stopped to see if the man would allow us to take a picture and he consented. I don't know if he was prompted by Esau or not; however, the plowman asked if Bill or I would like to sit on the camel and have our picture taken. We took turns, our first time atop a camel. We didn't ride the camel; we simply sat on the camel's back while he was still hitched to the plow! All, including the plowman, were amused.

We had a great time during the Easter break. Mr. and Mrs. Whitman were always glad to see us and always went out of their way to help us get the most out of our time there. We also found time to get extra sleep, which we needed, and to play a lot of bridge. Bill and I and his parents were a very compatible bridge foursome. They also included us in events for which they had received invitations. One of our last nights in Amman we attended an Easter party for Americans which was hosted by the US Ambassador and his wife. We didn't always have the right clothes for such events, but no one seemed to mind if we were more casual than some of the others in attendance.

Finally, the Easter vacation was over and we returned to Beirut. The ten-hour ride was tiring, but we thoroughly enjoyed the ride and the scenery. We talked about how content and comfortable we were, contrasting that with some of our first impressions when we had arrived the previous September. The weather had been good in Jordan; it was also nice and warm, although more humid, in Beirut. On the way from Damascas as we drove through the Bekaa Valley from the top of the pass to the sea level of Beirut, the change in the vegetation was remarkable. The country side was filled with growing crops, fruit orchards, olive groves, flowers, shrubs and fields of banana trees; pretty much in that order, all very colorful and aromatic.

Chapter 98

Meeting the Lebsocks

We were soon back in the routine of our classes and time flew by. Several of us organized a beach party, the first during our stay in Beirut, but not the last. About 30 young folks attended and we had a great time. The weather was warm, the water was a comfortable temperature, and the sandy beaches were clean. There was a Community School adjacent to the University. The school was a boarding school for young Americans whose parents were living and working principally in Saudi Arabia, but also in other parts of the Middle East.

Schooling for young Americans up to high school age was provided in Saudi Arabia by American companies, principally the Arab American Company (ARAMCO). Saudi Arabia was believed to have the largest oil reserves in the world and these companies were responsible for building and maintaining facilities for pumping, transporting by pipeline, refining, and shipping oil. A large number of American citizens were involved in the operations and many had moved their families to Saudi Arabia. Since no high schools for Americans existed in Saudi Arabia, those who finished the eighth grade went elsewhere. Many went to the Community School in Beirut, some to schools in Europe, and some went back to the United States.

The Community School in Beirut had an organized sports program. In the spring, an informal group of American students at AUB started playing soft ball. We occasionally played and usually lost to the Community School softball team. We also occasionally played and lost to a team composed of American Airways employees and AUB faculty members. I probably wasn't much help to the team, but we had fun and needed the exercise. Community School students were occasionally invited to our beach parties. Bill and I became acquainted with two of the Community School students: Donna Lebsock and Joan Hubbard. Joan's parents lived in Saudi Arabia and she boarded at the Community School.

Donna was from Colorado, the daughter of Harry and Hazel Lebsock. Mr. Lebsock had taken a job with a railroad operating in Saudi Arabia. After working enough time to be eligible for family housing, Harry brought his wife Hazel, daughter Donna, and son Kenneth to Saudi Arabia. Later he accepted employment with ARAMCO. His new employer required that he be employed a specified length of time before he was again eligible for family housing. Rather than return to Colorado, Hazel, Donna, and Kenneth moved into an apartment in Beirut, not far from the Community School and AUB. The year we met, Donna was a high school senior and Kenneth was in the seventh or eighth grade.

One of the American AUB students had told us about Hazel Lebsock, an American lady who had a nice apartment close to the AUB campus and was always delighted to have visitors. Bill and I started dropping in occasionally. Hazel loved to talk with us and others, frequently served snacks and always had cold beer on hand. Stopping by her apartment was a treat for us and provided a break from our routine. Whether I first met Donna at a soft ball game, a beach party or at her Mother's apartment, I can't be sure, as they all happened in about the same time frame. Soon we began to see each other more often. We were both serious students though, were concerned about grades, and had limited time for social activities.

One day I went swimming just off the University beach with a fellow student. We had borrowed homemade snorkeling gear so we could float. The water in this area always contained an interesting variety of tropical fish and an occasional small octopus. An octopus has a sharp parrot-like beak on the underside of its body and is capable of inflicting a nasty bite if you are not careful. We decided to try to catch one. The water was six to eight feet deep. Usually, by the time we dove down the octopus would have scurried into its hole. Finally, I was able to grab one without being bitten and I swam to shore. It was not large; the legs were ten to twelve inches long. I killed it with a rock as I had done at home with trout.

We had heard that octopuses were edible, so my friend and I went to Hazel Lebsock's apartment to see how we should proceed. Hazel didn't have any idea what to do. We cleaned it and removed skin as best we could in Hazel's kitchen sink. The octopus looked very tough and we attempted to tenderize it by pounding its legs with the edge of a heavy plate. After a while we fried the legs in a frying pan. It smelled good and actually didn't taste bad, although the meat was tough. We ate it all and were proud of the accomplishment. I have had fun over the years telling the story of catching an octopus with my bare hands and killing and eating it. I try to avoid disclosing its actual size.

Chapter 99

Travel Complications

During this time, I was looking at options for my return to the United States. Bill and I were hoping to spend the summer traveling in Europe, Also, I wanted to see Uncle Glen Wahlquist in Iran before I left the Middle East. I ran into problems with both.

Mother wrote to tell me that through some kind of a mix-up, I had received a draft board notice to report for a physical. Before I left Idaho, the draft board had assured me I would be deferred for the school year so long as I was a fulltime student receiving satisfactory grades. After much confusion, Mother wrote that I could postpone my physical until sometime in the summer; however, the exact date was not made clear.

Obviously, if I had to be back before fall, our travel time would have to be cut short. To complicate it further, travel during the summer, by plane or ship would be more expensive than after the tourist season. The coronation of England's Queen Elizabeth II occurred in 1953, the "Year of the Coronation," and resulted in increased travel between the US and the British Isles.

I checked with the military attaché at the US embassy and was advised that I might, with draft board approval, be able to take my physical at a military installation in one of the European countries. So many things up in the air made planning difficult. Finally, I decided to assume the best and, at least for the time being, I made tentative plans to return home in early fall and risk the consequences. I figured that the worst that could happen was that I would be ordered to take my physical immediately and be drafted.

I attempted to get a visa to allow me to travel to Teheran, Iran, to visit my Uncle Glen Wahlquist and his family, but there was a great deal of turmoil in Iran at this time. In 1951 the Iranian Parliament had voted to nationalize its oil industry. Under some pressure the Shah appointed a long time popular political figure, Dr. Mosaddegh, as Prime Minister. The new prime minister had considerable support among the Iranian people and had been the prime mover for nationalizing the oil industry. In 1952 Dr. Mosaddeg pressed for control of the Iranian armed forces and when the Shah refused his demand, Mosaddegh resigned. Immediately mass demonstrations took place in support of Dr. Mosaddegh followed by a period of countrywide rioting, and the Shah reluctantly reinstated Dr. Mosaddegh as Prime Minister.

Later, in the summer of 1953, Dr. Mosaddegh was ousted as Prime Minister in a coup which we now know was orchestrated and financed by the Central Intelligence Agency of the United States government. This coup was the first of several which the CIA undertook over the next several decades. This was at the height of the Cold War and the coup was in large part motivated by the mistaken belief on the part of the United States government that Dr. Mosaddegh and his supporters were controlled by the Communist Party of the USSR. President Eisenhower authorized the covert action after he was briefed by John Foster Dulles, the head of the CIA. Fear that the Communist Party and the USSR would control Iranian oil had much to do with the decision. Oil is still a major factor in US foreign policy in the Middle East. Little wonder that our Iranian student friends attending the American University of Beirut in 1952-53 had not wished to engage in political discussions!

So the process for obtaining an Iranian visa was very complicated and I was told it would take "several weeks" before I would know if the visa would be issued. There was a lot of anti-American sentiment there, but Uncle Glen was encouraging me to make the trip and for that reason, I felt confident the trip would be safe to take. However, I needed a visa. By contrast, we were able to obtain visas for travel to Syria, Turkey, Greece and Yugoslavia with little difficulty. We had been told that our US passports would be all that we would need in Western Europe.

I heard of several Point 4 officials who were planning to travel to Teheran about the same time; and also, that several of the Iranian students I had stayed with would also be returning to Iran after the semester ended. I made an effort, without success, to see if I could travel with either group. Bill planned to spend several days with his folks in Amman at the end of the school year before we left for Europe, and that was to be the window for my trip to Iran. Flying would be the easiest way, given the time constraints; however, I soon discovered that the cost of a round trip airline ticket from Beirut to Teheran would be quite expensive. It began more and more to appear that the trip to Teheran would not be possible.

A British member of the faculty at AUB owned a Model A Ford which he offered to sell to Bill and me for a reasonable price. He suggested we drive from Beirut to Western Europe. He was confident we could then sell the vehicle at a profit to an American serviceman. We became quite excited at the prospects until we learned about how bad many of the roads would be and how difficult it would be for us to find places to purchase gasoline or obtain any necessary repairs. We also recognized how limited our language and mechanical skills were. We wisely declined the offer. At one time, Mr. and Mrs. Whitman were considering the idea of driving a car, with the help of Esau, and taking us as far as Istanbul, Turkey, as part of a Point 4 inspection trip; however, the plan did not materialize.

We continued to be reminded of the deep resentment in the region of the policies of the United States. Late in the spring, US Secretary of State John Foster Dulles made a visit to the Middle East, including a stop in Beirut. The day Secretary Dulles and his party arrived in Beirut there was a large protest demonstration. The march started near the University and consisted mostly of students. As the protest demonstration proceeded through the city however, many others joined and when it arrived in downtown Beirut there was violence which resulted in some demonstrators being injured. Some were arrested. The protest march was not as violent as later reported in the US press, however it was a major protest. I was somewhat puzzled at the anti-American sentiment that was expressed; also by the fact that Dulles and his party were harshly criticized in both the Arab and Jewish presses.

The next day we received word that his motorcade would visit the AUB campus and we went out to watch. They drove in the main gate to the campus, moving fairly fast, made a loop through the campus, then drove out the same gate after no more than three minutes in all. Dulles was accompanied by perennial presidential candidate and former governor of Minnesota, Harold Stassen. I am not sure in what capacity Mr. Stassen was included in the group. I attempted to take a picture of Secretary Dulles, but due to the speed of his car, the picture was blurry and he was unrecognizable. We were reminded of the deep resentment in the region of the policies of the United States.

Chapter 100

The Kit Kat Club and an Overdue Debt

One night, Dick Shaheen took several of us downtown to visit the Kit Kat Club. The club consisted of a several-story-high building in an upscale part of Beirut. The building included several casinos, bars and restaurants and I am not sure what else. The complex was owned and operated by a wealthy Lebanese businessman we knew only as "Rajah." Dick had become acquainted with Rajah on a flight to Beirut a couple of years before and struck up a friendship that led to invitations to the Kit Kat Club. Rajah had a large international as well as a Lebanese clientele and ran a very successful enterprise. Dick Shaheen had heard rumors that he was gay although we never had any indication that it was true. He did like Americans to visit his place of business. I am inclined to think he was somewhat like the operator of Uncle Sam's, in that he thought having young Americans on the premises was good for his business.

The great thing about Rajah and his club was the fact that he would never let us pay for anything we ate or drank. When we showed up, he would welcome us and tell the hostess to give us anything we wanted. Not once did we ever pay anything. One time, when one in our party had a birthday Rajah sent one of his employees out to buy a birthday cake at midnight. To our amazement, the employee returned in half an hour with a large decorated birthday cake which we quickly consumed.

The last time I went to the Kit Kat Club was just before leaving Beirut. My friend from Montana, Dick Engan, and I were bored one night and to escape the heat, we went down to the air-conditioned Kit Kat Club. Bill was in Amman visiting his folks. School was over for many students and most of our other close friends had scattered. Dick Engan and I sat down and ordered appetizers and drinks. We waited for Rajah to appear and give his usual instruction to the hostess. Rajah never appeared. We continued to order and late in the evening we inquired of Rajah's whereabouts and we were told he was out of town on business for a few days. We didn't know what to do.

Ultimately, we were presented with a bill. Unfortunately, the total bill we owed far exceeded the Lebanese money we had between us. We decided we had no alternative other than attempt to leave without settling the bill. Each of us went separately to the bathroom on our floor, stayed a short time and then went down the stairway several flights to street level, exited the building and hurried down the street, fearful that someone would come running after us. I still feel guilty about the incident, although I am comforted somewhat by the fact that the owner was very wealthy and would have covered the bill had he been at the club.

I carefully watched the television coverage of the civil war that raged in Lebanon in the late 1980's and early 1990's and I am convinced that the Kit Kat Club and surrounding luxury hotels were destroyed. Someday I would like to go back and see if Rajah is alive, and if the Kit Kat Club has been rebuilt. If it has, I would happily settle the long-overdue debt.

Chapter 101

Pinned!

Donna and I were seeing more of each other. One weekend we went with another American couple we knew to the mountains on the way to Damascus to have lunch and spend the afternoon. The area we visited was a popular and very beautiful place for principally Lebanese people to visit in spring and summer to escape the heat of Beirut and the coastal areas of Lebanon. A number of nice-looking resorts and restaurants accommodated the people who came to the area, mostly the well-to-do. We had a nice lunch and walked around and then returned to Beirut. About this time I gave Donna my Sigma Chi pin which reflected our growing attraction for each other.

Donna was planning to attend Colorado Women's College in Boulder, Colorado in the fall of 1953. I hoped to connect with Orval when I arrived in the United States and ride with him to Idaho. Donna wanted to spend time with her family in Saudi Arabia during the summer and then to fly back to the States. I had mentioned the possibility of coordinating our plans to return to the United States so that Donna could ride back with Orval and me as far as Boulder. At the time, however, none of us, myself, Orval or Donna had made firm travel plans.

Donna's father, Harry, came to Beirut for Donna's graduation. Harry was a down to earth fellow with whom I felt comfortable. Harry and Hazel took Donna and me out to dinner in one of the nicer places in downtown Beirut. I believe it was the St. George Hotel. I remember I ordered frogs legs for the first time in my life, and also the last. The frog legs actually tasted pretty good as long as I didn't think about the fact that they were legs that had actually been removed from frogs!

Chapter 102

Bearing the Brunt of American Foreign Policy

Bill finished his exams and left for Amman. I also finished and was in the process of packing for our summer travels. When the final grades were posted, I was pleased with everything except the college math grade. The posted sheet showed me receiving a D which I knew was a mistake. College math was a four-credit course and one of the required courses back at the U of I. The grade would transfer, however it would hurt my grade point average and I was determined to have it corrected.

I had not found the course too difficult and I was quite certain I had received top grades on all of the exams given during the semester. I went to the professor's office. He was elsewhere, so I made an appointment through his secretary to see him. The professor did not show up for the appointment. I made another, and still I did not manage to find him. I tried several times and left notes and phone messages, all without success.

I need to provide some background. I was the only American in the math class which started at 7:30 AM on four days each week of the semester. My routine was to stop on my way to class for a cup of coffee and buy a daily newspaper printed in English, *The Beirut Daily Star*. I always sat in the back row. At the beginning of the first class, the professor came back to my desk, picked up the newspaper, and, in a raised voice, began speaking critically of the United States foreign policy with respect to Israel. He asked me several questions about my background and views. I could tell he was an angry man. Thereafter, at the beginning of each class, he would often make strong statements critical of the US as related to Israel, with emphasis on a variety of ongoing events in the Middle East and around the world. Sometimes he would borrow my newspaper, then key off on some headline or reported wire-service account of events. The Arab-Israeli conflict was the major news at the time and anti-American feelings ran high.

I learned that he was Palestinian from a well-educated and prominent family. He had been a professor at a college in Palestine; I believe his father had been a practicing physician. In1948, following passage of the United Nations resolution authorizing creation of the State of Israel, which was strongly supported by the United States, war broke out. As a result of the conflict additional territory beyond the scope of the UN resolution was seized by the Israeli military. The professor and all of the members of his family were forced from the homes they had occupied for generations; some family members were killed. He and members of his family who survived were the "lucky ones." They were able to relocate and find employment rather than be held in the "temporary" refugee tent camps.

The creation of the State of Israel was never intended to preclude the Palestinians from remaining. In 1953 the refugees were still waiting for the United Nations to demand that they be allowed to return to the areas from which they had fled. They are still waiting, decades later, for some just and fair resolution.

By the spring of 1953, I had become much more knowledgeable about the recent history of the Middle East and Israel than I had been when I first arrived in Beirut. I felt real sympathy for the professor whom I had found to be a fine teacher and a quality person; I respected him a great deal. Early in the semester, however, I learned to avoid any comments or responses to the professor's frequent commentaries. I tried to be almost invisible; in fact, we had almost no interaction during class. I studied hard and kept a low profile; and while I didn't keep any of the old tests, I am certain that I had done well. I believe the final exam grade counted for one third of the semester grade and I was confident I had done well on it as well. Frankly, I was expecting an A for my semester grade.

Bill was back from Amman and we were making final plans to leave Beirut. I was concerned that I would find it difficult if not impossible to straighten out the grade by correspondence when I had returned home. On my next to last day at AUB, I spotted the professor walking in the other direction at some distance across campus. I took off running to catch up with him. He turned around and faced me. I said I had been trying to reach him for several days, that there had been a mistake on my final grade in his class. He appeared to be enraged, and looking me straight in the eye said, "There was no mistake." Then he turned and I watched him walk away.

He was so full of rage at the United States that he could not hold it back. Being the only American in his class, I was the only person on whom he could express his rage. I don't think he could help himself. I believe this event exemplifies the depth of the anti-American sentiment that existed then and still exists, to a large degree, today. During my year in the Middle East I was spit upon by a fellow student during a demonstration, hit in the head by a small rock thrown at me when I was leaving a movie theater in downtown Beirut, and insulted many times.

The United States, the most powerful nation in the world and beacon of democracy, is widely believed to have failed in its responsibility to the Palestinian people. The pressure for a Jewish settlement following the Holocaust, leading up to and during World War II, created an emotional tide of support that could not be denied. Sadly, the tragic consequences to the Palestinian people have never been properly addressed.

Chapter 103

The Final Trek Begins

Bill and I had finalized our plans, at least in a general way. In early July, 1953 we planned to catch a second-class train from Beirut to Istanbul by way of Aleppo, Syria. Once in Istanbul, we hoped to stay at Roberts College which, like AUB, was administered by Americans. The dorms would be empty and we would most likely be allowed to stay there without charge. From Istanbul, we would figure out how to make our way to western Europe, hopefully, taking some time in Greece. Once in Europe, we intended to see as much as possible as we worked our way to London. I had reserved a one-way airline ticket from Shannon, on the west coast of Ireland, to Boston; Bill had a one-way ticket to Beirut from London a few days previous, in early September.

Donna planned to fly to London a day or two before Bill departed for Beirut. Then she and I would make our way to Shannon and fly to Boston where Orval planned to meet us for the trip west to Colorado and Idaho. That was the extent of our planning. We had concluded that any more detailed planning while we were in Beirut was not practical. We were also convinced that we could make the necessary arrangements for less money, as usual, by "winging it." We each had only a single bag because we intended to carry our luggage rather than entrust it to others. We were excited and full of confidence in our ability to meet any challenge we might face.

Based on advice we had received at the US Embassy in Beirut, Bill and I told our families to send letters to American Express offices in the major cities of Europe where we would likely be stopping. We, in turn, promised to write frequently to keep them advised of our whereabouts and the direction we were heading. We found that American Express was a great place to stop not only for mail, but to exchange dollars into local currency and to meet and exchange travel tips with other Americans.

Finally, in early July we made our way to the Beirut railroad station which we had not previously seen. We were not encouraged by what we saw. For $25 we each purchased a second-class ticket for the four-day trip to Istanbul. Actually, the first leg of the trip, to Aleppo, turned out to be third-class. The ticket agent spoke very little English and was surprised that Americans were buying such cheap tickets. He thought we would prefer something else, but we insisted.

When the train arrived, we boarded and realized why he had been surprised. It was a very old train and the cars were crowded with people, cargo, and several live sheep and goats. Smoke billowed from the engine and we discovered that most of the windows could not be closed which was just as well because the July heat was intense. All of the other passengers were local and appeared to be poor. The sounds and smells were quite interesting. Our fellow passengers seemed surprised and rather amused that Bill and I, who were clearly Americans, were on the train.

This part of the trip was neither comfortable nor relaxing. The train was slow, dirty and crowded, with many stops and a lot of people getting on and off. We had been warned about thievery and so stayed alert and held onto our luggage. We had left Beirut in the morning and arrived in Aleppo, Syria, that evening. We found a place to stay for the night and had something to eat.

In the morning, we walked around the city, took pictures and visited several ruins dating back to the Crusades. At noon, we caught the train for Istanbul, via Ankara, the capital of Turkey. It would take us about one and a half days to reach Ankara; from there, we were scheduled to continue, on the same train, to Istanbul without stopping.

The next train was an improvement. A small second-class Middle East train, it represented an upgrade from our first day of travel. The windows would open and close and the passenger cars were roomier and less crowded. A few of the passengers spoke some English. We soon became acquainted with a fellow from England who was also traveling to Istanbul. He was pleasant to talk with and provided us with a great deal of helpful information. The train was slow, the weather pleasant, and the scenery interesting. We began to relax and enjoy ourselves. Then two events occurred that jarred our composure a bit.

We had crossed the border from Syria into southern Turkey. I was sitting in a window seat with the window open, enjoying the ride, when all of a sudden, the slow-moving train started shaking and bouncing. I looked out the window and saw that something had been caught and was rolling under the train. When the train came to a stop, a cow was under it, its head sticking out over the rail on my side of the passenger car. A group of farmers working in the field a short distance away were shouting and running toward the train. They began to pull the cow out from under the train. I fully expected that the animal would be removed in bloody pieces.

Ultimately, the cow was removed and in a few moments it stood up and bawled loudly. I couldn't believe what I was seeing. I still have trouble understanding how the train stayed on the tracks and, even more, how the animal survived. I took several pictures of the cow half under the train and, later, standing near the train. We remained stopped for perhaps twenty minutes. When we left, the cow was being led away and did not appear to have any broken bones or to be bleeding anywhere.

Later during the same day Bill and I were enjoying the scenery and occasionally taking pictures from the train as we proceeded through southern Turkey. We rarely saw people or anything except what appeared to be open grazing land; occasionally there were crops. Our British friend, who was fluent in Arabic, came to us and said he had overheard a couple of the train crew talking about the fact that Bill and I were taking pictures while the train was passing through a military reservation. We had seen nothing to indicate anything military; however, at his suggestion, we stopped taking pictures and put the matter out of our minds. Later on, about an hour out of Ankara, our British friend said that the train officials had sent a radio message to the train station in Ankara, that Turkish officials were going to meet the train, and that Bill and I would be taken off the train for questioning.

The whole thing seemed a bit silly and we were sure nothing would come of it; perhaps at most our film would be taken from us. Our primary concern was that we were to take this train all the way to Istanbul. Depending on how long we stopped in Ankara, we might not be able to continue on that day. But our friend seemed worried about what might happen to us. We had been told at the US Embassy in Beirut, to avoid trouble whenever possible, but particularly in Turkey. We had heard horror stories about individuals who had been arrested in Turkey and held for extended periods of time without even being able to communicate with embassy officials or family. Turkey was the one place we were really cautioned about.

Ankara was a major railroad hub. As the train slowed down and approached the railroad station, we saw a number of trains in the station and large crowds of people on either side of the tracks our train was on. Obviously, they were there to meet passengers on approaching trains or to climb on board one of the departing trains. When the train came to a stop our British friend said, "Here they come." We looked out the window and saw thirty to forty uniformed soldiers wearing silver helmets and carrying weapons rushing in a tight formation toward our passenger car. They were forcing their way through the crowd and only about 50 feet away. We knew we were in serious trouble and without hesitation we each grabbed our bag, ran to the door on the opposite side of the train, and jumped out. Our friend shouted, "Good luck."

We worked our way through the crowd on that side and, moving as fast as we possibly could without running hard and calling attention to ourselves, we left the railroad station and hurried down a side street. We fully expected someone to shout for us to stop, and if they had we would have had no choice but to stop. It would have been futile to try to get away. By now we were really frightened.

Some distance away, we noticed a wide boulevard which went from the railroad station downhill to the center of Ankara. Although we had no map of the large capital city, the direction to go was obvious. We avoided the boulevard and crisscrossed several side streets as we made our way downtown. Once downtown, we found a cheap place to stay and to have a bite to eat. We began to relax and even did some sightseeing. Many of the buildings in Ankara were modern. Unlike most cities we had visited in the Middle East, the city had wide streets, an abundance of trees, and many parks. We decided Ankara would be an interesting place to visit, but we needed to keep moving.

The next morning we walked back to the railroad station to continue on to Istanbul. We were told that our tickets were only valid for a train which came through Ankara once a week. We asked if we could use the ticket on any other train to Istanbul and were told that we could not. This sounded unreasonable, as there had to be several trains that ran between the two largest cities in Turkey, but the agent in the station was adamant. To get to Istanbul, we would have had to purchase a new ticket at what seemed to us an exorbitant price, without any credit for the tickets we had.

We were totally frustrated and started walking around while we decided what to do. We thought maybe a different ticket agent would be more accommodating. At the same time, we did not want to call attention to ourselves in case the authorities might still be looking for us. A modern train bound for Istanbul was in the station with its engine running, obviously about to depart. We started walking along the side of the train and on impulse one of us flipped the door handle and the door opened. Without any discussion, we jumped on the train.

Once inside the passenger car, we saw a restroom which we entered and locked the door from the inside. I still find it hard to believe what we did and even harder to believe we thought we could get away with it, but we were desperate and acted strictly on impulse. We talked about trying to find empty seats after the train started. Maybe we thought we could simply apologize,

Obviously, what we did was dumb. I didn't tell Mother about the incident until sometime after I was home in Idaho.

In a few minutes the train, which was much fancier than we had been traveling on, started moving and picked up speed as it left the outskirts of Ankara. Soon someone, probably a passenger, tried to open the restroom door. We ignored the effort as we tried to figure out what to do. Suddenly there was loud knocking and an angry voice on the other side of the door. We unlocked the door and stepped out. The conductor asked for our tickets. I'm sure he knew before looking at our tickets that we were not authorized to be on this train. To make matters worse we were in a first-class car filled with well-dressed passengers and we stood out like sore thumbs.

The conductor spoke enough English to make it clear that he was going to have the train stopped and have us ejected. I remember looking out the window and by now the train was in a very desolate looking area of Turkey and many miles from Ankara. We were told to take a seat in the club car while the conductor left temporarily to check passenger's tickets and tend to his duties. Once again, we were scared to death. A well-dressed Turkish gentleman who appeared to be a businessman motioned us over. He spoke fluent English and asked us several questions about who we were, what we were doing in Ankara and where we were going. We answered all his questions at length. He said he lived in Istanbul, was traveling on business and regularly took this train.

He was very friendly, interested in the fact that we were American students who had spent a year attending the American University of Beirut with which he was familiar and that we were planning to spend the summer traveling in Europe. He seemed mildly amused about the whole incident. Soon the conductor returned to deal with us, and our new acquaintance started talking to him in Arabic. They talked at length and seemed to argue, and then both of them appeared to calm down. The conductor left again, apparently to tend to his duties. He returned a short while later and further conversation followed. Finally the conductor shrugged his shoulders and left. Our new acquaintance said we would be allowed to remain in the club car for the remainder of the trip to Istanbul.

We were relieved that we would not be thrown off the train. The conductor obviously did not like Bill and me, but he seemed to be acquainted with the gentleman who interceded on our behalf. The conductor by this time had our second-class tickets and we were not asked for any additional money. Our friend bought us a coke and went back to reading his newspaper. The scenery was mountainous and very beautiful as we came closer to Istanbul. Because this train was much faster than our second-class train, we were almost back on schedule. Our new friend wished us well as we left the train at the station in Istanbul.

It was getting dark when we arrived in Istanbul. We had brought maps and had directions to Roberts College. From the railroad station, we caught a ferry and crossed the Bosporus to the European side of Istanbul. When we landed, we took a streetcar north along the Bosporus; after a long ride, almost an hour in length, we reached the campus of Roberts College. It was late and we encountered a student who took us into a dormitory and showed us an empty room where we could stay the night

Roberts College was small compared to the American University of Beirut, with fewer modern buildings. We stayed at the college for four nights free of charge and spent three and one-half busy days touring the city and outlying areas. Our stay in Istanbul was one of the highlights of our trip. We were not spending time in jail nor walking along the railroad tracks in search of a place to stay. Life was looking up!

Chapter 104

Touring Istanbul

During the previous school year at AUB, Bill and I had taken courses in ancient history and also modern history of the Middle East. Both courses were taught by excellent professors. The ancient history was taught by a Turkish gentleman, Dr. Fuad Fuad, who was regarded at the time as one of the outstanding authorities in the world on the subject. The course was difficult, mainly because the history of the region is very complex and covers a span of thousands of years. What is now Istanbul had been a major settlement of the Phoenicians and later of the Greeks. It was also the capital of the Roman Empire in the third century AD and later the capital of the Byzantine Empire. For over seven centuries it was the capital of the Ottoman Empire and became known as Constantinople.

When Turkey became a Republic in the early 1920s through the efforts of Attaturk, widely known as the father of modern Turkey, the Ottoman Empire was overthrown. Constantinople became Istanbul, and the capital of Turkey was officially moved to Ankara. Other religions and cultures, including the Jewish faith, have been introduced and have left an imprint on the area. Before we started our summer trip, we had told Dr. Fuad about our summer travel plans and he gave us several suggestions on what to see and do in Turkey. Marlys Whitman had also given us suggestions. When we arrived, we had a good idea of the places we most wanted to see.. We hit the ground running.

Istanbul is a beautiful city built on seven small hills much like Rome, Italy. Because of its diverse history, Istanbul is filled with a variety of mosques, churches, synagogues, palaces and museums. The ancient structures and ruins span thousands of years of civilization. Each day we would take the long tram ride from Roberts College to the central part of the city. This actually gave us time to check our maps and guide books and become better oriented for sightseeing. We visited the famous Sultan Mosque (also known as the Blue Mosque) which was built by the Ottoman Empire conqueror and leader,

Suleiman the Great. We visited the St. Sophia Cathedral constructed under the orders of Justinian in the fifth century. There were many others, too numerous to mention.

We spent several hours in the famous Grand Bazaar, reputedly the largest covered bazaar or retail marketing complex in the world. The Grand Bazaar was spread over a vast area and contained row after row of shops and stalls offering for sale almost anything you could possibly imagine. We could have spent days and not seen it all. Late one afternoon we took a ferry up the Bosporus to the Black Sea, stopped for dinner, and caught another ferry back to Roberts College. The trip took a little over five hours.

Another time we went south of the city to see parts that remained of the original Wall of Constantinople, a major fortification which surrounded the old city of Constantinople. It was actually several parallel walls; a complex hundreds of feet wide. We also prowled around the city itself searching for and often finding ancient structures noted in our guide books.

The contrast between the east or Asian side and the west or European side of Istanbul was dramatic. The west side was modern and western or European in style and flavor. The east side was much less so, and had an Asian and Middle Eastern style and flavor. Each night we were exhausted but exhilarated when we returned to Roberts College to sleep. Initially, we had wanted to go on to Athens from Istanbul and we began checking bus schedules. Someone at the college mentioned that it was inexpensive to travel by ship. We checked and found a small ship that was leaving the next day for Piraeus, located a few miles north of Athens and its main port.

Chapter 105

To Athens on the SS Adana

The next day we thanked the people at the college who had been so hospitable, and we took a tram to the port where our ship, the SS Adana, was docked. We purchased our tickets for eleven dollars each and climbed on board. Our ship was small and had been in use for a long time. We were in a common area below deck which we shared with a number of other passengers, many of whom were about our age, but no other Americans. We settled into a spot; then we noticed that the other passengers had brought food on board.

We soon learned that no food was available on the ship. I watched our luggage and Bill ran off the ship and down the dock to buy a couple of loaves of Turkish bread, some cheese, cucumbers and fruit. He ran back and was on board in what seemed like barely minutes before the ship pulled away from the dock. I had been mentally trying to imagine what to do if it looked as if Bill would not get back in time and had decided I would jump off with both duffle bags to make certain we stayed together. We began to visit with the other young passengers who had watched Bill's frantic effort to get food. Everyone was friendly. We shared food with several others which helped to give us more variety at mealtimes. Another minor crisis had been overcome. After we ate, we found a spot to settle in for the night; actually, were able to get some sleep.

The next day we arrived at Izmir, Turkey, where we stayed for about six hours. We did some sightseeing, but we always stayed within sight and sound of the ship. The next day we reached Piraeus and made our way to the city of Athens where we located a place to stay and to eat. We always made sure we had a bed for the night before worrying about eating. Food was much easier to find.

We stayed in Athens for two days. The main attraction, of course, was the Acropolis, a large rock outcropping about 500 feet in height above modern Athens. From where we stayed, we could see the Acropolis and the next morning we took the short walk to the base and climbed to the top. On top of the Acropolis are the ruins off the Parthenon which was constructed in about 500

BC. Enough of the structure remained to provide a clear idea of what the completed structure looked like. This was also true of the remains of the Temple of Athena, constructed at about the same time. The Acropolis was the site of the capital and seat of government of ancient Greece. The top surface of the Acropolis was covered with ruins of what had been a variety of government buildings of that time. It was a thrill for us to actually be there and to imagine what life must have been like when the structures were in use by the Greeks. We visited other sites, but the Acropolis was our favorite. We were so fascinated that on our last day in Athens we again climbed the Acropolis and explored the ruins.

While in Athens, we began running into American servicemen, mostly young men about our age. It seemed good to interact with them and we had some great conversations. They expressed interest in what Bill and I had been doing in the Middle East and our travels since leaving Beirut. Through some of these servicemen, we were introduced to the US Military Post Exchange in Athens. For the first time in nearly a year, we went into a place that seemed like a stateside café and department store. We had our first "real" hamburger and milk shake since leaving the US. They tasted great! Everything in the PX was inexpensive, subsidized by the US government. We decided to keep our eyes open for military exchanges through the rest of our travels.

We needed to keep moving to meet our loose travel timetable, so we checked alternative transportation for traveling on to Europe. We needed to go north through Greece and the entire length of what was then known as Yugoslavia, to Trieste, Italy. The terrain north of Athens was rugged and mountainous with uncertain weather conditions, extremely poor roads and high passes. There had been reports of robberies and violence against travelers. That was enough information for us and given our time constraints, we bought the cheapest train ticket available.

Chapter 106

Through Yugoslavia on the Orient Express

The train we caught the next day was a portion of the train known as the Orient Express. Having read about the train and seen the spy movie "The Orient Express," we were delighted. As an added bonus, our tickets allowed us the option to stop along the way if we chose. The train, at least our section, was not fancy at all, but it was adequate. A few of our fellow passengers spoke English, and one was a former officer in the British army who had served in this region during World War II. He seemed to enjoy visiting with us and provided us with information about the area we were traveling through. He told us a few war stories as well. In the same car we met a German who had served in the German army during the Second World War. He was less talkative and the two former soldiers did not converse with each other at all.

The terrain in northern Greece was indeed rugged. After we crossed the border into Yugoslavia, the landscape changed from rugged mountains to much flatter terrain. From the train window, we began to see farms, growing crops, land for grazing, and people. From the quality of the crops, it was apparent that the land was fertile and productive. Grain and hay were being harvested. I found it interesting that the cut grain was tied into bundles which were put into shocks for drying, much as had been done when I was a small boy on the Airport Farm.

Food was available on the Orient Express, but to hold down expenses, we brought food with us and we were able buy to food at brief stops along the way. Making and altering plans as we went along was fun and added to the adventure of the trip. At the same time it was somewhat stressful and tiring not to know where we would stay, or when or how we would move on. This adventuresome spirit was what we had been doing and what we planned to do more of in Europe. In the meantime, though, it felt good to relax and rest up after the hectic pace of the previous ten days or so. To hold down expenses we planned to try hitchhiking once we arrived in western

Europe. Several of our friends in Beirut thought hitchhiking would be safe and practical and we were anxious to give it a try.

We left the train to spend a day and night in Belgrade, the capital of Yugoslavia. This was at the height of the Cold War and Yugoslavia was a Communist country. To stop there and look around would be an interesting adventure. The conductor assured us that after a one day stop we would be able to catch another train and proceed to Trieste.

Belgrade is one of the oldest cities in Europe and has a lot of Old World charm. After World War I, the Kingdom of Yugoslavia came into existence. The country suffered badly during the Second World War. In 1941, in an effort to stay out of the war, the king signed a pact with Germany and Italy which resulted in countrywide protests and violence and led to a military coup d'etat. The military leaders installed King Peter II who was under age and more of a puppet than ruler. In retaliation, Yugoslavia was heavily bombed and then invaded by Nazi Germany, Italy, and their allies in the Balkans. When the country was liberated by the partisans and the Soviet Army in 1944, partisan leader Marshall Tito became head of Yugoslavia and its Communist Party. In 1946 Marshall Tito proclaimed the country The Federation of the People's Republic of Yugoslavia.

Marshal Tito was a dictator who ruled the country with an iron hand. He was popular with the general population and well regarded by many in the West because he maintained a degree of independence from the Soviet leaders in Moscow. Although the country was a part of the Communist Soviet Bloc, Marshall Tito was able to chart a more independent course than other countries within the Soviet Bloc. The difficulty of Tito's task to rule the country and keep it intact became evident and better understood in recent years when civil war erupted in Yugoslavia and the country broke apart. The pieces of the former Yugoslavia, going south to north, include Serbia and Montenegro, Bosnia (location of Sarajevo, the site of Olympic winter games in recent years) and Herzegovina, Croatia, and Slovenia.

We had read about the Moscow Hotel in Belgrade and thought it would be an interesting place to stay. When we left the train, we walked to the hotel but discovered that rooms were expensive and so we took a couple of pictures and continued our search for a place to spend the night. We attracted the attention of a few people about our age who were very friendly and seemed to enjoy communicating with a couple of young Americans, a rare sight for them. In fact, during our time in the city, we didn't see any other Americans. Our new friends knew a few words of English; however, their pronunciation was difficult for us to understand.

During the previous year, we had discovered that much communication is possible without knowing a language, through facial expression and hand and shoulder movements. A hand on the stomach and a roll of the eyes says you are hungry; a hand to the side of the face coupled with a tilt of the head indicates you are tired and need a place to sleep and so on. With the help of our new friends, we found an inexpensive place to stay our one night in Belgrade. That night we found that our room was infested with bed bugs or fleas. Their bites were quite painful. Fortunately, we were able to shake out all of our clothing in the morning and avoided taking any away with us.

The next morning our new friends returned and said they wanted to take us somewhere. We couldn't understand what they were saying, much to their chagrin. It turned out they were saying "Donald Duck" and we followed them to a Communist Youth Building where we watched a few old Walt Disney cartoons. We didn't want to spend the limited time we had in Belgrade watching old Walt Disney films; and so we thanked them, shook hands, and struck out on our own. We went to a World War II museum. We found it very moving. It contained, among other things, numerous large graphic photographs showing atrocities inflicted by the partisans on the Nazi occupiers and then atrocities inflicted by the Nazis on the civilian population in retribution. The brutality inflicted by both sides was horrendous. There were many war memorials and statues around the city and in its many parks.

The red hammer and sickle emblem of the Communist Party and large photos of Marshal Tito were everywhere. We went to the Communist Party headquarters, but we were not allowed to enter. Instead, we took photos of the building and the guard at the door. Frankly, it simply looked like a drab multi-story office building. The following day, we caught the train bound for Trieste, Italy.

Chapter 107

Italy, Switzerland, and Austria

By the time we reached Trieste, we had successfully covered a lot of miles in areas we found more challenging than we had expected. We still had four to five weeks before we would reach London. We were within our budget; in fact, I was below budget. Our confidence was high; we were young and full of energy. I wanted to maximize the opportunity I had that summer. I was not sure if I would ever return to Europe. Given the circumstances, if I were repeating the adventure, I wouldn't do anything differently.

From Trieste we went straight to Venice where we located a youth hostel and stayed two days and two nights. We were starting to encounter English-speaking tourists our age, traveling in much the same fashion. We found it helpful to share information on places to stay, what to eat, and things to see and do. We, of course, rode a gondola on the Grand Canal, spent time at St. Mark's Square, and climbed up the tower to get a closer view of the famous clock. We also went to the beach and swam.

From Venice, we took the train to Lausanne, Switzerland, where we again stayed in an inexpensive youth hostel. We had maps and did our own walking tour of the city and went down to the lake to see the huge water fountain. After one night we moved the short distance to Zurich where we stayed another night. Switzerland was very beautiful, with high mountains, heavily wooded forests and many lakes. However, the country was expensive and the weather was cool and damp, so we moved on to Salzburg, Austria. Our train from Zurich to Salzburg passed through the tiny country of Liechtenstein where our passports were stamped at the border, but the train did not stop long enough to permit us to get off and look around.

We loved Salzburg and immediately identified the historic places we'd hoped to see. We encountered more young servicemen and their dependents and learned that the U.S. Army had a variety of free bus tours. If space were available, we were welcome to join, and we did on many occasions.

From Salzburg, we took the train to Vienna, Austria, where we spent three days and nights. Vienna had been divided into four separate zones, one controlled by the United States, one by Great Britain, one by France and one by Russia. We hopped onto an army bus at the railroad station and rode through the Russian zone where a large area had been reduced to rubble. Streets, covering many entire blocks, had been bulldozed in 1953; there were vast mounds of rubble, still. Much of Vienna had been destroyed; a lot of reconstruction had been completed or was in progress, but much remained to be done.

We saw some evidence of the damage caused by the war elsewhere, including parts of Munich later in the trip, but nothing compared to what we saw in Vienna. We weren't able to include Berlin in our travels, but we were told that the damage in Berlin had been even more extensive than Vienna, and much of it remained.

We hooked up with several army bus tours in Vienna. One day we rode into the countryside to the border of the Russian Zone of Austria which, given the Cold War atmosphere that pervaded, was kind of exciting. The border we reached, about 40 miles northeast of Vienna, was the westernmost location of the Iron Curtain, so named by Winston Churchill at the beginning of the Cold War. In fairness, when we passed through the Russian zone of Vienna we found the border guards to be friendly and polite. Most were just kids, like us.

We had seen the movie "The Third Man" which was partly filmed in Vienna and had included a scuffle between the good guy and bad guy on the largest Ferris wheel in the world. Naturally, we went to see the giant structure. It was operating at the time, so we took a ride. The passenger facilities were each the size of a medium sized street car and the ride afforded a magnificent view of the city of Vienna.

We visited the famous Vienna Opera House, which had been badly damaged during the war. It was being reconstructed. We toured the Imperial Palace, the main residence of the Hapsburg emperors, whose reign lasted until 1918 when the Austro-Hungarian Monarchy collapsed. We also toured the Schonbrunn Palace a short distance from Vienna, which was the official summer residence of the Hapsburg emperors. We went to the home where Mozart lived when he wrote the Marriage of Figaro, and we visited St. Stephan's Cathedral. Most of the places we visited in Vienna had suffered some damage during World War II and most were being restored.

We also discovered wine cellars which we visited in Austria and Germany, great places for inexpensive wine and a snack. All in all, Vienna was a great side trip. Because of the complex border situation, it was impossible for us to go anywhere from Vienna except back to Salzburg, so that is what we did.

Chapter 108

Germany and an Incredible Coincidence

In Salzburg we rode on an army bus to Berchtesgaden and into the mountains to see Adolph Hitler's retreat and hideout known as the Eagle's Nest. Most of the structures had been destroyed and the underground bunker had been blown up and its entrance sealed. The historical place was interesting to explore and we tried to imagine what it would have been like when Hitler and his entourage had been there. The Eagle's Nest provided a wonderful panoramic view of Berchtesgaden and the whole valley, looking back to Salzburg. As in Switzerland, we found the scenery in southern Austria and Germany to be absolutely spectacular.

On another day, we caught an army bus and went with a group of servicemen and families to Garmisch-Partenkirchen in southern Germany. We crossed a small lake by boat to visit King Ludwig's Palace. King Ludwig, who reputedly went mad, built an elaborate palace which, although smaller in size, was an exact duplicate of the Palace of Versailles located outside of Paris. King Ludwig died shortly after the palace was completed and it was never officially occupied. Fortunately, the castle had been carefully preserved and it was in "mint" condition.

From Salzburg, we headed to Munich, Germany, where we spent one night and a day. We ended up looking for a place to stay after dark in a section of Munich that still had extensive damage from the Allied bombing campaign. For the first time during the trip, and I believe the last time, we encountered anti-American sentiment from a few of the Germans who lived in buildings that had received extensive damage. These Germans were obviously suffering.

After we left Munich, we went west to Stuttgart and then north to Frankfurt. We were hitchhiking now, which provided a welcome relief from lower-class train travel. We had pretty good luck, thanks to the friendliness we encountered from the Germans we met and the number of US serviceman who were stationed in Germany. Only one time did we find ourselves out in the countryside after dark, with no place to stay for the night. We each had a duffle bag, but we had no camping gear whatsoever, not even a flashlight. We were between towns when the sun went down and the air started to cool. Traffic had been light and we simply could not get a ride. We walked until we found a small building, more like a barn or storage shed. Inside was a stack of what appeared to be wool or potato sacks which we used to pad the floor and pull over us, and we spent the night. The next morning we were able to catch a ride and we moved on.

We reached Frankfurt where a lot of US servicemen were stationed, which we always found to be a good sign. Frankfurt was a large, pleasant city with many historical sights. We again visited the US military PX where we purchased a small flashlight and a few other supplies. The weather turned cool and rainy and after a short stay, we decided to move on. To be able to start hitchhiking again, we had to cross the central part of Frankfurt and get to the outskirts. As we walked, we got really soaked. We kept waving our US passports hoping that an American would spot us and help us get across the main part of the city; however, no one would stop.

Finally, a small Volkswagen stopped and the driver motioned for us to get in. There was hardly room for the two of us and our bags, however the driver insisted. He was German, lived in Frankfurt and spoke a little English. We mentioned the highway we were trying to reach and he nodded. As we drove, he asked me, in broken English, where we were from. I said the United States and he asked where in the United States. We had found in our travels that very few people had heard of the state of Idaho, although some had heard of Sun Valley and of Idaho potatoes! Most people we met were familiar with New York and California, maybe Texas, but not Idaho. Not knowing what else to say I said we were from Idaho. He said, "Oh, have you ever been to Idaho Falls?" I almost fell out of the car and then explained that I lived there. He said, "Do you know a Henry Hurley in Idaho Falls?" I was dumbfounded. I said I grew up on a farm my parents had purchased from a Henry Hurley. That would have been the Airport Farm to which we moved when I was two years old.

As we drove along our driver explained that he had been taken prisoner of war by US military forces. He eventually wound up at Camp Rupert in southern Idaho. Due to the labor shortage in the United States, he and other prisoners were transferred to temporary detention camps in and around Idaho Falls to help with the potato harvest.

Our driver was sent to work on a farm owned by Mr. and Mrs. Henry Hurley who had emigrated from Germany many years earlier. He said they became good friends; he spent a lot of time talking with the Hurleys and was often invited to eat with them. He further said he had had some correspondence with the Hurleys after his return to Germany, but had lost touch in recent years. When Bill and I were dropped off at the outskirts of Frankfurt, our German friend gave me a card with his name and address and asked me to give his regards to Mr. and Mrs. Hurley. The following spring, after I returned to Idaho, I ran across the card, but sadly, I learned that both Mr. and Mrs. Hurley had passed away.

Proceeding north from Frankfurt, we had pretty good luck getting rides and made good time. At one point, we had the good fortune to be picked up by a couple of American servicemen on leave, who were on their way to Copenhagen, Denmark. When we mentioned we also hoped to visit Denmark, they said we were welcome to ride all the way to Copenhagen with them. Two days later, we arrived in Denmark and took a large ferry to the Island of Sjaelland on which Copenhagen is located. We drove the car onto the ferry and started the long ferry ride to the island. The cost of the ferry ride included a buffet lunch which consisted of a large assortment of meats, seafood, breads, cheeses and other food items as well as beverages. All four of us were starved and the food was delicious and very rich. We couldn't believe our good fortune and since the buffet was "all you can eat," we gorged ourselves.

When we arrived in downtown Copenhagen, we decided to do our own thing over the weekend and meet two days later. At that time our two new friends would be returning to Germany and offered to take us as far as Hamburg where we planned to head west to the Netherlands. Incidentally, when we got back together, we compared notes and it turned out we all had diarrhea that first night spent in Copenhagen, the result of overeating the rich sumptuous food on the ferry. We were much more careful about what we ate on the return ferry ride.

Copenhagen is a large and very beautiful city. Bill and I visited the Royal Palace and the changing of the guard ceremony in the square in front of the palace, and world famous Tivoli Park. We also walked to the harbor to photograph the famous bronze statue of "The Little Mermaid." We had read that the statute had been damaged by vandals who had actually removed the head of the mermaid; however, we found the mermaid's head was intact. I don't know if the original had been located or a duplicate forged. The statute is a must see for tourists and I am sure the repairs were done quickly.

Finally, we reconnected with the two servicemen who had kindly given us the ride to Copenhagen. We all boarded another ferry for our return trip. When we were dropped off on the west side of Hamburg, Germany, we were well rested and ready to start hitchhiking once again.

Chapter 109

The Netherlands

We headed west toward the Netherlands by way of Bremen, Germany. Once again, we were fortunate to be able to obtain rides with a minimum of waiting time. I remember one ride in particular. An obviously well-to-do middle-aged German driving a new Mercedes Benz convertible picked us up. We mentioned that we were heading in the direction of Groningen, Netherlands. He said he was waiting for his boat to be finished in a small shipyard at Bremen. When the boat was completed, he planned to sail it around the world. He apparently had little else to do, so he ended up taking us a considerable distance west.

He was a bit "full of himself"; however, he seemed to enjoy our company and was interesting to visit with. He loved to drive fast and frequently took short cuts on narrow side roads which were also used by farm equipment and a few farm animals. Once, he passed a farmer with a load of hay on a blind corner going at a high rate of speed. I'm sure he was aware from our body language that Bill and I were nervous; however, at the same time we were excited and having fun. After all we were barely twenty years old and invincible! Due to the single long ride and the short cuts taken by the driver, by late in the afternoon when he dropped us off, we were only about 100 miles east of Groningen. We had had another day of good fortune.

The next day we started later than we had planned. We were in a rural area and we had difficulty getting rides. Walking past what appeared to be a grocery store and bakery, we decided to buy something to eat. A large sign identified the proprietor as Hans Peter Hansen, the name of my paternal grandfather. I remembered the German who gave us a ride across Frankfurt and wondered if this was another miraculous coincidence. We went in and I located the owner. I told him about my grandfather and asked, if by chance, he and I were related.

The store owner laughed and said that we were not related. He acknowledged that he was Danish, then went on to explain the system of family names still commonly used by the Danes. For example, only about thirty-five to forty names had been used for centuries. If you were named Hansen it simply meant that you were the son of Hans, the first name of your father. Johnson would be the son of John, etc. Last names were not commonly used. As the population grew, this system simply became unworkable. He said the government was trying to get people to change; however, there was still resistance to a system that would perpetuate last names rather than first names, as done for years in most other countries. Bill and I bought a small bottle of milk and a pastry and continued on our way.

It took us all day to reach Groningen, located in the northern tip of the Netherlands about 40 miles from the Grand Dike which separates the North Sea from the Zuider Zee. We have all read the children's story about the little boy who stuck his finger in the dike to hold back the waters of the North Sea. He saved Holland! The Grand Dike is the largest of a whole complex of dikes and pumping projects which have been constructed to drain and reclaim much of the land area of the Netherlands.

In February of 1953, the Netherlands experienced a one-in-a-hundred-year storm. Many of the dikes were breached; many of the pumping complexes used to pump water back into the sea were severely damaged. Vast areas were once again under water. We were able to see some of the damage and flooded areas. It was a sad sight. A massive effort was underway to restore the breached dikes and to replace or repair the damaged pumping equipment in order to reclaim the land. What we saw was a reminder of just how vulnerable this small nation is to natural catastrophe.

The route we took provided an interesting side trip; however, the roads were narrow, had much less traffic and the towns were few and far between. As a result, hitchhiking became more difficult and our progress slowed considerably. After crossing the Grand Dike, we headed south to Amsterdam which was on our list of things to see. We were exhausted when we arrived in Amsterdam. It was after dark and we had been dropped off in the center of the city. We found a room and went to sleep. We slept late and when we woke up, we found that our room was part of a multi-story building in the "Red Light District" of Amsterdam. As we left the building, we noticed several women hanging out of upper story windows, soliciting their customers.

We spent most of a day in Amsterdam, a clean and beautiful city with several canals that served as streets, as in Venice, but we decided we needed to keep moving and elected not stay another night. We inquired as to how we could get to Marken Island. We had been told that the people who lived on Marken Island lived much as the people in Holland had many years before.

They lived in colorful houses, used windmills to grind grain and pump water, and wore traditional clothing, including wooden shoes.

We found all of this to be true; however, we also learned that the residents needed to diversify their gene pool rather than continue intermarrying within such a small population. It was also evident that the whole project was subsidized and maintained by the government as a tourist attraction. I felt somewhat like I was visiting a zoo, except these were real people. The experience was kind of sad and disappointing. From conversations we had with several citizens of Netherlands, Marken Island was not something they recommended tourists visit. They actually seemed embarrassed about its existence and promotion as an attraction.

Chapter 110

Through Belgium and Luxembourg and on to Paris

Since we were now some distance south of Amsterdam, we headed south to Belgium and Luxembourg on our way to France. We were watching the calendar and mindful of when we had to be in London to meet Donna.

Still trying to make our way by hitchhiking, we did well traveling to Brussels and on to Liege, Belgium. However, traffic slowed down when we continued south to Luxembourg. Luxembourg was not high on our list, but I believe we felt it would be one more country. I don't remember that we were "counting" countries, but that may have been a subtle consideration.

As in northern Netherlands, we were in a rural area; the rides were less frequent and often short local hops. We did a fair amount of walking. Then we really started having difficulty getting rides when we entered France. One evening when we were about one hundred miles east of Paris, we finally gave up hitchhiking and caught a train to take us the rest of the way into the city.

Paris was one of the cities we really wanted to visit. We had a mental list of the places we planned to see if at all possible, the major attractions that all visitors try to see. When we arrived in Paris, France was undergoing a general strike which included most public transportation facilities. Fortunately, everything we wanted to see we could reach by walking, the only exception being the Palace of Versailles.

We went to the Louvre and saw its fabulous collection of art and sculpture; we climbed to the top of the Arc de Triumph; we toured the Notre Dame Cathedral and climbed the stairway as high was we could. We toured some of the underground catacombs near the Cathedral. We walked to the Eiffel Tower and climbed all the way to the top, rather than take the elevator. We wanted to save money, but we also wanted to see if we could make the climb and we wanted to count the steps. We visited the beautiful Church of the Sacred Heart. We spent one evening at the Moulin Rouge, (literally the Red Mill) which was a nightclub that was the subject of a current popular song and movie. We had to pay a cover charge to enter the nightclub, and the drinks were expensive. We ordered cokes and nursed them for a couple of hours. Our waiter kept coming to our table and expressing his displeasure that we were occupying good seats and not spending more money.

We also went to see a performance of *Romeo and Juliet* at the famous Paris Opera House. The Opera House was spectacular. We were pleased to find out that *Romeo and Juliet* was being performed, entirely in Italian. We were vaguely familiar with the story, or at least thought we were, but we really could not follow the story line. To make matters worse, the opera started late and we were exhausted from racing around the city during the day. As a consequence, I think we both were nodding off a great deal. We discussed leaving early, but we had paid for the tickets and we decided to stick it out.

One morning we visited the Palace of Versailles which was a few miles outside of the city, and also, a large museum near the Palace. I recall that we took a tram to the Palace, notwithstanding the general strike. The Palace had served as the residence of several of the kings of France until the time of the French Revolution in 1789-1790. The last King to occupy the Palace was King Louis XVI who was captured while attempting to flee France. He was returned to Paris where he was condemned to death and sent to the guillotine in 1793. The Palace is now maintained as a national museum.

The Palace was grand and the surrounding grounds and gardens were beautiful. Bill and I kept making comparisons with "mad" King Ludwig's Palace in southern Germany. Many of the features, including the Hall of Mirrors, were the same, though larger in size. We spent most of a day on our tour of the Palace and surrounding area. We could have spent much more time there, but we were on the move.

Because of the general strike and time constraints, we cut our stay in Paris by one day and decided to move on to London. We were able to purchase inexpensive tickets for the train to Calais, France. At Calais we located and boarded a ferry for the trip across the English Channel to Dover, England. Then we had another piece of good luck. We struck up a conversation with a young man who had just put his car on the ferry. He said he was driving to Glasgow, Scotland, and said we were welcome to ride with him. We jumped at the chance. We had planned to go directly to London; however, this opportunity was just too good to pass up. We still had a few days until Donna arrived in London and we would still have time to see some of the sights there before we had to leave.

When the ferry reached Dover, we tossed our duffle bags into our new friend's car and we all headed north to Scotland and another adventure. Our friend did not plan to stop along the way, which was fine with us. He had a fairly new car, was a fast although careful driver, and was familiar with all the roads. He bypassed London and the other major cities along the way. We made excellent time and arrived after dark in Glasgow, where he dropped us off. Try as we might we could not find a place to stay. This was the height of the tourist season and was also the Year of the Coronation for young Queen Elizabeth II of England. A taxi driver directed us to a private home which sometimes was available for tourists as a bed and breakfast establishment. This turned out to be very fortunate for us. Our luck seemed to be holding out.

 The door was opened by an elderly lady who was a widow and lived alone in a very modest house. She obviously was someone of limited financial means. As it turned out, she was also a wonderfully warm person and an excellent cook. In spite of the late hour she insisted on fixing us tea and something to eat. We agreed on a very reasonable charge for staying in her house. In response to her inquiries, we told her we had no particular plans for our stay in Scotland, other than perhaps wanting to see Edinburgh and whatever else she might suggest.

 Our landlady took it from there. By the time we woke up in the morning, she had been on the phone and gone out to gather maps, bus and tram schedules and guide books for us. Over breakfast she gave us suggestions for places to go that day and how our travel could best be accomplished. I am sure she could tell from our clothing, our luggage, and simply by talking with us, that we were on a tight budget.

 Each morning, she helped us plan the day to cover as many places of interest as possible, outlined the public transportation and schedules we needed to connect with, packed a nice lunch for us, and sent us on our way. When we returned in the evening she always fixed hot tea and had food for us. She asked us a lot of questions to make sure all had gone as planned and that we had enjoyed ourselves. She loved to visit and wanted to know about our families and our life in the United States. She treated us like her grandchildren, and yet she was not intrusive. She was truly wonderful.

 We could not have been more fortunate. We really received three full meals a day and although we tried, she wouldn't take any extra money. I believe she was delighted to have some company. I think she also appreciated the fact that we didn't smoke or drink, were polite, were interested in Scotland and appreciative of everything she did for us. Bill and I did smoke a few cigarettes at the time, but never in or around her house.

 One day she had us take a bus into the Lake District, where we visited several lakes, or lochs as they are known in Scotland, including Loch Lomond, which we had heard much about over the years. We passed through a countryside filled with heather in full bloom, which was spectacular. At one of the bus stops we were treated to bagpipe music. One day we took a bus to Edinburgh to spend the day. Edinburgh is a beautiful city. It was full of flowers and had been especially decorated in celebration of the Year of the Coronation of Queen Elizabeth II. I have a picture of a huge clock made entirely of flowers of various types and colors which was part of the Coronation festivities. Another time we took a bus to Dundee and saw the Firth of Forth and an old bridge that had been the scene of a spectacular train wreck years before.

When we left our landlady, she gave us each a big hug and a piece of paper on which she had written her name and address. She asked us to write to her when we returned home and we promised that we would. By the time I did arrive home, I had misplaced the paper and never did keep my promise, something I still feel guilty about. We took a public bus to London. We considered trying to hitchhike, but the weather was rainy and cool and we had stayed in Scotland longer than we had originally planned. Donna would soon be arriving in London and we had promised that we would meet her.

Chapter 111

London, Shannon, and Going Home

We arrived in London and found a place to stay in the center of the city that could accommodate the three of us, and Donna arrived late the next day. We had arranged to meet at the base of the statue of Lord Nelson on Trafalgar Square. This was long before cell phones, and public phones were rare and not very reliable. Donna had written letters which we had picked up at American Express offices in major cities, and I had written to her periodically to indicate the likely direction we were traveling. It worked, miraculously, and we found each other.

The three of us spent three nights and most of three days in London. As with other cities, we had a mental checklist of the places we had heard or read about, and we moved about quickly to see as many as possible. We watched the colorful changing of the guard at Buckingham Palace. We also toured the Tower of London and went to the Parliament building; unfortunately, it was not open to the public at the time.

We went to Number 10 Downing Street, the official residence of the British Prime Minister. We listened to Big Ben sound the hour in the deep long bongs we had heard many times on the radio during World War II. We walked along the Thames River to see the famous London Bridge of nursery rhyme fame. We received blank looks as we inquired of the local Brits as to the whereabouts of London Bridge. We learned that there were several "London Bridges" which spanned the Thames River and many looked the same as all the others.

Whenever possible we rode on the red "Double Decker" buses London was famous for. Bill and I had read about London's Windmill Theater. According to the accounts, the theater had remained open throughout the war, despite German bombing raids and V-1 and V-2 rocket attacks which caused much destruction and loss of life. The three of us attended an afternoon performance.

After our whirlwind tour of London, it was time for us to move on. Bill Whitman was due to return to Beirut and Donna and I had reservations to fly to New York City from Shannon, Ireland, in two days. Donna and I packed up, said goodbye to Bill and boarded a bus which took us through Wales to a coastal town and onto a ferry for the crossing to Ireland, and finally on to the city of Dublin, Ireland which we found to be a rather drab city.

Shortly before we arrived in Dublin, we started talking about getting married while we were still in Europe. Once in the city, we actually stopped a priest on the street to inquire about the requirements for getting married. I don't exactly remember the conversation, but I do recall that he seemed somewhat less than friendly as he looked us over. He gave us to understand that the process for foreigners to get married in Ireland would be fairly complicated, and I believe he suggested we consult someone at the US Embassy. We decided to continue on to Shannon.

In retrospect, the notion that we might get married on the way home was really quite naïve. Donna was 18 and just out of high school and I was barely 20 and had only two years of college behind me. Life was exciting and the setting rather romantic, however. Whether we would have gone ahead with marriage, if such had been possible, I don't really know. We may have simply been expressing the depth of our feelings. In any event we caught the bus and went on to Cork, Ireland.

While at Cork, we took a short bus ride to the town of Blarney to visit Blarney Castle. We toured the Castle and at the top located the "Blarney Stone" which was also known as the Stone of Eloquence. Anyone who kissed the stone, and most tourists did, was said to receive the gift of eloquence. Kissing the stone is not as simple as it sounds. In order to reach the stone which was part of a large stone wall, you had to hang upside down holding onto iron hand rails while someone held your legs, for safety reasons. We have color slides of each of us performing the feat. When looking at the pictures, I still have difficulty deciding the correct way to hold the slides.

We didn't have time to do much more sightseeing, however we enjoyed the beautiful countryside as we rode the bus from Dublin to Cork and on to Shannon, located on the west coast of Ireland. Once we reached Shannon, we went directly to the airport to check in and make certain all was set for our flight back to the States.

Ours was a night flight from Shannon to New York City where Orval would pick us up and then we would all head west. The plan was to drop Donna off at Colorado Women's College in Boulder where she was already registered for the fall term; then for Orval and me to drive on to Idaho Falls. We boarded a

Lockheed Constellation, a beautiful four engine craft with triple tail fins, known as the "Connie". The inflight service was elegant. I was always fascinated with airplanes and tickled to be able to fly on this particular one. After a nice dinner, we read, talked for a while and then fell asleep. In the morning we landed, but we were not in New York City; we had landed in Reykjavik, the capital of Iceland!

We were told our plane had experienced mechanical trouble during the night flight and that we had been diverted to the nearest airport which was at Reykjavik, almost due north from where we had taken off the night before. While we stayed in Reykjavik a good part of the day, we were told that our departure time was uncertain and that we needed to stay at the airport rather than go into the city. Ultimately, we again boarded the plane and continued on to the States; however, we were now told that our plane would land at Boston rather than New York City as originally scheduled. Orval had planned to pick us up at New York City and we had no way to contact him. We simply hoped that he would have checked with the airline and would meet our plane in Boston.

The rest of the flight was interesting. We were now much further north than our original flight would have taken us. Now our flight path took us over the southern part of Greenland. We had found Iceland to be filled with vegetation. From the air, as we took off and circled, the landscape of Iceland was a variety of green color and quite pretty. When we flew over Greenland, it looked like a solid block of white ice. The weather was clear and sunny and we could easily see the ice floes that were falling off glaciers and into the Atlantic Ocean, a process known as "calving." It was a beautiful sight to see the ice bergs drifting south from the coast of Greenland and spreading out over the ocean. The unexpected stop in Iceland ended up providing us with spectacular views of areas we had not even thought of being able to see. Somehow it seemed an appropriate finale to a truly amazing year.

Chapter 112

Our Luck Holds

Our luck held out as Orval was at the Boston airport to meet our plane. Orval had packed his car and was ready to head west. Donna and I picked up our luggage and we took off on one of Orval's marathon cross-country drives. All of us were anxious to reach our destination. We had only gone a short distance when Orval suggested to Donna that she enroll at the University of Idaho rather than at Colorado Women's College. After what now seems like an amazingly short discussion, she agreed that she would in fact enroll in the U of I. Although she was pre-registered at CWC, she was not aware of anyone she knew who would be attending the college. We made a brief stop in Brush, Colorado, where Donna had lived prior to moving to Saudi Arabia. She said hello to some of her relatives, explained the change of plans, and we proceeded on to Idaho Falls.

During the short time we were home, Donna took steps to have her high school transcript sent to the University of Idaho. I discovered that the draft board in Idaho Falls had agreed I could enroll at the University and that when I received my draft notice, I could go to Spokane for my induction physical examination. I spent a lot of time visiting and introducing Donna to family members and friends. In the late spring, I had asked Reed to sell my car so I would have enough money to finish the year at AUB and spend the summer traveling in Europe. This was the first time I had not had my own car since I had been in ninth grade. Ultimately, we packed up, caught a ride with friends to Moscow, and we both enrolled at the University of Idaho for the fall semester.

Although encouraged to do so by my sister Mary and our friend Vonda Jackson, Donna decided not to pledge with a sorority and arranged to live in Hays Hall. I spent a short time at the Sigma Chi house. The house was full, and I volunteered to find a room off campus, although I continued taking many of my meals at the fraternity house. I found that I was experiencing a "culture shock" in reverse, not quite the same as when I first arrived in Beirut, however in many ways, just as profound.

I was surprised at how much I had changed. I was more anxious than ever to get on with my life. I had enrolled in General Agriculture my freshman year without giving my future a great deal of thought. At the time, what I studied didn't seem terribly important. Now I wasn't sure it would lead me anywhere I wanted to go, and at the same time I was unsure where I really wanted to go. I knew that I wanted to obtain my degree in as short a time as possible and that Donna and I were quite serious about getting married, although we didn't have any specific plans.

I had come to the conclusion that the farm, which seemed quite large a few years earlier, did not seem as large and, in a sense, was growing smaller. Norman was married and had started a family. Reed had dropped out of school after Dad passed away and seemed committed to remaining on the farm. Mother depended on the farm for a source of income. Rightly or wrongly, she had used most of the money from the sale of the Ford agency to pay down farm debt. It was starting to become clear that without major expansion, the farm would not be able to support all of us; it was still carrying a fair amount of debt.

I had many good friends at the Sigma Chi house and elsewhere at the University. I discovered that while it was good to be reacquainted with my friends, I no longer enjoyed the hoopla and pranks that had seemed so much fun the year before. I found that I was bored with the fraternity rituals. I did not in any way feel superior to anyone else; I simply didn't feel as comfortable as I had before. It was more like I didn't belong and I pulled back some.

During the previous twelve months, I had really undergone a life changing experience, a change which I did not, as yet, fully understand. I had been exposed to such a variety of different races, cultures, religions and political environments. I knew that I had come away with a better understanding and a sincere respect for all I had seen; however, the experiences left me somehow unsettled. I probably needed some time to work through all of this and to talk with someone who could relate to what was going on in my head. Unfortunately, the end of the trip was abrupt, our stay in Idaho Falls was much too brief, and now I was back in school, needing to sort out the "rest of my life."

When I enrolled in the fall of 1954, I changed my major to agricultural economics. I had thoroughly enjoyed the economics courses and the statistics course I took at AUB. I wasn't sure where a degree in agricultural economics would lead except to a Bachelor of Science in two more years; while a transfer out of the college of agriculture would have lengthened the time for me to obtain a four year degree, something that I quickly ruled out. An additional two years seemed like an eternity. I was in a hurry even though I wasn't sure where I was going! The scenario almost seems humorous, as I reflect on all of this today.

Occasionally, I considered the possibility of getting a bachelor's degree and then going on to law school; however, law school seemed pretty much out of reach at the time. I checked into the possibility of applying for a Fulbright Scholarship for study abroad, with the idea of returning to the Middle East, possibly back to AUB. Donna was not sure what she wanted to study. She enrolled in the Home Economics Department with the idea of pursuing nutrition; however, without any specific purpose in mind. We were both restless.

The idea of going overseas appealed to both of us, particularly returning to Beirut. I found that the fact that I had spent a year in the Middle East studying at the American University of Beirut would strengthen my application for a Fulbright scholarship; however, the competition was great. I was told that my odds would be improved if I had an outline for a planned course of study and a four-year degree. At the time, I had neither. While all of this was going on I was expecting any day to receive a letter from the draft board for me to appear for a physical and my likely induction into the military service.

I rented a place to live inside of a commercial woodworking business that was just off campus. The rent was cheap, partly because I served as an informal night watchman. The rented room did not have any cooking facilities. I gradually adjusted and became more relaxed. I believe it helped me to be living off campus. It gave me a chance to get away from the fraternity hubbub.

Donna and I took part in the fraternity dances and other social activities. I was "tubbed" as a result of having given Donna my fraternity pin to wear; and she in turn was duly serenaded at Hays Hall by the members of the fraternity. We caught a ride to Idaho Falls for Thanksgiving break.

After the short holiday break, I received notice from the draft board that I was to report to a facility in Spokane, Washington, for my induction physical. Round trip transportation from Moscow to Spokane was provided by the military. I, along with others, was given a thorough physical and written exam. Later I was called out, as were I believe a few others, for an interview with two regular Air Force officers. I was told that I did well on my exams and was asked if I would be interested in attending officer candidate school for flight crew training. They explained that upon successful completion, I would receive a commission with the rank of Second Lieutenant. I said I was surprised that I would qualify, given my near-sightedness. I was told that the eye sight requirements were lower for non-pilot duties, such as those of a flight engineer, bombardier or navigator.

I thought about all of the advantages and said I would be pleased to participate in the program. I would receive more schooling, some of which would be accepted as credits toward a bachelor degree. I would receive higher pay and better housing benefits than if I were an enlisted man, and I would be doing something challenging, while at the same time having more time to ponder my future.

Following discharge, I would be eligible for the G.I. Bill which would provide help with future college expenses. Finally, it might just lead to an opportunity for me, and perhaps Donna and me, to go abroad again and go with a decent salary. I was ready to go into the service right then; however, I was told to continue in school until I was notified to report, which would probably be in a few weeks. I was excited about the opportunity, and when I told Donna I believe she was excited as well.

The next few weeks flew by. We went home for Christmas vacation which was two full weeks, enough to provide a meaningful rest and break from school. We relaxed and had fun. Donna was well liked by my family and friends, and she was fond of Mother and all of the others. She seemed to fit right in. I was mentally adjusting to the idea of entering the service and was relieved to have my life settled for at least a period of time. The fall semester would not be completed until the middle of January and the final exams came the latter part of the month. Consequently, following the vacation break, the month of January was always a frantic time.

Chapter 113

Everything Changes

When the semester ended, I had not heard from the Air Force. I decided to go ahead and enroll for the second semester. Early in February, I received a call from Mother who told me that Norman and Reed had been in a serious car accident and had been taken to the hospital. John Beal, a long-time key employee who was in charge of the Grade A dairy operation, had been riding in the car with them and was also in the hospital. I quickly packed a bag and flew home.

Reed had been driving the car on a stretch of road in Teton County, Idaho. The road was suddenly covered with "black ice" and Reed had collided with an oncoming vehicle. The other car had been driven by a woman who was killed instantly. Apparently both cars had started skidding and the impact was impossible to avoid. Reed was in critical condition, and Norman and John Beal were in serious condition. No one could predict whether Reed would survive or how long Norman and John Beal would be laid up, or what their ultimate recoveries would be. In addition to operating the Grade A dairy, a full time and a major operation, the fall potato crop needed to be sorted and sacked, and the potatoes hauled to town for shipment to market. I told Mother that I would drop out of school and come home to help out. She didn't ask me to, but she didn't protest my decision. The necessity was obvious. My year abroad and return to the University had been accommodated, and now I was needed on the farm. It was that simple.

I returned to the University, withdrew from my classes and packed my things. I explained the situation and my decision to Donna. I did not know when or if I would be returning to school. It occurred to me that if Reed survived, he might be the one who would need to return to the University to complete his degree rather than resume farming. Everything was suddenly up in the air. Donna wondered if she should also drop out of school and we discussed the possibility of getting married. In retrospect, I think it is fair to say that it would have been more prudent for me to go home and for Donna to finish the semester and then to take a look at the situation during the summer.

By summer things would look much different. All three men would be on their way to what appeared to be a full recovery. John Beal and Norman would be back working. Norman would still be having some problems with his leg, but overall, he would be doing quite well. Reed would be out of the woods and expected to make a full recovery. At the end of the summer, I would be planning to return to the University after being out just one full semester.

I know her parents Harry and Hazel would have preferred that Donna continue in school. She was a good student and the first child in her family to have the opportunity to attend college. But without looking back, Donna and I both dropped out of school and returned to the farm. We decided to get married as soon as the work schedule on the farm permitted.

In the meantime, I worked harder that I had ever worked in my life. I frantically loaded and hauled, sorted and sacked potatoes to take to town. The men on the sorting crew, some of whom I knew and liked, knew I was an out of shape "college boy" and they pushed me hard to see how much I could take. I think they wanted me to ask them to slow down and maybe I should have, but being stubborn, I did not. It became a test of wills, what might be called a silly "guy" thing. The only rest I had was driving to town and back for another load.. When I was back, they stopped sorting and lifted 100# bags onto the bed of the truck as fast as they could for me to stack and load, tier by tier. I thought I was going to die; however, we finally finished the job and by this time, I was beginning to get into pretty good physical condition.

February and March of 1954 were busy months; however, the pressure subsided somewhat. In early April, we were planting grain and when that was completed we would have a break in the farm work until we started irrigating and planting potatoes in May. Donna and I began making plans to get married after the grain had been planted.

Chapter 114

Married!

We set a date: April 16, 1954. I know Mother was relieved. She had never said anything about Donna's decision to leave school or our decision to get married. But she thought Donna had been put in an unfair situation and she was not comfortable with Donna's having to deal with something as vague as "…when we get caught up with the farm work…." She felt protective of Donna; she worried that we boys were not sufficiently sensitive to the issue, and she probably was right.

Neither Donna nor I had much experience with religion. I had seldom attended church and while she had gone a number of times with a variety of friends, she had not formally joined any church. Her mother had practiced Christian Science. Donna asked if I had any objection to having a Christian Science practitioner perform the marriage ceremony and I said that I did not. When she inquired however, she was told that marriage ceremonies were not performed by Christian Science practitioners. We were both pretty naïve about organized religion.

We asked Mr. Albert Dew, who was then bishop of the Osgood Ward of the Church of Jesus Christ and the Latter Day Saints, to perform the ceremony and he agreed. His wife, Verda Dew, also attended. We were married at home on the farm on Good Friday, April 16, 1954. Mary was bridesmaid and Reed was best man. Following the brief ceremony in the living room, we borrowed Reed's car and headed south to the Grand Canyon. We stopped in Salt Lake City and visited with Farrel and Alice who took us to dinner.

From Salt Lake City, we drove south to the Grand Canyon by way of the Painted Desert and the Petrified Forest. On our return, we drove through western Colorado and visited the ruins at Mesa Verde. The weather was warmer than at home, the scenery was nice, and it felt good to get away from the farm work for the first time since leaving school.

Following our return, we had a reception which provided an opportunity for more people to meet Donna and to offer congratulations. Then we settled back into the farm routine. During the previous couple of months, Donna and I had spent time getting the basement ready for us to move into. Norman and Clem had previously moved out of the basement and into the house built just off the highway to the north. Mostly we cleaned and painted; we used some wild colors.

1954 was a busy year in more ways than one. Reed had been dating Marilyn Hoff for some time and in June they eloped to Elko, Nevada. Marilyn's parents, Mark and Onita Hoff, were long-time friends of my mother and dad and were fairly well acquainted with Reed. They approved of the marriage; however, I am confident they would have preferred a church wedding for their oldest child and only daughter. Later, in November, of the same year my sister Mary and George Freund were also married.

In the summer of 1954, Farrel finished his surgical residency and received his Board Certification in General Surgery. He and his wife Alice moved to Idaho Falls to live and establish a medical practice. Norman, Reed and I took a farm truck to Salt Lake City, helped load up all of their furniture and belongings. We all returned to Idaho Falls; Farrel, Alice and their two small children, Connie and Scott, followed in their car.

They soon located a house on Garfield Street in the newly developed Bel Aire Subdivision. Farrel and Alice were a great addition to the social activities that we enjoyed with family and close friends. We were all very busy; however, we found time for family dinners, couples poker nights, and other informal social events, and even an occasional swim in the Great Western Canal at the farm. We were all on tight budgets, but we were young and thoroughly enjoyed each other; we had some great times together.

Chapter 115

Back to School

Donna and I left for Moscow in September, 1954. This time we had our own transportation. Mother loaned us her car, a 1952 Ford sedan. The plan was for me to return to school and Donna to look for work to help cover the expenses. Harry and Hazel Lebsock offered to pay the expense for Donna to enroll at the University and finish her education; however, we declined the offer. I remember that I felt very strongly that having made the decision to get married we should pay our own way. I believe Donna agreed. I remember that she was not really excited about the Home Economics Department and its curriculum. In retrospect, it may have been a mistake. Her parents were sincere and really wanted Donna to get a college degree. I think I was stubborn; perhaps we both were. We probably should have given it a try; at least discussed it with someone else, perhaps Mother, but we did not do so.

I had saved most of the money I earned while working on the farm. We brought a large quantity of frozen meat and canned goods from the farm with us when we returned to Moscow. We found a place to live, on the second floor of a home in Moscow. There was an outside entrance from the back yard. Our landlords were Mr. and Mrs. Goettche.

In the fall of 1954, Bill Whitman returned to the University with his new bride Joan Hubbard. Joan and Donna had been friends at Community High School in Beirut. Donna graduated in 1954 and Joan a year later. Joan's parents also lived in Saudi Arabia where her father was employed.

A friend and colleague of Bill's father was a professor at the University of Idaho and was on a year's sabbatical. He and his wife owned a lovely two-story colonial house in Moscow which they offered to Bill and Joan rent free. We spent a lot of time with Bill and Joan that year. We shared many pictures, memories and experiences. Joan had two sisters, Marcia who had graduated from high school with Donna, and Trudy who was younger and lived with Bill and Joan and attended high school in Moscow for the school year 1954-55.

Bill Whitman worked part time in a butcher shop in Moscow. In the fall I went hunting and was successful in getting a deer. I took the carcass to Bill and he arranged for the deer meat to be mixed with generous portions of beef and pork and had the entire meat mixture ground into hamburger. I had never cared much for deer meat because it was often tough and had a strong "game" flavor. It is very important how you "dress" or butcher the animal and how you handle the carcass. The skill of the cook in dealing with wild game meat is very important as well. The hamburger meat was the best I have ever had and took some pressure off of our food budget. We had meatloaf in all shapes and forms and it was excellent. The mixture was very low in fat content, and the usual "gamey" flavor was almost totally eliminated by the addition of the pork and beef.

The 1954-55 year at Moscow was very enjoyable. We spent considerable time with Bill and Joan, and the four of us also took part in some of the social events at the Sigma Chi fraternity, mainly the formal dances. Donna worked at Rogers Ice Cream Parlor. Bill and I were busy at school and both had part time jobs, Bill at the meat market and me at the University plant lab. Joan kept busy looking after the large house and her younger sister Trudy. Still we seemed to have plenty of time to get together for a game of bridge or otherwise to do something fun. We were young and made the most of our time and energy. We all got along very well.

Chapter 116

Mary Marries George Freund

We drove home for the short Thanksgiving break. My sister Mary had, for some time, been dating George Freund who worked at the Argonne National Laboratory at what we called the Site on the desert west of Idaho Falls. The official name I believe was still the National Reactor Testing Station, a place for the development, construction and testing of various types of nuclear reactors. Mary had been working for Westinghouse Corporation, one of the major contractors at the Site.

At the time, Westinghouse Corporation was involved with building and testing a prototype for an operational nuclear submarine. George lived in Illinois and was in Idaho on assignment with the Argonne National Laboratory which was affiliated with the University of Chicago. Mary and George often rode the same bus to the site; both shared an interest in playing bridge, which was a common pastime of bus riders; and they occasionally bumped into each other during the work day.

George proposed to Mary sometime in the fall, after Donna and I had left for Moscow. They were kind enough to schedule the wedding date during the Thanksgiving weekend so that we could be present. Donna was Mary's matron of honor, and I was George's best man. As with our marriage ceremony the previous April, it was a small family affair which took place in the living room of Mother's house on the farm. After they were married, Mary and George moved to Illinois.

An entire book could and should be written about George Freund someday. In the future, hopefully, one of his children will take on the project. George passed away in June of 2006 following a series of serious health problems. George was born in Vienna, Austria in 1926 or 1927. His parents were Jewish and George was raised in the Jewish religion. After his mother died he went to live with grandparents in rural Austria. In 1939, when the persecution of the Jews by Adolph Hitler and the Nazi regime became truly alarming, his grandparents made arrangements for George to leave the country and travel via England to New York City to stay with an aunt. Shortly after they left, the borders were sealed and no one else was permitted to leave.

Several years ago, Mary and George traveled to Vienna and researched records which had been meticulously kept by Nazi Germany. George learned for the first time that his grandparents had been sent to the infamous death camp at Auschwitz located near Krakow, Poland, and to its gas chamber and crematorium. The entire tragic story of the life of George Freund should be documented. His mother died shortly after he was born; his father, who was a lawyer who practiced law in Vienna, died when George was eight years old. After his father died, his maternal grandparents picked George up and took him to live with them. Several years ago, I had the opportunity to travel to Krakow and visit the Auschwitz "death" camp and museum. It was a gruesome reminder of the enormity of the tragedy of the Holocaust.

Chapter 117

Happy Holidays Lead to a Happy Arrival

When we returned to Moscow after Thanksgiving, we brought a turkey Mother had given us, along with other food supplies. Donna had not cooked a turkey before and wrote to her Mother in Saudi Arabia to get instructions along with a recipe for dressing. We invited several friends over for a potluck buffet-style dinner. To seat everyone, we set up card tables along the wall in the small living room. The walls were slanted because it was an attic apartment. This was our first attempt at entertaining and all in all we felt it was successful. Most of our guests were newly married and living on limited budgets much like we were. I am sure we made too much noise; however, this was a rare occasion and our landlords, who lived downstairs, did not complain.

Donna and I drove to Idaho Falls to spend the Christmas vacation which always included a major New Year's Eve party in the basement of the house Norman and Clem lived in on the farm. We had some really great parties which included dancing and singing until the early hours of the morning. We always had a huge crowd of friends and relatives and almost everyone dressed up in elaborate costumes. We normally had a "decorating party" several days before New Year's Eve which was also well attended and almost as much fun as the party to follow. In those days, Norman was making "home brew" beer and generally had a supply on hand. It was pretty good, although he did not have a centrifuge and sediment settled in the bottles after they had been filled and capped. You had to be very careful when tipping the bottle to not unduly disturb the sediment. The best thing about Norman's home brew, of course, was the fact that it was free!

The tradition of having a "costumed" New Year's Eve party with ever more elaborate costumes continued for years and years thereafter. The parties were generally attended by the younger crowd, the generation of me and my siblings, but others attended as well and everyone had fun. I remember one year, as the evening progressed, suddenly four ladies and a gentleman, all dressed in elaborate costumes, showed up in the basement and slowly walked around the large room. The music stopped and everyone stared to see who had arrived. We couldn't tell who they were until one or more of the ladies began laughing and they lifted their masks.

The strangers were Mother, Lottie Danner, Veva Jackson and Clara Jensen, accompanied by Ralph Danner-- "The Foursome," plus Ralph. They had obviously spent a lot of time and effort to disguise themselves as four harem ladies escorted by an Arab sheik. They were determined to fool us and they really did. In those days everyone worked very hard, but when we found the time, we enjoyed ourselves and had a great deal of fun.

Donna and I returned to Moscow. She continued to work at Rogers Ice Cream Shop. I believe about this time she received a raise and was getting forty cents an hour! I attended classes and continued to work at the Plant Pathology lab. Most of the time I was sorting, washing and bundling strawberry plants that had been grown on the University farm adjacent to campus. The building I worked in was cold, as was the water used to wash the plant roots, and the pay was low. I had work, but it was a job typical of that available to students. I envied those students who were receiving the GI Bill benefits.

When we got married, Donna and I had decided that we would postpone starting a family until I had finished getting a bachelor's degree. I remember that after a while we began to wonder whether we would be able to have children. I am not sure why we started worrying, perhaps it was because some of our friends were having babies. In any event, we became less cautious and sometime in January, 1955, Donna became pregnant. Donna stopped working at Rogers Ice Cream parlor because it required her to be on her feet most of the time. She began working at the University of Idaho Dairy Science Research office. She learned to use a Friedan calculator and continued working there until the semester was finished and we went back to the farm for the summer.

That was pretty much our routine. I went to school, we both had jobs in Moscow, and we returned to the farm where I worked until it was time to leave to return to school in the fall. When we returned in the fall, and from holiday visits, we always brought a supply of frozen beef from the farm cold storage locker, as well as a variety of canned goods and a sack of potatoes. In spite of our initial thoughts of postponing having a family we were both pleased that Donna was pregnant and looked forward to the new challenge. We didn't have any savings and were just barely getting by, but this didn't seem to cause us any undue concern. We were young and healthy and we had good family support, and we both knew how to work. We were confident everything would work out fine, and it always seemed to.

Harry and Hazel Lebsock and their son Kenneth came to visit us on the farm during the summer of 1955. They were still living in Saudi Arabia and Harry was still working for ARAMCO. Donna's parents and brother were delighted to see her for the first time in almost two years. They seemed genuinely pleased to meet Mother and the rest of the members of my family and we enjoyed a good visit. Harry and Hazel looked forward to becoming grandparents. When Harry and Hazel left for Colorado to visit members of Harry's family, Kenneth stayed with us on the farm until his parents returned. Kenneth wanted to learn to drive a car so I took him out a few times, with limited success. At one time, he wasn't able to stop the car and drove it into an irrigation ditch much to his embarrassment. He quickly lost interest and the lessons stopped.

When they left, Harry and Hazel gave Donna a small portable GE television set so she would have something to watch both before and after the baby was born. We had the set for many years thereafter, although we were not able to watch it for another year. The apartment complex we next moved into, the Burr Apartments, did not have TV hookups, and the built-in antenna would not pull in enough signal from Spokane. I discovered that the cost of installing a large pole and antenna was prohibitive, at least for our budget, and might not have pulled in a strong enough signal anyway.

In the fall, we resumed our routine, except that Donna did not go back to work. We were now living in a ground floor unit and awaiting the arrival of the baby. Mike Heppler and his wife also lived at Burr Apartments. Mike, whom I had known slightly, was a member of the Sigma Chi house. As we became better acquainted, we discovered a mutual interest in making "home brew" and we decided to make a batch. The result was not bad and we had a lot of fun doing it. Donna was not totally comfortable with the odor of the process, so we usually placed the crock in the Heppler apartment until it was time to fill and cap the bottles.

We were expecting the baby around the first part of October; however, Linda Sue Hansen was not born until October 16, 1955, at Gritman Memorial Hospital in Moscow. Linda weighed 8 pounds and 14 ounces at birth. Donna was small and the delivery was not easy, but the baby was healthy and she and Donna soon recovered. Despite her exhausting delivery, Linda was a beautiful baby. As I remember Hazel was able to stay with us for a few days when we first brought Linda back to the apartment. Later, Mother came to Moscow to stay with us and help out for a while. We knew practically nothing about raising a baby, however, with their help, we quickly learned.

Chapter 118

An Unexpected Opportunity

I was not able to work very many hours for the University, so I answered an ad for a job at the *Daily Idahonian*, the daily paper published in Moscow. The newspaper was looking for someone to run the "second mailer" machine. I accepted the job and worked at the paper until I finished law school. The pay wasn't great; however, I enjoyed the work atmosphere and the people I worked with. I was the only college student who worked at the paper and I think my coworkers appreciated the fact that I was willing to work and that I was dependable. In the beginning, I worked only a couple of hours or so in the late afternoon, but I worked six days each week and was able to make more than I had at my weekend job at the University. I also received a free paper and could read the comic strips for the whole week in advance if I chose!

My job as second mailer consisted of running an ancient machine located near the printing press. I would pick up a stack of papers from the press and run them through the machine, which stamped individual papers with the name and address of subscribers who received a paper by mail. Each page of the paper was set up by old linotype machines, where operators typed one letter at a time onto pieces of lead, then arranged them in a large square pan the size of an entire newspaper page. Someone would put ink on the filled pans with a hand roller and the pans were then placed in the press.

When the press first started, the ink was thick and the first papers were tossed away until the ink thinned out and the pages became readable. Occasionally, the roll of paper on which the paper was printed would break, making it necessary to stop the press and rethread the paper through the rather complicated machine. A skilled operator was needed to make certain the tension, the amount of ink and speed of the machine were just right to continue operating without interruption. While I worked at the paper, I worked with different operators, some more skilled than others.

Occasionally, we had the excitement of hearing someone yell, "Stop the Press!" because something had just come over the wire that the publisher thought was important. Immediately, one of the linotype operators would be handed a piece of paper and frantically type out the breaking news on pieces of lead. A new piece of freshly typed-on lead would be substituted for a section of equal size in one of the pans in the press, inked, and the press would start rolling again. If we hadn't already heard the nature of the "breaking news," we would quickly grab a freshly printed paper to find out what all of the excitement was about. When enough papers had been printed, the press was stopped, the heavy pans lifted out and the lead removed to be melted and used again.

About this same time, Bill Nixon, a member of the Sigma Chi fraternity, and I arranged to get the contract to deliver the *Argonaut* to the various housing units and other buildings around campus. The *Argonaut* was the University's student newspaper that was published each Friday at the *Idahonian*. We weren't paid very much as I remember; however, we received enough money to make the effort worthwhile. In those days every extra dollar we could pick up helped. We picked up the papers early Friday afternoon, and if we hurried, I could make my next class. I occasionally came to class late and usually with fresh printer's ink on me.

Donna, the baby, and I went to Idaho Falls for the Christmas break. Farrel's wife, Alice, had also given birth that fall to their son Jeff. George and Mary's first child, a daughter named Ruth was born in Illinois, a few weeks before Linda was born. Reed's wife Marilyn had recently given birth to their son Marcus. A lot of babies were born over the next few years. Fortunately, all of the babies were healthy. We still had frequent informal family gatherings and the babies were now included and occupied center stage. Our lives changed somewhat; this was a new experience for us and one we thoroughly enjoyed. We continued to have good times and to enjoy each other's company.

After the Christmas break, we went back to Moscow and our usual routine. I worked hard and also did well in school. I had taken electives whenever possible within different colleges and departments. For some reason, I took a class in Range Management in the College of Forestry and found I enjoyed it. The last two years of undergraduate studies involved taking many of my classes in the College of Letters and Science. One of my electives was a course in Chinese history taught by Dr. Hosack, who was considered one of the outstanding professors on campus. The course was difficult; however, I worked hard and received an A. I also did a lengthy term paper on land reform in ancient China. I remember this because I was given permission to use a modified version of the paper for a term paper requirement of an upper level agricultural economics course.

Dr. Foltz was the head of the Department of Agricultural Economics, and an outstanding teacher and advisor. I took a required senior seminar course from Dr. Foltz. He encouraged me to undertake a study and an analysis of the potato processing industry in Idaho. For years, Idaho grew and shipped fresh potatoes, exclusively. During World War II, a few plants were built to process dehydrated potatoes for the military. During the war, the technology for freezing some foods successfully was developed at first by Birds Eye Food Company. Equipment was being developed to process and freeze a French-fried potato product, increasingly in demand by fast food establishments. Also, the technology was being developed to successfully make potato flakes which, when reconstituted with water, made mashed potatoes, a product increasingly in demand by working housewives.

No statistics existed on the scope of the developing Idaho industry. I made a list of all the concerns in Idaho that were involved in any operation for processing fresh potatoes into a different form and compiled and sent a questionnaire to each. The questionnaire was an effort to find out the types and quantities of potatoes being processed, and the amount and type of processed product being marketed. I also had a variety of questions that I hoped would give some indication of the future growth of the industry and the new products that were being developed or contemplated. In my cover letter, I pointed out that the questionnaire form did not require disclosure of the name of their business, and I gave assurance that all I wanted were the statistics for a statewide analysis. I enclosed a self-addressed stamped return envelope. As I was about to mail out the letters, I realized I would not know which companies had replied and which would need a follow-up letter. I put a small code number on the back of each questionnaire and mailed them. In a few days, I received a reply from a large concern, I believe it was the J. R. Simplot Company, asking why I had coded the questionnaire, if the identity of the processor was to be kept confidential. Somewhat embarrassed, I wrote back and explained and they promptly sent the information.

Actually, I found out that those who were in the industry were quite interested in the information I was gathering and were awaiting the results of the statistical analysis. In reality, there were not many processors in Idaho at the time, and many of their products and the relative size of their operations were fairly well known. It would not have been difficult to determine the source of the information furnished, at least in most cases. I received an excellent response and compiled the information in the form of an article complete with graphs and charts, which was included with the results of several other seminar projects, in an Agriculture Economics publication. I sent the article to each of the companies to which I had sent a questionnaire. This was the first comprehensive report on the relatively new industry. For a number of years, I would occasionally read a newspaper account which provided statistics on the Idaho potato processing industry, often using the base line of information I had compiled in 1956.

I took a couple of courses from Dr. Erwin Graue, who had emigrated from Germany and was nationally recognized in the field of economics. Dr. Graue had a very stern and gruff demeanor which intimidated many of his students, myself included. He demanded a lot of his students and most responded. In the spring of 1965, I took a required course from Dr. Graue which met three times a week, the last on Friday afternoon. It was his class I would race to after Bill Nixon and I finished delivering the student newspaper around campus.

Unfortunately, my seat was in the front row and I always came to class out of breath, with smudges and traces of printer's ink on me. More than once, I was late for class. I sensed Dr. Graue was not pleased when I entered the classroom and sat down. I worked hard, liked the class, and did well. On the last day of the semester we had our final exam, a "blue book" exam which, like all of the tests he gave, was challenging to say the least. I was made very uncomfortable by the fellow seated next to me who kept trying to see what I was writing. I was pretty sure Dr. Graue was aware of it, too; he was constantly walking around the room as the exam was taking place.

The next morning I received a telephone call from Dr. Graue who said in his usual gruff voice that he wanted me to come to his office that morning. I was immediately fearful that he thought I had cheated on the exam and that he intended to give me a failing grade. If that happened, I would not receive the required credits for graduation. I had been working hard and was anxious to graduate and get on with my life. I was very nervous when I reached his office. He said I did very well on the final exam and that he was giving me an A grade for the course. He went on to say that he was in a position to guarantee me a Teaching Assistantship for the following year at Brown University which would pay me enough to cover living and school expenses while pursuing a graduate degree in Economics. He said to think about the opportunity and let him know as soon as possible and that was the end of the conversation. I couldn't believe it.

I had wanted to study at an eastern university, and in the back of my mind I had thought about going there, if I ever went to law school. Now that I was married, with a young baby and no money, I had about given up on the idea.

The assistantship would make it possible to go east, but to study economics rather than law. I was familiar with and really enjoyed the field of economics. On the other hand, I really knew nothing about the field or the practice of law.

Donna and I talked it over. We were both very practical in our approach. If I went to law school in the fall, we would return to Moscow and I would enroll in the College of Law at the University and could continue to work on the farm during the summers. By this time we were pretty sure we would prefer to live, work and raise our family in Idaho. At the time employment opportunities in the field of Economics seemed to me to be limited to teaching or perhaps working for a state or the federal government.

I was flattered with the offer from Dr. Graue. However after thinking and discussing the alternatives, Donna and I decided that my going to law school, as we had tentatively planned, made more sense for us. Sometime the following week, I went back to see Dr. Graue. I thanked him for the offer and explained our decision and how we had arrived at it. He seemed to understand and wished us well and said little else. He was not one for small talk. I do think he at least approved of the way we had reached our decision and the fact that we did have a plan of sorts. I have often wondered what course our lives might have taken had we gone back East. I have never had any second thoughts however, about the decision we made in the spring of 1956.

Chapter 119

A Family Summer Before Law School

After the graduation ceremonies, Donna and I bundled up Linda and packed the car for the trip to Idaho Falls where I again worked on the farm during the summer. Life on the farm was busy, as usual, and the summer went by quickly. I enjoyed farm work and it was nice to be away from school and back among family and old friends. While my wages were modest, we had a place to stay and our expenses were low so I could save most of my earnings for the following school year. Linda was growing fast and fun to be with; Donna spent time with Alice, Clem, Marilyn and Mother, enjoying all of the new additions to the families.

Our unit at the Burr Apartments was quite small with few windows and there was limited area outside for kids to play safely. The apartment was fine for a couple who were away much of the time, but not for young children. Donna and I had been thinking about a different living arrangement for the next three years while I was attending law school. We did not have time to look around Moscow before we left for the farm. By the time we returned in the fall, the better options would have already been taken. We had friends in Moscow who were living in a trailer house and were quite satisfied. We decided to investigate purchasing a trailer house, something we could do while we were in Idaho Falls for the summer.

Donna located and we ended up buying a used 32 foot Columbia Trailer house that was in good condition. It was well constructed with many windows which let in a lot of natural light and had a well-designed floor plan. We were confident the unit would serve our purposes better than the apartments we had rented, and it did. To save money Norman offered to help me pull the unit to Moscow with a farm pickup.

We made the trip, although the trailer was much heavier to pull, and the trip took longer, than we had anticipated. We really could have used a pickup or truck with more horsepower. We literally crawled up Monida Pass on the Montana border and Lookout Pass in north Idaho, but we eventually reached Moscow. We pulled the trailer onto a space in a trailer park just off the east side of the University campus where our friends were also staying; then Norman and I drove back to Idaho Falls.

When it was time to enroll in school, Donna and I once again put Linda and all of our belongings in the car and headed north to our new home. We were law school-bound.

John (on right) left the camaraderie and comfort of his Sigma Chi house at the University of Idaho to traipse off with his fraternity brother Bill Whitman (left) to Lebanon and enroll in the American University of Beirut. There, he met another American--Donna Lebsock (below).

Donna, Harry and Hazel Lebsock's daughter, was in her last year of high school in the Community School, a school for Americans whose parents were living and working in the Middle East. John claims he and Donna were serious students, with little time for socializing.

American students enjoyed visiting Hazel's apartment in Beirut--a little taste of "home," usually with snacks and a cold beer available. John was no exception. The mustache and goatee cost forty-five cents to trim, along with a haircut.

Let the Record Show by John D. Hansen

Bill (on the left) and John (on the right) found time for a trip to Egypt between semesters. They hired a small boat in Luxor to take them across the Nile to the Valley of the Kings and Queens.

Two days were not enough to cover the wonders of the Valley with its statues and obelisks that overwhelmed John as he tried to imagine what life was like for the people entombed in this valley.

John and Bill brought the overseas adventure to an end with an exciting trip through Europe that included escaping the Turkish army.

Photo Gallery 2

Another adventure began for John--his courtship of Donna who returned to Idaho with him. They married in 1954--between planting the grain and irrigating the potatoes. It was a busy time.

Linda Sue was born in Moscow, Idaho, October 16, 1955. John, finishing his undergraduate degree, enjoyed his new role as a dad, and he and Donna continued to enjoy good times and each other's company.

Patricia Ann, arrived hale and healthy August 12, 1958, but required a bit of monitoring for a potential RH factor problem. Big sister Linda wore her winter mittens to celebrate the occasion when she went with Daddy to pick up the new baby.

Steven, born March 18, 1961, required a complete blood exchange minutes after his birth. Thankfully, a Type O blood donor was found, and Steven thrived. Here he is with his sisters and John.

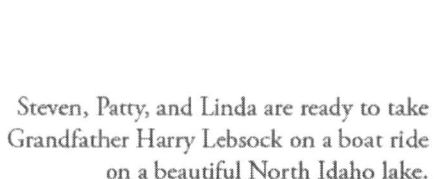

Steven, Patty, and Linda are ready to take Grandfather Harry Lebsock on a boat ride on a beautiful North Idaho lake.

Let the Record Show by John D. Hansen

LET THE RECORD SHOW

Part III:
The Law Years

Chapter 120

First Semester

On our arrival in Moscow in the fall of 1956, I leveled the trailer and secured it on blocks with the help of the trailer park manager. I was able to purchase a small shed-like structure which someone had built and given or sold to the trailer park manager. The structure was open on one side and had a door, roof, and floor, and it was fairly well insulated. I blocked and pressed it tightly against where the rear door was located, just off the main bedroom at the back end of the trailer. The door to the addition became the back door of the trailer. Though not a large addition, about four feet deep and six to eight in length, it held a small desk I had built, a chair and lamp, a bookcase and a small floor heater; and it left enough room to enter or exit.

I had built the desk in the evenings while we were on the farm the previous summer. I had used a small chest of drawers and a nice piece of wood that had been the top of an old dresser. The "study" was a great addition to our home. I was able to spend most evenings studying at home, in a quiet setting, without being disturbed or disturbing anyone else. Otherwise, I would have had to go to the law library because the trailer was small and we now had a baby, Linda. With our new move, we were finally able to receive a decent signal and enjoy the GE television set Donna's parents had given her the year before. We had used the television set in the basement at the farm, however, had not been able to use it in Moscow. Now Donna could watch television in the evenings without disturbing me. I would occasionally take a study break and watch a show. That small portable black and white TV set lasted for many years and served us well.

When I enrolled in law school, I had been advised not to try to work, at least for the first year. Law school was known to be hard and very demanding. In those years, it was easier to gain admittance to law school than is the case today; however, the attrition rate was high. Grading was done on the "class curve" rather than a finite number scale. Quite consistently, about one half of the students who started as freshmen did not finish law school, and most of those who did not finish simply flunked out. I decided to heed the advice I was given. We did not have any time to waste and were both anxious for me to finish school. Even three years sounded like a long time. Donna continued to work at the University of Idaho Dairy Science Research Office and the American Suffolk Sheep Society, and she also did some babysitting for friends. I did little else except go to class and study.

A fairly high percentage of the students in my freshman class were married; some were veterans, and several had small children. They all approached law school as I did, feeling somewhat insecure and determined to succeed. The best way to accomplish that was simply to study hard and be prepared for class. I remember looking around and thinking that if only one half of the students in the freshman class survive three years of law school, a lot of good students would be washed out. I was certain that most of the other students were smarter than I. Only about one half of my class graduated after three years, as had been predicted. My freshman class started with thirty-five freshmen, and seventeen of the original students actually graduated. Our freshman class was the largest class in several years; the classes ahead of us started with about half as many freshmen. All of the students in the law school were male when I entered, and there were no female law students during the entire time I attended law school. All of the faculty members were also male. In fact, there were only two females in the law school: the Dean's secretary and the law librarian!

My first year, the entire law school, including class rooms, offices for the Dean, faculty members and staff, and the law library, occupied a small wing on the second floor of the old U of I Administration. The old University library was located on the floor immediately below. All law classes then, as now, were taught by the "case" method. The text books consisted of summaries of actual cases designed to illustrate points of law. The standard practice was for the students to review and prepare summaries of the cases likely to be covered in class the next day, and to be prepared to be called upon in class to explain the facts of a particular case and the point of law it illustrated.

No student knew in advance when he would be called upon, and as a consequence, we all tried hard to be prepared for every case assigned. On rare occasions, a student would acknowledge being unprepared for a particular case and ask to be passed over; but it was not considered wise to allow yourself to be in that position. When called up, the student didn't simply recite his understanding of a particular case, he often was subjected to a series of questions from the professor who often challenged his statements or conclusions.

One reason for the pressure felt by law students was that only one exam was given for each course and it was at the end of the semester. That one final exam determined your grade for the course and whether you passed or failed. To fail a course was serious, since most classes were progressive. A student had to pass one course in order to take the course that followed. A particular course given in the fall or in the spring term for example, could not be repeated until that term the following year. Summer classes were not offered. Every class was conducted in the same way and the material was covered rather rapidly. You had no way of knowing for sure how well you were grasping the information until the results of the final exam were received. Freshmen were given what was referred to as a "practice" exam about nine weeks into their first semester. The exam did not count officially but served to give students an opportunity to better understand the type of exam to be given and what the professor expected of them. The practice exam I took early in the first semester of my freshman year was reassuring. I did well and felt I could handle law school, if I continued to work hard.

All law school exams consisted of a series of hypothetical law cases. The student was expected to read, understand, and correctly identify the legal issues and render a decision in the case and justify the result. Recognizing and identifying the issues in a particular case, and the reasoning for your decision, was generally more important than reaching the correct decision, that is finding in favor of A or B. The exams were long and could be either written or typed, whichever the student preferred. By this time, I typed everything, including my class notes and the case summaries I prepared for class. Many times, I said a quiet "thank you" to Mrs. Holmgren who had talked me into taking a typing class when I started my senior year in high school. By this time, I was a good typist and my thought processes and my typing speed were in sync. I don't think I could have survived if I had been writing long hand.

The final exam for each course lasted three to four hours without a break. An individual student could take a break, but seldom did any one leave except to use the restroom. When the exam time had elapsed, everyone stopped, whether finished or not. Many would not finish completely. Seldom did anyone turn a test in before the time allotted for the exam had expired. There was never enough time to finish and fully review what had been written. That was probably just as well, as the temptation was usually to frantically make last minute changes.

I found that for me, at least, the best approach was to read a particular question a couple of times, give it some thought, jot down a few notes and then start writing. I usually typed the legal issues I had identified, the decision I had reached, and my rational for the conclusion without stopping and then moved on to the next question. I thought I was better off to try to finish the entire exam, and I could always go back and review my answers if I had additional time. Sometimes I did go back for a review, however I found that I was better off to simply go with my first approach.

Law students taking exams fell into one of two categories. Some immediately left the test area and didn't want to talk with anyone. Quite often, different conclusions would have been reached or different issues identified. Some could not resist doing "post mortems" with other students. They engaged in frantic conversations with others asking questions like "How did you decide the such and such case, and what issues did you find?" and so on. Discussion of the just-taken exam would often lead to looks of sheer panic on the faces of students from a fear of having failed the exam and the entire semester course.

I probably fell somewhere in between and more often visited with a few other students who were close friends. We knew that the cases in the exams usually reflected close questions of law and that in most cases, your answer would be judged more on the analysis and reasoning than for which way you decided a case. In addition, most cases selected for the exams contained many issues, some carefully hidden, and a student would seldom recognize all of the issues on an exam. Each law student was assigned a number for exam purposes, and when the grades were posted, you would check your number to find out the grade. Only you knew what your grade was, although word soon got around as to who got top grades and who failed a particular course.

The final exams for the first semester of law school occurred the last half of January. Donna's birthday fell on the twenty-second of the month. I had always had a difficult time remembering the date, and it was even worse when I was in law school than before. It helped when the kids were old enough to remind me, but that would be a few years away. Donna was pretty good about my shortcoming and we would try to celebrate after exams were finished. We celebrated both the birthday that year and the fact that I had passed my first semester of law courses.

Chapter 121

An Ambitious Work Schedule

Since I had done well overall my first semester of law school, I felt that I needed to be earning money, and I decided that I could devote time to working and still be able to manage the academic load. I had developed good study habits and became more comfortable with the routine and demands of law school. I talked with my friend, Bud Hagen, who had initially discouraged me from working my first year. He was pleased with my grades; however, he still felt I should devote all of my time to law school and he discouraged me from taking on more work.

In spite of Bud's advice, I decided to look for work, confident that if my grades suffered, I could reduce my work hours. Few law students worked while attending school. Several had served in the military and were receiving G. I. Bill benefits, some had spouses who were able to work full time, and some were otherwise able to make it without earning extra income. Donna was working as much as we thought was prudent while taking care of Linda. Right or wrong, we still believed quite strongly, that we should do it on our own. We were determined to ask for help only in an emergency; we did not want to leave school owing debts if at all possible.

A fellow law student, Jack Barrett, was a veteran with benefits under the G. I. Bill and he also had part time work. He had a motor route to deliver newspapers for the *Spokane Daily Chronicle* which was an afternoon paper. Out-of-town newspapers usually had more scattered coverage than a local newspaper. Since a larger area had to be covered, much of the distance was covered by both driving and walking. Jack mentioned to me that the *Lewiston Tribune*, a daily newspaper published in Lewiston, Idaho, was looking for someone to take over a motor route in Moscow. While the *Chronicle* was delivered in the afternoon shortly after classes were out, the *Tribune* was a morning newspaper. I decided to give it a try.

My motor route was all that part of the City of Moscow east of Main Street which was a large area to be served. The papers were dropped off at the Moscow Hotel around 4:30 a.m. by a Greyhound bus traveling north through Moscow. Coverage of the route required one-and-one-half to two hours, if I moved quickly. My routine was to wake up at 4:45 a.m., dash to the hotel to pick up my bundles of papers, and then take off. I drove to a point from which I could stop and deliver several papers on foot. My habit was to grab the necessary number of papers and take off running to the subscribers' scattered houses, often a block or two. Then I would cross the street, circle back, and deliver as I made my way back to the parked car. I then moved on to another somewhat central point and repeated the process until I was finished with my deliveries.

If all went well, I could finish my deliveries and get back to the trailer before 6:30 in the morning. If I was really quiet, I could enter the trailer and climb back into bed for another half hour of sleep without waking Linda. (Later Linda and Patricia.) Usually, all went well; however, sometimes due to weather problems or problems with the presses in Lewiston, the papers were late getting to the hotel or I was slowed down in making my deliveries. The motor route was not a glamorous job, but it helped to pay the bills. I continued on with my motor route for the *Lewiston Tribune* until I graduated from law school in the spring of 1959, summers excluded. I lost weight; however I was in excellent physical shape, probably better shape than I have been in since.

I continued running the second mailer machine at the *Daily Idahonian* in the afternoon. In the spring of 1957, my supervisor at the *Idahonian* asked me if I would also consider driving the company panel truck to deliver sacked bundles of papers to boys for delivery in the small towns north and east of Moscow. The deliveries could be made when I had finished stamping addresses on papers to be mailed to out-of-town subscribers. In addition, I was given a route for newspaper subscribers who lived along the highway between Moscow and the grocery store at Princeton, Idaho, my last truck stop. The extra duties meant extra money and I accepted the offer to drive the truck and handle the highway route. I also continued doing this until I graduated from law school.

The delivery route along the highway was a challenge. I had customers on both sides of the highway and generally I tried to complete these deliveries on the way to Princeton, before I turned around to return to Moscow. The customers had newspaper tubes secured to posts, similar to mailboxes. Most of the tubes were along the highway; however, a few were not. I became quite good at inserting a paper into the tube without stopping the truck. To cover both sides, on the way up I would go back and forth across the highway, keeping a watchful eye out for traffic which always included logging trucks. It was easier to "hit" the tube on the left side of the highway than on the right, but I usually was able to hit the tubes on the right side. Years later, I have had occasion to drive along the same stretch of highway. I swear I could still deliver most of the route. The biggest problem I had was collecting for the newspaper each month. This was in the rural area with mostly farms, and often I would not find anyone in the house to collect from.

I don't remember just how much I earned with my various jobs; however, it was not a lot. Part time jobs for university students were limited and none of the jobs paid very well. As my economics professor would have said, "It's just a matter of supply and demand." I understood the concept but wish I had not had to experience its practical application in such a personal way! Looking back, I probably tried to take on more work than was prudent. With the early morning stint with the *Lewiston Tribune* and the longer afternoon responsibilities with the *Idahonian*, I really had almost no time for study until in the evening following dinner. During the week, the evenings were short because 4:45 a.m. came awfully early. I remember that I tried to keep up with my case reviews on the weekends.

I probably should have tried to work out another approach, but it all seemed to work. Donna and I were both young and healthy. Perhaps I should have laid out a year to work and then returned, but that would have delayed graduation. I have often reflected on the life Donna and I lived while I was attending law school full time. I have wondered if I would do it again the same way, or if I would have expected anyone else, one of my kids for example, to do the same as we had.

Under all of the circumstances I do believe I would do it again in much the same way; although I would make a real effort to find better paying jobs and work hours that were more compatible with the academic load. I really envied my friend Jack Barrett and his afternoon motor route, but on the other hand, I had the added income from my work at the *Idahoan*. Without a doubt, I would not have expected any of my children to carry the same work load while attending school; however, the circumstances were much different when they actually were attending college. To their great credit, each of my children did contribute significantly to the expense of college. Each of them has developed a very good work ethic.

My grades probably did suffer somewhat, although when I graduated I was in the low end of the top third of the class. I always thought I could have done better, and I probably could have. I was not asked to be a part of the Law Review Program which was started for the first time with my class during the third year. I guess I would have liked to have been asked; however, I am not sure how I would have found the time to make a meaningful contribution. Those who decided which students to invite into the program may have realized my time constraints. Anyway, I was pretty sure that I wanted to practice law, probably in Idaho Falls, and I believed that a willingness to work hard and discipline oneself was equally, if not more important, than grades in the practice of law. If I had been interested in teaching or working for a large corporation, having top grades would have been more important; however, I had no interest in either of those pursuits.

I did participate in the Moot Court program which I believe all first-year students who were not "struggling" were asked to do. Following the first round, I was asked to participate as a member of the Moot Court team representing the University of Idaho Law School. Our team made several trips to compete with other law schools in Montana, Oregon and Washington. Other than Moot Court and Practice Court during my senior year, I simply went to school, worked and studied. Donna and I did occasionally attend a movie or get together with friends for a game of bridge or a picnic on the weekend. Most of the other law students were in pretty much the same boat: short of time and money. At the time we did have fun; however, Donna and I were gradually worn down by our routine.

Chapter 122

Summer of 1957 and the Palisades Family Venture

Our summers were pretty much the same as when I was in my undergraduate years. When the term ended in the spring of 1957, we packed up the car and drove back to the farm in Idaho Falls. Before leaving we had arranged for our trailer to be moved to a newly constructed trailer facility, Terrace Gardens Trailer Court, located south of Moscow. The trailer park had paved streets and sidewalks, and large lots on a southern slope. The new location would be more a more pleasant place to live and a safe place for Linda to play. Life was always busy on the farm and the summer of 1957 was no different. We quickly fell into the summer routine which, while hectic, was also a pleasant change from the routine of law school and work in Moscow.

For years our family had talked about having a cabin someday which would give us a place to get away and relax. Dad had often talked about how much fun it would be to have a cabin for family use. During the early summer, we started talking seriously about the possibility. Orval and his wife, June, were now living in Idaho Falls where Orval was engaged in the practice of law with the St. Clair firm. Orval and June had arrived in Idaho Falls in early 1956. Farrel and his wife, Alice, were also living in Idaho Falls where Farrel was developing his medical practice. I think their return gave new impetus to the idea of a family cabin. The new dam and reservoir were under construction in Palisades, east of Swan Valley. The area was certain to develop into a new recreational area in close proximity to Idaho Falls, and we began to check out possible cabin sites.

We looked at the cabin site areas which were being developed for lease by the US Forest Service. With the size of our family and the fact it was growing, we began to look for a deeded acreage. We learned about a tract of land being offered for sale by Worth and Afton Smith. The 120-acre tract was located along the highway overlooking Indian Creek at the point it would flow into the new reservoir created by the dam under construction. We attempted to purchase a few acres; however, Worth Smith said he would not divide the 120-

acre tract. We discussed the matter as a family and decided to buy the total 120 acres. We obtained the $25,000 by increasing the mortgage on the farm. We believed that this purchase would give us plenty of room for our growing family. Also, much of the tract could be subdivided into lots and sold for cabin sites. Suitable deeded land was limited, and when the dam and reservoir were completed, it would be in demand, or so we rationalized.

During the summer of 1957, we were busy with the usual demands of the farm. In addition, we began to make plans for the Palisades property. We arranged to have a person do a topography survey, which resulted in a map showing the elevations of the property. The surveyor suggested such a map was essential to evaluating development prospects. I think we all later agreed it was a waste of time and money. This was due in part to the fact that he marked the elevations with wooden lath which soon rotted out. Also, the changes in elevation on the property were relatively minor. The location of possible roads and cabin site areas could easily be selected with the naked eye and a little common sense. We were inexperienced in land development and were bound to make a few mistakes. The topography survey was our first.

As a note of interest, the surveyor who suggested that a topography map was the essential first step in developing, had no experience in developing land. He was employed by the US Soil Conservation Service. He also persuaded us to survey some of our sloping fields on the farm to allow us to plant potatoes in rows that followed the contour of the field. The theory was that running rows on the contour would greatly reduce and possibly eliminate erosion from irrigation. The theory sounded good; however, we soon discovered that to plant on the contour resulted in many rows that did not have access to the ditch that provided the irrigation water. Also, many rows did not end at the low point of the field to allow waste water to drain away. This greatly complicated the all-important step of irrigating the crop, as well as cultivating the rows to eliminate weeds and providing a furrow for the irrigation water to flow through. Obviously, we also learned a lesson here as well. I will resist making any comments about the competency of the government.

We arranged for a house mover to move one of the houses across the street that had been used to house farm help to the Palisades property. It was the two-room bunk house Dad and Mother had purchased for Grandma Wahlquist. She had never moved in, and the house had been moved across the street. As payment for moving the bunk house, we gave the mover the end house across the street. We had as many as five houses at one time and this brought us down to three houses for farm help. Changes in farming practices had reduced the need for help.

Chapter 122: Summer of 1957 and the Palisades Family Venture | 343

Farrel identified a site for the bunk house and arranged for a dozer tractor to level the spot. As a result of unusually heavy rain, the mover became stuck and was unable to reach the intended site for the bunk house. It was left where the mover was stuck, which is its present location. Some of us made a homemade sign which we put on the site. The sign read "Farrel's Folly" and it remained there for several years until it disappeared. We kidded Farrel a lot about this. Actually, the final location was fine, probably as good as the intended one.

That summer we used the bunk house some although it was temporarily on blocks. We dug a pit and erected an outdoor privy a short distance away. In addition, we had a well drilled and cased, and installed a hand pump as a source for water. A reasonable source of water was reached at over 200 feet below. We were able to lift water to the surface with the hand pump, but to do so was hard work. We encouraged the younger kids to take turns at the pump and they did so eagerly, in an effort to prove that they could.

We found that the mosquitoes were bad for several weeks in late June and early July. We sprayed the area around the bunk house with DDT which was still legal to use, and it helped quite a bit. If you walked out of the area sprayed however, they were thick again. Nonetheless we were excited and enthused about the property, and we all spent as much time there as we could squeeze in. In the spring, when I was still in Moscow, thousands of seedlings purchased from the University of Idaho Experiment Station were planted on the property. The dominant established tree on the property was the Lodgepole Pine. The seedlings were intended to provide a mix which included Colorado Spruce, Ponderosa Pine and other varieties.

The planting of seedlings was done over several years. Many of the seedlings died, and for a time we were afraid that all had died from lack of water at critical times. To offset the drought problem, we even carried water to some of the seedlings during the summer. Years later, to our surprise and delight, the results of the planting efforts began to grow and show. It takes a long time for a seedling to become established and grow high enough to be seen above the grass and other growth. We can now clearly see the results of the efforts fifty years ago. The planted trees, now mature, are providing seeds for new seedlings. Lodgepole Pine no longer totally dominates the property.

We arranged for another surveyor to stake out proposed cabin site lots toward the other end of the location of the bunkhouse. Our intentions were to keep the one end of the property for future family use. Our family was growing fast. We planned that someday everyone in the family who wanted one, could have their own cabin site. The property we intended for family use also had some of the best views of the new Palisades reservoir. Orval was then practicing law in Idaho Falls, and he undertook the task of having a plat prepared of the lots for sale, filing the plat with the Bonneville County authorities, and preparing and recording restrictive covenants. We were careful to take all of these steps before selling any lots. We also made arrangements to have another well drilled to provide a source of water for the benefit of the building lots.

I was asked by the family to take the main responsibility for showing lots to prospective buyers in the new subdivision and to oversee the well drilling. I did make several quick trips to the Palisades property during the summer to show lots. In order to keep our development costs down, as well as the asking price for lots, we had decided to simply cap the well that had been drilled for the new subdivision of twelve lots. Our plan was to sell with each lot, an undivided one-twelfth interest in the capped well. We would leave it to the new lot owners to take on the responsibility of forming an association of owners and of developing the well and providing distribution lines to each of the subdivision lots.

We soon discovered that it took a lot of time to show lots located seventy miles from home. We also learned that the lots as platted were smaller than most people desired. Further, we ultimately decided that it was a mistake not to develop a water system and install distribution lines before attempting to sell lots. Most prospective buyers were turned off by having to deal with the financing and operation of a water system themselves. This was particularly so in the early stage of development and until all of the lots had been sold. In retrospect, we would have been wiser to have put a water system together and increased the asking price of the lots. This would have required that we also operate the system until all the lots were sold and the system could be turned over to the owners. The down side would have been the responsibility of operating a small water system from a long distance.

We discovered that land development is more expensive and complicated than we had envisioned in the beginning. Ultimately we did sell all the lots and the new owners did take on the responsibility for water, but it took much time and, overall, was not a profitable venture. Many of the buyers purchased two lots for a single summer home. Also, we ultimately decided that we would be better off to hold the undeveloped land for investment. If and when the value of the land and demand for cabin sites warranted development, then we probably would sell a large tract to an experienced developer. We also considered keeping all of the remaining unsold property within the family. As I said, land development turned out to be quite complicated.

Chapter 123

The Cold War Escalates

Year 1957 was at the height of the Cold War. The United States and the USSR were in a tense arms race. Each country had developed both an atomic bomb and the more powerful hydrogen bomb. The United States developed these weapons first; however, the USSR followed suit within a relatively short time. Both countries were stockpiling these sophisticated weapons, and both countries had large bombers capable of delivering the weapons. Each country was afraid the other would start World War III with the use of these new weapons. The use of the A-bomb in August 1945 brought an end to World War II and made everyone aware of the terrible devastation that would result from such a conflict. President Eisenhower had been elected to a second term in the fall of 1956. It is hard to describe the tension that everyone felt during that time. We in the United States took pride in being stronger and technologically more advanced than the Soviet Union, or so we thought. Certainly, that was the widely-held view. Anticommunist propaganda touted the superiority of democracy over communism. Suddenly a dramatic event occurred.

I was driving home from Palisades in the late summer of 1957, by myself, and listening to the radio. I can still remember where I was on the Antelope Flat stretch of the highway when the news flash came on. The USSR had just announced the successful launch of a long-range ballistic missile, an intercontinental ballistic missile (ICBM). The news report went on to say that the large rocket traveled a distance of 6000 to 8000 miles, and that it landed in the ocean within six to eight miles of the intended target area.

This was a huge development. Obviously, with such a rocket the USSR could deliver an A-bomb or H-bomb a long distance in a matter of minutes. To deliver such weapons with an accuracy of just a few miles was astounding considering the area of devastation that would result. Imagine an H bomb hitting within a few miles of the center of New York City. The conventional bombers of the United States, the only delivery system we had then, would take hours to travel the same distance. The Cold War advantage had dramatically shifted to the USSR. More evidence of this became known later that fall.

The summer of 1957 went by quickly and soon Donna and I, together with Linda who was growing up fast, left for Moscow and my second year of law school. When we arrived, the trailer had been moved to our new location at Terrace Gardens Mobile Home Park south of Moscow. We settled into our new surroundings, the routine of law school, and our various jobs. We were pleased with the new location and the facilities available to us, a vast improvement over the previous year. Our friends Merlin (Duke) and Mary Powell and their new baby had moved to the same trailer facility, and we soon became acquainted with other residents. Most of the people we became acquainted with were attending the university or working to support a spouse who was a student, or both.

Each lot even had a buried trash bin with a lid flush to the ground which you raised by stepping on a small pedal. A few days after we arrived, I heard Linda crying. I looked around, but was unable to find her. I followed the sound and discovered that she had stepped on the trash bin pedal and fallen in head first. The lid was partially closed but I could see one of her shoes sticking out. I couldn't help laughing when it was obvious that she was unhurt. Linda was not amused, although I doubt that she had any idea what had happened. Donna and I spent some time showing her how the lid worked and what not to do. As far as I remember she never fell in again!

During the first week of October, 1957, the USSR, using the same rocket that had been test fired the previous August, successfully launched Sputnik 1 and placed it in orbit around the earth. In early November, 1957, Sputnik 1 was followed by Sputnik 2 which placed a larger satellite into orbit. The satellite contained a compartment that held a small dog named Laika. By now it was clear that the USSR, our adversary in the Cold War, had gained a huge strategic advantage over the United States.

A sense of urgency, almost panic, prevailed in this country. Sputnik 1 officially ushered in the start of the space age and a host of new political, military, technological, and scientific developments. Then, Sputnik 1 and 2 caused a political furor which prompted Congress to pass legislation leading, among other things, to the creation of the National Space and Aeronautics Administration (NASA). The events also lead to a careful analysis of the performance of our education system, and a recognition of the need to place more emphasis on and allocate more resources for science and technology training. The achievements of the USSR stunned the world and dominated the news everywhere.

Periodic reports were given on the condition of the dog, Laika. The times when the orbiting satellites would be visible in certain locations were regularly provided by the news media. One night in early November, I set the alarm and around 3:30 a.m. I got up, dressed and walked down our street to a point where I could get an unobstructed view of the portion of the southern sky Sputnik 2 was expected to pass through. I remember feeling a little bit foolish; however, in spite of the cold, I continued to wait and watch. Suddenly the orbiting satellite was indeed visible, a bright light moving at a slow, steady pace across the entire night sky. It was thrilling to see, and to realize it was an object made and placed in orbit by man, in a sky otherwise filled with stars, planets and constellations. I listened very carefully; however, I was unable to hear any barking by Laika! I went back to bed, glad I had made the effort to see Sputnik 2.

About the time Sputnik 2 was orbiting the earth, Donna became pregnant, although I don't really believe that there was any connection between the two events. In spite of the fact that our financial resources were limited, we were both pleased at the prospect of having another baby. We had talked about the need to have our children reasonably close together and having Linda and the new baby three years apart seemed about right to us.

The 1957-1958 school year seemed to pass by quickly. I continued to deliver the *Lewiston Tribune* in the early mornings and work at the *Idahoan* in the afternoon running the second mailer machine and making deliveries afterwards. Donna did some baby sitting and also continued to work part time for the Suffolk Sheep Society. As in the previous year, we occasionally got together with some of our married friends for a game of bridge or just to visit, but we mostly worked, studied and slept. Linda developed fast and was fun to be around. Aside from a bout of colic shortly after she was born, she was a happy and healthy child who played well with other children. We returned to Idaho Falls for a few days during the Christmas holidays, but remained in Moscow the rest of the time.

Chapter 124

Summer of 1958

At the end of the school year, we closed up the trailer and returned to Idaho Falls for the summer. By this time, Donna was almost seven months pregnant. Even though I planned to work on the farm, we decided it would be easier for Donna if we found a place that was on one floor and had a fenced yard. We checked around and located a house on Merritt Drive in Idaho Falls that had both and was available for the summer.

In addition to helping on the farm, I also spent time at Palisades. The family decided that we should remodel the bunkhouse for use as a family cabin. By this time Farrel had purchased a small camp trailer which was parked near the bunkhouse. We hired a couple of carpenters and I worked with them a good deal of the time. Often I would stay on the property at night, utilizing the camp trailer. Ray Nickerson was one of the persons I worked with. He was a most interesting person. He was totally honest and capable of doing almost anything. Ray had built a cabin for Worth Smith from whom we bought the property and had been highly recommended by Mr. Smith. The other person who helped at Palisades was a fairly competent carpenter; however, he had a serious drinking problem and often failed to show up for work.

With Ray's help and supervision, we mixed concrete and put the structure on a concrete foundation. We replaced all of the windows, installed log siding on the outside walls, and put on a new roof. We went to a rock quarry near Ririe, Idaho, and secured chunks of rather beautiful rock for a fireplace. Ray had all of the appropriate hand tools and showed us how to split the rock into the right size and shape for the fireplace. The fireplace was really interesting with a variety of colors and rocks that were shaped into a calf head, a crescent, and other interesting figures on the inside, above the fireplace screen. Ray really was an amazing fellow.

I became well acquainted with Ray and his wife who lived in Swan Valley, Idaho. We developed a friendship that lasted until Ray died many years later and his wife Bernice, after a time, moved to Arizona. She was also a fascinating person. For years she raised mules. Like Ray, she was a hard worker. Ray and Bernice owned a one-horse buggy that was almost a duplicate of the buggy Doc used in the TV series "Gunsmoke." Many people tried to buy the buggy over the years, however Ray refused to sell it. One day he said he would sell it to me, and I bought it. Reed and Marilyn were looking for a buggy and I immediately sold it to them. I am not sure what eventually happened to it. I hope it was restored to new condition.

We installed a sink in the "cabin" kitchen and left a place for a bathroom, however that was all. Ray said he did not do plumbing and we decided we would finish the cabin in stages. Farrel had a friend who worked at the National Laboratory west of Idaho Falls (commonly called the "Site") who wired the cabin for us. By the end of the summer, we had insulated the walls and ceiling and had installed a Majestic cook stove in the kitchen. The Majestic was similar to the one Mother used on the Airport Farm. The fireplace worked well, and we had an outdoor privy. Reed and Marilyn made a table with benches and a couch, mostly out of log materials found on the property. While the cabin was somewhat primitive, it was quite usable, and we did use it as often as we could, summer and winter.

I divided my time between Palisades, working on the cabin, showing lots, and working on the farm wherever I was needed. One summer farm chore I remember doing during the time I was in law school, was operating the field hay chopper. We continued to field chop our alfalfa hay as feed for the dairy herd. About this time, we started using a swather to cut and windrow the hay in one operation. The swather also made a looser windrow which allowed the cut hay to cure faster and more uniformly. With the new self-propelled swather, we did not need to cut and windrow the hay quite as far ahead of the chopper as when we mowed and raked in two separate operations. This seemed to prevent the hay from becoming overly dry in the event rain fell on the cut hay and delayed haying operations.

Hay wagons constructed for the chopped hay were transported to and from the field, two wagons in tandem. I hooked an empty wagon to the hitch on the back of the chopper and proceeded down the windrows one at a time until the wagon was full. Then I would hook up another and continue on. When two wagons were full they were towed by a tractor to the stack yard near the milking parlor. The hay chopper had a large and rather temperamental engine. Often, I had to stop and wait for empty wagons to arrive; particularly when I was in a field at the west end of the farm, a distance of close to two miles from the stacking yard. I generally put the chopper into neutral and left the engine running. I had learned that if I shut the engine off, it was often difficult to restart.

To leave the engine running was not a safe practice but, as I was generally the only one around and understood the equipment rather well, I thought it was a reasonable tradeoff. I also routinely greased the machine while the engine was running. Occasionally, something would plug the cutting chamber and stop the rotating heavy blades which cut the hay into small pieces. I learned to remove whatever stopped the cutting, a large piece of wood or a large wad of green alfalfa, without shutting down the engine. Sometimes this involved reaching into the cutting chamber.

I know this was not the safest practice, but I was careful. I think I learned to unplug the chopper without turning off the engine from Norman, who had operated the chopper in previous years. Nothing was more frustrating than to try to spend an hour trying to start a hot engine on a hot afternoon while the entire haying crew stood around without anything to do. I always checked carefully to make sure no one was standing near the lever which engaged the rotation of the blades in the cutting chamber.

I kept the tool box of the chopper filled with back issues of *US News and World Report* that Mother subscribed to. While I was waiting for empty wagons to arrive in the field, I read the issues cover to cover. I didn't have much time for discretionary reading while I was in Moscow working and attending law school. In those days, the magazine was a much better source of in-depth news than it is today. I was amazed how timely most of the material was, though it had been published weeks and months before. I didn't want others in the crew waiting for me; however, I actually enjoyed having time to read while waiting for empty wagons. Reading helped make the time pass.

We enjoyed living on Merritt Drive. Linda played in the fenced yard, often with other kids including her cousins. Donna did not have the worry of traffic on the farm or the nearby open ditches and canal. When I came home for dinner I stayed home for the evening. When we stayed on the farm there was always something to do after dinner, such as servicing a tractor or repairing equipment or helping with the livestock. Living in town was an interesting change for us. Linda was fun to be around and excited about the new baby which was due soon. I did stay overnight at Palisades occasionally, but no more than necessary. It was quiet and boring, especially when the workmen left at five o'clock in the afternoon. The camper did not have electricity, only a butane light to read by. A couple of times Donna and Linda came up and stayed with me in the camper. Usually I drove back to Idaho Falls in the evening and returned to Palisades in the morning.

Patricia Ann Hansen was born on August 12, 1958. I don't remember if it was possible in those days to determine the sex of the baby prior to birth, however I think it was. We always waited. We wanted to be surprised. Patty was smaller at birth than Linda had been, however she was a full-term, healthy baby. Linda, who was not yet three years old, was excited at the prospect of having a sister, and was very sweet with the new baby. Linda wore her winter mittens when she and I went to the hospital to pick up Donna and Patty because it was such a special occasion.

We were made aware of a potential concern, should we have additional children. We had known that Donna's blood type was A negative and mine was B positive. This combination meant that we had an RH blood problem which showed up in our babies. Linda exhibited no symptoms; however, Patty showed signs of jaundice, one of the indicators of the blood incompatibility. The doctor monitored her, and no serious problems developed. We were advised that the problem would be more pronounced should we have more children.

About a week after Patty was born and soon after she and Donna were settled in the house on Merritt Drive, the owners came back unannounced and wanted to move back into the house. They had originally planned to be gone all summer and to return after we left for Moscow. While this was inconvenient to say the least, with Mother's help we moved back to the farm and into the basement apartment. After a few weeks, it was time for the four of us to pack up, and drive to Moscow and settle into the trailer. I registered for my third and last year of law school and classes began. Once again, I went back to the *Idahoan* and took up where I had left off the previous spring; and I resumed delivery of the early morning motor route of the *Lewiston Tribune*. The good news was that I was in my last year of law school and I could see "light at the end of the tunnel."

Chapter 125

Graduation in Sight; Panic Sets In

We soon fell into the usual routine of school and work. Patty fit nicely into our family routine. She was a healthy and happy baby, and she and Linda got along well. Linda was very protective and in her own way, was helpful and attentive. While the trailer was small it was compact and efficient and worked well for the four of us. There were two bunk beds along the walkway in the center with a curtain for privacy. Linda graduated to the top bunk when Patty was finally old enough to move to the lower bunk from her small bassinet in our bedroom.

During the previous summer, the law school had been moved from the cramped quarters of the third-floor wing of the old Administration building to the first-floor space which previously housed the university library. The area had been totally remodeled and included more and larger classrooms; also, a model court room to be used for Moot Court competition and for Practice Court, a senior level course. Practice Court was the only offering during the three years of law school that exposed students to something that involved the practical side of the practice of law. Everything else we did involved studying the law based on the case method that I described.

With the exception of Practice Court there was nothing exceptional during my senior year at law school. I did enjoy the experience of Practice Court. Senior law students worked in teams of two on "canned" cases we were assigned. Some cases were criminal; others were civil. We students were quite competitive and worked hard to advance our side of the case. The exercise was good experience and helped us to build our confidence. The witnesses and jurors were university students from outside the law school who were selected or who had volunteered. Everyone, including the witnesses and jurors, took their responsibilities seriously.

We often were able to watch at least parts of some of the practice court trials of other students. At some point after each trial had been completed, one or more of the faculty members gave a detailed critique of the handling of the proceeding. After so much academic theory we were all hungry for this taste of "real" law practice and an opportunity to test ourselves. I was impressed with the fact that the real key to success was preparation, preparation, preparation. There is no magic to the practice. One cannot overprepare, but it is quite possible to underprepare. This lesson stayed with me, aided by the fact that I was an insecure farm kid who assumed everyone else was better and smarter and that my only hope was to work harder in my preparation.

For years, I had harbored some notion that I might like to become a lawyer, beginning with the suggestion of Mrs. Roach, my social science teacher when I was in the ninth grade at O.E. Bell Jr. High School. I found the study of the law interesting and a challenge which I really did enjoy. However, sometime during my senior year of law school, it occurred to me that I had never been inside a law office and really had no idea what the practice of law was all about. Suddenly I felt a sense of panic.

I was twenty-six years old and had a wife and two children to support. I started to worry about what I would do if after graduation I discovered that I did not really like the profession I had chosen after all. Orval had graduated and was now in practice; however, I had had limited contact with Orval while he was attending law school and even after he had returned to Idaho Falls. He and I had not really discussed the practice and I had never visited his office or met any of his partners. It seems strange, looking back; however, I was extremely busy during the summers I spent in Idaho Falls. I was starting to become anxious about what I would do after I graduated. What had seemed far away for so long was now just around the corner. And I had no plans.

One or two of my classmates planned to leave the state and pursue a master's degree in law. A couple of students had military obligations to perform and would enter the JAG (Judge Advocate Program). The Idaho Attorney General always hired two or three new deputies. Most of my fellow students were planning to look for a job in a private law firm or start a practice. Unlike today, very few firms came to the law school to recruit graduating senior law students. The Federal Bureau of Investigation was the only recruiting entity that I remember. My general plan on graduation was simply to return to Idaho Falls, study for the bar exam, and, if and when I passed the bar, to practice law in the area.

I learned that Joe Anderson, a local attorney who held the part time position of Police Judge for the City of Idaho Falls, was planning to give up his duties as police judge and devote full time to his law practice. I thought that if I could pick up that position, it would give me some regular income while I tried to develop a private law practice. At the time I knew of no law firm in Idaho Falls that had plans to hire a new lawyer.

While we were in Idaho Falls for the Christmas vacation, I arranged for an interview with Idaho Falls Mayor O'Bryant. While there had been no commitment from the mayor, our conversation went well, and I went away thinking my prospects for being appointed the Police Judge following graduation were pretty good. Shortly before graduation I received word that William 'Bill" Black, had been appointed to the position. Bill Black was ahead of me in law school and had served as Police Judge for the City of Moscow. His father was and had been for many years City Engineer for the City of Idaho Falls. Bill and I ultimately became good friends, but I remember being extremely disappointed when I received the word. I had no back up job plan. I guess I had just assumed I would get the position of Police Judge and if not, that something else would work out.

Looking back, I really should have been more aggressive in my efforts to find a paying job upon graduation. I reconciled myself to working on the farm and studying for the bar exam which was to be given in September. Thereafter, I would start a solo law practice, commonly called "hanging up a shingle." At this point in my life, I remember being physically and mentally exhausted from the routine of work and study, and I have to admit I was quite discouraged. I am sure however, that I did not share my concerns with anyone else.

Two or three weeks before the end of my senior year of law school, I finally gave up delivering the *Lewiston Tribune* in the early morning. I usually woke up just before the alarm clock went off and would quickly shut the alarm button off. I probably was afraid I would sleep in and also that the alarm would wake up Linda and Patty. The first morning after I gave up the motor route I remember wondering if I would still wake up at 4:45 a.m. It was not a problem. That first morning and every morning for the remainder of the year, I slept soundly until 7:00 a.m. If I have to get up I can, but if not, I am a sound sleeper. The same thing had been true when I was a young boy at home on the farm and would get up early to milk cows and do chores. On my occasional day off, I had no trouble sleeping late into the morning.

For the first time in the history of the University of Idaho School of Law, members of my graduating class were allowed to wear a graduation gown and hood during commencement denoting the academic rank of Juris Doctor. Our class, with the support of the faculty members, successfully lobbied university officials for the privilege of wearing the hood. The law students believed, rightly so, that the three years of law school should count for as much as either a master's or a doctorate degree. I don't remember being very worked up about the issue, although I supported the effort as a matter of principle. Interestingly, our degree was identified on the diploma we received as a Bachelor of Laws, the same as in prior years.

To my surprise, Mother and my brothers, Farrel and Norman arrived in Moscow to attend the commencement ceremony. I was moved that they took the time to drive all the way from Idaho Falls to see me graduate from law school. Donna, and I believe Linda and Patty, also attended. Mother, Farrel and Norman drove home the next day.

It is interesting to note that several years later, the graduating law students began receiving a Juris Doctor, which is now the standard degree awarded. A short while later when I was engaged in the law practice, I received a letter from the Idaho State Bar advising that upon payment of forty-five dollars I could receive a Juris Doctor degree to replace the Bachelor of Laws degree I had received in June, 1959. I declined the offer.

Chapter 126

Back Where We Started

After graduation, Norman came up with a farm pickup and together we pulled the trailer back to Idaho Falls. At first, we parked the trailer on the farm, but of course we had no sewer hookup. Shortly thereafter, I arranged for a space at the Uptown Trailer Court behind Stoddard Mead Ford on West Broadway, formerly the Hansen Allen Ford agency.

So here we were, back in Idaho Falls and living in a trailer court that was much less desirable than the one we had moved from in Moscow. I had a law degree and no job prospects. At least I again had a job on the family farm. Suddenly, life seemed much more complicated than when I was a student. I needed to start studying for the bar exam that would be given in September. I was tired of school and found it difficult to begin studying. At the time, there was no bar review course for Idaho students anywhere in the state. The graduates from law school simply prepared for the exam on their own.

Where there were several graduates in the same city or community, sometimes they studied together; however, to my knowledge I was the only graduate in the Idaho Falls area. Actually, I often preferred to study on my own to avoid distractions. In June of 1959, I needed motivation, not companionship. Orval gave me the materials he had used when taking a bar review course in Washington D.C. These materials were helpful to me in getting started and, together with all the case summaries I had typed for my law classes, I had plenty of materials to review.

About this time, I received a call from "Bud" Hagan who had been a mentor at the Sigma Chi Fraternity during my first year of law school. Bud had moved to Boise following his graduation in 1957, had passed the bar, and was employed with a prominent Boise firm. Bud asked if I had a job and I said I did not. He went on to say that the Boise firm of Marcus and Evans was looking for a law graduate. Bud said that Claude Marcus and Blaine Evans were both well respected lawyers, and he strongly recommended that I interview with them.

Apparently, they had planned to hire; however, they had delayed making a decision until all of the graduates in the Boise area had been hired by other firms.

I immediately called Mr. Marcus; I drove to Boise and interviewed a couple days later. I was impressed with both gentlemen and with their staff. They offered me a job at a salary of $350 per month. At the time this was considered a good starting salary. I learned that it was slightly higher than any of the other members of my graduating class. The reason for the salary really had nothing to do with my scholastics or class standing. They needed help and I was the only one available. As my economics professor had said, "It is all about supply and demand."

I told them that I planned to ultimately return to Idaho Falls. They didn't seem concerned. If things worked out, I am sure they felt I would change my mind. Also, another young lawyer had been slated to come into the firm; however, he had decided to serve another two-year term as Ada County Prosecuting Attorney. I was elated with the offer, and I knew Donna would be. From our conversations, it was clear that she would prefer to live in Boise than in Idaho Falls, although she was agreeable to living in Idaho Falls.

I felt strong family ties and was pleased that Orval and Farrel had returned to the community to live and work. All family members got along well and had fun together and were excited about developing the property in Palisades. Idaho Falls seemed to me to be the right place to settle permanently. I probably should have been more open-minded, but I was not. Boise was to be an opportunity for a couple of years of experience and then we would return to Idaho Falls.

I believe I accepted the offer from Mr. Marcus and Mr. Evans on the spot. Blaine Evans suggested I look at Boise Hills Village as a possible place to rent. Boise Hills Village was constructed north of downtown Boise as housing for returning veterans and other young families. It was a two-story U-shaped complex with a large grass area and playground in the center. I took a quick look at the apartments and thought it would work fine for us. I spoke with Donna on the phone, and she seemed comfortable with my description of a two-bedroom unit which I asked to be held pending her inspection and approval. The rent was reasonable, and all utilities were included.

Before returning home, I talked briefly with Jack Barrett and Howard Humphrey who were in the same law school graduating class. I also visited with Bud Hagan to thank him for the suggestion that I apply for a job with Marcus and Evens. All of them and their wives were close friends of Donna and me. They seemed pleased and offered suggestions and help in finding a place for us to live in Boise. On the drive home, I realized I had gone from feeling discouraged to feeling relief and excitement about the new opportunity in Boise. When I returned home, we put an ad in the newspaper for the sale of our trailer and started preparing for the move to Boise.

The trailer that had been our home during the law school days was in good condition and sold quickly. We loaded up a rented trailer with just about all we owned, which was not much. We also loaded several articles of furniture that Mother and several family members had given to us, as well as the inexpensive pine bedroom set which was in my room in the farm house when I was fifteen years old. Donna and I, along with Linda and Patty, headed for Boise, excited that the future was coming into focus, at least for a couple of years.

Donna and the girls approved of the apartment at Boise Hills Village. Linda and Patty were excited about having their own beds and their own room, which was a big step up from their bunk beds in the hallway of the trailer! We set up the maple bedroom set and other items of furniture we had brought from Idaho Falls. We went shopping for a couch and purchased an attractive one with a white Naugahyde covering that was reasonably priced. It looked nice for a while. However after several days the shape of the couch changed dramatically. We discovered that the frame had been made with "green" wood causing the shape of the couch to change as the wood dried out. Fortunately, the store took it back and gave us credit on another. Like most young families, we had a mixed variety of furniture, but we didn't really care. We were getting settled and had more room to spread out. After we were settled in the apartment, I began working for the law firm.

Chapter 127

Practicing Law

I found both Mr. Marcus and Mr. Evans delightful to work with, and they made me feel like I was an equal. Both went out of their way to introduce me to friends and clients. Mr. Marcus had had a large mining law practice and maintained his home and office in Idaho City for many earlier years. He had a very successful office and trial practice. Mr. Evans had been Ada County Attorney and had prosecuted several high-profile criminal cases, including at least two that resulted in the death sentence. Both had served in the Idaho legislature: Mr. Marcus as a legislator from Boise County years prior and Mr. Evans as a senator from Ada County. They were active in the Bar Association, in politics, and community affairs. They soon became Claude and Blaine. I appreciated the fact that they went out of their way to review with me legal matters they were handling and routinely sought my advice. I enjoyed being included in client conferences and case reviews. I know they were trying to acquaint me with how a firm operates, or should operate, something not available during the law school years.

On the first or second day, I was shown my new office which had a nice outside window with a view of downtown Boise and the State Capitol in the background. I had book cases but nothing else. I went with Claude and Blaine to look at furniture and they purchased a new wooden desk and chair and two side chairs for my office. The office looked and felt great. I was introduced to the two office secretaries. Mary Jean had worked for Claude for many years and Belva had been working with Blaine since he entered private practice. They were told that my work was to be given the same priority as my superiors, which I know was intended to make me feel like an equal. I knew however that these "pros" knew which work had priority.

I was given a Dictaphone, which I used primarily for legal research, most of which I did at the Idaho State Library located in the State Capitol Building. The firm had some research materials; however, the state library had practically everything, even more than the extensive library at the law school. I spent many hours there, often in the evening after our office was closed. I usually found other young lawyers from my graduating class also doing legal research in the evenings at the state library.

Mr. Marcus encouraged me to give dictation directly to a secretary as often as possible. This was a new experience for me, and I still remember how nervous I was when I dictated my first letter to Mary Jean. She sat very patiently, looking at her steno pad and not directly at me which I appreciated. When I struggled for a word or phrase, she would quietly make a suggestion and I began to relax. After a while, I preferred giving direct dictation, and I think it helped me to condense my thoughts better. When using a dictating machine, I know that I had a tendency to ramble; when I looked at a draft of my dictation, I usually chopped out about half of what I had dictated. I still enjoy giving direct dictation to a secretary; however, shorthand is no longer taught in secretarial schools or to court reporters for that matter, and its use has essentially died out. Very few secretaries are able to take shorthand. The machines have improved a great deal, and their use has become more efficient.

I soon became acquainted with the other lawyers in Boise and in the bank building in which we were located. All of the firms in Boise were small, consisting of two or three lawyers, generally. The Eberle firm was the largest with about five or six lawyers. Down the hall was the firm of Davidson, Copple and Davidson with three members. The older Mr. Davidson no longer practiced; however, he came to the office almost every day and met with clients. One day he asked me if I was related to a Hans Peter Hansen with whom he had been acquainted. I told him my grandfather on my father's side was so named. The next day he gave me an eight by ten glossy photo of my grandfather doing volunteer work in an LDS Church cannery in Boise not too long before he died. I later showed the photo to my mother and then gave the photo to my brother Farrel to include in the family archives.

Another day, I was talking with Mr. Davidson when he mentioned something about the Empire Building. I asked him where the Empire Building had been located and he said we were in it! The Idaho First National Bank Building had once been called the Empire Building. He said it originally had four stories and when purchased by the bank two additional stories were added and the building had been remodeled.

When Mother was about sixteen years old, she dropped out of school in Murray, Utah, and went to work for the Metropolitan Life Insurance Company in Salt Lake City to supplement the family income. Her sister Anna worked for the same office. The insurance firm needed someone to fill an opening in its office in Boise. Anna had more seniority; however, she was newly married, and her husband was employed in Salt Lake City. Mother offered to take the transfer. Mother enjoyed working for Metropolitan and often talked about her experiences there. She often mentioned that the office was located in the Empire Building which had the only elevator in Boise at that time. I now realized that I was working in the same building my mother had worked in many years before. She and I both enjoyed the coincidence that our working careers started in the same location. I often had a smile on my face when I came into the building lobby in the morning and entered the elevator to reach my office on the sixth floor, as my mother had done to reach her office on the fourth floor. She later met Dad at a church gathering in Boise.

One day Claude asked me to research a legal question. I thought I knew the answer from law school; however, I did some light research and reported back. He suggested that I dig a little further which I did, somewhat impatient because I had several other projects to do. I reported back to Claude and again he suggested I "dig a little deeper." I returned to the State Law Library and discovered that my tentative conclusion was totally wrong. Claude was pleased when I came back with the final research product. I have often wondered if he knew the answer all along and was just testing me. I learned a valuable lesson which benefited me throughout my years in the practice of law. There is no substitute for preparedness. In the pressure and time constraints of the practice, one can be a tempted to cut corners to conserve time. It is always a mistake. An extra level of preparation can make the difference in an opinion, a brief, and in the court room. It also provides an attorney a level of confidence that is helpful, especially when dealing with a more experienced lawyer on the other side. Claude was a strong advocate of preparation.

Early on Claude let me handle the insurance defense of a suit brought by an older attorney. Although the case involved less than $1,000, I worked hard and told Claude I thought the matter could be resolved by a motion for summary judgment. A summary judgment motion is an effort to resolve a case without an evidentiary hearing, simply on a question of law. Such motions are seldom granted early in a lawsuit, as fact questions are generally disputed. Anyway, I prepared a motion and submitted a brief and an affidavit on which I had worked very hard. I filed the papers with the court and set up a hearing date.

The opposing lawyer was a real nice fellow. He was kind to me in our dealings, although I know he thought I was wasting his and the court's time. Just before the hearing, he had encouraged me to make him a settlement offer. After a brief argument, the presiding judge, having read the brief and in all likelihood having checked the law himself, granted the motion and dismissed the lawsuit. The opposing lawyer was astonished. He had been so sure of his position that he hadn't thoroughly researched the legal issues.

Chapter 128

Life Before the Bar

We arrived in Boise in late June or early July, and the bar examination was scheduled for a date in September. The University of Idaho law school did not provide a summer bar review course of study for those intending to take the examination. Some individuals chose to study with someone else or in a small group of recent graduates. I preferred to study on my own. As mentioned earlier, I still had most of the case summaries I had prepared for classroom use while in law school, and I still had the materials Orval had obtained when he attended a formal bar review course in Washington DC following his graduation from George Washington Law School. I studied most often at the apartment and occasionally at the office after hours. I avoided The State Law Library, mainly because other law graduates were usually there, and it too was easy to engage in a "bull session."

One night I was at the apartment studying after the kids had gone to bed. I was sitting in a straight chair which I had leaned against the outside wall which faced the grassy courtyard. Suddenly the apartment building started swaying dramatically for several seconds. Although I had never experienced an earthquake, I knew that was exactly what was occurring. People exited the building complex and gathered on the grass. Donna and I stayed in the apartment and the kids slept through it. We were surprised to read in the paper the next morning, that the rather severe quake had occurred in the Hebgen Lake area north of Island Park in eastern Idaho. It caused the lake to tip and triggered a huge rockslide which formed a dam causing water to back up creating Crater Lake. We later learned that between twenty and thirty campers had been buried by the slide.

We occasionally got together with our friends and their young families for picnics. Donna and I particularly enjoyed taking Linda and Patty to Ann Morrison Park in the late afternoon or evening to feed the ducks and play on the equipment. The park, which ran along the Boise River, had just been completed and was a gift to the City of Boise from Ann Morrison, the widow of the founder of Morrison-Knudson Construction. The construction firm had built many major projects around the world, including Boulder Dam and Grand Coulee Dam.

Leisure time was limited. I put in long hours at the office trying to bring in enough fees to cover my salary and expenses, though I doubt that I ever did. Also, as the time for the bar exam approached, I began to feel added pressure. Being married with two children, I suddenly realized the importance of passing and being sworn in as a member of the Idaho Bar. My value to the office would be diminished were I to fail the exam which was given only twice a year. Failure to pass would also have been a major blow to my ego, even though a certain percentage of recent graduates had failed. Those who had failed the exam at least once often became some of the outstanding members of the bar. We were told it was not a disgrace to fail the exam; however, I don't think we really believed it.

The night before the exam was to begin, I put all of the study materials away and decided to go to bed early in order to be refreshed the next morning. I was keyed up and had a hard time falling asleep. A party was taking place in our end of the building, and the noise helped to keep me awake. Late in the evening, I grabbed a pillow and drove downtown to the office and slept on the couch in the waiting room. I didn't really sleep well, and early in the morning I went home to have breakfast. Then I drove to the federal courthouse building where the exam was to be given. I was not well rested, and I remember feeling a sense of panic.

Fortunately, when the exam started I calmed down at least somewhat. I followed the same procedure I had used in law school. I read the question, made a few notes to record the issues I could identify and started typing. After I had completed an answer, I quickly reread what I had typed and moved on to the next question. I tried to resist inserting new ideas into what I had already written. Fortunately, I was a pretty good typist and my thoughts and typing speed were usually in sync. I hoped a typed answer with reasonable sentence structure and good spelling would count for something.

As had been my habit in law school, I tried to avoid "kibitzing" with other exam takers at the noon break and at the end of each day. What others would say always sounded better than what I remembered having written for my answers. When I finally finished the three-day exam, I was exhausted. While one can never be sure, and I didn't want to say it out loud, I thought I had done pretty well. In due course, I learned that I had passed the exam and was sworn in as a member of the Idaho Bar.

Chapter 129

My Turn with Judge Chase Clark

Shortly after I had finished taking the bar exam, Claude asked me if I would handle a criminal matter for him in US District Court. At that time, members of the bar association were assigned to handle the criminal defense for defendants who were without means to employ an attorney. All lawyers were included, without exception, and when a federal judge assigned a criminal case to a lawyer, the lawyer was obligated to undertake a defense pro bono, or without a fee, for the person charged. It was considered to be an obligation of the profession and all lawyers, from the youngest to the oldest, were expected to accept such assignments and did so willingly. Claude was particularly busy and asked me to handle this one and I was eager for the experience.

    I went to the federal courthouse to see the US Attorney and explained that I was filling in for Mr. Marcus and that this was my first time to appear in federal court. I soon discovered that the defendant was charged with two counts under the Federal Mann Act, transporting women across state lines for purposes of prostitution. One count of the indictment involved a married woman and the other a sixteen year old girl. The US Attorney told me, just before the hearing, that I should have the defendant enter a formal plea of not guilty which would give me some time to investigate the facts, interview the defendant privately, and decide how to proceed. When the defendant was brought into the courtroom for his arraignment, I advised him to enter a plea of not guilty which he did, and the judge, US District Judge Chase Clark accepted the plea and set a date for the next procedure. I was starting to feel like a real lawyer! My first time and I was in federal court and handling a major felony case. Several arraignments were also scheduled on the same afternoon, so I arranged a time to review the file more extensively and interview the defendant, and then I returned to the office.

A tough old Democrat, Judge Clark had previously served as mayor of the city of Idaho Falls, and as governor of the state of Idaho. President Harry Truman had appointed him to the federal bench, a lifetime appointment. It was late in his career and I was told he was short-tempered. There are many colorful stories about Judge Clark told by the older members of the bar. I would soon have my own to tell.

A short time later, I went back to the federal courthouse, reviewed the charges against my client, and learned more about his prior offenses. I interviewed him and found him to be a fairly reasonable fellow, although he had a long record of prior offenses and had served time in a number of penal institutions, most recently McNeil Island Federal Penitentiary in the state of Washington for offenses similar to the ones now pending. Although he acknowledged that he was guilty of the charges filed, he did not want to go back to McNeil Island. I met again with the US Attorney who said he would be willing to drop the charge involving a minor female in exchange for a plea of guilty to the charge involving a married woman. Back at the office I reviewed the matter with Claude and Blaine who both believed that the defendant had no chance of being found not guilty and that he would be wise to accept the plea offer.

The next time I interviewed the defendant, he was surprisingly reluctant to enter a plea of guilty. At the same time, he acknowledged that he would undoubtedly be found guilty, and if convicted by a jury on both counts, he would probably receive a longer sentence. His record of prior offenses reflected that he had been in reformatories as a youth and in a number of adult institutions on a variety of offenses for most of his adult life. He mentioned that he had never, even as a youth, received probation or a withheld sentence. I told him that if he were willing to enter a plea, I would ask the judge to grant him probation and he agreed. We both knew that it would be a "hard sell" but I thought at least I had an argument for probation, and he seemed interested in the fact that I was willing to try.

I worked hard on my presentation to Judge Clark. I intended to acknowledge that the defendant had a long criminal record, and while many might think him undeserving or unable to meet the conditions of a parole, everybody deserved at least one chance. Throughout his life the defendant had never once been given the opportunity of probation; on each offense he was simply incarcerated. I would ask the judge to give the defendant his chance to prove himself and would stress that by doing so "…the defendant would have the key to the jail in his pocket." If he failed, he would simply be placed in jail, but at least for the first time in his life he would have been given the opportunity to prove himself. The more I worked on my presentation, the more I thought I had a fighting chance for probation. I can't remember where the "key to the jail" idea came from, but I thought it sounded pretty good.

The morning of the sentence hearing, the court room was crowded with attorneys waiting for their cases to be called. Mine was the first case called. I went to counsel table and the defendant was brought in and sat beside me. The US Attorney was present. I noticed Claude Marcus in the back of the courtroom. I wasn't sure if he was there on another matter or simply to observe me. Judge Clark asked the defendant to stand and we both stood. The US Attorney moved to dismiss the one count which involved a minor female. Judge Clark then asked the defendant how he intended to plea to the second count and he said, "Guilty, Your Honor." Immediately the judge slammed down his gavel and said, "Ten years in McNeil Island" and called for the next case. He hadn't even acknowledged my presence.

I was flustered, but I quickly addressed the court. I said I was the defendant's lawyer and that I had planned to make remarks on his behalf before sentence was pronounced. I know I was shaking, at least on the inside, but I was also unhappy with the way I was being treated. The judge glared at me and finally said, "All right I will hear what you have to say, but I want you to know that I consider a violation of the Mann Act to be more reprehensible than the crime of murder." I gave the judge the whole pitch I had worked up. I think the fact that I felt I had been professionally mistreated by the judge (and I had!) helped me in my presentation.

At the end of my remarks the judge said, "Well the sentence of ten years will stand; however, I will put in the order that the authorities at McNeil Island Penitentiary shall have discretion to grant the defendant probation if they choose to do so." I thought for a second, that perhaps I had gained a little something, but the defendant knew and the US Attorney later shared with me, that probation would never happen. The defendant thanked me for speaking on his behalf. Mr. Marcus gave me a pat on the back for having the guts to go forward with my planned remarks. He also thought Judge Clark had been out of line. That was my first experience in federal court. After I returned to the office, I realized that I had not yet been admitted to practice in the federal courts, a separate procedure from being admitted to practice in the state courts. Blaine Evans went back with me to the federal courthouse to have me formally sworn in to rectify the matter.

Not long thereafter, I received a call from the federal court to advise me that I had been appointed to represent another defendant charged with a federal crime. I reviewed the file and learned that my client was charged with transporting stolen automobiles across state lines. He also had a long criminal record and had spent a considerable part of his life behind bars. I interviewed the defendant who told me he was guilty and did not want to contest the charge. He also said that he in fact looked forward to returning to prison where he had friends and actually felt more comfortable than he did on the "outside."

I was beginning to learn that prison time is not really a deterrent for many ex-cons who have a long history of criminal activity. You and I would do anything to avoid the shame and stigma of incarceration for committing a crime. Many ex-cons are more comfortable in prison than trying to function in society. I remembered discussing this at length with Paul Boyd who practiced down the hall from our firm. He had a private practice and also served part-time as the Idaho Bankruptcy Judge. Earlier in his career, he had been a US Attorney for many years and had extensive experience with criminals.

When the date for plea and sentencing arrived, I went to federal court and sat beside the defendant and US Attorney and again I was in front of Judge Chase Clark. I planned to have the defendant enter a plea and then make a few remarks before sentence was pronounced, but I really didn't plan on saying very much. Before asking how the defendant would plea to the charge, Judge Clark declared a recess and invited counsel to come to his chambers. I didn't have a clue what he wanted. For a second I wondered if he was going to caution me on any remarks I might make. As soon as we all sat down, the judge ignored me and started working on the US Attorney to reduce the charge from a felony to a misdemeanor, a lesser charge. If there ever was a case that warranted a reduction, it was not this one. It was open and shut, as they sometimes say, and the federal prosecutor knew it. The judge however was persistent and finally the prosecutor relented and agreed to reduce the charge.

Back in the courtroom, the prosecutor made the motion to reduce the charge to which the defendant entered a guilty plea. He was sentenced to be incarcerated for a fairly short time. The defendant was as confused as the prosecutor and I were. Afterwards, I asked the prosecutor what had occurred. He thought that the judge had treated me unfairly during my first court appearance, and that perhaps today, he decided to give me a break. The justice system is not perfect!

Chapter 130

First Experiences

The time I spent in the law practice in Boise was personally very rewarding. Every day I learned something new, and I was gaining valuable experience. I became acquainted with many very fine lawyers who, without exception, were helpful and gracious to me. This was probably due in part to the high respect they had for Claude and Blaine who were quick to give me opportunities I would not have expected so early in my legal career. I will probably spend an extra amount of time, perhaps too much, discussing some of my "first" experiences because they were exciting learning experiences and provided a real adrenalin rush. Over the years, the experience becomes more routine, although often the routine still offers something new and different, which makes the practice interesting.

One day Blaine brought in one of his prospective clients, a young businessman, who had been arrested a few days earlier for DUI. He drove a vehicle which struck a woman on a bicycle. That morning, the newspaper reported that the woman had died from her injuries. Blaine asked me to take the client out to a justice of the peace whom Blaine had been acquainted with since his days as Ada County Prosecuting Attorney. He suggested that I ask for a reduction of the charge of DUI to negligent driving, which surprised me. In those days, justices of the peace handled misdemeanor criminal offenses. Probate judges handled estates, guardianships and adoption, and also criminal misdemeanors. Often the judges were laypersons. Later reforms were implemented replacing these forums with magistrate courts, and today all magistrate judges must be lawyers.

Blaine's client and I drove out to the house where the elderly justice of the peace lived and held court. Without any formality whatsoever, the judge reduced the charge to negligent driving, accepted a guilty plea, imposed a fine of about $300 and sentenced the client to serve 5 days in jail which the judge immediately suspended. That was all. I had barely said a word. Apparently,

Blaine had arranged for the disposition of the case with a phone call before we had arrived. I am sure Blaine felt a quick resolution of the criminal case would reduce the likelihood that the charge against the client would be changed to negligent homicide, even though the new charge would still be available in view of the death which had occurred. No other criminal charges were ever filed. A civil suit for monetary damages was probably filed on behalf of the woman's family, although I don't know that for sure. I remember feeling uncomfortable with the outcome.

Late in the fall, Blaine asked me to help him with a client who had brought his three children to Boise from his home in the state of Washington to visit relatives during Thanksgiving. Shortly after his arrival, case workers from the Idaho Children's Home, as it was then called, picked up and took custody of the children. The officials refused to return the children to their father or to disclose their whereabouts. I don't remember all of the details; however, I believe that relatives of the father's former wife had arranged for the children to be picked up. Blaine thought we should consider filing a writ of habeas corpus against the Children's Home which was an agency of the state of Idaho. Such a writ, if issued, would require that the Children's Home come to the district court and show cause for the taking. The writ means literally "produce the body" although in this case, the children were not required to be present for the hearing. It is a seldom-used procedure in modern times, but one that all law students study in school.

Blaine suggested I talk with Bill Eberle, the attorney for the Children's Home, to see if the release of the children could be arranged without a formal proceeding. Mr. Eberle was a highly-regarded lawyer who had served as Speaker of the House in the Idaho Legislature at the same time my brother Orval served in the legislature. He advised me that the children would not be returned unless such was ordered by the judge. As a consequence, Blaine and I prepared a writ of habeas corpus supported by affidavits and a brief which we filed with the court and then asked for a hearing at the earliest possible date. The case was assigned to Judge Merlin S. Young, considered one of Idaho's finest District Court judges. Blaine asked me to sit in with him when he interviewed prospective witnesses and the client shortly before the hearing date.

On the morning of the hearing, I went to the office early. I had never accompanied Blaine in a court proceeding and was anxious to see him perform in a trial. I was particularly pleased to have been asked to sit with him and the client at counsel table. At the last minute, Blaine said he had something he had to do. He asked me to walk the client to court and said he would catch up with us shortly. I carried the files and when we arrived, I sat at counsel table with the client and waited for Blaine to show up. He never did. At the time set for the hearing, Judge Young asked for a brief statement from both sides.

I was familiar with the facts and made a few remarks outlining why we had filed the writ and what we hoped to accomplish. Counsel for the Children's Home also gave brief remarks. Judge Young asked for the petitioner to call its first witness. We represented the petitioner in the writ. I looked frantically over my shoulder and said to Judge Young that Blaine was to present the matter in court and that he said he would be here shortly. The judge said rather sternly that the time for hearing had arrived and that we should proceed. I called the client to the stand. As I started my examination of the client, I periodically looked towards the back of the court room for any sign of Blaine.

I was frantic. I had never appeared in District Court and had never before interrogated a witness or offered an exhibit in evidence. I was as green as I could be. My only prior experience had been in practice court during my senior year in law school. There was a small crowd in the seating portion of the courtroom which included officials from the Children's Home and several witnesses ready to appear, as well as a reporter from the *Idaho Statesman*. We were into the holiday season and the case involving a father trying to obtain custody of his children from the state of Idaho had apparently generated some local interest. Fortunately, I had worked on the case from the beginning, was familiar with the facts, and had helped research the law governing the writ.

Even in later years, when I had a contested hearing or a trial, I would carefully outline my interrogation of witnesses, at least key areas of testimony, and carefully review the basis for establishing a proper foundation for expert witness opinions and the introduction of documents to be made a part of the case record. All of this preparation would be done to avoid or overcome likely objections from opposing counsel in advance of the court proceeding. In this case, I had not even thought about any of these things, believing I would simply be present to listen and learn from experienced lawyers.

The client was called to the stand and put under oath, and I proceeded. In my excitement, I frequently asked questions which were leading or otherwise in improper form to which opposing counsel objected; in most cases the objections were sustained by Judge Young. I remember being so focused on my questions that I didn't always hear the basis of the objection, which made it difficult for me to oppose the objection. I also remember wishing the judge would relax the technical rules in the interest of getting the relevant facts out. That did not happen, and I have to assume opposing counsel rather enjoyed "rattling" me with a barrage of objections. It was a very traumatic experience for me, and I was afraid the client would feel that his case was being badly handled. If he felt that way, he kept it to himself. As noon approached I repeatedly tried to have a critical document introduced into evidence and each time I offered it an objection was made which the judge sustained, agreeing with opposing counsel that "I had failed to lay a proper foundation." I was totally frustrated. Judge Young called for the noon recess and said the court would take up again at 2:00 p.m.

I literally ran back to the office some 6 or 8 blocks away. Neither Claude nor Blaine was at the office. I raced down the hall to see if Paul Boyd was in. His secretary said he was in a meeting in his conference room. Just then Paul happened to open his conference room door. He saw the look of panic on my face, told the group in the conference room that he had an important meeting with a fellow attorney and invited me into his office. He directed me to sit down and asked me what the hell was wrong. I believe he thought something drastic had happened down the hall.

I explained the whole situation and about my efforts to have the document placed into evidence. Paul Boyd handed me a yellow legal pad and told me to write down what he was going to say. He outlined a series of the key questions for laying a proper foundation for the introduction of the document. Based on what I had told him about the proceeding, he gave me additional advice on how to proceed. All of this served to calm me down. He also said if I ran into another jam to ask for a recess and give him a phone call. I thanked him and returned to the courtroom.

When court resumed, I put the petitioner back on the stand. I laid a proper foundation as Paul Boyd had outlined and the exhibit was readily admitted into evidence. My confidence level increased and I proceeded to present our case. I was careful with my questions and had fewer objections to deal with. During a court recess in mid-afternoon, I was out in the hall and the reporter for the *Idaho Statesman* came up and asked me a few questions about the case which I tried to answer without giving the matter much thought.

Later in the afternoon, Judge Young inquired of both counsels as to how many more witnesses we intended to call. It was obvious we could not conclude that day and the judge had a full calendar for several days thereafter. The hearing was continued and reset in two weeks. Judge Young said he wanted to have testimony on the suitability of the petitioner as a custodial parent, something in the nature of a "home study." His comments gave me a glimmer of hope.

Back at the office, our client and I sat down with Blaine to evaluate what had taken place and how to proceed when the hearing resumed. Blaine suggested an agency that would be able to provide the type of study Judge Young was interested in. We made arrangements to have it completed by the next hearing date. The next morning Claude showed me the article which the *Statesman* had published which contained several quotes from me about the case. Claude told me that it was quite improper for me to have talked to the press in the middle of a court proceeding. He said in all likelihood, Judge Young would not be pleased and that I should be prepared to offer an apology should the judge mention the incident when the hearing resumed.

When the hearing resumed, to my relief, the matter of my having talked with the press was not raised. I called the case worker, who had completed the study we had requested, to testify. The report was favorable to our client. After laying a proper foundation, her official report was admitted into evidence. We also requested that Judge Young interview the children in his chambers located behind the courtroom. The children were deemed too young to be sworn in and testify in open court. Judge Young declined to interview them. As the hearing went on, it became fairly clear that the people who caused Children's Home case personnel to take custody of the children had had a vendetta against the father over the circumstances of the marriage and divorce of the parents of the children. The relatives had hoped to eventually have custody awarded to an aunt who lived in Boise. At the conclusion of the second hearing, Judge Young ordered the three children be immediately returned to their father.

Our client and I were both delighted. We were into the Christmas season and the *Idaho Statesman* wrote a nice human-interest story about the outcome. This time I was not quoted! I had been better prepared for the second hearing, aware that I would be handling the case, and things went smoother than during the first hearing. Blaine did not offer to accompany me, and our client seemed confident with my continuing to handle his case. Neither Blaine nor I ever commented on the fact that although he had said he would be in court shortly, he had never appeared at the first hearing. I still believe that Blaine was wrong to put me in that position and that the client's cause was put at some risk as a consequence. Fortunately, everything turned out well in the end. Blaine was a great guy, a wonderful teacher and mentor. We enjoyed a close personal and professional relationship until he died a couple of years ago. I can only assume that he had had confidence that I was ready and able to handle the matter.

Chapter 131

Representing Don Antone

One day, a young fellow came to Blaine asking for help. I still remember his name: Don Antone. He had been working part time for a local plumber and claimed to have injured his back while working on the job. Shortly after his injury, Don had been terminated by his employer. Blaine brought the young man into my office and asked me to handle his case. This was my first workman's compensation case. I took his statement, talked briefly with his treating physician, and concluded that his claim, though not large, had merit. Don had not had much schooling; however, he was a decent sort of a guy. With Blaine's help, I prepared the forms and filed a claim for compensation with the Industrial Commission.

In due course a hearing was scheduled. As I remember, the employer who had failed to carry workers' compensation insurance, which Idaho law required, did not appear for the hearing. I put Don on the stand, as well as his treating physician, who was kind enough to appear without the customary advance fee for testifying. After taking the matter under advisement, the commission mailed an order awarding compensation, which included an allowance for attorney's fees and costs. An employer who fails to provide insurance coverage for employees is subject to severe penalties including revocation of their state license to engage, in this case, in the plumbing business. To avoid the penalty, the plumber, in due course, paid the compensation award in cash and also obtained insurance coverage on the employees. The commission sent a check to the office in full payment of the award, costs and attorney fees. I was elated and quickly paid the treating physician his fee for appearing at the hearing. I had experienced a new area of the law and had become acquainted with the commissioners and staff.

Sometime later, I received a telephone call from my client, Don Antone. He was in the Ada County jail and said he needed my help. I visited him and learned that he had been charged with forgery, a felony. I reviewed the Ada

County Prosecutor's file and learned that Don had picked up a blank counter check at a local bank and filled it out made payable to him for a couple hundred dollars. He wrote in the maker of the check as The Northwest Pipeline Company, all in his own handwriting. Don told me he had worked briefly for the company which had a contract to bury gas pipe for The Intermountain Gas Company. When he tried to cash the check, the cashier called the authorities and Don was arrested and put in jail. He readily admitted to me what he had done. When I discussed the matter with Claude Marcus he wondered if, under the circumstances, what Don had done rose to the level of a completed crime. I decided to do some research.

I discovered that one element of forgery was the "fraud" perpetrated on the maker of the check. Many of the reported cases held that fraud involves intent to deceive. Clearly Don intended to deceive his former employer; however, his attempt was rather crude. I found some older case laws that suggested the effort to deceive had to be such as would deceive a reasonable person. I questioned whether a reasonable person would have actually accepted the check for payment. Claude said I should make an effort to have the criminal charge dismissed. I prepared and filed a motion and brief with the Ada County District Court. Ultimately, the matter came before Judge Merlin Young who had presided over my first court case, the custody matter.

At the hearing, I argued that the attempted forgery was so crude and amateurish that no one to whom the check was presented for payment should have been deceived. Certainly, the cashier to whom Don handed the check was not fooled and had immediately notified a bank official who called the authorities. A deputy county attorney appeared on behalf of the state of Idaho. Judge Young granted my motion to dismiss the criminal charge and ordered that Don be released from custody. After the hearing was concluded, Judge Young asked me to come back to his chambers. Once there he complimented me on my efforts on behalf of Don and told me the case was what the legal profession was all about. He said lawyers have a professional duty to make certain that a person charged with a crime and is, in fact, guilty of a crime, receive the full protection of the law regardless of the defendant's ability to pay a fee. He was aware that Don lacked the money to retain a lawyer and that I was representing him *pro bono*. I know I was at least a foot taller when I walked back to the office to report to Mr. Marcus.

There was a final chapter to the story of Don Antone. Late in the spring, I received another call from him. Don was once again in the Ada County jail and charged with the crime of forgery. Apparently, he had learned something from his prior experience and this time he was successful. I said I would help him, and I did; however, I could not establish any legal defense. I appeared with him in court when he entered a guilty plea. This time he was sentenced to serve time. I never heard from him again. I made very little money representing Don; however, I had gained valuable experience.

Chapter 132

Learning from the Masters

Paul Boyd and Claude and Blaine were close friends and went to have coffee at a nearby drugstore almost every day. As soon as I started working, I was always invited to go with them. I really enjoyed being accepted by them and listening to their discussions about legal matters, politics, community affairs, and anything else that came up. I became quite close to Paul Boyd and often consulted with him whenever I had a question on my mind and neither Claude nor Blaine was readily available. I appreciated his willingness to help me and I like to think he enjoyed our contacts as well. I also became acquainted with his wife Mary.

One time, Paul told me that he and Mary were going to adopt a child and he asked me to handle it for them. I was extremely flattered. This was the first adoption I had handled. Adoptions are usually not complicated; however, there is a process to be followed. Pleadings must be prepared and filed, an agency home study obtained which supports the adoption; and a court hearing held in order to obtain the final order of adoption. When the final hearing was concluded, the adoption was granted and we all went to a nearby coffee shop and had root beer floats.

After I returned to Idaho Falls, I saw Paul fairly often as he frequently came to eastern Idaho to handle federal bankruptcy matters held in the federal courthouse in Pocatello. He appointed me receiver and trustee in a number of business bankruptcy cases in this part of the state. One day Paul invited me to lunch and told me he would soon retire. He asked if I wanted to return to Boise and take over his private law practice. I was flattered; however, such a move at that time would not have been practical. Paul died of cancer about a year later.

I worked closely with Blaine on a number of his personal injury cases. One in particular involved a suit against a local construction firm for injuries sustained by a small boy in a fuel tank explosion. The construction company stored some of its equipment on a tract of land on which it also dumped construction "debris" including a couple of huge underground fuel tanks that had been dug up and replaced. The tract of land was along the Boise River and was fenced. Several young boys who lived in the vicinity entered the property. One boy climbed on one of the large fuel tanks. Curious as to what might be inside, he lit a match and attempted to look down the uncapped filler pipe. The tank exploded causing serious injuries to the boy. The parents of the injured boy came to Blaine Evans for advice.

Blaine and I inspected the site of the explosion and talked to some of the residents who lived nearby. Several confirmed what the young boys had told us. They said that young children often entered the property by crawling under the enclosure fence. The children would then play on and around the items stored there by the construction company. The frequency with which this occurred, suggested that children were on the premises at times when workmen employed by the owner of the property were present. It appeared that little or no effort was made to keep young children from entering the premises.

Obviously, the children were trespassers; however, Blaine believed that under the circumstances, the legal doctrine of "attractive nuisance" would apply. If someone maintained property that would tend to attract children onto the property and expose them to potential harm, and they knew or should reasonably have known that children did in fact enter the property, and failed to take reasonable steps to prevent such entrance, the property owner could be held legally liable for any resulting damages for injuries.

The parents of the badly injured boy could not afford to pay for a lawyer to handle their case. Blaine agreed to handle their case on a contingent fee basis. Under this arrangement, the attorney would act on their behalf and receive as a fee a percentage of any recovery of monetary damages, by settlement or following a trial. If no recovery was made, the lawyer would not receive a fee. This was the first of many instances I would be involved in, where deserving people with limited financial means would not have received legal help except for the contingent fee arrangement. The contingent fee is often maligned and misunderstood by some members of the public; however, it does serve a commendable purpose. Most lawyers would prefer to be paid for their time on a regular basis, but some clients simply do not have the means to obtain legal help without the option of a contingent fee.

Blaine aggressively pursued the case on behalf of the injured boy and his family. He arranged for the boy to be examined and have his condition evaluated by several medical specialists. I was able to sit in on several of his subsequent interviews of the examining physicians. Blaine also arranged to take the depositions of several of the employees of the defendant construction company, as well as persons who lived in the vicinity of the area of the explosion and an expert on the hazards of abandoned fuel tanks that had not been properly decontaminated. Ultimately, settlement negotiations ensued and resulted in a settlement favorable to the boy and his parents. I still remember the office conference when the settlement was finalized. Blaine reduced the contingent fee originally agreed upon when he had accepted the case. The parents literally had tears in their eyes and were most appreciative of the hard work Blaine had done on their behalf. They would never have been able to retain a lawyer without the contingent fee.

Chapter 133

Introducing Vernon K. Smith

The insurance defense practice usually was undertaken by the older, more established law firms. The law firms who had insurance company clients guarded them jealously. Claude and Blaine had a few such clients. An insurance defense case came into our office where an insurer had been named in a major damage lawsuit. I don't remember the details of the suit. What I vividly remember is that one day Claude came into my office and asked me if I would help him with the defense of the lawsuit, and of course I was delighted with the opportunity. Ultimately, he asked if I would be willing to handle the matter myself. I had been in the practice not quite a full year. Claude was not being careless with the interest of a valued client. It turned out that our insurance client provided "excess coverage," and the insurance company with the "primary coverage" for the damages had a policy with high limits and was separately represented. In other words, after evaluating the plaintiff's claim for damages, Claude concluded that it was unlikely our insurance company client would be called upon to participate in any jury award that might result. The claims agents for our client concurred with Claude's assessment and approved of my handling the matter. They probably saw it as a way to save on defense costs. I was excited to have the experience.

The primary insurance carrier was represented by Vernon K. Smith. He was known as one of Idaho's top trial lawyers and was renowned as a colorful criminal defense lawyer, too. V.K. Smith was a sole practitioner who had a busy practice and traveled a lot. He did most of his trial preparation in his office during the evening hours. I spent many nights with him in his office. He constantly asked my opinion on points of the law and defense strategy and provided me with a wonderful experience. With Mr. Smith, I had the opportunity to have contact with and become acquainted with the plaintiff's attorney who was with a major Boise law firm. Ultimately the case settled within the limits of the primary insurance policy. Our insurance client only paid its own legal fees and costs.

V.K. Smith was a very skilled lawyer who also had a reputation for "cutting corners," so to speak. Several times during our evenings together, he regaled me with some of the noted cases he had handled. I remember one in particular. He was defending a person in a felony criminal matter. During the trial, he tried very hard to have a certain exhibit introduced and each time his effort was objected to by the opposing attorney and the objections were all sustained by the judge. He made one more unsuccessful try at the end of the trial. By this time, he told me that he knew the jury really wanted to see this document that had been the subject of so much controversy. I am sure that is why he attempted so many times to have it entered as an exhibit. He happened to walk by the empty jury room the jurors would soon enter to begin its deliberations. V.K. Smith said he simply tossed the disputed document onto the conference table where the jurors would surely find it. This had been a serious breach of ethics and could have resulted in a disciplinary proceeding by the Idaho State Bar, had it come to their attention.

V.K. Smith later ran for governor twice on the Democratic ticket as a strong advocate for legalized gambling in Idaho. The issue was not popular with everyone and he lost both times. He and his gambling issue were believed by some to have been responsible for the defeat of others who, though not in favor of legalized gambling, were also running for office on the Democratic ticket. He was a colorful person. He also was a big stakes gambler himself. One time at a Christmas bar party at the Plantation Golf Course club house in Boise, I watched him playing at the crap table. At one time, Vernon who had had a fair amount to drink, had a $2,100 side bet on the person rolling the dice. I did not understand the game at all and still don't; however, I remember that he held onto his money and several lawyer friends persuaded him to stop gambling and get something to eat.

The last time I saw him was many years later in Idaho Falls in the early morning. He had been arrested for refusing to sign a ticket for jay walking. He had crossed C Street, in the middle of the block, while on his way to the Idaho Falls jail and police department to interview a client. Both facilities and the fire department were then all located in the old City Building at the corner of C Street and Shoup Avenue. I saw Vernon on the sidewalk right after he had been arrested. He was furious and frustrated. I told the rookie police officer that I knew Mr. Smith and would vouch for him on his promise to come to the station on his own. I then asked Vernon if I could be of any help. He remembered me;

however, he declined any help. He was going in to raise hell with the chief of police, and he did.

I later found out that he was just having a little fun with the young officer over the prospect of the ticket. The inexperienced officer became angry and felt obliged to make an arrest. All charges were dropped. I later had occasion to talk about the matter with Chief Bob Pollock, who was an outstanding chief of police. He just laughed about the whole thing and said it was a good learning experience for the rookie officer. V.K. Smith died a couple of years later. I enjoyed the several experiences I had with this brilliant, controversial, unpredictable and thoroughly charming man.

Chapter 134

Decision Time

My time in Boise went fast. I spent a lot of time at the office on law matters, and I gained a wealth of valuable experience and self-confidence. The longer I was in Boise the more I found I enjoyed the city and the legal profession and what they had to offer us. Though the law practice dominated much of my time, Donna and I, and Linda and Patricia did find time to enjoy Boise, some of the surrounding area, as well as our many friends who lived there. I had been adamant that I wanted to return to Idaho Falls to practice law. I also had felt that Idaho Falls was a good place to raise our young family.

Farrel had returned to engage in the practice of medicine and Orval had returned to practice law. We had ambitious plans for developing the Palisades property. In addition, the Idaho National Laboratory, then known as the National Reactor Testing Station, was bringing in people from other parts of the country and changing the character of Idaho Falls in a positive way. Notwithstanding all of these factors, I must confess that the longer we stayed in Boise the more difficult it was for me to leave.

I know Donna would have preferred to live in Boise; however, she understood my feelings and was a good sport. We really never discussed the subject after our decision to go to Boise for a couple of years at the most. If we had, we would have found it even more difficult to leave Boise, and might possibly have talked ourselves into staying. I know Claude and Blaine would have liked me to stay. I had accepted their offer on the basis that it would be temporary, and they did not put pressure on me to change my mind. The St. Clair law firm in Idaho Falls had recently expressed an interest in my working for them and had named the salary they could offer me.

About this time, I received a phone call from Lloyd Haight who was general counsel and corporate secretary for the Simplot Corporation. Mr. Haight had been active in the Idaho Republican Party and the Bar Association. I had met him on several occasions, although I did not know him well. He asked me to stop by his office. I had no idea what he wanted to talk to me about. When we met, he said that he was looking to hire an attorney to help handle legal matters for the corporation. He said that his corporate responsibilities were taking more and more of his time. At this time, he was the only lawyer employed by the Simplot Corporation.

I don't remember what salary he was offering, but it did represent a substantial increase over what I was then receiving and what I had been offered by the St. Clair firm. He also said much of what I would be doing would involve working directly with J. R. Simplot. The Simplot Corporation was then totally owned by Mr. Simplot and his immediate family. He described the type of practice I would be engaged in. Giving a laugh, he said advising Mr. Simplot could be frustrating. He explained that a number of times Mr. Simplot would ask him if he could or should do this and so, and after advising him not to, Jack would go ahead and plunge into the venture anyway and it would turn out to be very successful. He said Mr. Simplot loved the challenge of new ideas and had a unique ability to analyze and take advantage of new opportunities.

I remembered that Dad was a friend and admirer of Mr. Simplot. The prospect of being the number two lawyer in the large and successful corporation was intriguing. It would have been an exciting opportunity and potentially very rewarding. The legal department of the corporation was soon to grow larger than many law firms. Several of its attorneys later served as president of the corporation. It was a big decision for me. I talked with Claude Marcus who likewise was intrigued with the possibilities. Like Mr. Haight, Claude thought Mr. Simplot could be difficult to work with. Although he didn't say so, I sensed that Claude did not have a high opinion of Jack Simplot. He suggested I not reject the opportunity out of hand.

I talked with my brother Orval about the offer. Even though we had made a tentative agreement to come back to Idaho Falls, Orval said it was my decision to make and suggested I talk with Sandor and Edith Klein who lived in Boise at the time. Orval was first acquainted with "Sandy" when he was a well-known newspaperman in Washington DC. He later met and married his wife, Edith, who was an attorney and a partner in a prominent law firm in Boise. She also served in the Idaho Legislature. I called and was invited to meet with Sandy and Edith at their lovely home on Warm Springs Avenue one evening to further discuss the offer from Lloyd Haight. They did not advise me one way or the other; however, they helped me better understand the type of law practice I would be engaged in, were I to accept the Simplot offer.

After a few days I finally concluded, and Donna agreed, that I would be happier in a more varied practice of law, much as Claude and Blaine had developed, which I anticipated would be available to me in Idaho Falls. Over the years, I have had many opportunities to do work for and with the legal department and some of the corporate officers of the Simplot Corporation. I have often wondered what "would have been," had I accepted Mr. Haight's offer; however, I have had no regrets with the direction I chose. By now I had firmly accepted the offer from the St. Clair law firm in which Orval was now a partner, and they were anxious for me to start with them. A starting date with the new firm was agreed upon. In the fall of 1960, Donna and I began to make plans for the move back to Idaho Falls.

Chapter 135

First House and a Son

By now we knew that Donna was expecting our third child, due to be born around the middle of March of 1961. Donna was experiencing morning sickness. Patty had a bad urinary tract infection and had been on sulfa drugs for months. We both had our hands full, Donna at home and me at the office. I know she would have preferred to remain in Boise where she now had many close friends with young children as well as a nearby college, Boise Junior College, where she could have resumed her college education someday. Looking back, I am surprised that we did not even sit down to review the decision made two years earlier, to return to Idaho Falls, but we did not. Perhaps in the back of our minds, we did not have the energy, or simply believed that doing so would not lead to a different decision. I am still not sure.

Once again, we loaded a rented trailer with all of our belongings and the four of us drove to Idaho Falls. Upon our arrival, we stayed with Mother and started house hunting. I believe we were shown around town by Louis Boyle with L A. Hartert and Company, a client of the firm I was joining. We looked at several newer houses and finally at an older house: 128 - 11th Street. The house was at least fifty years old. We had no cash and with a baby coming we were not anxious to incur any more debt than necessary. Against the recommendation of Mr. Boyle, we decided to try to buy the house. As I remember our offer of $8,000, conditioned on our ability to get financing, was accepted by the owner, the widow of James Hurley. Her late husband, by coincidence, was the brother of Henry Hurley from whom Dad and Mother had purchased the Airport Farm in 1935.

Though old and badly in need of redecorating, the house had three bedrooms, a living room and dining room, a large glassed-in sun porch just off the small kitchen and a large detached double garage. There was one bathroom with old fixtures, a full basement, and old steam radiators throughout the house heated hot water from an oil-fired boiler and furnace. The house had lots of windows and the lot had many large trees, established shrubs and a big unfenced back yard which we immediately made plans to fence. The house was in a nice neighborhood and was located within walking distance to a drug store, Hawthorne Elementary school, a nearby YMCA swimming pool and Kate Curley park. The location and lot really sold us and made it easier to overlook the condition of the house itself.

I went to First Federal Savings and Loan to see about financing the purchase. I was told by Mr. Worth Wright, the manager, that as I had a job, a loan was available; however, we would need to put down cash to cover a 10% down payment and closing costs, a total of about $1000. We had no cash whatsoever. I was able to borrow about $500 on a small life insurance policy Mother and Dad had taken out on each of the children. On the suggestion of my sister Mary, I reluctantly approached my brother-in-law George for a personal loan for the difference. He readily agreed and we settled on an interest rate and repayment plan. I immediately prepared a written promissory note which provided for small monthly payments. I still remember how appreciative we were to receive this help from George and Mary. A couple of years later the note was paid off and we had a "note burning" ceremony.

We moved into our new home sometime in October and began steaming and stripping many layers of wall paper, sanding hardwood floors, hanging new wall paper and painting the walls and woodwork. Redecorating was a bigger project than either of us had anticipated, but we were excited to be in our own home and to see it take shape. By Christmas we were pretty well finished and settled. We decorated a large Christmas tree and really enjoyed the holidays in our new home.

We had a cold winter with a lot of snow. The house faced north, and ice built up under the shingles just above the eave. When the snow started melting we noticed a wet spot on the living room wall. I was able to chip some of the ice off the roof and fortunately the plaster was not damaged. The next year, I paid close attention to the ice buildup.

We gradually discovered other "joys" of owning an older home. Once I tried to fix a leak in the bathroom, only to discover that many of the pipe and drain joints had been "fixed" with putty and string, and while trying to fix one leak more leaks appeared. I worked most of a day out of the office and I finally had to call a plumber. He took care of the problems and recommended that all of the plumbing in the bathroom be replaced. We declined his suggestion and crossed our fingers.

In early March, the weather warmed up and we decided to take down the storm windows and put up the screens. The storm windows had not been taken down for many years and we had considerable difficulty removing them.

Around the middle of the month, Mother came in to tend Linda and Patty, and I checked Donna into Parkview Hospital on Boulevard. On March 18th, Steven was born. The delivery went well, and he was a healthy baby. Shortly after he was born however, problems developed due to the RH blood incompatibility we'd been made aware of: my blood type is B positive and Donna's is A negative. As we knew, the problem increases with each pregnancy. There were no complications when Linda was born; and only a minor problem with Patty which was monitored but did not require any procedure.

Steve, however, began to become extremely jaundiced and we were told he required a complete blood exchange immediately. He needed a transfusion of O negative blood which is the type that is most rare, and the hospital did not have any. A search began for a donor. I remembered that my brother Reed had O negative blood and called his house. Reed was quickly located and got on the phone. I explained what we desperately needed and started crying. He raced to the hospital, but before he arrived, another donor had been located and the transfer was in progress. Steve immediately started to regain a normal color and was fine. It was a close call. Donna and I were advised by our doctor that we should not attempt to have any more children and we readily agreed. Three seemed like a good round number to us!

Chapter 136

Practicing Law in Idaho Falls

The experience I had working with Claude Marcus and Blaine Evans served me well in Idaho Falls. I was comfortable in both office practice and trial practice. I still believed most other lawyers were more skilled than I, which gave me the incentive to work extra hard in preparation, and thorough preparation is what it is all about. I sought advice from older lawyers whenever I had the chance. In those days, almost every lawyer was willing to give young lawyers the benefit of their expertise.

I began practicing law with the firm of St. Clair, St. Clair and Hansen on the second floor of the Hasbrook building on Park Avenue above a men's clothing store. The firm had been founded by Clancy St. Clair who had recently passed away. His two sons, Bob and Gilbert (Skinny) St. Clair, and Orval were the firm partners. I was an associate. Paul Petersen, an older lawyer, practiced law in a room on the second floor and shared a secretary with the firm. Jim Marshal, a farm loan agent with John Hancock Insurance Company, also had an office on the same floor.

I very much admired and respected Paul Petersen. He no longer handled court cases, and he turned over to me any cases which required going to court. Orval did some trial work; however, he had a busy office practice and so I did most of the trial practice while I was with the firm. I found practicing in Idaho Falls to be quite different from what I had experienced in Boise. As a matter of fact, I was quite disappointed at first and wondered if I had made a mistake by coming back; however, the move had been completed and I felt there was no turning back.

In the summer of 1962, Blaine Evans approached me at the Idaho State Bar convention in Sun Valley. He told me, in confidence, that he would be leaving Claude Marcus to join Carl Burke, Jr. to form a new firm in Boise and they would like me to join them as number three. I was really flattered. Carl Burke's dad and Frank Elam had started a very reputable firm, however both had since passed away. This would have been a great opportunity and if the offer had happened before I left Boise, I would have accepted.

Donna and I talked it over and to pull up stakes and return was just too complicated. Orval and I were talking about setting up our own practice as of January 1, 1963. Blaine and Carl went on to put together one of the largest and most successful firms in Boise. I often wondered what life would have been like had I felt comfortable in accepting the position in Boise; however, I was confident we made the right decision and never looked back.

Chapter 137

Growing the Law Firm of Hansen and Hansen

In the summer of 1962, Orval had been in a tough election campaign trying to unseat Ralph Harding who was finishing his first term in Congress and running for the second time. Ralph had defeated ten-term Congressman Hamer Budge in an upset in 1960. Ralph Harding won his seat back, and Orval was out of politics, at least temporarily. So, in early 1963, Orval and I opened the firm of Hansen and Hansen in a small three-room complex north of the Bonneville County Courthouse.

Fred Ochi painted a sign which we hung under the overhang adjacent to our front door. (I still have the sign.) We rented from Jerry Staker who owned Staker Floral with which we shared a wall. Winnie Hearn who had been Orval's secretary at the St. Clair firm came with us. Winnie was a great help. She handled our secretarial work and also kept the books.

The separation with the St. Clair firm was amicable. Some legal work followed us, and some work Bob and Gilbert St. Clair asked us to finish up. I respected them both; however, there had always been a level of friction between the St. Clair brothers, and I enjoyed the new atmosphere. Orval and I worked well together. Orval handled most of the office practice, I handled most of the trial work. We shared a developing estate practice and worked together on the more complicated trial practice. We both had young families to support and worked hard to develop the practice. When we closed the books at the end of the first year, we had each taken home, after all expenses, sums significantly greater than we had earned the previous year with the prior firm. We were bullish about the future.

In the spring of 1964, Winnie Hearn informed me that Orval had decided to run for a seat in the Idaho Senate. The Legislature had been reapportioned and one of the House seats was eliminated and the Senate seat was "open." Rather than pit two incumbents in a primary, Orval offered to run for the open seat. I had no idea that he was thinking about returning to the Legislature, where he had served for six years. I walked into Orval's office to ask him if what I had just learned was true and he confirmed that it was. Frankly, I was disappointed that he hadn't discussed the matter with me before making the decision; however, he assured me he would still be able to handle a significant amount of law work while the legislature was in session. And he did. Orval was a great guy, a good lawyer who worked hard at whatever he did. When he wanted to do something, he just did it!

The firm had two monthly retainers. The New Sweden Irrigation District had been a long-time client of Paul Peterson, then went to Bill Holden at the Holden, Holden Kidwell firm, and then to me. The monthly retainer was small, but the work load grew rapidly and I would bill over and above the retainer on a quarterly basis. The District gave me exposure in the agricultural community and a lot of good referral work. Orval and I were both comfortable working with the folks in agriculture.

The other retainer was The Idaho Potato Growers, the potato cooperative for which Dad had served as general manager from 1936 to1946. We both had a good relationship with management. IPG came to Orval as a client as soon as he returned to practice law in Idaho Falls and stayed with us for many, many years. The IPG retainer always paid a fair portion of our office overhead. Orval and I both had a good relationship with its board of directors, management and key employees. The board of directors met at least monthly, sometimes more, and insisted that either Orval or I attend each board meeting. Our contacts with IPG also led to referrals to the firm. The matters we handled for IPG ranged from the routine to several exciting legal matters.

After a period of time, we moved from our quarters behind Staker Floral to larger quarters on Capital Avenue, across from the Bonneville County Courthouse. We had hired a second secretary and we had more legal files to accommodate. The previous office was just not big enough. There was now space for our small library and a conference room. We each had a larger office, a room for two secretaries, and an extra office for possible expansion. In the meantime, the extra office was occupied by our brother-in-law George Freund. George had left his job at Argonne National Laboratory and was starting up his own consulting firm, Western Nuclear Corporation.

We were located in the center of a half-block long building, the Dennis Building. The suites on either side of us were occupied by lawyers. John Ferebauer and George Barnard, Sr. had offices on the south end; Boyd Thomas and Jack Voshell were in the north end of the building. All three firms shared their small libraries. The new arrangement worked out very well for all of us.

John Ferebauer was a very experienced trial lawyer with an extensive insurance defense practice. Mr. Barnard had been a very experienced appellate lawyer. He had argued several cases before the United States Supreme Court before coming to Idaho. He did very little law practice at this time; however, Mr. Barnard had a wealth of experience and was very generous with his time and advice, as was Mr. Ferebauer. Jack Voshell was the Prosecuting Attorney of Bonneville County. Boyd Thomas was a respected member of the bar and would soon become a District judge. We were in good company!

Chapter 138

Taking on the Corporate World

Soon after I returned to Idaho Falls, Eugene Bush was the Prosecuting Attorney for Bonneville County. Gene's father, Harold Bush, was principal of the Riverside Elementary School. He was my sixth-grade teacher and one of the finest teachers I think I ever had. Gene had graduated from the University of Idaho Law School. Gene asked me to be his deputy prosecutor, primarily to handle misdemeanors, and I accepted at a salary of $200 a month. The work was routine, but it gave me a chance to get better acquainted with the judges and other lawyers in the local bar association.

I also was "second seat" to Gene in a few felony jury cases tried in district court. He and his family lived on 11th Street, a short distance from our home. Gene Bush was a very good friend, very competitive, and an excellent lawyer. We often sought each other's advice on legal matters, principally regarding trial tactics and strategy and the value of personal injury cases.

One time a client of mine, Dale Graves who was the local manager of U-Haul in Idaho Falls, commented on the fact that right after World War II, he had gone to work with Sam Shoen the founder of U-Haul International when the company was just starting up. He said Sam was making trailers in his home garage, which Dale would then take to various cities across the nation in an attempt to set up dealerships. Dale said the concept was new and most of the folks he contacted thought the idea was crazy. Gradually, the idea started to catch on and a company was born that provided a cheaper way for people to move their house goods across the country.

In the early years, U-Haul was not making much money, so Dale received stock in the company. He was a young bachelor and was able to get by on his travel expenses. The same was true with several others who were involved in the early years of the company. Dividends were never paid on the stock; however, those early stockholders received many other opportunities within the company with the expectation that in time they would receive value for their stock. Other benefits were gradually eliminated, and at the same time the parent company was extremely profitable. Dale and a friend of his by the name of Tom O'Donnell who lived in Portland, Oregon, brought in boxes of old company records and asked if I would help them receive fair value for their stock. The company was privately held, mostly by its founder Sam Shoen, members of his family and, of course, those early employees.

I reviewed the records and consulted with Gene Bush and a CPA. We determined that U-Haul International held huge cash reserves, and had done so for many years, far beyond its demonstrated capital needs. As a result, the company was at risk of being assessed a tax on the excess reserves, an imputed tax. The excess reserves were never subjected to income tax; however, if paid in the form of stock dividends the cash would have been taxed as income when received by the shareholder. Gene and I made demand on the parent company to either pay a fair dividend or purchase the stock at a fair price. We were literally told to "go to hell" and we promptly filed a class action lawsuit in US Federal District Court in Pocatello, Idaho. In truth, one of the corporate attorneys for U-Haul International said that when Sam Shoen received our proposal for settlement, he told the attorney to tell the plaintiffs and their attorneys to "go f… a dog!" This particular attorney seemed to enjoy getting out of the corporate headquarters in Phoenix, Arizona and coming to Pocatello, and we became fairly good friends. The private firm lawyers who came to Idaho were a different breed, however.

Neither Gene nor I had been involved in a class action suit before, and I believe this was the first such case ever filed in the Idaho federal courts. We were barraged with motions from the defense lawyers, and each time we had a proceeding in federal court, a number of attorneys from out of state came to Pocatello to participate. The presiding judge ultimately ruled that we had sufficiently identified a "class" of individuals to qualify the suit for further proceedings. It was obvious, however, that the judge had a busy caseload and wasn't particularly pleased to have this new and complicated case on his docket.

The case which Gene and I took on a shoestring was beginning to take a lot of our time. Our two clients were thoroughly enjoying the proceedings; however, they were sensitive to the costs of the lawsuit. The lawsuit was also expensive for U-Haul International; however, its biggest concern was not the expense per se, but fear that the suit would get the attention of the Internal Revenue Service and result in an effort to subject the excess reserves to income tax for the current, as well as past years. The newspaper coverage of the lawsuit and its colorful founder would be much greater in Phoenix than in Pocatello where it was hardly mentioned in the local newspaper.

The defendants were making a strong case for having the lawsuit transferred to the US District Court of Arizona on the basis of "forum non conveniens," arguing that it would be more convenient to the parties if it were tried in Phoenix. We resisted, saying it would only be more convenient for the very profitable corporation defendant as all other parties were scattered throughout the United States. At this stage, the class of plaintiffs had not been "certified," that is, identified as individuals, and thus notified of the right to join as plaintiffs, so Gene and I still only had to deal with our clients Dale Graves and Tom O'Donnell.

In this atmosphere, we ultimately negotiated a settlement. Dale and Tom would sell all of their company stock for an agreed upon value and receive payment in cash. I think everyone was happy. Dale and Tom received less than their stock was probably worth, but they were pleased that they held the company accountable and finally received value for the stock. And we all had fun along the way. Tom was a very interesting fellow. He owned several restaurants in the Portland, Oregon, area and was fairly well-to-do. He had been a B-17 pilot during World War II, and in fact, he flew his twenty-five combat missions in the airplane now exhibited in the National Air and Space Museum in Washington DC.

He and Dale were involved in several joint investments, including the purchase and operation of the Champagne Creek Ranch located on Champagne Creek in Butte County. I did a fair amount of legal work for both of them over the years. Dale now lives on a small ranch along the river just east of Darby, Montana. We have visited Dale at his ranch in Darby and once we stopped by his place in Mexico, near Nuevo Guemes. Dale occasionally stops by when he comes to Idaho Falls to see old friends.

Chapter 139

Idaho Lawyer Meets the Mob

The Idaho Potato Growers provided us with some interesting legal work. The cooperative was a large producer of a variety of frozen and dehydrated potato products as well as a shipper of fresh potatoes. As such, they were frequently adopting trade names for new products, so we began learning the practice of trademark, copyright and patent law. I am sure the practice was easier to engage in then, than would be the case today. One day the IPG manager, M. A. Peterson, asked me to accompany him to Chicago. IPG was furnishing frozen french fries to a new start-up chain of drive-ins called Golden Point. Golden Point was distinguished by a tall gold-colored obelisk, and was competing with another new chain called McDonald's, identified by its large gold-colored arches.

We visited the well-furnished headquarters of Golden Point. The company seemed to be doing well, although it was heavily in debt with start-up costs. Golden Point eventually went into bankruptcy; only a nominal payment on the debt was ever received by IPG. Meanwhile, McDonald's continued to prosper.

On another occasion M.A. Peterson, whom I called Pete, came into the office and asked me to again accompany him to Chicago the next day. He had already purchased our airplane tickets. IPG produced a lot of frozen french-fried potatoes which were its most profitable product. The total product the co-op shipped nationwide was handled by a single broker, a fellow named Charles Windle who operated a brokerage firm based in Chicago. The brokerage firm sold the product and also collected the money from the customers, and in turn remitted to IPG. Mr Windle's account receivable with IPG had grown quite large and was now several hundreds of thousands of dollars delinquent. When pressed, Mr. Windle always claimed that he was having difficulty collecting from his customers. One day one of his large customers called Mr Peterson to ask why he had to pay cash on delivery for the product he purchased. We were going to find out what was going on.

The weather was bad in Idaho Falls and also in Chicago. I did not have a decent overcoat and borrowed one from my brother Reed. When we left, we did not have hotel reservations. We did not know how long we would be gone, and Pete was confident that Charles Windle, who was always called Charlie, would meet us at the airport and be able to help us find a place to stay. We flew on Western Airlines to Minneapolis, where we transferred to a smaller plane and then flew on to land at the Chicago Midway Airport.

Thus began one of the most amazing experiences of my entire life. Charlie did in fact meet us at the airport, but he was not alone. He was accompanied by two fellows, neither of whom Pete knew. This disappointed Pete because he wanted to have a private conversation with Charlie and perhaps some of his key staff members, particularly, a fellow named Jerry Waxler. Charlie Windle was visibly uncomfortable when he met us at the airport.

We learned the names of the strangers, but nothing else as to who they were and why they were with Charlie. One was Lou Rosanova and the other was Jake Summerfield. Lou was a large man, over six-foot six-inches tall, and he weighed at least 300 pounds, and all of it appeared to be muscle. His hands were about the size of baseball mitts, and he was not what you would call an attractive man. Jake was small of stature and was obviously better educated than his companion, Lou. It became obvious that Charlie had not wanted us to meet these two individuals, but equally obvious that they very much wanted to get acquainted with us. It took a while to find out why.

Pete mentioned that we had not made hotel reservations before leaving, and one of the two strangers recommended a hotel. They drove all of us directly to the Saint Clair Hotel where we checked in and put our bags in the room. Charlie and the other two stayed in the lobby. Again, we had hoped Charlie would come up to the room, but he did not do so. When we came down to the lobby, the three were waiting for us. Pete and I had not eaten other than a light breakfast on the plane. Pete said we would like to have lunch and perhaps we could get together later. He obviously hoped that we might have an opportunity to meet alone with Charlie, but it was not to be.

Our new friends took us to a restaurant in the area and all five of us had lunch together. The conversation during lunch was awkward to say the least and consisted mainly of small talk. Pete and I were asked a lot of questions about us, our work, the business operations of Idaho Potato Growers, and the weather in Idaho. Throughout the long lunch, Charlie said almost nothing. I had never met him before, however Pete had known Charlie for years and had described him to me on the flight as being outgoing and affable. He was a great sports fan and traveled all over the country to see sports events, and on occasion, would charter a plane to fly his favorite team to some exotic place. By all accounts, he was a wealthy and generous individual who lived and traveled in the "fast lane."

I watched Charlie and his "friends" closely during lunch trying to pick up on what was going on. I was unsuccessful, other than to conclude that Charlie was in some kind of financial trouble and that Lou and Jake were somehow involved in his business affairs. After lunch, much to our dismay Charlie insisted that he had matters he needed to attend to, and that he would see us later. Charlie implied that Lou and Jake knew all about his brokerage business and could provide us with more information. Lou and Jake said they wanted Pete and me to meet someone who was identified as their legal adviser, and away we went: Pete, Lou, Jake, and I. Pete and I had not had a chance to talk privately with Charlie or even to talk privately to each other since arriving at the Chicago Midway Airport.

When Pete and I had talked at length in the office before our trip and also during the flight, we both assumed Charlie was in some kind of financial trouble. The large amount of money he owed the Idaho Potato Growers was seriously delinquent and yet customers were being pressed for payment on delivery of the product. Charlie was out of his brokerage office a lot of the time and Pete dealt primarily with an employee by the name of Jerry Waxler. Pete had called Jerry Waxler in an effort to find out more about what was going on with the accounts. Pete was told that while he, Jerry Waxler, handled the sales end of the business, Charlie handled the collections and therefore he could not provide meaningful information.

So, we wanted to ascertain the true amount of debt owed IPG for frozen potato product and how Charlie would propose to bring the account current. We expected to work out some type of payment arrangement, perhaps obtain a promissory note from Charlie, and set up a different arrangement for collecting from the customers.

Pete was obviously concerned about collecting the sizeable debt. He explained, however, that of greater importance was maintaining a market outlet for the large volume of frozen potato products IPG produced. The value of product produced and shipped each month was staggering, at least to me. Any interruption of the sales of this volume of product would cause a severe financial blow to IPG. Should it be necessary, finding a new broker would take time and probably involve having to locate and set up a number of brokers around the nation. There were several large producers of the product who would be quick to solicit IPG's existing customers.

For all of his faults, Charlie was a tremendous salesman and from his office in Chicago he sold and directed shipment of product to customers all across the

United States. Over the years, he had built up a good business, both for himself and for the Idaho Potato Growers. Except for the last year or so, he had kept current his account with IPG.

We arrived at an office building and took the elevator several floors up to the office of the "legal advisor." We were introduced to the gentleman whose name I don't remember. The lettering on the door indicated he was an accountant. He impressed me as having a legal background, but I saw nothing on the walls that indicated a law degree or membership in a bar association. He seemed surprised to see all of us, and Jake explained who Pete and I were and said that we had a few questions. Again, this was a very awkward situation. After some small talk the "legal adviser" made the connection between us, the Idaho Potato Growers, frozen potato products, and our national sales broker Mr. Windle, and he seemed to understand why we were in Chicago.

Some months earlier, he said he had prepared a promissory note to evidence a short-term loan that was being made to Charlie Windle. We were shown a copy of the note. The loan had been in excess of $100,000, and it had been executed by a corporation rather than Mr. Windle personally. We had understood Charlie Windle had operated his business as a sole proprietorship. The accountant explained that the "lender" insisted that Charlie incorporate his business before the loan was made. The interest rate on the note was many times the legal rate of interest under Illinois law. Still not sure exactly who the fellow was, I commented on the extremely high the rate of interest which was, in fact, usurious.

The accountant said Mr. Windle's brokerage business had been incorporated before the loan was completed. Under Illinois law the usury laws do not apply to corporations! He added that Charlie had also signed a personal guaranty of the promissory note. He gave me a copy of the note and said he had no idea what the balance of the note was at that time. Mr. Summerfield said he would verify the current balance for us. Even though pretty hefty monthly payments had been made, due to the exorbitant rate of interest being charged, it was obvious that the principal balance owed would not have been reduced much, if at all.

The four of us left the accountant's office and sat in the waiting room for a few minutes. Pete and I very much wanted to get away from these fellows, but they insisted we had to reach some kind of agreement as to how ongoing profits from the brokerage business and the proceeds from the sale of Charlie's assets would be shared between IPG and our new, as yet unidentified, "partner." Pete explained the structure of the Idaho Potato Growers and emphasized that only its board of directors could make a binding agreement. Therefore, Pete said, we would need to go back to Idaho to meet with the board. This was true; however, we desperately wanted to get back to the hotel, and by ourselves, so we could privately try to make sense of the events since our landing at the airport earlier in the day. We still did not have all the information we would need to report to the board of directors.

We reached an agreement on when we would meet again, in Chicago. Lou and Jake were pressing for a quick meeting and Pete and I were pushing for a later meeting to give us a chance to gather and assess more information as to what was going on. The continuation of the brokerage business was critical for IPG to move the potato products nationwide. We agreed to meet again in three to four weeks.

Though nothing was specifically said, all of us were concerned about the health and state of mind of Charlie Windle. He was somewhat overweight and obviously under tremendous stress; in short, a candidate for a heart attack or stroke. We learned from our new friends that Charlie, his wife and one small child lived in an expensive mansion. Also, he owned an airplane, a couple of summer homes, exclusive country club memberships and other valuable assets, all of which needed to be preserved and hopefully liquidated in some orderly fashion. None of us felt comfortable leaving Charlie in control of all of his assets for any length of time, given his apparent state of mind. Our new friends said they would keep a close watch on matters until we returned and reached some type of liquidation agreement.

As we left the waiting room and approached the elevator to leave the building, Lou Rosannova and Jake Summerfield made eye contact and I swear Jake gave Lou a nod. Then Lou sort of "frog walked" me backwards to the elevator some distance from Mr. Summerfield and Pete. My back was against the closed elevator door and he leaned down real close, just inches away from my face and said in a low voice; "Hansen, we don't fuck around. You need to understand that. When we get back together again an agreement will be reached, period. No more delays." I mentioned that the obligation owed us was the personal obligation of Mr. Windle and being based on embezzlement, the debt could not be discharged in bankruptcy, while the promissory note evidencing the loan to Mr. Windle would be discharged. Lou Rosanova replied, "Look, we have an insurance policy on Windle's life. We will collect our money one way or the other." I was frightened, and yet the whole scene seemed like a Grade B Movie. A fleeting concern at that moment was that I might start laughing, not out of any bravery on my part, but uncontrolled emotion. Fortunately, I did not.

Lou and Jake drove us back to our hotel and left. We went to our room and just stared at each other for a few moments. We knew we were involved with some pretty rough characters and that Charles Windle was in very big trouble. It was obvious that in desperation he had borrowed a large sum of money to pay on his account with IPG, probably trying to buy time, and now his problems were worse than ever. Pete, while concerned about collecting the large debt owed IPG, was even more concerned about what could happen to IPG's national sales market. Pete was well acquainted and impressed with Charlie's chief sales broker Jerry Waxler who was the key person who handled the IPG account. We decided we still needed more information and we were convinced the information would not be coming from Charlie Windle.

Pete called Jerry Waxler at his home in Skokie, Illinois, some distance north of Chicago. He asked if we could get together for a private conversation that same night. Jerry suggested we meet at a particular all-night restaurant located somewhere between Chicago and Skokie. Pete and I hailed a taxi. By now it was late and we selected a table in the middle of the room where we would not be overheard. Jerry knew that his boss, Charlie, was in some financial trouble and that his account with IPG was seriously delinquent, but little else.

In confidence, we related the bizarre happenings since our arrival that morning. When we mentioned the names of Lou Rosanova and Jake Summerfield, Jerry turned pale and became visibly frightened. He said they were part of an organized crime syndicate: the Mafia. These fellows were for real and played rough. Jerry believed that Charlie was not only in financial trouble, but that his life was in danger. If the Mafia decided to take over Charlie's brokerage business, Jerry wanted no part of it.

Pete and I were dumbfounded!

Pete and Jerry talked in detail about the IPG account. Jerry said that he and his co-workers really handled the frozen potato product sales for IPG and even without Charlie, the sale of product could be handled at the customary monthly volume. Something would have to be worked out quickly in regard to collecting money from the purchasers. At this point, Pete acknowledged that IPG had had complete trust in Charles Windle; therefore, IPG had not required that Charlie carry a personal fidelity bond even though he handled large sums of money. I was surprised, as was Jerry Waxler, to learn that IPG did not have the protection of any bond whatsoever.

When Pete explained the customer calls complaining about having to pay for product on delivery, Jerry understood why relations with some customers had become strained. Jerry assured Pete that he would continue to handle all of the accounts and would keep in close touch with Pete on a confidential basis while IPG tried to reassess its business plan. The sales he handled were a very profitable part of the brokerage business, and Jerry didn't believe anyone else was in a position to take over sales. However, the Mafia was a large and diversified operation and it probably could take over and operate Charlie's brokerage business. Jerry again emphasized that if that should that happen, he would not stick around.

It was now 2:00 am. I could almost see the wheels spinning in Jerry's mind as he assessed what he had learned. He was a young man with a young family and acknowledged that he was concerned about what could happen if Lou Rosanova and Jake Summerfield suddenly appeared at the brokerage office and announced their organization was taking over the business. He was very concerned about his personal financial situation in such event, as he would terminate his employment immediately. The fears Jerry expressed greatly concerned Pete. Jerry told us to be very careful and assured Mr. Peterson he would keep in contact and would not leave the brokerage firm without prior notification. We all shook hands. Jerry returned to his home in Skokie, and Pete and I hailed a cab and returned to our hotel.

Pete and I collapsed on our beds. We could hardly believe what had happened. Pete told me that when he first met Charlie Windle he worked for a brokerage firm in Kansas City which handled all of IPG's nationwide sales of frozen potato product. Charlie was primarily responsible for the IPG account at that firm. The Kansas City firm had been started by two retired FBI agents and had grown into a large and successful national operation. The firm handled many food products and enjoyed an excellent reputation. Pete had great admiration for the two founders of the firm.

At a point in time, the owners of the brokerage firm advised IPG that they were no longer going to broker sales of frozen potato products. They said Mr. Windle would be allowed to take the IPG account and that he could start up his own brokerage business. Pete told me that they praised Mr. Windle and strongly recommended that IPG continue to have him handle their nationwide sales. Pete said it was on the strength of their endorsement that IPG continued on with Charlie without requiring the protection of a fidelity bond. Before we fell asleep, Pete had decided that on our way home we should fly to Kansas City. Pete wanted to explore the possibility the Kansas City firm might once again take over the national sales for IPG, in the event the Chicago firm owned by Charles Windle ceased to exist or was unable to continue operations.

In the morning, Pete called the Kansas City brokerage firm and spoke to one of the two owners of the firm. Without giving any details, Pete said we were coming through Kansas City and would like to get together with them. Both partners would be pleased to meet with us. They offered to take us to dinner that evening if we were available, and of course, we were. We arranged for tickets for the flight, and without meeting or talking with anyone else in Chicago, we packed our bags and took a taxi to the airport.

I know we both felt better to be leaving Chicago after a fairly good night's sleep. I remember we flew to Kansas City on a new Boeing 707, which was the first pure jet airliner I had ever flown on. We went directly to a hotel where Pete had booked rooms. After we "freshened up," the two owners of the Kansas City firm picked us up and took us to a private club for dinner. After a few preliminaries, Pete, in confidence, gave them the full details of what led up to our trip to Chicago and all we had learned the day before. They expressed surprise. At one point one in our conversation, one of the fellows mused out loud to the other something to the effect that it was "Charlie Windle's propensity for dishonesty" that persuaded them to ask him to leave their firm years earlier. Pete was stunned, and so was I. Pete said nothing, but I could tell he was not at all happy to learn of the circumstances of Charlie Windle's leaving the Kansas City firm.

Here were the same two men who recommended IPG continue with Mr. Windle, and based on their high recommendation IPG had done so without requiring a fidelity bond. IPG would not have allowed Mr. Windle to take over all nationwide accounts under the same arrangements had they been told of the reason Mr. Windle was terminated.

Charlie was obviously a good salesman. Based on his record as a salesman, even with full disclosure from his former employers, he might well have been given the opportunity to handle all of IPG's product sales. Without a doubt, however, IPG would have setup a different arrangement for collecting the sales proceeds. In fact, I learned that in the produce brokerage business, sales and collections are more commonly handled by separate entities. Certainly, the frank and honest comments of these two retired FBI agents would have greatly influenced that ultimate business decision.

During the rest of the evening, Pete explored the possibility that the Kansas City firm might again assume the role of broker for IPG's frozen potato products. Without much discussion, the two owners made it clear that they were not interested. Whether it simply no longer fit their firm's business model, or whether the prospect of a possible struggle with the Mafia influenced the decision, we were not told. I suspect the answer is probably some of both.

After our brief stay in Kansas City, Pete and I flew back to Idaho Falls. We gave a lengthy report on what had transpired and what we had learned on our trip. The board members and key personnel who attended the meeting were astounded to say the least. Concern was expressed that any interruption of the volume of sales from frozen potato products nationwide would be a severe financial blow to the Association. The sales and accounting divisions of the Association provided data to confirm just how serious the problem could be.

Jerry Waxler, not Charles Windle, was the one person that sales and accounting had always dealt with, and they liked and trusted him. Everyone quickly came to the conclusion that to enter into a business relationship with a new broker or brokers would be a lengthy process and would risk losing customers. The brokerage business was very competitive and some of the largest customers were already unhappy with having been pressed to pay for product on delivery. The best solution, if possible, was for Jerry Waxler to set up and staff his own brokerage business to handle the frozen product of the Association without any interruption. To explore this preferred alternative would require a face to face meeting with Mr. Waxler in Chicago as soon as possible. This meeting had to be held before our next meeting with Mr. Rosanova and Mr. Summerfield.

Pete called Jerry Waxler and said we would like to come back to Chicago as soon as possible to talk privately with him. At the meeting of the Association board of directors, it was suggested we should establish contact with a Chicago attorney. Pete received a recommendation from someone that he should contact a Mr. Peter Giachinni in Chicago. I checked the name in Martindale and Hubble, which provides information about attorneys and law firms, and found that he practiced by himself in an office in Chicago and also owned a small bank in Maywood, Illinois, south of Chicago. Mr. Peterson called Mr. Giachinni and explained briefly the purpose of our trip and the need for the trip to be kept strictly confidential.

Pete and I took a late afternoon flight that arrived in Chicago in the evening and took a taxi directly to a private club where Mr. Giachinni had arranged for us to stay. We were still on edge from our prior trip only a few days before, and very much wanted to slip in, firm up a relationship with the attorney, meet with Jerry Waxler, and return to Idaho. The last thing we wanted was to run into our "friends," Lou Rosanova and Jake Summerfield. I didn't sleep very well. Early in the morning when I was still in bed I noticed the door to the hall open slowly. Even without my glasses I could tell someone was coming into our room. I jumped up like I had been shot from a cannon and lunged towards the door. I scared the hell out of a woman who was responsible for cleaning the room. I was as frightened as she. I quickly apologized. I am sure she thought I was crazy.

We took an early morning commuter train to Maywood and walked the short distance to the bank, arriving before the bank was open for business. Mr. Giachinni met us, escorted us to a small conference room and said he would be back shortly. After a few minutes, the conference room door opened and in walked Lou Rosanova and Jake Sommerfield! They both had wide smiles on their faces. Pete and I were totally overwhelmed to put it mildly. Mr. Rosanova said "How are things in Idaho? We heard you were coming back to Chicago." It was obvious that they were enjoying our reaction to their unexpected appearance. We said we had some Association business to take care of, and that we were still planning to come back to Chicago to meet with the two of them as previously agreed.

Mr. Rosanova then began to tell us that he knew we had met with Jerry Waxler in a café midway between Chicago and Skokie late at night during our previous trip to Chicago. Lou then began to relate some of the details of our conversation. They also knew of our side trip to Kansas City. I had my hands on my lap under the conference table we were seated around. At the time I smoked cigarettes, and I wanted one badly. I noticed my right hand was shaking.

I believe I have the ability to remain or at least to appear calm in tense situations even if I am not calm on the inside, so to speak. But the shaking of my hand was an involuntary reflex. I did not want to pull my right arm out from under the table to reach for a cigarette, fearful it would give a clear signal how unnerved I really was. I concentrated on calming my arms and hands, particularly the right one, so I could bring them out from under the table, reach for, and light a cigarette. Finally I was able to, and that calmed me down somewhat.

Pete and I mentioned that since our last visit we had visited with the former brokers of the Association, and also had met with the board of directors in Idaho Falls as well as key people in the production, sales and accounting divisions of the Association. We explained that the board had not yet reached a decision but would do so before the meeting scheduled in Chicago in a couple of weeks.

We said we were simply doing our due diligence to look at every available brokerage alternative in an effort to protect the Association's share of the national market. As to the secrecy of our current trip, we explained that the national frozen potato product industry was extremely competitive. We had moved quickly and quietly to identify and act on our best option to minimize the risk of competitors picking off our key customers and making inroads on the market share of the Association. All of this was the truth.

Jake Summerfield, in particular, asked a lot of questions, exhibiting a fair amount of business savvy. Much of the tension seemed to leave the Maywood bank conference room. Pete and I calmed down somewhat, although not entirely. We agreed to keep in contact, and Lou and Jake left the bank. Attorney Giachinni returned shortly. He said Mr. Rosanova and Mr. Summerfield simply showed up at the bank and wanted to meet with Mr. Peterson and myself. Mr. Giachinni was a very distinguished looking man with a reassuring manner. We still believed that he was on the up and up and was representing us.

The unexpected appearance of Lou and Jake was unnerving; however, we were getting a better understanding of our adversaries, who they were, and how they operated. We told Mr. Giachinni that were going to meet with Jerry Waxler and explore the possibility that he might set up his own separate brokerage business. We agreed to meet with Mr. Giachinni after we met with Jerry and before we returned to Idaho Falls. Pete and I caught the local train and returned to the private club where we were staying. We had lunch and called Jerry to arrange a meeting.

On a later occasion, Jake Summerfield shared with me that he supervised several of the business ventures of the "organization" he worked for. He also explained that Mr. Rosanova was simply used occasionally to "impress" people with the importance of meeting their commitments to the organization, i.e. repay money that had been loaned. Obviously, Lou and Jake were taken aback and suspicious of our unexpected return to Chicago, fearing I am sure, that we were not playing square with them. The discussion in the conference room of the bank in Maywood, Illinois, seemed to reassure them. We were doing what we could to protect the interests of our client, at the direction of its board of directors. We were not dealing with them in an underhanded way.

How did Mr. Rosanova and Mr. Summerfield know so much about our meeting with Jerry Waxler in the middle of the night miles from Chicago, our side trip to Kansas City, and that we were coming or were back in Chicago? We later learned from several sources, including an article in either "Life" or "Look" magazine, that the St. Clair Hotel was owned and operated by the Mafia. (I may still have a copy of the article somewhere.) You will remember that Charlie Windle, Lou and Jake picked us up at the airport on our first trip and took us to the St. Clair Hotel. Obviously, the phone in our hotel room had been tapped, so someone knew we were planning to meet Jerry that night and exactly where.

I am convinced that some type of "bug" or listening device was used in the all-night café where we met with Jerry Waxler. When Pete had called Jerry at his home in Skokie he simply said that it was very important for us to meet with him that night. The details of the conversation which Lou and Jake related to us with such dramatic effect, could only have been known as a result of a "bug." Over the subsequent few years we dealt with Mr. Summerfield, other pieces fell into place to help us understand what had happened earlier. My wife, Donna, said on the day I had left home to go to the airport and on to Chicago she answered our home phone and a man asked to speak to me. She told him I was on my way to Chicago. She did not recognize the voice, and the man did not leave his name or a message. We later assumed the caller was probably either Jake Summerfield or Lou Rosanova attempting to verify the timing of the second trip.

We met with Jerry Waxler several times during that second visit. He was quite interested in setting up his own brokerage business. Actually, the business was quite lucrative if managed properly and represented a lifetime opportunity for him. Pete had confidence in Jerry and knew that he was liked by the customers. Jerry had the ability to conduct the operation, provided he could keep at least some of the existing sales staff. He said Mr. Windle was absent from the business frequently and seldom was involved in sales. Charlie's primary role was handling collection of accounts receivable, making all bank deposits and remitting and accounting to the Association headquartered in Idaho Falls.

Jerry's main concern was the Mafia. His firsthand knowledge of the Mafia really frightened him, and it showed in his face and in his voice. He said he had fully expected someone from that organization to simply walk into the office and say that they were Mr. Windle's new partner and were taking over the business. That had not occurred to Pete; however, as a result of talking with Jerry, he also became concerned about the possibility and the consequences to the Association if such a thing were to happen. It seemed likely this also was least one reason the two gentlemen in Kansas City were not interested in the business, profitable though it was.

Before we left Chicago, we conferred by phone with people in Idaho Falls and met with Jerry Waxler a couple more times. We reached a tentative agreement whereby Jerry would set up his own business and handle all of the nationwide product sales and do it at a reduced commission, at least until we recouped the amount owed by Mr. Windle. The tentative agreement was conditioned on the Association's being satisfied the arrangement for reduced commission was legal, and by Jerry's being satisfied that the Mafia would not interfere with his setting up the new brokerage. We were fairly confident the next meeting with Mr. Summerfield and Mr. Rosanova would give us the answer to Jerry Waxler's main concern, one way or the other.

Chapter 139: Idaho Lawyer Meets the Mob | 409

Later Pete and I met with Mr. Giachinni over dinner. We told him we had reached a tentative agreement with Mr. Waxler subject to certain conditions which we didn't explain in detail and he didn't inquire about. Mr. Giachinni agreed to help us; however, he acknowledged that he had no knowledge or experience in the law governing cooperative marketing corporations. We still believed he was representing us and was trustworthy. Nonetheless, we were still puzzled by the coincidences we had experienced and how they had occurred.

The next day Pete and I flew directly back to Idaho Falls. We reported on the events of the previous trip. We met several times to prepare for the meeting with Lou Rosanova and Mr. Summerfield that we had agreed to just outside of the elevator on our first trip to Chicago. We had all committed to reaching a final agreement regarding payment on our respective debts. We were feeling somewhat more comfortable that Jerry Waxler would be able to put together an organization to take over and handle the brokerage business, if the Mafia did not interfere. The IPG sales staff had high confidence in Jerry Waxler's ability to do so with little or no loss of retail customers.

Ultimately, we decided to propose that IPG and the Mafia set up an arrangement to liquidate Mr. Windle's considerable assets in an orderly manner and that the net proceeds be shared on the basis of our respective debt balances. That was the concept. We realized the details of how to accomplish this were yet to be determined.

While we could not predict what our "friends" would do and how they would react to our proposal, we took some comfort in the fact that they had not yet said anything that would indicate an interest in taking over the brokerage business. They gave the impression that they simply wanted their loan repaid. We would learn more as soon as we returned to Chicago.

When we arrived at the airport in Chicago, we expected to be met by Lou Rosanova and Jake Summerfield, however, this time it was only the latter. We never did see Lou Rosanova again. We had made our own hotel arrangements. We drove to the hotel, where Charlie Windle joined us, to discuss an agreement. As it turned out, we had been thinking along the same lines.. We were given a list of Charlie's assets which included an equity in his personal residence, an airplane, a summer home in upstate Illinois, and a country club membership.

Mr. Summerfield said he was very familiar with the assets and would take charge of selling. We agreed that all sales would be cash, and that no sale would be finalized until we had been provided written confirmation of the sale price and had specifically approved the sale. Charlie said very little, except that he wanted the assets to be sold for reasonable value. He pledged to cooperate. We agreed to confirm our understanding by an exchange of letters and Pete suggested that I be the contact person for Mr. Summerfield as liquidation progressed.

We indicated that we were meeting with Jerry Waxler to finalize an arrangement for him to set up a new entity to take over all brokerage business operations, theretofore handled by Charlie who seemed to accept that as inevitable. Mr. Summerfield seemed comfortable with our plans, giving a clear indication for the first time that the Mafia had no interest in becoming involved in the business. We all shook hands and agreed to keep in close touch. Charlie was not happy, but he was still young and obviously very talented. If all went well, the mess he was in would be taken care of by others, and he would have a chance to start over.

As it turned out, I never did prepare a formal agreement. We felt we had to trust Jake Summerfield, as he would be as interested as anyone in maximizing the returns. Pete and I were impressed that Mr. Summerfield was experienced in business matters, which was confirmed as our relationship continued.

Following our fairly short meeting, Jake Summerfield left. Pete and I expressed interest in seeing Charlie's residence which appeared to be a major asset, and he agreed to give us a tour. On the drive, he explained that the house had been built by Mr. Sears, the co-founder of Sears and Roebuck, as a wedding present for his daughter. The house was really a mansion located in a very exclusive section of Chicago. In the large kitchen, we met Charlie's young wife and a pre-school age daughter. His wife was young, attractive and unsmiling. She seemed to sense that our presence indicated that all was not well. I had the distinct impression that she was uncomfortable living in such plush surroundings. She and her young daughter remained in the kitchen while Charlie gave us a tour. It reminded me of a mansion such as one might see in a Cecil B. DeMille movie. After touring the downstairs, we went up a wide circular stairway to the second floor. I cannot remember for certain the number of bedrooms, I believe 10 to 12, and each spacious and well-furnished bedroom was connected to a large and beautiful, mostly marble bathroom.

Jerry Waxler was excited about the opportunity to put together his team and new business relationship. He knew the potential of the business and recognized it gave him a once in a lifetime opportunity. Pete and I did not believe our share of the asset sales would cover the outstanding debt owed to IPG, so Pete discussed an arrangement whereby Jerry would reduce the brokerage fee until our share of assets sales and reduced fees equaled the full amount of the debt owed by Mr. Windle. Thereafter, the regular brokerage fee would apply. Ultimately, this was the arrangement agreed to by both parties.

Pete and I returned to Idaho Falls. Our third trip to Chicago had gone more smoothly than we had feared might be the case. The members of the IPG board of directors were pleased with the outcome and the sales personnel were delighted at the prospect of Jerry Waxler's handling the nationwide sales of frozen potato products with no interruption. Mr. Summerfield and I exchanged letters outlining the agreement we had reached. Jerry Waxler quickly put his team together under a new entity in a new location and commenced to do business. Jerry agreed to furnish a fidelity bond in an agreed-upon amount.

I regularly received telephone calls from Jake Summerfield keeping me up to date on his efforts to sell the Windle assets. Few of the assets were paid for, so it was a matter of recovering equities. He constantly asked my advice which I found reassuring. One of the assets was a membership in the exclusive Thunderbird Country Club in Palm Springs, California. Mr. Summerfield said he would be interested in purchasing the membership personally. In due course, we received our share of the membership sale. In a conversation later, I mentioned the membership, and to my surprise Mr. Summerfield said he had not purchased the membership. I later learned from Jerry Waxler that the Thunderbird Country Club did not permit persons of the Jewish faith to become members. Jake Summerfield was Jewish, as was Jerry Waxler.

The airplane and the summer home in upstate Illinois sold. The personal residence turned out to be the most difficult asset to sell, partly because of its price and uniqueness, but mostly because Charlie had an unrealistic idea of its value. Pete and I encouraged him to cooperate with efforts to sell the property. Mr. Summerfield expressed frustration that Charlie was not being reasonable. Finally, after several months, Mr. Summerfield informed me that a written offer had been obtained. Charlie confirmed that the sales price was acceptable to him.

I prepared the deed and related sales documents and made arrangements to fly to Chicago to obtain Charlie's signature in order to complete the sale. Charlie met me, as agreed. However, to my surprise, he was unwilling to sign the papers, saying the sales price was too low. After a lengthy discussion, he left. Shortly thereafter, Jake Summerfield arrived, and after a warm greeting asked if I had the signed deed. I told him I had the deed, but that Mr. Windle had refused to sign. Mr. Summerfield said, "Give me the papers," whereupon he left. Within an hour, he returned and with a big grin he gave me the papers which had been signed by Charlie Windle and properly notarized by a notary public. He didn't offer any explanation and I made no inquiry.

Jake Summerfield and I spent considerable time talking on a variety of subjects, and he seemed to enjoy working with me. He gave me an update and review of sales to date and a full accounting of the proceeds. I was impressed. In the business world, he was in his element. We relaxed, and we both seemed to enjoy the conversation and our relationship. I had not seen Mr. Rosanova since our second trip to Chicago and asked if he was still involved in the matter we were dealing with. He said he was not. It was apparent as he talked about Mr. Rosanova, that he did not care for him. While I don't remember the specific words, he made it clear that Mr. Rosanova was essentially a "muscle" man and was brought into our dealings to make sure Mr. Peterson and I appreciated the seriousness of matters.

I decided to ask Mr. Summerfield about his responsibilities. He explained in general terms that he was the manager of a number of businesses and business interests. It was apparent to me that he was a businessman and was proud of what he did. In addition, he felt strongly the organization he was employed by was engaged in business activities which were legitimate and that the aggressive tactics used at times were necessary and appropriate, much like collateral taken by automobile dealers or credit agencies.

Either my brother Orval or I usually were asked to attend the monthly meetings of the Idaho Potato Growers, and often Mr. Gil Karst would attend as well. At some subsequent time, Mr. Karst felt that for tax purposes it would be important for IPG to have a signed affidavit from Charlie in which he acknowledged the fact and amount of his embezzlement. When I talked with Charlie I assured him it was not our intention to prefer criminal charges, but only to have a document in the IPG files to show the IRS, should there ever be any question about the money we were receiving. He indicated he would have no objection to signing such a document. I prepared a lengthy affidavit which contained the language Mr. Karst suggested, and both he and I flew to Chicago to obtain Charlie's signature on the document.

After Charlie read the document, he said he wanted to talk with an attorney before he decided whether or not to sign. He invited Mr. Karst and me to accompany him to see the lawyer he had selected, a Mr. Witte, the head of a sizable law firm. Mr. Witte had a high rating from the American Bar Association. I remember being nervous. It became apparent that Mr. Witte had no idea why we were there, and that this was the first time he had in fact met his new client, Mr. Windle.

After an awkward few minutes, Charlie mentioned the affidavit he was being asked to sign. I handed the document to Mr. Witte, and he became very quiet as he read it. I did my best to explain the past relationship between IPG and Mr. Windle's brokerage business. Mr. Windle said almost nothing. Mr. Karst explained the reason the document was important to IPG from a tax standpoint. I added that the repayment plan we had worked out with Mr.

Windle's lender was working satisfactorily. We wanted the plan to continue and believed criminal prosecution would not serve anyone's best interests.

I assumed Mr. Witte would ask Mr. Karst and me to step out of his office in order that he could talk with Mr. Windle in private; however, he did not do so. He simply turned to Charlie and said, "Well…?" Charlie said he didn't like the explicit nature of the language in the affidavit. Mr. Witte said, "Mr. Windle did you take their money?" And when Charlie stammered that well yes, he guessed he had, Mr. Witte simply said to him, "Sign their document!" He knew that if we had wanted to have criminal proceedings filed against Charlie we could do so with or without the document. He also recognized our purpose was legitimate and that it was in Mr. Windle's best interest to cooperate with us.

As we were leaving, Mr. Witte motioned me back. He was interested in our relationship with the attorney Peter Giachinni. Mr. Witte told me that Mr. Giachinni had a reputation for representing the interests of the Mafia!

That evening Charlie, a big sports fan, invited Mr. Karst and me to join him in watching a professional hockey game. The Chicago Black Hawks were in the final series of the Diamond Cup. I had never been to a professional hockey game; however, Mr. Charlie explained the game to us. We had choice reserved seats and I found it exciting to watch. As I recall, Chicago won the game and the Diamond Cup, the first time in several years we were told. I vividly remember the noise and how physical the game was played. Apparently, Mr. Witte was also a big hockey fan. We saw him sitting a short distance away and he seemed astounded when he noticed and acknowledged Charlie, Gil Karst and myself together at a sports event, only a few hours after our rather tense meeting in his office.

The wrap up of our dealings with the Mafia continued for some time and for the most part was uneventful. For years, I would receive a Christmas card from him signed simply, "Jake and Babe." I never met Jake's wife, Babe, but wish that I had. The liquidation of Charlie's assets did not cover the full debt of either IPG or the Mafia. In the course of a conversation with Mr. Summerfield toward the end of our dealings, I made reference to the fact that a portion of the debt had not been paid and he simply said, "We collected all of our debt."

I did not ask any questions; however, I was not overly surprised. I never learned the source of the final payment of the debt owed the Mafia. By the same token, I am not sure we ever expressly acknowledged to them the details of our reduced brokerage arrangement with Jerry Waxler. All the disclosed assets had been sold and accounted for properly. In truth, IPG ultimately recouped all the funds Charlie had embezzled.

On my last trip to Chicago, I spent a fair amount of time with Mr. Giachinni. The night before I left for home, he took me to dinner at a very nice restaurant. At dinner, he mentioned that his responsibilities as owner and manager of the Maywood bank was taking the bulk of his time and he wanted to pull back and slow down. He was proud of the law practice he had developed and felt he was neglecting and asked if I would be interested in moving to Chicago and taking over his practice which included representing his bank.

I told him I was content with the practice my brother and I were developing in Idaho, however that I was flattered by the offer which I would consider and discuss with my wife. I was reluctant to flatly reject the offer, however in truth, I had absolutely no interest in moving my young family to Chicago. I remember Mother had mentioned to me once that when Dad was in the potato business, he had received a fairly attractive offer that would require moving the family to Chicago. She said the two of them quickly concluded they did not want to do so. I remember as a small boy thinking how much fun it would be to live in a large city like Chicago. Now I had a much better understanding of why Dad rejected the offer. That was the last time I saw Mr. Giachinni. I suspect that he, in fact, had connections to the Mafia and that the surprise meeting at Mr. Giachinni's bank in Maywood had not been a surprise to him. I never had the courage to bring up the subject.

Pete and I often reminisced about our experiences in Chicago. In his capacity as General Manager of IPG, he traveled all over the United States. One time, after a trip to Los Angeles, he brought back two newspapers that had articles about our old "friend," Lou Rosanova. He had risen in the Mafia organization and was living in Los Angeles. The paper called him a "mobster" and referenced his alleged activities and the territory he controlled for the Mafia. Several pictures of Lou were in the articles and it was clearly the same person with whom Pete and I had dealt. He appeared heavier and had grey hair; however his looks had definitely not improved. Members of the Mafia who have achieved some notoriety commonly assume a nickname. The articles referred to him as Lou "The Snake" Rosanova.

Over the years, Jerry Waxler and the team he assembled continued to do an excellent job of handling the marketing of IPG's national frozen potato products, and Jerry prospered. Jerry had received an opportunity of a lifetime and IPG had also benefited. I saw Jerry a couple of times later when he visited the IPG operations in Idaho Falls. Seeing him brought back my experience of dealing with the Mafia, now long gone, but never forgotten.

John and his brother, Orval, opened their law firm in Idaho Falls in 1963. The firm outgrew its original office and moved to larger quarters on Capital Avenue across from the courthouse. The new offices provided space for a small library where John looks right at home.

Outdoor recreation was important to John; the Palisades property provided a retreat for the family. Patty shares some outdoor time with her dad.

Steve and his dad shared outdoor adventures. This one looks cold--perhaps a climb in the Idaho mountains.

A long time away from the trailer homes of earlier years, the family home grew along with the family. Here, the young-adult children join their parents in front of the fireplace, John and Donna in front, backed by Steve, Linda, and Patty.

Photo Gallery 3

Back on the Airport Farm, a very young John sits in the driver's seat of the Model T. On the right, a grown-up John drives the fully-restored Model T, his pride and joy. After winning prizes and acclaim wherever it went, the Model T is scheduled to be exhibited in the Museum of Idaho, Idaho Falls.

Lily Hansen, John's mother, was an inspiration to her family, encouraging them to be their best and supporting them, however she could, to meet their goals. She lived to be nearly ninety-seven years old.

John loved the mountains and climbed many of them with his brothers. This may be the summit of one of those climbs.

Let the Record Show by John D. Hansen

Lily Hansen, in the front, is backed by her six children: Reed, Orval, Mary, Farrel, Jr, Norman, and John.

It looks like the brothers may have just come off a climb, with uncharacteristic beards to show for it: John, Reed, Orval, and Farrel, Jr.

John often told people he was "just a farm kid from Osgood." He loved the land, he loved the hills, he loved learning and the law, and he loved his family. This picture, perhaps at the Palisades, shows John as he is remembered by those who loved him.

Photo Gallery 3

EDITOR'S NOTE

The Final Chapter

John will never see his story as the book you've just read--not on this earth, anyway. Nor will many of the folks who populate the story. But John makes it clear in his author's note that this story is not for those who lived it. It is his gift to those who have come along since--children, grandchildren--that they might know this part of the heritage that is theirs.

As I edited this manuscript, I came to know John, whom I had never met. I heard his voice as clearly as if he were sitting in his arm chair, telling his tales on a sunny afternoon in Idaho Falls. I also came to understand he was telling a story about more than just himself.

Let the Record Show is a story about Idaho and the ethics of hard work and independence, hallmarks of the state he loved and served. He doesn't talk much about his accomplishments as a public servant; that could have been Part IV. But in this story, we hear the gifts he brought to the statehouse--humor, intelligence, respect, honesty, kindness, and yes, humility.

Early in the editing of Let the Record Show John's son, Steve, sent me a quote from an author he and his dad shared back and forth. Steve wrote, "I'd like to think it encapsulates most of what's in Let the Record Show."

"Like other Americans uncertain of who they are, I take a firm hold on the certainties of where I am from. I can say to myself that a good part of my private and social character, the kinds of scenery and weather and people and humor I respond to, the prejudices I wear like dishonorable scars, the affections that sometimes waken me from middle-aged sleep with a rush of undiminished love, the virtues I respect and the weaknesses I condemn, the code I try to live by, the special ways I fail at it and the kinds of shame I feel when I do, the models and heroes I follow, the colors and shapes that evoke my deepest pleasure, the way I adjudicate between personal desire and personal responsibility, have been in good part scored into me by that little womb-village and the lovely, lonely, exposed prairie of the homestead."

(Wallace Stegner, Marking the Sparrow's Fall)

Steve recognized his father's heart in Stegner's quote. John's world expanded beyond Idaho Falls, beyond Idaho, beyond our nation's shores. But at its core we find "that little womb-village" scored into him and passed on to his descendants, for whom this book was written.

The manuscript ended abruptly, without any real closure. In talking with Steve, I said, "I'm sure your father did not run out of stories, so he must have run out of time."

Steve chuckled. "No," he said. "I think he ended it right where he wanted–with his favorite lawyering story." John's widow, Michele, concurs that John enjoyed telling about his brush with the mafia, and he told it often. It was a good place to stop.

The extended Hansen family along with friends and relatives of the people whose lives touched John's have a piece of their history in these chapters. It was John's fervent wish to see them published. Thank you, Michele, for seeing that it was done and for giving me the privilege of editing it. And thank you, John, for telling your story.

Dorothy Read, Editor

MORE ABOUT JOHN

Born in 1933, the youngest of Lily and Farrel Hansen's six children, John Hansen had vivid childhood memories of the Great Depression and the World War II years in rural Idaho. In 1951 he began his studies at the University of Idaho, with a year's interlude at the American University of Beirut in Lebanon where he met and later married Donna Lebstock. He earned a law degree from the University of Idaho in 1959. He began his law career in Boise but soon moved back to Idaho Falls where he and Donna raised their three children.

Hansen's many awards and recognition include the Distinguished Lawyer Award from the Idaho State Bar Association. Hansen served in the Idaho State Senate for twelve years, focusing on the interests of the environment and education and serving as the Senate Education Committee chair.

In recognition of his tireless efforts, the Idaho Education Association presented him with their Friend of Education Award. Widely read and widely traveled, Hansen never lost his appreciation of education, as his memoir reflects. John D. Hansen succumbed to a heart attack in 2017. Honoring one of his last requests, his widow, Michele Hansen, published *Let the Record Show* in 2019.

Made in the
USA
Lexington, KY